Giving Well

Giving Well

The Ethics of Philanthropy

EDITED BY

Patricia Illingworth, Thomas Pogge, and
Leif Wenar

OXFORD
UNIVERSITY PRESS

OXFORD
UNIVERSITY PRESS

Oxford University Press is a department of the University of Oxford.
It furthers the University's objective of excellence in research, scholarship,
and education by publishing worldwide.

Oxford New York
Auckland Cape Town Dar es Salaam Hong Kong Karachi
Kuala Lumpur Madrid Melbourne Mexico City Nairobi
New Delhi Shanghai Taipei Toronto

With offices in
Argentina Austria Brazil Chile Czech Republic France Greece
Guatemala Hungary Italy Japan Poland Portugal Singapore
South Korea Switzerland Thailand Turkey Ukraine Vietnam

Oxford is a registered trade mark of Oxford University Press
in the UK and certain other countries.

Published in the United States of America by
Oxford University Press
198 Madison Avenue, New York, NY 10016

© Oxford University Press 2011

First issued as an Oxford University Press paperback, 2013.

Library of Congress Cataloging-in-Publication Data
Giving well: the ethics of philanthropy / edited by Patricia Illingworth,
Thomas Pogge, and Leif Wenar.
    p. cm.
ISBN 978-0-19-973907-3 (hardcover); 978-0-19-995858-0 (paperback)
1. Charities—Moral and ethical aspects. I. Illingworth, Patricia M. L.,
1954– II. Pogge, Thomas Winfried Menko. III. Wenar, Leif.
HV41.G525 2010
174'.93617—dc22   2010008770

Printed in the United States of America
on acid-free paperr

Contents

Contributors

KENNETH ANDERSON is a law professor at Washington College of Law, American University, and Hoover Institution Task Force on National Security and Law fellow. Professor Anderson was formerly general counsel to the Open Society Institute and director of the Human Rights Watch Arms Division, and currently chairs the boards of two global philanthropies. His book on U.S.–UN relations, *Returning to Earth*, will be published in 2010.

ELIZABETH ASHFORD teaches in the Department of Moral Philosophy at the University of St. Andrews, Scotland. She has held visiting fellowships at the Harvard University Edmund J. Safra Foundation Center for Ethics and at the Oxford University Centre for Ethics and the Philosophy of Law. Her publications include *Utilitarianism, Integrity and Partiality* (2000); *The Demandingness of Scanlon's Contractualism* (2003); and *The Duties Imposed by the Human Right to Basic Necessities* (2007).

ALEX DE WAAL is a program director of the Social Science Research Council and senior fellow of the Harvard Humanitarian Initiative. He has written or edited 13 books on humanitarianism, conflict, and HIV/AIDS in Africa, especially Sudan, most recently *Darfur: A New History of a Long War* (2008). He has served as adviser to the African Union mediation team for the Darfur peace talks (2005–2006) and the African Union High-Level Panel on Darfur (2009). He was awarded an OBE in the New Year's Honors List of 2009, and was on the Prospect/Foreign Policy list of 100 public intellectuals in 2008 and on the Atlantic Monthly list of 27 "brave thinkers" in 2009.

THOMAS W. DUNFEE (1941–2008) was the Joseph Kolodny Professor of Social Responsibility in Business at the Wharton School. He served on the editorial board of six leading journals and was the president of both the Academy of Legal Studies in Business and the Society for Business Ethics. His 1999 book with Thomas Donaldson, *The Ties That Bind*, is the canonical statement of their widely influential Integrative Social Contracts Theory, and has been called the bible of business ethics. Dunfee authored more than 50 articles and almost a dozen books on a wide range of topics, including corruption, social investment, duties to rescue in catastrophes, Asian business practices, and the ethics of travel agencies. We honor his distinguished career and his pioneering life's work on morality within the marketplace.

JON ELSTER is the Robert K. Merton Professor of Social Science, Columbia University. He also holds the Chaire de Rationalité et Sciences Sociales at the Collège de France. His publications include *Alchemies of the Mind* (1999), *Ulysses Unbound* (2000), *Closing the Books: Transitional Justice in Historical Perspective* (2004), *Explaining Social Behavior* (2007), *Agir contre soi* (2007), and *Le déntéssement* (2009).

PATRICIA ILLINGWORTH is associate professor in the Department of Philosophy and in the College of Business Administration at Northeastern University. She is also a lecturer in law at Northeastern University School of Law. Illingworth has held fellowships at Harvard Law School and at Harvard Medical School. She is the author of *Trusting Medicine: The Moral Costs of Managed Care* (2005), and a coeditor of *The Power of Pills* (2006) and *Ethical Healthcare* (2006). She is currently a visiting scholar in the Harvard Program in Ethics and Health.

DEVESH KAPUR is the director of the Centre for Advanced Study of India, and is the Madan Lal Sobti Associate Professor for the Study of Contemporary India, University of Pennsylvania. He is the coauthor of *The World Bank: Its First Half Century* (1997), *Give Us Your Best and Brightest: The Global Hunt for Talent and Its Impact on the Developing World* (2005), and *Public Institutions in India: Performance and Design* (2005). His most recent book, *Diaspora, Democracy and Development: The Impact of International Migration from India* (Princeton University Press, 2010). He has a BTech and MS in chemical engineering and a PhD in public policy from Princeton University.

THOMAS POGGE is Leitner Professor of Philosophy and International Affairs, Yale University; professorial fellow at the Centre for Applied Philosophy and Public Ethics, Australian National University; research director, Centre for the Study of Mind in Nature, University of Oslo; and adjunct professor at the University of Central Lancashire. His recent publications include *World Poverty and Human Rights* (2nd ed., 2008) and *Politics as Usual: What Lies behind the Pro-Poor Rhetoric* (2010). Pogge's current work is focused on a team effort toward developing a complement to the pharmaceutical patent regime that would improve access to advanced medicines for the poor worldwide (www.healthimpactfund.org).

ROB REICH is an associate professor of political science and, by courtesy, in philosophy at Stanford University. He is the codirector of Stanford's Center on Philanthropy and Civil Society. He is the author of *Bridging Liberalism and Multiculturalism in American Education* (2002) and is completing on a book on ethics, philanthropy, and public policy.

ROGER C. RIDDELL is a board member of Oxford Policy Management, a principal of the Policy Practice, and a member of an independent advisory committee to the UK's Department for International Development. He has degrees in economics from the University of Zimbabwe and development studies from the Institute of Development Studies at the University of Sussex. He was international director of Christian Aid from 1999 to 2004 and, earlier, chair of the first Presidential Commission of Inquiry following Zimbabwe's Independence in 1980. His publications on foreign aid include *Foreign Aid Reconsidered* (1987) and *Does Foreign Aid Really Work?* (2008).

JAMES SHULMAN is the president of ARTstor, a nonprofit organization that provides digital images, software, and services to colleges, universities, museums, and schools around the world. He received his PhD from Yale University, and has written about decision making in books about renaissance epic poetry (*The Pale Cast of Thought: Hesitation and Decision in the Renaissance Epic*, 1998) and about university admissions and policies (*The Game of Life: College Sports and Educational Values*, 2002), and in a number of articles about strategy for innovative nonprofits.

PETER SINGER is Ira W. DeCamp professor of Bioethics at the Center for Human Values at Princeton University and laureate professor at the Centre for Applied Philosophy and Public Ethics at the University of Melbourne. He is the author of many books, including most recently *The Life You Can Save* (2009).

LEIF WENAR holds the Chair of Ethics at King's College London. He received his bachelor's degree from Stanford, his doctorate from Harvard, and has recently been a visiting professor at Princeton. His most recent publications include "Property Rights and the Resource Curse" (2008), "Realistic Reform of International Trade in Resources" (2010), and (with Branko Milanovic) "Are Liberal Peoples Peaceful?" (2009).

Acknowledgments

As editors and contributors, we would like to thank the colleagues, teachers, friends, students and family members who have inspired, critiqued and supported our work on this volume. We are grateful in particular to Matt Peterson for doing most of the editorial work on the proofs and for supervising work on the index, to student assistants Carolyn Lux and Christina Schlegel for their help with the index, and to Stephanie Zelman for her bright idea of putting a well on the cover. We also wish to thank our Oxford University Press editors Peter Ohlin and Lucy Randall, who have been enormously helpful at each stage of the publication process. Peter Singer's opening essay first appeared in the *New York Times* on December 17, 2006.

Giving Well

Introduction

The Ethics of Philanthropy

Patricia Illingworth, Thomas Pogge, and Leif Wenar

> To give away money is an easy matter and in any man's power. But to decide to whom to give it, and how large, and when, and for what purpose and how, is neither in every man's power nor an easy matter.
>
> Aristotle

Philanthropy—the "love of humanity"—has surged into public view. The spectacular sums given by Warren Buffett and Bill Gates captured headlines, as did the high-profile charitable campaigns by George Soros, Ted Turner, and Oprah Winfrey. The rocketing wealth of the richest (since 2006, the Forbes 400 list has contained only billionaires, with a total worth of more than $1.5 trillion in 2008) has clashed sharply with the widening inequalities among compatriots (the richest 1% of Americans captured 50% of the real per-capita growth of the U.S. economy between 1993 and 2007). Simultaneously, globalization and the spread of information technology have spotlighted the massive disparities of wealth between the affluent countries and the nearly half of humanity that lives on, at most, $2.50 (2005 international dollars) a day. In our world today, every 3 seconds a child dies from poverty-related causes, and many have asked whether rich and even ordinary citizens of affluent countries should do more. The heightened attention to the urgency of unfulfilled human needs has spurred the "New Philanthropy," more focused on giving that is targeted and effective than on giving that merely salves the conscience or advertises the donor's name.

Yet despite the recent attention on philanthropy, there is little consensus on how to answer the basic *ethical* questions it raises. For example, during their lives, Americans give 60% of their charitable donations to religious organizations and only 2% to international aid, whereas the British give 14% of their donations to international aid and only 8% to religious organizations. Americans give more than twice as much to charity than Canadians do, and 10 times more than do the French.

However, surveys show that Europeans are more likely to believe that their moral duties are better fulfilled through paying taxes to the government than through the "arbitrary" channels of private donations. These differences reflect disagreements about means as well as ends. Indeed, even the most basic ethical questions about philanthropy are unresolved. Is there good reason to give money to charities at all? And if people are going to give, is it acceptable for them to give to whatever causes might strike their fancy? Can reasoned argument reach conclusions about how people should give? Or are such arguments ungrateful intrusions into donors' rights of free choice?

A new field of inquiry—the ethics of philanthropy—would address these crucial questions, and many more besides. Books should be written, journals started, dissertations published; the issues are vital and fresh. Philanthropic practices should be changed, regulations revised, and economic and political agendas reformulated. We hope to make readers confident that there is an unusually important domain to be investigated here, defined by the most basic ethical questions: Who should give? How much should they give? To whom should they give? For which purposes and why? Among the many issues within the ethics of philanthropy are those listed in the following sections.

WHO SHOULD GIVE?

- "The day is not far distant when the man who dies leaving behind him millions of available wealth...will pass away unwept, unhonored, and unsung....Of such as these the public verdict will then be: 'The man who dies thus rich dies disgraced.'" Do the very rich have a special obligation, as Andrew Carnegie insisted, to give their money to purposes "best for the good of the people"?[1]
- Should the poor give to charity? An American in the bottom 5% of the U.S. income distribution is richer than two thirds of the people in the world. Should such a poor American feel obliged to help the much poorer people in other countries?
- Corporations enjoy many of the advantages and protections of the law. Do corporations have a social responsibility to give some percentage of their profits—say, 10%—to charitable causes? Do shareholders have a moral duty to require "their" corporations to give? Or was Milton Friedman right that the only social responsibility of business is to increase profits within the rules of the market?
- The Catholic Church engages in a wide range of poverty relief and educational activities around the world. Yet the Church has also accumulated billions of dollars worth of artistic treasures and historical artifacts. Jesus said: "Sell all that thou hast, and distribute unto the poor" (Luke 18:22). Do Christian principles demand that the Church sell off its luxuries, and use the proceeds to relieve human suffering?

HOW MUCH?

The Institute for Philanthropy has suggested that people give 1.5% of their income. The traditional Judeo-Christian tithe is 10%. Islamic law requires 2.5% of wealth to be given—and Shi'ites have a separate requirement to give 20% of income beyond living requirements. Bill Gates has given away approximately 35% of his vast fortune. Veronica Atkins, the widow of Dr. Robert Atkins, has given half a billion dollars, keeping $60 million for herself. Real estate tycoon Zell Kravinsky gave away nearly all his $45 million savings—and one of his kidneys to a stranger, as well. Yet these are exceptional cases. Studies show that, on average, the higher a person's income the *less* she gives as a percentage of her wealth.

Philosopher Peter Singer once suggested that people should give down to the level at which, if they gave more, they would cause as much suffering to themselves as they would relieve for an impoverished person.[2] Other philosophers have argued that each person need only do his share of satisfying the needs of others—even if each is certain that most other people will never do *their* share.

Is there *any* defensible answer regarding how much one should give?

TO WHOM? FOR WHICH PURPOSES?

- May donors do whatever they like with their money? Is it morally acceptable for donors to give money to an art museum or to a poetry magazine, to an animal shelter or to their alma mater when the money could be used to save human lives instead?
- Should donors give locally or globally? Given that the poor in rich countries are so much richer than the poor in poor countries, can donors in rich countries rightly keep their money within the borders of their city, state, or nation?
- Is it an insult to people's dignity to offer them charity? Should donors prefer causes (such as the environment) for which no disadvantaged person has to be in the position to accept their charity? Or is it condescending to attempt to decide for the disadvantaged what is consistent with their dignity?

WHY?

- Why give to charity? Is this a moral requirement, a religious obligation, or just a matter of personal preference? Is someone who gives to charity going beyond the call of duty or simply doing what is required of any decent person?
- Nobel Prize–winning economist Herbert Simon estimated that at least 90% of what people "earn" in rich countries could be

attributed to "social capital"—to the technology, social networks, and good government in their country. "On moral grounds," Simon wrote, "we could argue for a flat income tax of 90 percent." Is there any real sense, then, that individuals deserve to keep most of their income? If Simon is right, should it not be a requirement on every person to "give a lot back to the community"?[3]

- Is the ultimate reason for giving to charity really self-interest? Thomas Hobbes said that he gave to beggars to relieve his own pain.[4] Today economists and psychologists talk about the "the warm glow of giving." Many people seem to give to charitable causes for the sake of self-promotion or to ward off criticism of their business dealings. If philanthropic giving is guided by self-interest, is there anything commendable about it? Is the moral character of a gift enhanced if it is given anonymously?

HOW SHOULD THE MONEY BE RAISED?

- Charities find that they can often raise significantly more money when they allow street canvassers (disparagingly called *charity muggers* or *chuggers*) to keep a percentage of the money they collect. Similarly, in raising money for breast cancer research, the Avon Foundation found that it ended up with three times less money after it replaced a for-profit company, whose chairman was very well paid, with its own nonprofit staff. Does this reflect market rates for excellence in leadership, or corporate opportunism? Must charitable fund-raisers themselves be innocent of the profit motive—even at the expense of less funds raised for good causes?
- Should charities put ever-greater efforts into fund-raising if their gains will come at the expense of donations to other charities? Isn't such a zero-sum fund-raising "arms race" collectively self-defeating?
- How much deception is permissible in fund-raising, if any? For example, is it acceptable for a charity to distribute misleading advertisements that make potential donors believe that their contributions will sponsor a *particular* poor child? One-to-one sponsorship is extremely inefficient and, in fact, no large charity attempts to match individual donations to specific children. However, the idea of one-to-one sponsorship is quite compelling to potential donors, and campaigns based upon it tend to raise more money. Is it morally permissible for nongovernmental organizations (NGOs) to mislead potential donors into thinking they are sponsoring a particular child, as long as the money raised by the campaign in fact goes to helping poor children?
- Should there be any constraints on the images that are shown in fund-raising? Pictures of emaciated listless villagers covered in flies, especially children, are often effective in fund-raising. However,

they also reinforce the Western stereotype that certain peoples (particularly Africans) are mostly helpless, passive victims. Should charities avoid "the pornography of poverty?" Or is such advertising justified by the fact that it will raise more funds?

- Should charities accept "tainted" donations—say, from foreign dictators or corporations involved in human rights violations? On the one hand, the donations could be used to further good causes. On the other hand, the charity may be seen to be wrongly legitimizing the donor or to be accepting blood money. Are there some sources from which charities should never accept donations?

- Should countries encourage philanthropy by giving tax incentives (for example, allowing relief for gifts in kind, "split interest trusts")? Or should they tax the public to pay for causes that would otherwise be left to individual choice? Is it justifiable to give large tax incentives to donors when this means that the government will have significantly less revenue to distribute to needy organizations and individuals? The U.S. government loses $50 billion in tax revenue a year by subsidizing donations—and some of these donations do not reduce inequality in America overall.[5] Is this just? Should we even call this *philanthropy?* Or, does the charitable deduction provide government with an opportunity to monitor and structure giving in a way that is more likely to meet human needs by steering the money into specific areas, some of which are preferable to those that individuals might choose without such incentives?[6]

- Should the deductibility of a charitable donation be based on the recipient charity's demonstrated success in fulfilling its mission?

HOW SHOULD CHARITABLE ORGANIZATIONS SPEND THE MONEY THEY RAISE?

- Should charitable funds only be dedicated to saving human lives and relieving human suffering as much as possible? What could possibly be more important than saving lives and relieving suffering? How could we justify spending money on anything else?

- Charitable organizations are agents of the donors who fund them. Should charities be more transparent and accountable for how they spend their money and whether they produce results? Is self-regulation enough? Is new legislation required?

- Is charitable giving effective at all? After several decades of giving, the evidence that foreign charitable aid has done significant good (or even more good than harm) is, at best, incomplete. Should we just "wrap up" the effort to improve the world through charity, having found that we do not know how to help? Or are there reforms that can counteract some of the hazards of aid?

BOOK OVERVIEW

This volume is the first major contribution to the new field of the ethics of philanthropy. The authors have vast experience in philanthropy: its theory and practice, its past and future, its design and execution, both in fund-raising and *ex post* evaluation. Each author spotlights one dimension of philanthropy with the light of his or her own expertise, and by so doing illuminates wider issues in the ethics of giving.

The essays here offer overlapping and reinforcing views on the ethical demands on individuals, corporations, NGOs, states, international organizations, and aid workers in the field. They cover the motivation for, creation of, sustainment of, legitimation of, and effectiveness of organizations that engage in philanthropic activities. Both the positive and negative sides of philanthropy are explored in this volume: altruism and selfishness, satisfaction of unmet needs and power without accountability, the promotion of pluralism, and the wasting of resources. These essays approach the topic of philanthropy and ethics with a seriousness that reflects the weight and importance of the moral issues at stake. Most notable about this interdisciplinary volume is the ethical and practical wisdom the essays convey. The range and depth of their discussions are remarkable, and together the essays in this volume present an unmatched introduction to the ethical issues surrounding giving.

In his essay, Peter Singer asks: What should a billionaire give—and what should you? Starting with a basic moral premise that all humans are equal, he questions whether we can really claim to believe this while living in a land of plenty while so many children die of easily preventable diseases overseas. This thought motivated Bill Gates to start giving away his massive fortune; yet, after all the giving, he will still have a huge amount of money at his command. Does Gates give enough? Or Warren Buffett? Or Zell Kravinsky, the man who gave one of his kidneys to a total stranger? Does America as a whole give enough, given the tiny amount of its resources that would be needed to reach the desperately urgent Millennium Development Goals? Singer journeys to the foundations of morality and returns with specific, action-guiding answers.

Although dramatic emergencies like the 2004 Asian tsunami capture headlines and open floodgates of charitable donations, it is a fact that chronic poverty kills many times more people each year than do all natural disasters combined. In fact, as Roger Riddell reports in his essay, the ratio of chronic poverty to emergency deaths each year is between 150:1 and 200:1. Elizabeth Ashford builds on Singer's work to distinguish our duties to disaster victims and our duties to those suffering from the injustice of severe poverty. She argues, with philosophical precision, that although we are under stringent duties to help both groups of individuals, the massive systematic injustice of poverty means that our duties to benefit the impoverished are, in fact, the more imperative.

International aid NGOs should try to "do good" overseas. It is important to think systematically about what NGOs' moral priorities should be. Yet is it really morally defensible for an NGO merely to protect some badly off people from harm—even if a larger number of people who are worse off could be protected elsewhere at the same cost? Should large NGOs divide their efforts "fairly" among developing countries? Or should they focus on those places where they can do the most good? When (if ever) is it acceptable for NGOs to compete for limited funding? And should NGOs incorporate the objectionable (say, racist) priorities of their donors into their planning? Thomas Pogge's rigorous, provocative essay shows how the consistent application of basic moral principles might require us to revolutionize our understanding of how international NGOs should understand their missions.

Jon Elster enlists the latest methods to probe an ancient question: Why do people give to charity? Is giving fundamentally altruistic, motivated by a disinterested concern for others? Or is giving at base egoistic—an indirect strategy to maximize the giver's material well-being? Elster uses game theory to cast suspicion on whether either of these explanations can account for the amounts and kinds of giving we actually see in the world. He turns to consider a third type of motivation, and one that seems to be supported by the latest brain imaging studies. This motivation is that people give egocentrically. They act from a desire to feel good about themselves—for the sake of the "warm glow." Although egocentrism may well explain a good deal of the giving that we observe, Elster uncovers its distinctive irrationality, for most types of egocentric givers must be self-deceived. Egocentric givers will only get the "warm glow" of giving if they believe they are not acting egocentrically.

Globalization's "networking of the world" has vivified the massive amount of severe poverty that still exists on the planet, and has raised hopes that new opportunities may exist to alleviate it. Those concerned with global poverty must decide how to divide their resources between private action and pressing their governments to increase foreign aid. Roger Riddell presents a masterful overview of foreign aid. He surveys the most critical issues in official development assistance—how much we know about what aid works, and what new challenges donor states are likely to face in the future as they try to provide aid effectively. Riddell is neither an aid "skeptic" nor a "booster"; he gives a clear-eyed assessment of development based on his years of study and practice in the field.

Leif Wenar returns to Peter Singer's call for affluent individuals to send money to aid NGOs to help save the lives of the world's poorest. He surveys the tremendously complex environment—political, economic, and social—that stands between the affluent person writing a check and the poor person whom this money is meant to benefit. He concludes that those wanting to act to alleviate the moral crisis of global poverty must do so without confidence that their actions will help those in need—and indeed must weigh in their deliberations the possibility that their actions may make some of the poor even worse off.

Alex de Waal turns the camera around to examine how aid workers and peacemakers are viewed by the people they are meant to be helping. Taking Sudan as his central case study, de Waal shows how surprising such an "ethnography of philanthropy" can be for those who fund philanthropic organizations. Far from being victims to be helped and passive recipients to be aided, many Sudanese use these organizations as sources of employment, as refuges from government repression, and as bases to campaign for political office. In short, philanthropic organizations and their resources are often co-opted to play a role in the power and patronage networks of the country's politics. De Waal does not decry what he sees as this inevitability, yet the predictability of this co-opting does raise unique ethical quandaries.

Fierce battles within the development community have recently been fought over the question of accountability. Although some protesters have complained bitterly about the lack of accountability of multilateral institutions like the World Bank and the International Monetary Fund to the world's poor, David Rieff has countered: Who elected the NGOs? Kenneth Anderson traces the history of transnational humanitarian organizations leading up to Rieff's query. From their origins in the mid-19th century through the Cold War to the age of globalization, NGOs have asked for philanthropic support on the grounds that they perform needed tasks that neither states nor individuals can. Yet after the crucial, shattering events of the Seattle protests against the World Trade Organization, "global civil society" organizations proved unable to redeem their promises either to legitimate a new model of global governance or even merely to represent the people of the world better than national governments were able to do. Anderson's engrossing narrative yields a sobering lesson to those tempted to direct their philanthropy toward transnational NGOs on the basis of their grand, yet sometimes hollow, public presentations.

Accountability is not, of course, merely a matter for international financial institutions and NGOs. In a pathbreaking essay, Devesh Kapur takes up the issue of the accountability of a key institution that rarely receives such scrutiny: the universities. Academics in the rich world have profound effects on the lives of the world's poor. They advise poor-country governments, educate poor-country elites, design drugs for tropical diseases, and set much of the development agenda. In its totality, "the portfolio of ongoing international development-related projects by U.S. universities exceeds that of the World Bank." Yet, what mechanisms make sure that academics fulfill their responsibilities? Kapur demonstrates how accountability weighs in the balance with the undeniable value of academic freedom. His essay raises the possibility that charitable donors who understand the many roles of universities in development could themselves become agents of accountability in the ways that they direct their giving.

Rob Reich takes a panoptic view of U.S. tax laws allowing deductions for charitable donations, and queries what their possible justification could be. A free society should surely allow its citizens to give away their money, but why should society give up tax revenues to encourage them to do so? Reich vets and discards what might seem the most natural responses to this challenge and settles on an unexpectedly satisfying reason. Allowing deductions for charitable donations is a way that the people of a free society can help to foster a flourishing, pluralistic democracy.

Patricia Illingworth looks at how charitable tax law can be used to increase giving. She focuses on the connection between social capital and philanthropy, and argues that a consideration of the impact of the law of charitable deduction on social capital may result in both enhanced social capital and greater giving. She also argues that the water's edge policy, which limits the charitable deduction to charities created or organized in the United States, is problematic from the perspective of cosmopolitan ethics and may undermine already scarce, but important, reservoirs of global social capital.

One high-profile group that may be incentivized by the tax structure consists of wealthy individuals who wish to start an entirely new charitable enterprise. A person of means (or a foundation) deciding to establish a new nonprofit organization will have a vision, but should also reflect upon what mechanism is the right one to carry out that vision, who else is affected by that choice, and indeed what they have let themselves in for. Drawing on his extensive experience with such undertakings, James Shulman leads the reader through the practical challenges faced by the "funder–founder." From building a new institutional identity, to weaving the nonprofit into the life of a community, to relinquishing operational control, Shulman gives a fascinating primer on the perils and rewards of bringing a new charitable institution to life.

Turning from the nonprofit to the for-profit world, Thomas W. Dunfee refutes both critics on the Left (who distrust that corporations can have any genuinely philanthropic goals) and on the Right (who don't believe that corporations should be in the charity business at all), and takes a balanced view of corporate philanthropy. Although many corporations do genuinely try to serve the community, the real potential of their efforts is often frustrated by bad planning, a lack of focus, and disconnected management. Dunfee sets out firm, directive precepts for corporations that want to maximize the good they do, such as applying business methods to charitable projects, staying close to core competences, and increasing transparency during all steps of the project.

Even this rich collection of essays can address only a fraction of the pressing questions of the ethics of philanthropy. Answering these questions is crucial not only for improving the philanthropic enterprises already underway, but also to give practical guidance to donors in the future.

Affluent people often think extremely carefully when investing money for themselves, but most of those who make donations lack a credible ethical framework for choosing charitable causes and know little about the actual impact of the organizations they support. Serious work in the ethics of philanthropy can provide orientation, information, and even inspiration for those who give.

Thomas W. Dunfee, Joseph Kolodny Professor of Social Responsibility and Chair of the Department of Legal Studies and Business Ethics at the Wharton School, died while this volume was in preparation. We are saddened by his death, and grateful to have his insights included in this volume on the relations between philanthropy and two topics on which he did pioneering research: business ethics and corporate social responsibility. Tom Dunfee left us too early; it is up to us now to travel farther down the trails he blazed for us.

Notes

1. Andrew Carnegie, *The Gospel of Wealth and Other Timely Essays* (New York: Century Co., 1901), pp. 19, 42.

2. Peter Singer, "Famine, Affluence, and Morality," *Philosophy and Public Affairs* 1 (1972), pp. 229–243.

3. Herbert A. Simon, "UBI and the Flat Tax," in *What's Wrong with a Free Lunch?*, eds. Joshua Cohen and Joel Rogers (Boston: Beacon Press, 2001), pp. 34–38. See also Branko Milanovic ("Global Inequality of Opportunity: How Much of Our Income Is Determined at Birth?" [working paper, Development Research Group, World Bank, Washington, D.C., 2008]), who estimated that 60% is determined by country of birth and 20% is determined by parental social class (precisely, ventile in the income hierarchy).

4. John Aubrey, *Brief Lives*, edited by Richard Barber (London: Penguin, 2000), p. 446.

5. Stephanie Strom, "Grab Bag of Charities Grows, Along with U.S. Tax Breaks," *New York Times* (December 6, 2009), p. A1.

6. *Bob Jones University v. United States*, 461 U.S. 574 (1983).

1

What Should a Billionaire Give—and What Should You?

Peter Singer

What is a human life worth? You may not want to put a price tag on it, but if we really had to, most of us would agree that the value of a human life would be in the millions. Consistent with the foundations of our democracy and our frequently professed belief in the inherent dignity of human beings, we would also agree that all humans are created equal, at least to the extent of denying that differences of sex, ethnicity, nationality, and place of residence change the value of a human life.

With a large proportion of humanity still trapped in conditions of life-threatening poverty, we might ask ourselves how these two beliefs—that a human life, if it can be priced at all, is worth millions, and that the factors I have mentioned do not alter the value of a human life—square with our actions. Perhaps this year such questions lurk beneath the surface of more family discussions than usual, for it has been an extraordinary year for philanthropy, especially philanthropy to fight global poverty.

For Bill Gates, the founder of Microsoft, the ideal of valuing all human life equally began to jar against reality some years ago, when he read an article about diseases in the developing world and came across the statistic that half a million children die every year from rotavirus, the most common cause of severe diarrhea in children. He had never heard of rotavirus. "How could I never have heard of something that kills half a million children every year?" he asked himself. He then learned that in developing countries, millions of children die from diseases that have been eliminated, or virtually eliminated, in the United States. That shocked him, because he assumed that if there are vaccines and treatments that could save lives, governments would be doing everything possible to get them to the people who need them. As Gates told a meeting of the World Health Assembly in Geneva last year, he and his wife, Melinda, "couldn't escape the brutal conclusion that—in our world today—some lives are seen as worth saving and others are not." They said to themselves, "This can't be true." But they knew it was.[1]

Gates's speech to the World Health Assembly concluded on an optimistic note, looking forward to the next decade when "people will finally
accept that the death of a child in the developing world is just as tragic as
the death of a child in the developed world."[2] That belief in the equal
value of all human life is also prominent on the website of the Bill and
Melinda Gates Foundation, where under "Our Values" we see: "All lives—
no matter where they are being led—have equal value."[3]

We are very far from acting in accordance with this belief. In the same
world in which more than a billion people live at a level of affluence
never previously known, roughly a billion other people struggle to survive on the purchasing power equivalent of less than US$1 per day. Most
of the world's poorest people are undernourished, lack access to safe
drinking water or even the most basic health services, and cannot send
their children to school. According to UNICEF, more than 10 million
children die every year—about 30,000 per day—from avoidable, poverty-
related causes.

Last June, investor Warren Buffett took a significant step toward
reducing those deaths when he pledged $31 billion to the Gates Foundation
and another $6 billion to other charitable foundations. Buffett's pledge,
set alongside the nearly $30 billion given by Bill and Melinda Gates to
their foundation, has made it clear that the first decade of the 21st century
is a new "golden age of philanthropy." On an inflation-adjusted basis,
Buffett has pledged to give more than double the lifetime total given
away by two of the philanthropic giants of the past—Andrew Carnegie
and John D. Rockefeller—put together. Bill and Melinda Gates's gifts are
not far behind.

Gates's and Buffett's donations will now be put to work primarily
to reduce poverty, disease, and premature death in the developing
world. According to the Global Forum for Health Research, less than
10% of the world's health research budget is spent on combating conditions that account for 90% of the global burden of disease. In the
past, diseases that affect only the poor have been of no commercial
interest to pharmaceutical manufacturers, because the poor cannot
afford to buy their products. The Global Alliance for Vaccines and
Immunization (GAVI), heavily supported by the Gates Foundation,
seeks to change this by guaranteeing to purchase millions of doses of
vaccines, when they are developed, that can prevent diseases like
malaria. The Global Alliance for Vaccines and Immunization has also
assisted developing countries to immunize more people with existing
vaccines; 99 million additional children have been reached to date. By
doing this, GAVI claims to have already averted nearly 1.7 million
future deaths.[4]

Philanthropy on this scale raises many ethical questions: Why are the
people who are giving doing so? Does it do any good? Should we praise
them for giving so much or criticize them for not giving still more? Is it
troubling that such momentous decisions are made by a few extremely

wealthy individuals? And how do our judgments about them reflect on our own way of living?

Let's start with the question of motives. The rich must—or so some of us with less money like to assume—suffer sleepless nights because of their ruthlessness in squeezing out competitors, firing workers, shutting down plants, or whatever else they have to do to acquire their wealth. When wealthy people give away money, we can always say that they are doing it to ease their conscience or generate favorable publicity. It has been suggested—by, for example, David Kirkpatrick, a senior editor at *Fortune* magazine—that Bill Gates's turn to philanthropy was linked to the antitrust problems Microsoft had in the United States and the European Union.[5] Was Gates, consciously or subconsciously, trying to improve his own image and that of his company?

This kind of sniping tells us more about the attackers than the attacked. Giving away large sums, rather than spending the money on corporate advertising or developing new products, is not a sensible strategy for increasing personal wealth. When we read that someone has given away a lot of their money, or time, to help others, it challenges us to think about our own behavior. Should we be following their example in our own modest way? However, if the rich just give their money away to improve their image, or to make up for past misdeeds—misdeeds quite unlike any we have committed, of course—then, conveniently, what they are doing has no relevance to what we ought to do.

A famous story is told about Thomas Hobbes, the 17th-century English philosopher, who argued that we all act in our own interests. On seeing him give alms to a beggar, a cleric asked Hobbes if he would have done this if Christ had not commanded us to do so. Hobbes replied that he would, that he was in pain to see the miserable condition of the old man, and his gift, by providing the man with some relief from that misery, also eased Hobbes's pain. This reply reconciles Hobbes's charity with his egoistic theory of human motivation, but at the cost of emptying egoism of much of its bite. If egoists suffer when they see a stranger in distress, they are capable of being as charitable as any altruist.

Followers of the 18th-century German philosopher Immanuel Kant would disagree. They think an act has moral worth only if it is done out of a sense of duty. Doing something merely because you enjoy doing it, or enjoy seeing its consequences, they say, has no moral worth, because if you happened not to enjoy doing it, then you wouldn't do it, and you are not responsible for your likes and dislikes, whereas you are responsible for your obedience to the demands of duty.

Perhaps some philanthropists are motivated by their sense of duty. Apart from the equal value of all human life, the other "simple value" that lies at the core of the work of the Gates Foundation, according to its website, is: "To whom much has been given, much is expected." This suggests the view that those who have great wealth have a duty to use it for a larger purpose than their own interests. However, while such questions of motive may be relevant to our assessment of Gates's or Buffett's character, they pale into insignificance when we consider the effect of what Gates and Buffett are doing. The parents whose children could die from rotavirus care more about getting the help that will save their children's lives than about the motivations of those who make that possible.

Interestingly, neither Gates nor Buffett seems motivated by the possibility of being rewarded in heaven for his good deeds on earth. Gates told a *Time* interviewer, "There's a lot more I could be doing on a Sunday morning" than going to church.[6] Put them together with Andrew Carnegie, famous for his freethinking, and three of the four greatest American philanthropists have been atheists or agnostics (the exception is John D. Rockefeller). In a country in which 96% of the population says they believe in a supreme being, that's a striking fact. It means that, in one sense, Gates and Buffett are probably less self-interested in their charity than someone like Mother Teresa, who as a pious Roman Catholic believed in reward and punishment in the afterlife.

More important than questions about motives are questions about whether there is an obligation for the rich to give and, if so, how much they should give. A few years ago, an African American cabdriver taking me to the Inter-American Development Bank in Washington asked me if I worked at the bank. I told him I did not but was speaking at a conference on development and aid. He then assumed that I was an economist, but when I said no, my training was in philosophy, he asked me if I thought the United States should give foreign aid. When I answered affirmatively, he replied that the government shouldn't tax people to give their money to others. That, he thought, was robbery. When I asked if he believed that the rich should voluntarily donate some of what they earn to the poor, he said that if someone had worked for his money, he wasn't going to tell him what to do with it.

At that point we reached our destination. Had the journey continued, I might have tried to persuade him that people can earn large amounts only when they live under favorable social circumstances, and that they don't create those circumstances by themselves. I could have quoted Warren Buffett's acknowledgment that society is responsible for much of his wealth. "If you stick me down in the middle of Bangladesh or Peru," he said, "you'll find out how much this talent is going to produce in the wrong kind of soil."[7] Nobel Prize–winning economist and social scientist Herbert Simon estimated that "social capital" is responsible for at least 90% of what people earn in wealthy societies like those of the United States or Northwestern Europe. By social capital, Simon meant not only natural resources, but, more important, the technology and organizational skills in the community, and the presence of good government. These are the foundations on which the rich can begin their work. "On moral grounds," Simon added, "we could argue for a flat income tax of 90%." Simon was not, of course, advocating so steep a rate of tax, for he was well aware of disincentive effects. However, his estimate does undermine the argument that the rich are entitled to keep their wealth, because it is all a result of their hard work. If Simon is right, that is true of, at most, 10% of it.

In any case, even if we were to grant that people deserve every dollar they earn, that doesn't answer the question of what they should do with it. We might say that they have a right to spend it on lavish parties, private jets, and luxury yachts, or, for that matter, to flush it down the toilet. But we could still think that for them to do these things while others die from easily preventable diseases is wrong. In an article I wrote more than three decades ago, at the time of a humanitarian emergency in what is now Bangladesh, I used the example of walking by a shallow pond and seeing a small child who has fallen in and appears to be in danger of drowning. Even though we did nothing to cause the child to fall into the pond, almost everyone agrees that if we can save the child at minimal inconvenience or trouble to ourselves, we ought to do so. Anything else would be callous, indecent, and, in a word, wrong. The fact that in rescuing the child we may, for example, ruin a new pair of shoes is not a good reason for allowing the child to drown. Similarly, if—for the cost of a pair of shoes—we can contribute to a health program in a developing country that stands a good chance of saving the life of a child, we ought to do so.

Perhaps, though, our obligation to help the poor is even stronger than this example implies, for we are less innocent than the passerby who did nothing to cause the child to fall into the pond. Thomas Pogge, a philosopher at Yale University, has argued that at least some of our affluence comes at the expense of the poor.[8] He bases this claim not simply on the usual critique of the barriers that Europe and the United States maintain against agricultural imports from developing countries, but also on less familiar aspects of our trade with developing countries. For example, he points out that international corporations are willing to make deals to buy natural resources from any government, no matter how it has come to power. This provides a huge financial incentive for groups to try to overthrow the existing government. Successful rebels are rewarded by being able to sell off the nation's oil, minerals, or timber.

In their dealings with corrupt dictators in developing countries, Pogge asserts, international corporations are morally no better than someone who knowingly buys stolen goods—with the difference that the international legal and political order recognizes the corporations, not as criminals in possession of stolen goods, but as the legal owners of the goods they have bought. This situation is, of course, beneficial for industrial nations, because it enables us to obtain the raw materials we need to maintain our prosperity, but it is a disaster for resource-rich developing countries, which turns the wealth that should benefit them into a curse that leads to a cycle of coups, civil wars, and corruption, and is of little benefit to the people as a whole.

In this light, our obligation to the poor is not just one of providing assistance to strangers, but one of compensation for harms that we have caused and are still causing them. It might be argued that we do not owe the poor compensation, because our affluence actually benefits them. Living luxuriously, it is said, provides employment, and so wealth trickles down, helping the poor more effectively than aid does. However, the rich in industrialized nations buy virtually nothing that is made by the very poor. During the past 20 years of economic globalization, although expanding trade has helped lift many of the world's poor out of poverty, it has failed to benefit the poorest 10% of the world's population. Some of the extremely poor, most of whom live in sub-Saharan Africa, have nothing to sell that rich people want, whereas others lack the infrastructure to get their goods to market. If they can get their crops to a port, European and U.S. subsidies often mean that they cannot sell them, despite—as, for example, in the case of West African cotton growers who compete with vastly larger and richer U.S. cotton producers—having a lower production cost than the subsidized producers in the rich nations.

The remedy to these problems, it might reasonably be suggested, should come from the state, not from private philanthropy. When aid comes through the government, everyone who earns above the tax-free threshold contributes something, with more collected from those with greater ability to pay. Much as we may applaud what Gates and Buffett are doing, we can also be troubled by a system that leaves the fate of hundreds of millions of people hanging on the decisions of two or three private citizens. However, the amount of foreign development aid given by the U.S. government is, at 22 cents for every $100 the nation earns, about the same as a percentage of gross national income as Portugal gives and about half that of the United Kingdom. Worse still, much of it is directed where it best suits U.S. strategic interests. Iraq is now by far the largest recipient of U.S. development aid; and Egypt, Jordan, Pakistan, and Afghanistan all rank in the Top 10. Less than a quarter of official U.S. development aid—barely a nickel in every $100 of our gross national income—goes to the world's poorest nations.

Adding private philanthropy to U.S. government aid improves this picture, because Americans privately give more per capita to international philanthropic causes than the citizens of almost any other nation. Even when private donations are included, however, countries like Norway, Denmark, Sweden, and the Netherlands give three or four times as much foreign aid, in proportion to the size of their economies, as the United States gives—with a much larger percentage going to the poorest nations. At least as things now stand, the case for philanthropic efforts to relieve global poverty is not susceptible to the argument that the government has taken care of the problem. And even if official U.S. aid were better directed and comparable, relative to our gross domestic product, with that of the most generous nations, there would still be a role for private philanthropy. Unconstrained by diplomatic considerations or the desire to swing votes at the United Nations, private donors can more easily avoid dealing with corrupt or wasteful governments. They can go directly into the field and work with local villages and grassroots organizations.

Nor are philanthropists beholden to lobbyists. As *The New York Times* reported, billions of dollars of U.S. aid is tied to domestic goods.[9] Wheat for Africa must be grown in America, although aid experts say this often depresses local African markets, reducing the incentive for farmers there to produce more. In a decision that surely costs lives, hundreds of millions of condoms intended to stop the spread of AIDS in Africa and around the world must be manufactured in the United States, although they cost twice as much as similar products made in Asia.

In other ways, too, private philanthropists are free to venture where governments fear to tread. Through a foundation named for his wife, Susan Thompson Buffett, Warren Buffett has supported reproductive rights, including family planning and prochoice organizations. In another unusual initiative, he has pledged $50 million for the International Atomic Energy Agency's plan to establish a "fuel bank" to supply nuclear reactor fuel to countries that meet their nuclear nonproliferation commitments. The idea, which has been talked about for many years, is widely agreed to be a useful step toward discouraging countries from building their own facilities for producing nuclear fuel, which could then be diverted to weapons production. It is, Buffett said, "an investment in a safer world."[10] Although it is something that governments could and should be doing, no government has taken the first step.

Aid has always had its critics. Carefully planned and intelligently directed private philanthropy may be the best answer to the claim that aid doesn't work. Of course, as in any large-scale human enterprise, some aid can be ineffective. However, provided that aid isn't actually counter-productive, even relatively inefficient assistance is likely to do more to advance human well-being than luxury spending by the wealthy.

The rich, then, should give. But how much should they give? Gates may have given away nearly $30 billion, but that still leaves him sitting at the top of the Forbes list of the richest Americans, with $53 billion. His 66,000-square-foot high-tech lakeside estate near Seattle is reportedly worth more than $100 million. Property taxes are about $1 million. Among his possessions is the Leicester Codex, the only handwritten book by Leonardo da Vinci still in private hands, for which he paid $30.8 million in 1994. Has Bill Gates done enough? More pointedly, you might ask: If he really believes that all lives have equal value, what is he doing living in such an expensive house and owning a Leonardo Codex? Are there no more lives that could be saved by living more modestly and adding the money thus saved to the amount he has already given?

Yet we should recognize that, if judged by the proportion of his wealth that he has given away, Gates compares very well with most of the other people on the Forbes 400 list, including his former colleague and Microsoft cofounder, Paul Allen. Allen, who left the company in 1983, has given, over his lifetime, more than $800 million to philanthropic causes. That is far more than nearly any of us will ever be able to give. However, Forbes lists Allen as the fifth-richest American, with a net worth of $16 billion.

He owns the Seattle Seahawks, the Portland Trailblazers, a 413-foot ocean-going yacht that carries two helicopters, and a 60-foot submarine. He has given only about 5% of his total wealth.

Is there a line of moral adequacy that falls between the 5% that Allen has given away and the roughly 35% that Gates has donated? Few people have set a personal example that would allow them to tell Gates that he has not given enough, but one who could is Zell Kravinsky. A few years ago, when he was in his mid 40s, Kravinsky gave almost all of his $45 million real estate fortune to health-related charities, retaining only his modest family home in Jenkintown, near Philadelphia, and enough to meet his family's ordinary expenses. After learning that thousands of people with failing kidneys die each year while waiting for a transplant, he contacted a Philadelphia hospital and donated one of his kidneys to a complete stranger.

After reading about Kravinsky in the *New Yorker*, I invited him to speak to my classes at Princeton. He comes across as anguished by the failure of others to see the simple logic that lies behind his altruism. Kravinsky has a mathematical mind—a talent that obviously helped him in deciding what investments would prove profitable—and he says that the chances of dying as a result of donating a kidney are about 1 in 4,000. For him this implies that to withhold a kidney from someone who would otherwise die means valuing one's own life at 4,000 times that of a stranger, a ratio Kravinsky considers "obscene."

What marks Kravinsky from the rest of us is that he takes the equal value of all human life as a guide to life, not just as a nice piece of rhetoric. He acknowledges that some people think he is crazy, and even his wife says she believes that he goes too far. One of her arguments against the kidney donation was that one of their children may one day need a kidney, and Zell could be the only compatible donor. Kravinsky's love for his children is, as far as I can tell, as strong as that of any normal parent. Such attachments are part of our nature, no doubt the product of our evolution as mammals who give birth to children, who for an unusually long time require our assistance to survive. However, that does not, in Kravinsky's view, justify our placing a value on the lives of our children that is thousands of times greater than the value we place on the lives of the children of strangers. Asked if he would allow his child to die if it would enable a thousand children to live, Kravinsky said yes. Indeed, he has said he would permit his child to die even if this enabled only two other children to live. Nevertheless, to appease his wife, he recently went back into real estate, made some money, and bought the family a larger home. However, he still remains committed to giving away as much as possible, subject only to keeping his domestic life reasonably tranquil.

Buffett says he believes in giving his children "enough so they feel they could do anything, but not so much that they could do nothing."[11] This means, in his judgment, "a few hundred thousand" each. In absolute terms, that is far more than most Americans are able to leave their children and, by Kravinsky's standard, certainly too much. (Kravinsky says that the hard part is not giving away the first $45 million, but the last $10,000, when you have to live so cheaply that you can't function in the business world.) But even if Buffett left each of his three children a million dollars each, he would still have given away more than 99.99% of his wealth. When someone does that much—especially in a society in which the norm is to leave most of your wealth to your children—it is better to praise them than to cavil about the extra few hundred thousand dollars they might have given.

Philosophers like Liam Murphy of New York University and my colleague Kwame Anthony Appiah at Princeton contend that our obligations are limited to carrying our fair share of the burden of relieving global poverty.[12] They would have us calculate how much would be required to ensure that the world's poorest people have a chance at a decent life, and then divide this sum among the affluent. That would give us each an amount to donate and, having given that, we would have fulfilled our obligations to the poor.

What might that fair amount be? One way of calculating it would be to take as our target, at least for the next 9 years, the Millennium Development Goals set by the United Nations Millennium Summit in 2000. On that occasion, the largest gathering of world leaders in history jointly pledged to meet, by 2015, a list of goals that include

- Reducing by half the proportion of the world's people in extreme poverty (defined as living on less than the purchasing-power equivalent of US$1 per day)
- Reducing by half the proportion of people who suffer from hunger
- Ensuring that children everywhere are able to take a full course of primary schooling
- Ending sex disparity in education
- Reducing by two thirds the mortality rate among children younger than 5 years of age
- Reducing by three quarters the rate of maternal mortality
- Halting and beginning to reverse the spread of HIV/AIDS, and halting and beginning to reduce the incidence of malaria and other major diseases
- Reducing by half the proportion of people without sustainable access to safe drinking water

A United Nations task force, led by Columbia University economist Jeffrey Sachs, estimated the annual cost of meeting these goals to be $121 billion in 2006, rising to $189 billion by 2015. When we take account of existing official development aid promises, the additional amount needed each year to meet the goals is only $48 billion for 2006 and $74 billion for 2015.[13]

Now let's look at the incomes of America's rich and superrich, and ask how much they could reasonably give. The task is made easier by statistics recently provided by Thomas Piketty and Emmanuel Saez, economists at the École Normale Supérieure, Paris-Jourdan, and the University of California, Berkeley, respectively, based on U.S. tax data for 2004.[14] Their figures are for pretax income, excluding income from capital gains, which for the very rich are nearly always substantial. For simplicity I have rounded the figures, generally downward. Note, too, that the numbers refer to "tax units"—that is, in many cases, families rather than individuals.

Piketty and Saez's top bracket comprises 0.01% of U.S. taxpayers. There are 14,400 of them, earning an average of $12,775,000, with total earnings of $184 billion. The minimum annual income in this group is more than $5 million, so it seems reasonable to suppose that they could, without much hardship, give away a third of their annual income, an average of $4.3 million each, for a total of around $61 billion. That would still leave each of them with an annual income of at least $3.3 million.

Next comes the rest of the top 0.1% (excluding the category just described, as I shall do henceforth). There are 129,600 in this group, with an average income of just over $2 million and a minimum income of $1.1 million. If they were each to give a quarter of their income, that would yield about $65 billion, and leave each of them with at least $846,000 annually.

The top 0.5% consists of 575,900 taxpayers, with an average income of $623,000 and a minimum of $407,000. If they were to give one fifth of their income, they would still have at least $325,000 each, and they would be giving a total of $72 billion.

Coming down to the level of those in the top 1%, we find 719,900 taxpayers with an average income of $327,000 and a minimum of $276,000. They could comfortably afford to give 15% of their income. That would yield $35 billion and leave them with at least $234,000.

Finally, the remainder of the nation's top 10% earn at least $92,000 annually, with an average of $132,000. There are nearly 13 million in this group. If they gave the traditional tithe—10% of their income, or an average of $13,200 each—this would yield about $171 billion and leave them a minimum of $83,000.

You could spend a long time debating whether the fractions of income I have suggested for donation constitute the fairest possible scheme. Perhaps the sliding scale should be steeper, so that the superrich give more and the merely comfortable give less. And it could be extended beyond the top 10% of American families, so that everyone able to afford more than the basic necessities of life gives something, even if it is as little as 1%. Be that as it may, the remarkable thing about these calculations is that a scale of donations that is unlikely to impose significant hardship on anyone yields a total of $404 billion—from just 10% of American families.

Obviously, the rich in other nations should share the burden of relieving global poverty. The United States is responsible for 36% of the gross domestic product of all Organization for Economic Cooperation and Development nations. Arguably, because the United States is richer than all other major nations, and its wealth is more unevenly distributed than wealth in almost any other industrialized country, the rich in the United States should contribute more than 36% of total global donations. So somewhat more than 36% of all aid to relieve global poverty should come from the United States. For simplicity, let's take half as a fair share for the United States. On this basis, extending the scheme I suggested worldwide would provide $808 billion annually for development aid. That's more than six times what the task force chaired by Sachs estimated would be required for 2006 to be on track to meet the Millennium Development Goals, and more than 16 times the shortfall between that sum and existing official development aid commitments.

If we are obliged to do no more than our fair share of eliminating global poverty, the burden will not be great. But is that really all we ought to do? Because we all agree that fairness is a good thing, and none of us like doing more because others don't pull their weight, the fair-share view is attractive. In the end, however, I think we should reject it. Let's return to the drowning child in the shallow pond. Imagine it is not one small child who has fallen in, but 50 children. We are among 50 adults, unrelated to the children, picnicking on the lawn around the pond. We can easily wade into the pond and rescue the children, and the fact that we would find it cold and unpleasant sloshing around in the knee-deep muddy water is no justification for failing to do so. The "fair-share" theorists would say that if we each rescue one child, all the children will be saved, and so none of us have an obligation to save more than one. But what if half the picnickers prefer staying clean and dry to rescuing any children at all? Is it acceptable if the rest of us stop after we have rescued just one child, knowing that we have done our fair share, but that half the children will drown? We might justifiably be furious with those who are not doing their fair share, but our anger with them is not a reason for letting the children die. In terms of praise and blame, we are clearly right to condemn, in the strongest terms, those who do nothing. In contrast, we may withhold such condemnation from those who stop when they have done their fair share. Even so, they have let children drown when they could easily have saved them, and that is wrong.

Similarly, in the real world, it should be seen as a serious moral failure when those with ample income do not do their fair share toward relieving global poverty. It isn't so easy, however, to decide on the proper approach to take to those who limit their contribution to their fair share when they could easily do more and when, because others are not playing their part, a further donation would assist many in desperate need. In the privacy of our own judgment, we should believe that it is wrong not to do more. However, whether we should actually criticize people who are doing their fair share, but no more than that, depends on the psychological impact that such criticism will have on them, and on others. This in turn may depend on social practices. If the majority are doing little or nothing, setting a standard higher than the fair-share level may seem so demanding that it discourages people who are willing to make an equitable contribution from doing even that. So it may be best to refrain from criticizing those who achieve the fair-share level. In moving our society's standards forward, we may have to progress one step at a time.

For more than 30 years, I've been reading, writing, and teaching about the ethical issue posed by the juxtaposition, on our planet, of great abundance and life-threatening poverty. Yet it was not until, in preparing this article, I calculated how much America's top 10% of income earners actually make that I fully understood how easy it would be for the world's rich to eliminate, or virtually eliminate, global poverty. (It has actually become much easier throughout the past 30 years, because the rich have grown significantly richer.) I found the result astonishing. I double-checked the figures and asked a research assistant to check them as well. And they are right. Measured against our capacity, the Millennium Development Goals are indecently, shockingly modest. If we fail to achieve them—and, given current indications, we well might—we have no excuses. The target we should be setting for ourselves is not halving the proportion of people living in extreme poverty, and without enough to eat, but ensuring that no one, or virtually no one, needs to live in such degrading conditions. That is a worthy goal, and it is well within our reach.

Notes

1. Bill Gates, speech to Fifty-eighth World Health Assembly (Geneva, Switzerland, May 16, 2005), www.who.int/mediacentre/events/2005/wha58/gates/en/index.html.

2. Ibid.

3. Originally located at www.gatesfoundation.org/AboutUs/OurValues/default.htm, this statement no longer appears on their site. A similar formulation, "Our belief that every life has equal value is at the core of our work at the foundation," can be found at www.gatesfoundation.org/about/Pages/overview.aspx (July 24, 2010).

4. Marc Hofstetter, "Scaling Up Financing for Access to Health" (lecture, Global Health Forum, Geneva, Switzerland, August 31, 2006), www.ghf06.org/ghf06/files/ps02/ghf_pl023_hofstetter.pdf.

5. David Kirkpatrick, interview by Jeffrey Brown, PBS Newshour, PBS (June 16, 2006), www.pbs.org/newshour/bb/social_issues/jan-june06/gates_06-16.html.

6. Walter Isaacson, "In Search of the Real Bill Gates," Time 149 (January 13, 2007), pp. 44–55.

7. Quoted in Janet C. Lowe, Warren Buffett Speaks: Wit and Wisdom from the World's Greatest Investor (New York: Wiley, 1997), p. 165.

8. In, for instance, Thomas Pogge, Politics as Usual: What Lies Behind the Pro-Poor Rhetoric (Cambridge: Polity, 2010).

9. Cecilia Dugger, "Kenyan Farmers' Fate Caught Up in U.S. Aid Rules That Benefit Agribusiness," New York Times (July 31, 2007), p. A8.

10. Nuclear Threat Initiative, "Nuclear Threat Initiative Commits $50 Million to Create IAEA Nuclear Fuel Bank" (press release, Vienna, September 19, 2006), nti.org/c_press/release_IAEA_fuelbank_091906.pdf, p. 10.

11. Warren Buffett, interview by Charlie Rose, *Charlie Rose*, PBS (June 26, 2006), http://www.charlierose.com/view/interview/345.

12. Liam Murphy, *Moral Demands in Nonideal Theory* (New York: Oxford University Press, 2000), p. 76, and Kwame Anthony Appiah, *Cosmopolitanism: Ethics in a World of Strangers* (New York: Norton, 2006), pp. 164–165.

13. UN Millennium Project, *Investing in Development: A Practical Plan to Achieve the Millennium Development Goals* (London: Earthscan, 2005), pp. 249–256.

14. The figures that follow can be found on Emmanuel Saez's website, elsa. berkeley.edu/~saez/

2

Obligations of Justice and Beneficence to Aid the Severely Poor

Elizabeth Ashford

In his hugely influential and controversial essay "Famine, Affluence and Morality," Peter Singer argues that our individual obligations to help those whose vital interests are threatened by chronic severe poverty are morally analogous to the stringent obligation to rescue a child we were to pass drowning in a pond.[1] A common objection to Singer's argument is that the analogy he draws between the obligation to rescue the drowning child and the obligation to aid the severely poor fails, because of key differences between the two contexts. In the latter case, an individual agent is responding to a small-scale emergency, which is random, rare, and episodic, whereas chronic severe poverty is a systemic problem that presents an ongoing threat to the basic interests of the members of a vast group and can only be adequately addressed by a scheme of institutionalized collective action. It is often suggested that Singer's account of our obligations of aid to the severely poor is unreasonably demanding in virtue of giving no intrinsic weight to these differences.

I argue here that these are certainly crucial differences, and, moreover, that it is principally in virtue of them that the threat to persons' interests posed by chronic severe poverty, unlike the threat posed by a random emergency, constitutes a fundamental injustice. However, I maintain that it is a strength of Singer's argument that he focuses our attention on a simple and urgent moral relation that also obtains between individual relatively affluent agents and particular individuals in severe need in just the same way as in a rare and episodic emergency situation, that grounds stringent obligations of beneficence over and beyond obligations of justice. Thus, although the plight of those suffering chronic severe poverty differs from the plight of the drowning child in constituting a systemic injustice that demands an institutional response, Singer's lifesaving analogy nevertheless also holds. Furthermore, I argue that insofar as the plight of chronic severe poverty differs from a standard emergency situation—understood as rare, episodic, and random—in constituting a systemic and ongoing threat to members of a particular group, the moral principles that underlie obligations of beneficence toward those suffering chronic severe poverty are *more* demanding than those that underlie obligations of beneficence in response to emergency situations such as the pond case. As I argue, Kantian contractualist accounts of obligations of beneficence as avoiding the extreme demandingness of the utilitarian approach with which Singer is associated tend to assume implicitly that the status quo is basically just. As a result, these arguments fail to apply to the context of the demandingness of our individual duties of beneficence toward those suffering chronic severe poverty.

I aim to show, then, that although global extreme poverty does indeed constitute a fundamental injustice that demands institutional reform, this does nothing to undermine Singer's account of the stringency and demandingness of our individual obligations of beneficence toward those suffering such poverty. On the contrary, the moral reasons that ground stringent obligations of aid in the pond case equally obtain, and insofar as the threat to basic interests posed by extreme poverty arises from a systemic injustice rather than a random emergency, our duties of beneficence to give aid are more demanding.

I begin by giving a brief overview of obligations of justice and beneficence toward those in severe need. I then, in the next section, analyze Singer's account of the stringency and demandingness of our obligations toward those whose basic interests are threatened by chronic severe poverty. In the third section, I defend his account against the objection that the lifesaving analogy fails. In the last section, I argue that insofar as chronic severe poverty differs from a random emergency in constituting a systemic injustice that presents an ongoing threat to the basic interests of members of a particular group, individual duties of beneficence toward the severely poor are more demanding than duties of beneficence that arise in random emergencies.

OBLIGATIONS OF JUSTICE AND BENEFICENCE TOWARD THOSE SUFFERING CHRONIC SEVERE POVERTY

It is very difficult to offer a firm distinction between obligations of justice and obligations of beneficence.[2] Moreover, according to utilitarianism, all obligations can be seen as ultimately derivative of obligations of beneficence; obligations of justice designate a particular subset of such obligations. It is sufficient for my argument if I identify some of the key features of both kinds of obligations, and show that on even a modest account of the purview of these obligations, we are under obligations of both kinds to redress the plight of those suffering chronic extreme poverty. I intend to leave open the possibility that there may be overlap between the two kinds of obligations.

I am taking obligations of beneficence to be simply obligations to show adequate practical concern for others' interests.[3] A classic example of such an obligation is the obligation to phone for an ambulance if someone collapses on the street in front of you. The rationale for this obligation is that failure to take this easy step to save the person's life would show a grossly insufficient practical concern for that person's vital interests.

The core feature of obligations of justice is that they correspond to rights. Accordingly, obligations of justice are owed to particular individuals who are entitled to the fulfillment of such obligations, and these obligations are justifiably enforced (principally by social institutions). Human rights are rights that are held by everyone in virtue of the universal moral status of human beings. I take the class of basic human rights to mark out a set of rock-bottom rights that are particularly morally urgent, and I take the role of such rights as protecting persons' basic interests against standard threats, where basic interests are those interests that are essential to being able to realize a minimally decent life.

When we consider obligations of justice toward those suffering chronic severe poverty, clearly a crucial class of these are negative obligations not to contribute to such poverty.[4] My focus in this discussion is on positive obligations to aid the severely poor. I take these positive obligations to include obligations of basic justice; I take the right to subsistence to be a basic human right that imposes positive as well as negative obligations.[5] Positive obligations corresponding to the right to subsistence are obligations to protect people from being deprived of the opportunity to earn a subsistence income, and obligations to assist those who have already suffered such a deprivation or who are unable to obtain a subsistence income for some other reason (such as disability).[6]

What is distinctive of obligations of justice to aid those suffering chronic severe poverty is that they correspond to rights, and that, accordingly, they ought to be institutionally articulated and enforced. If there is a basic human right to subsistence, then each person is entitled to reasonably secure access to such subsistence. Corresponding to such a right there is a duty to ensure that different agents' positive obligations are specified, allocated, and enforced in such a way as to ensure that each person is guaranteed reasonably secure access to a subsistence income. Institutional coordination of these obligations is demanded, because they must together constitute a scheme of collective action that will ensure the universal fulfillment of the right to subsistence. Coercive enforcement of the obligations is also demanded to secure compliance with them, again to ensure to a reasonable degree of security that each person's right is actually fulfilled.

In contrast, imperfect obligations of beneficence toward those in severe need are not owed to every human being. Each agent has latitude over whom to help and what kind of help to give, and if different agents' individual obligations of beneficence are not sufficient or are not coordinated in such a way as to aid every destitute individual, this need not constitute a failure of any obligation. For any particular destitute individual, he or she has no moral claim to be helped, and would have no ground for complaint if they did not receive help.[7] As Jeremy Waldron argues:

Jones and his philanthropic friends may think that something has gone wrong if all of them end up (accidentally) lavishing their charity on the same few persons or if, after all of them have fulfilled their imperfect duties, some indigents have still not received any benefit at all. We may want to express this... as follows.... each of the potential beneficiaries has a right to assistance.[8]

As I have argued more fully elsewhere,[9] the claim that the right to subsistence is a basic human right that imposes positive as well as negative obligations follows from each of the two dominant contemporary theories of justice: utilitarianism and Kantian contractualism. One way of showing this is to consider the widely held claim that the fundamental role of obligations of justice is to secure an equitable resolution of competing interests (at least insofar as benefits and burdens are unchosen and subject to social control).[10] As Thomas Pogge emphasizes,[11] these interests are judged from a probabilistic, *ex ante* perspective. From the outset, those who do not enjoy the right to subsistence face a drastically stunted life and, likely, premature death. The threat to basic interests posed by the lack of subsistence is one that could feasibly be eradicated at a small cost, given the level of overall global wealth.[12]

Utilitarian and Kantian contractualist accounts of justice differ over cases in which a few persons' basic needs are at stake that could only be protected at considerable aggregate cost, such as cases of certain severe disabilities or rare medical conditions.[13] According to utilitarianism, the interests of the small group might be outweighed by the total cost to others of protecting such interests, whereas Kantian contractualism prohibits such interpersonal aggregation. However, it follows from both accounts of justice that social institutions that do not recognize a human right to subsistence are so far from securing an equitable resolution of competing interests as to be incompatible with the most minimal concern for persons' well-being or respect for their dignity as rational autonomous agents.

According to utilitarianism, given the extremity of the suffering caused by lack of subsistence and the number affected, and the extreme cheapness of redressing this, failing to do so is incompatible with a minimally adequate acknowledgement of the moral importance of each person's well-being. According to Kantian contractualism, principles under which agents have an obligation to redress this plight cannot be reasonably rejected, and principles under which this obligation is not taken to be an obligation of justice corresponding to a human right are unacceptable from the point of view both of individuals in severe need and of relatively affluent agents.

From the point of view of individual victims of extreme poverty, a set of principles under which they are not taken to be entitled to the help is completely unjustifiable (given the extremity of the burden imposed on them by lacking secure access to subsistence, and the small cost on other individuals of securing it). From the point of view of agents under an obligation of aid, a particularly salient feature of obligations of justice is that

they are held to be justifiably coercively enforced. Both because of the
unfairness of facing an extreme burden of aid as a result of other agents'
failure to do their share, and because of the far greater efficiency of an
institutionalized coordinated response, a principle under which other
agents' compliance with the obligation of aid is coercively enforced cannot
be reasonably rejected.[14]

If the basic human right to subsistence were fulfilled, in conjunction
with the right to physical security and any other basic rights, the status
quo would be such that each person's basic interests would be protected
against standard threats.[15] Accordingly, from the probabilistic ex ante perspective, setting aside the cases of rare medical conditions I mentioned
earlier, each person would have a reasonable chance of leading a decent
life. Conversely, until the right to subsistence has been secured, some
from the outset are likely to die prematurely and are precluded from any
realistic chance of leading a minimally decent and autonomous life, even
though this plight could be feasibly and cheaply prevented. For these
individuals, the existing distribution of competing benefits and burdens is
completely unacceptable.

To sum up, I take the core feature of obligations of justice to be that
they correspond to rights. Obligations of beneficence, by contrast, do not
entail corresponding rights. The primary focus of obligations of justice is
the shape of social institutions. First, the purview of obligations of justice
is the equitable resolution of competing interests across the community
as a whole, or, in the case of human rights, across global social institutions
and the international community. Second, obligations of justice ought to
comprise a scheme of institutionally articulated, coordinated, and enforced
collective action that ensures the corresponding rights are universally
fulfilled. Accordingly, although responsibility for implementing obligations of justice ultimately lies with single individuals, these obligations
are commonly and plausibly understood as fundamentally collective, and
individual agents' obligations may accordingly be taken to be derived
from the underlying collective obligations.

By contrast, the primary focus of obligations of beneficence is what an
individual agent owes to other particular individuals out of practical concern for those individuals' interests. An obligation of beneficence may give
rise to a secondary obligation to seek to coordinate with other agents and
to seek institutional reform, if this is the most effective way of implementing it. However, as I will argue, the primary and underlying obligation is most plausibly taken to be an individual one.[16]

I will now turn to Singer's account of our obligations to aid those whose
vital interests are threatened by chronic severe poverty. One of the most
striking features of Singer's argument (and the one that has been particularly subject to critical scrutiny) is that he bases it on an analogy with a
context in which an individual agent encounters an emergency in which
she is in a position to save a particular individual's life at a small cost. The
threat to life posed by emergencies of this kind is one that is random, rare,

episodic, and on a small scale. As Singer originally presents the example, the agent is the only individual on the scene. Chronic severe poverty, by contrast, is an ongoing threat to the basic interests of a vast number, and can only be adequately redressed—and, indeed, eradicated and avoided— by coordinated institutional action. It has been argued that because of these important differences, Singer's analogy fails.

In accordance with the account of obligations of justice I have outlined, it is in virtue of these differences that positive obligations to redress and eliminate chronic severe poverty, unlike the obligations that arise in the pond case, ought to be seen as obligations of basic justice. Because emergencies such as the pond case are rare, random, and on a small scale, the threat they pose to each person's vital interests, from the probabilistic *ex ante* perspective, is remote, and, moreover, this is not a threat that could feasibly or reasonably be institutionally prevented. In contrast, the threat to vital interests posed by chronic severe poverty is not random; it affects members of a particular group and is on a vast scale. From the outset, members of this group likely face death and are precluded from any reasonable chance of a minimally decent life, and this threat to their basic interests could be feasibly and cheaply prevented. For these reasons, I have argued, chronic severe poverty is a fundamental injustice.

Nevertheless, as I will now argue, Singer is right that there is also a crucial similarity between the two scenarios, in virtue of which in both cases we are under stringent obligations of beneficence over and beyond our obligations of justice. I will begin by offering an analysis of Singer's argument. I will then offer an analysis of the main line of objection to his analogy and will defend his argument against it.

AN ANALYSIS OF SINGER'S ARGUMENT

Singer's argument appeals to an analogy with a situation in which an agent passes a child drowning in a pond and is easily able to rescue the child at the mere cost of getting his trousers muddy. As Singer points out, it is clear that in such a situation the agent is under a highly stringent obligation to rescue the child. Singer's central claim is that the reasons it would be wrong not to rescue the drowning child equally support the view that it is wrong for us not to help those whose vital interests are threatened by chronic severe poverty.

The first premise in his argument is the uncontroversial claim that suffering and death are bad. Singer then argues that the most obvious explanation of why it would be wrong not to rescue the drowning child is grounded in the badness of the harm the child stands to suffer if he is not helped, and the smallness of the cost to the agent of giving that help. Singer expresses this as the general moral principle that if an agent can prevent something bad from happening, without thereby sacrificing something of (comparable) moral significance, he ought to do so. I will

refer to this second premise of Singer's argument as "P2" (and will shortly
discuss the two versions of it he offers). Singer then argues that this principle equally applies to the context of relatively affluent agents' duties of
aid to those suffering severe poverty. Chronic severe poverty causes
suffering and death, and the agent is in a position to prevent persons'
suffering or to save their lives at a small personal cost by, for example,
donating to a nongovernmental organization (NGO). Singer concludes
that every relatively affluent agent is under an obligation to give aid to
those whose basic interests are threatened by extreme poverty that is just
as stringent as the obligation to rescue the drowning child.

In the context of chronic severe poverty, given the vast number of
people whose vital interests are threatened whom the agent could help at
a relatively small personal cost, P2 continues to apply over and over again.
It therefore soon threatens to become extremely demanding. Singer offers
two versions of P2, the second of which is less demanding, and asks the
reader to choose between them.

The first version and the one he favors is this: "If it is in our power to
prevent something bad from happening, without thereby sacrificing
anything of comparable moral importance, we ought, morally, to do it."[17]
This implies that the agent ought to continue donating until the point at
which the cost to herself of giving a further donation would be as great
as the cost she could prevent by giving the donation. However, it should
be stressed that Singer does not invoke the requirement, advocated by
some versions of utilitarianism, that we ought to maximize the impersonal good:

> It follows from some forms of utilitarian theory that we all ought, morally,
> to be working full time to increase the balance of happiness over misery.
> The position I have taken here would not lead to this conclusion in all cir-
> cumstances, for if there were no bad occurrences that we could prevent
> without sacrificing something of comparable moral importance, my argu-
> ment would have no application.[18]

Rather, Singer is appealing to the obligation that we prevent something
bad—suffering and death from lack of food, shelter, and medical care. The
demandingness of this obligation arises from the fact that there is currently so much suffering and death we are in a position to prevent. It is
because of the extremity of the plight imposed by chronic severe poverty
and the fact that the agent could save or transform an individual's life by
giving the further donation, and because this same relationship obtains
between the agent and a huge number of other individuals in dire straits,
that the first version of P2 will require her to donate until the cost to herself is extreme.

The alternative version of P2 that Singer offers is: "[I]f it is in our
power to prevent something very bad from happening, without thereby
sacrificing anything morally significant, we ought, morally, to do it."[19] It
has been objected that while the first version of P2 is unreasonably

demanding, the second version is so undemanding as to be fairly empty, given that even trivial sacrifices can be plausibly described as having some moral significance, and that this version is therefore unable to establish the conclusion for which Singer is arguing. For example, Singer is keen to establish that it is wrong for us to spend money on trivial luxury items, such as fashionable clothes, in circumstances in which we could save people's lives by donating the money. However, it might be reasonably claimed that although occasionally buying fashionable clothes is clearly not of comparable moral significance to saving someone's life, neither is it of *no* moral significance (because it can enhance our well-being to have clothes other than what we need to stay warm).

However, the core of Singer's argument is to appeal to the widely held view that it would be wrong not to rescue the drowning child, and then show that there is an analogy between this obligation and our obligation to aid those whose vital interests are threatened by extreme poverty. This suggests that to arrive at the most charitable interpretation of his argument so as to best evaluate its force, we should take the version of P2 that we view as offering the most plausible account of our intuition that it would be wrong not to save the drowning child. In offering a second version of the principle that is close to being at the opposite end of spectrum from the first version of it with respect to the extent of its demandingness, and inviting the reader to choose for herself between them, Singer's strategy can be taken as leaving open the question of precisely how demanding is the principle that explains our obligation to rescue the drowning child, and showing that wherever we take the required level of sacrifice to fall between these two opposite ends of the spectrum, the principle has radical implications when applied to the context of absolute poverty.

It seems that prevalent moral thinking would not accept the claim that the agent would be under a stringent obligation to rescue a child if the risk to her own life were considerable, even if the child were certain to drown unless rescued, or if it would involve the agent's losing a limb or suffering some other serious permanent debility. Prevalent moral thinking, therefore, seems to reject the utilitarian principle that the agent is required to sacrifice her own interests up to the point at which this sacrifice is on a par with the cost to someone else, where the agent would be able to prevent that cost. On the other hand, prevalent moral thinking does seem to require an agent to rescue a child at a significant financial cost (it would certainly, say, require her to rescue the child at the cost of ruining her only smart suit). One understanding of P2, therefore, is a middle position between the two versions Singer offers that combines elements of both, and interprets "comparable moral significance" as meaning, roughly, "in the same moral ballpark." This is a vague category, but plausibly a significant risk of loss of life or limb or a cost that would mar one's life would be in the same moral ballpark as the victim's loss of life, whereas a significant financial cost would not be. This interpretation, moreover, is suggested by Singer's statement that the first principle does not require the agent to give up family relations, because most people find such relations necessary to a flourishing life, so that to sacrifice them would be a sacrifice of great moral significance, "Hence, no such sacrifice is required by the principle for which I am here arguing."[20] It is also in line with Singer's most recent expression of the principle as the claim that "[i]f it is in your power to prevent something bad from happening, without sacrificing anything nearly as important, it is wrong not to do so."[21] Singer there also explicitly states that this is a deliberately vague principle, so that the reader can choose for herself what interpretation of it she judges most reasonable.

On this interpretation, therefore, when we apply P2 to the context of chronic severe poverty, the agent is obliged to keep donating time and money to save persons' lives (or other basic interests) until the point that she can honestly claim that the cost to herself of doing more would be in the same moral ballpark as the terrible harm she could prevent by doing so. What is striking about P2, as Singer presents it, is that it applies iteratively to every instance in which the agent is able to save someone's life (or other basic interests). The more the agent donates to an NGO, the greater the cost she will incur by giving a further donation, given diminishing marginal utility. However, even when she has already donated a great deal, it will be hard for her to claim that the loss of a further few hundred dollars is in the same moral ballpark as having one's life saved or of avoiding some calamitous harm (such as the death of one's child), and so P2 implies that it will be hard for her to justify not giving that further donation; and the same applies to the next donation, and so on. The sacrifice this second version of P2 requires is therefore still hugely demanding. I will nevertheless now defend Singer's appeal to the life-saving analogy and to his iterative principle of beneficence against the objections that have been made.

A DEFENSE OF SINGER'S ANALOGY

A common objection to Singer's argument is that the analogy he draws, with a small-scale emergency situation in which the agent is under a stringent obligation to save another person's life directly, fails. In this kind of emergency situation, it is appropriate to focus on what steps that individual agent should take to save the person's life. Chronic severe poverty, by contrast, is a systemic problem that can only be adequately addressed by a coordinated institutional response. In this context, it is therefore inappropriate to focus on what steps an individual relatively affluent agent ought to take to go to the direct aid of particular individuals in severe need.[22]

It is difficult to pin down the precise objection to Singer's argument expressed in this line of argument against it, and I will try to elucidate various ways of understanding the objection. Taken as a criticism of the implications of Singer's argument for how we ought to implement our obligations of aid, the objection completely misses the mark. Singer is the first to stress that we ought to implement these obligations as efficiently as possible. If this involves seeking to coordinate with others to bring about institutional reform rather than donating to NGOs, then that is what we ought to do.[23] Singer's central claim concerns the stringency and demandingness of our obligations of aid, and, clearly, obligations to seek institutional reform can be just as stringent and demanding as obligations to donate to NGOs.

Therefore, to have any bite, the objection must be directed at the implications of Singer's argument for the stringency and demandingness of the obligation of aid he advocates. It is this criticism, therefore, on which I focus. According to this objection, we cannot plausibly be morally required to make such large sacrifices as the ones the iterated application of P2 implies. Stringent obligations to help in an emergency are not unreasonably demanding, precisely because such emergencies are rare, random, and short term. In contrast, according to this line of objection, it is not plausible to take agents to be under a comparably stringent obligation to respond to the ongoing threat to the vital interests of a vast number posed by chronic severe poverty.

One way of understanding this objection to the demandingness of Singer's account is that in the context of chronic severe poverty, unlike that of random emergencies, our focus ought to be on obligations of justice rather than of beneficence, and that the former are less demanding than the latter. Obligations of justice, as we have seen, may be plausibly construed as collective obligations that ought to be institutionally allocated and enforced. If a scheme of institutionalized coordinated action to redress and prevent chronic severe poverty were in place, this would be vastly more efficient than individual agents' attempts to help those in severe need, so that the total cost of addressing chronic severe poverty would be much smaller. Moreover, because coercive mechanisms would be in place to ensure that each agent fulfilled her fair share of the obligation (such as taxation), this burden would be fairly distributed among agents. Therefore the cost to any individual agent would not be onerous.

When our focus is on the question of what would constitute an adequate response to the problem of chronic severe poverty, clearly the institutional implementation of obligations of justice is first and foremost. If just institutions were in place to ensure that persons had their just economic entitlements in the first place, they would generally have adequate opportunities to earn a subsistence income, with provision for those unable to do so. Obligations of beneficence to respond to the plight of those suffering chronic severe poverty would not even arise. As I have argued, this institutional scheme would be vastly preferable to the existing one from the point of view of both those in need and relatively affluent agents. However, in the actual situation that currently obtains, another key question for the individual moral agent concerns how she ought to respond to the actual plight of those who are suffering chronic severe poverty as a result of the unjust social institutions that are actually in place. In this context, three important considerations arise.

The first point to note is that a systemic injustice can give rise to obligations of beneficence as well as of justice. These obligations of beneficence may be centrally important, even though they would not have arisen in the first place if just social institutions were in place. This point can be illustrated by considering a variation on Singer's pond analogy. Suppose several children's lives have been put in danger as part of a government campaign to intimidate opponents by threatening members of their families. In this case, the threat to the children's lives would constitute an injustice rather than a random emergency. If an agent were to encounter one of these children and could easily save his life, then on some accounts of justice that agent might not be under an obligation of justice to save the child (perhaps because she had already fulfilled her fair share of the obligation to oppose the government and its tactics, or because she was a foreigner who was not implicated in the injustice), but she would certainly be under an obligation of beneficence to do so, in just the same way as in Singer's original pond example.

Second, in the current nonideal world context in which just institutions are not in place, obligations of justice toward those in extreme poverty may, in fact, be close in nature to obligations of beneficence toward them. In this context, the comparison is not between the agent's obligation of justice to contribute her fair share to an institutional scheme to prevent chronic severe poverty (through taxation for example), on the one hand, and her open-ended obligations of beneficence to donate a huge percentage of her income and time to support NGOs, on the other. Rather, the content of obligations of justice and of beneficence may be similar. As we have seen, obligations of beneficence as well as of justice may be directed at seeking institutional reform. Conversely, as Liam Murphy has argued, when unjust social institutions are in place, obligations of justice may be directed at donating to NGOs in circumstances in which this would protect persons' basic interests more efficiently than by seeking institutional reform.[24]

Turning to the demandingness of the two kinds of obligations, it might be claimed that because obligations of justice are fundamentally collective, individual agents are not required to fulfill more than their fair share of such obligations even in circumstances of widespread noncompliance, when coercive institutional mechanisms to compel compliance are not in place. This claim, however, is far from obvious when applied to the obligations of justice corresponding to the human right to subsistence. The view that agents ought to fulfill their fair share of obligations of justice is plausible when those obligations correspond to special rights that are grounded in membership of a reciprocal group. These rights are earned in virtue of contributing to the common good, and can be appropriately forfeited by those who fail to contribute their fair share (to prevent their free riding on others' contributions). However, basic human rights such as the right to subsistence are too urgent to be either earned or forfeited, and are held by everyone simply by virtue of the universal moral status of human beings. Moreover, those who would suffer if the agent fulfilled only her fair share of the obligation of justice are not the ones who have failed to contribute their fair share. Far from being fellow members of a community of agents interacting on a basis of reciprocity, they lack the preconditions for the exercise of rational autonomous agency.

This argument is controversial, and an adequate defense of is beyond the scope of this essay, so I will set it aside; but it brings me to the third point: that one advantage of obligations of beneficence in this context is that they may be easier to identify than obligations of justice. There is very little dispute that an agent would be under an obligation to save a child she passed who was drowning in a pond, on the ground that failing to save the child would show a completely deficient degree of concern for the child's interests. What Singer's argument highlights is that whatever the complexities of the institutional causes of and solutions to chronic severe poverty, the moral reasons that underlie the obligation to save the drowning child's life obtain in the context of chronic severe poverty in just the same way, and so equally ground a stringent obligation of aid.

It should also be stressed that, in the current situation, obligations of justice are just as liable as obligations of beneficence to give rise to the thought that any action toward implementing them that an individual agent can take is grossly inadequate and inefficacious in comparison with what is needed. The primary focus of obligations of justice is the shape of social institutions, and when unjust social institutions are in place, these obligations are primarily directed at institutional reform. However, an individual agent may be unable to achieve significant institutional reform, and, furthermore, the effort she puts toward it is likely to have little or no impact on any actual victims of chronic severe poverty. In one respect, obligations of beneficence have an advantage in this regard. The primary focus of such obligations is on what we as individual agents owe to particular individuals in severe need simply out of practical concern for their interests. Consideration of the institutional causes and remedies for such poverty enters secondarily, when we consider how best to implement this obligation. It is a strength of Singer's argument that it focuses on a simple and urgent moral relation that obtains between an individual relatively affluent agent and particular individuals whose basic interests are threatened by chronic severe poverty, in just the same way as in the pond case, a situation in which we would feel ourselves to be under a stringent moral obligation to give aid. In both cases, we as individual agents are in a position to save or transform the lives of particular individuals at a small personal cost.[25] In the context of global poverty, this relation tends to be obscured by the scale and complexity of such poverty.

I suggest, then, that in the current situation, in which just social institutions that would prevent chronic severe poverty are not in place, obligations of beneficence as well as obligations of justice play a crucial moral role. Although these two kinds of obligations have different groundings, they may both, as we have seen, have a similar content: Implementing both may involve donating to NGOs and seeking institutional reform. Each of these responses can lead to what Peter Unger calls "futility thinking," given the scale and complexity of chronic severe poverty.[26] When we consider how much to donate to NGOs, it is tempting to feel that a substantial donation will involve a fairly futile sacrifice, given that it will help only a tiny fraction of these in need and will not combat the root institutional causes of chronic severe poverty. On the other hand, when we consider how to go about seeking institutional reform, this addresses the root problem, but there is risk that as individual agents we will not be able to advance such reform significantly, and that our efforts in this regard will have no impact on the lives of any particular victims of chronic severe poverty. There is a danger that we will fluctuate back and forth in this way and end up implementing neither of these responses. Both kinds of obligations play an important role in combating this futility thinking, from different, complementary perspectives. The role played by obligations of beneficence is to focus our attention on the fact that we are in a position to prevent the death or extreme suffering of some individuals in severe need, at a small personal cost, and that this has just as much moral significance in the context of global severe poverty as it does in a small-scale emergency, where we would feel morally compelled to give help.

Another way of understanding the objection to Singer's lifesaving analogy is as the claim that it leads him to offer an implausible analysis of our obligations of beneficence themselves. In the pond case, the individual agent is the only person on the scene. The obligation of beneficence is therefore an individual one. By contrast, it may be argued, in the context of chronic severe poverty, in which a vast number of agents are able to help, the obligation of beneficence ought to be understood as a collective one.

A particularly sophisticated defense of this understanding of the obligation of beneficence as a collective one has been offered by Liam Murphy.[27] Murphy argues that obligations of beneficence are collective obligations owed by the whole group of agents who are able to help to "those in need" considered as a group. Each agent is required to fulfill only her fair share of the collective obligation, even if other agents are failing to fulfill their fair share. Thus, the level of sacrifice that an individual agent is required to make does not exceed the level that would be optimal under full compliance.

On this view, the interests of those in need belong to a pool of potential beneficiaries that the agent addresses purely as a member of a group of potential benefactors, and the amount of aid the agent should give is determined solely by what would be the fair division of the burden of aid among those benefactors. Thus, the interests of those in need are pooled and the agent is not required to respond to any of these interests directly, but rather to a proportionate share of that pool—however small would be the cost to the agent of fulfilling more than that proportionate share, and however great the harm she could prevent by doing so.

Singer considers a variation on the pond case in which there are several children drowning and several agents who could rescue them, most of whom fail to do so. On Murphy's cooperative principle of beneficence, the agent is required to rescue only her fair share of the children. The agent is not under an obligation to respond to the plight of the other children on the grounds that this would exceed her fair quota of aid, regardless of the severity of the harm those children stand to suffer if the agent fails to help them and the smallness of the cost to her of doing so. Singer points out, however, that in this scenario it would not be plausible to say that the agent ought to rescue only her fair share of the drowning children. If she were to do so, this would seem to show insufficient weight to the interests of the other children she left to drown; and the reason for this is that, in the case of each of these children, she could prevent their drowning at such a small cost. In this context, then, it is more plausible to hold that P2 applies iteratively to each of the children the agent is in a position to rescue at a small cost than to take the agent to be under an obligation to rescue a proportionate share of the drowning children considered as a group.

The next question is whether the analogy holds between the pond case in which there are several agents on the scene most of whom are refusing to rescue their fair share of the drowning children, and the standing problem of chronic severe poverty. The same considerations that led to the conclusion that it would demonstrate a failure of beneficence of the agent to give only her fair share of help in the pond case equally apply to this context. If we suppose that the agent could save or transform the lives of a vast number at an extremely small cost by giving more than her fair share of aid to the severely poor, then to fail to do so would again seem to show inadequate concern for their interests. Murphy does concede that there might be an exception to the claim that agents ought to do only their fair share of aid in a situation of "catastrophe on an unprecedented scale."[28] However, this can plausibly be construed as the situation that relatively affluent agents currently face. The current situation, in which there are 18 million annual poverty-related deaths and the lives of many more millions are drastically stunted as a result of chronic severe poverty, while far from being unprecedented, can be plausibly described as morally catastrophic.[29]

It should also be noted that obligations of beneficence to aid those whose basic interests are threatened by chronic severe poverty would not arise in the first place if just social institutions to prevent such poverty were in place. Obligations of beneficence, therefore, only arise because obligations of justice to bring about institutional reform and ensure that persons have adequate economic opportunities and entitlements have not been fulfilled. It follows that if we acknowledge any such obligations of beneficence toward those suffering chronic severe poverty—as Murphy does—we are already acknowledging that agents may be under an oner-ous moral demand to respond to the plight persons actually face as a result of other agents' failing to act as they should. In deciding the extent of these obligations of beneficence themselves, it seems arbitrary to limit them to the amount of aid that would be needed if there were full com-pliance with them, regardless of the plight persons face as a result of other agents' noncompliance and of the smallness of the cost to the agent of helping them.

I conclude that Singer is right that the features of emergencies that ground stringent obligations to prevent persons' suffering or death also apply to our situation in relation to those whose basic interests are threat-ened by chronic severe poverty. Despite the differences between these two contexts, P2 applies in each case. However much aid the agent has given, it remains the case that she could save or transform the life of another individual in dire straits at an extremely small personal cost (say, $200), an individual who will not otherwise be helped. If we do consider this particular individual's plight, it is indeed hard to justify the agent's duty of beneficence not extending to this individual, too. In this bizarre situation relatively affluent agents currently face, in which literally every $200 they spend could save or transform someone's life if they gave it to a reputable NGO, it is, I suggest, appropriate that it should be hard for agents to justify not making that further sacrifice and that there should be no morally comfortable stopping point, precisely because P2 does keep applying. Until a just status quo has been brought about, Singer's pond analogy reflects the urgent moral relation that obtains between the individual agent and individuals in severe need in just the same way as in the drowning child scenario.

Moreover, as I will now argue, insofar as chronic severe poverty differs from Singer's pond example, in constituting an ongoing threat to the basic interests of particular individuals and a systemic injustice, the principle governing individual duties of beneficence toward them is more demanding than the principle governing duties of beneficence to protect persons' basic interests in random emergencies.

THE DEMANDINGNESS OF OBLIGATIONS OF BENEFICENCE TO PROTECT PEOPLE FROM SYSTEMIC AND NONRANDOM THREATS TO THEIR BASIC INTERESTS

Objections to the demandingness of Singer's account of duties of benefi-cence toward those suffering chronic severe poverty, and to the utilitarian theory with which he is associated, have often been made from the per-spective of Kantian contractualism as the main rival impartial moral theory. However, defenses of Kantian contractualism as being only mod-erately demanding have often implicitly assumed that the status quo, against which the benefits and burdens imposed by candidate principles are assessed, is basically just. They, therefore, fail to apply to the context of our obligations to aid those suffering chronic severe poverty.

The assessment of candidate principles governing obligations of beneficence is principally determined by comparing the costs to the agent in a position to give help imposed by a demanding principle of aid, and the cost to individuals in need imposed by less demanding principles.[30] The cost imposed by moral principles is not limited to their impact on individuals' well-being, but will include considerations such as the impact such principles have on the degree of control individuals have over their own lives. In addition, when assessing these principles we need to consider the general character of the social world in which different kinds of conduct are prohibited or permitted, rather than focus simply on the costs to the agent giving help or the person in need of help imposed by a particular action or omission on a particular occasion.

Arguments that Kantian contractualism can provide a less demanding alternative to Singer's approach have often assumed that the status quo against which these costs are measured is one in which the different individuals are all in a position of equality. Rahul Kumar, for example, in his defense of a moderately demanding Kantian contractualist account of obligations of aid, discusses obligations of aid that arise in the context of emergencies, where the threat to persons' basic interests is random.[31] The example he focuses on involves a rabid dog whose bite will be lethal to the person he is threatening to attack, and who can only be stopped by the agent's interposing himself between this person and the dog, at the cost of the agent's losing his arm. Because such emergencies occur at random, the individuals who are considering candidate principles are all in an equal position: Those who stand to be burdened by a less demanding principle (by not being saved in such an emergency) also stand to be benefited by it, by being under less onerous duties of aid. The randomness of these emergencies, in conjunction with their rareness, also means that from the probabilistic *ex ante* perspective, the chance for any particular individual of being in a position in need of lifesaving aid in an emergency is remote. Therefore, the reduction in life expectancy imposed by a less demanding principle of aid governing such an emergency is likely not to be very significant. Each person may therefore judge the cost imposed by a less demanding principle of not being helped in such an emergency to be outweighed by the cost imposed by a more demanding principle, of having a lesser degree of control over their lives.

However, in the context of considering principles governing obligations of beneficence toward those suffering chronic severe poverty, the individuals raising objections to candidate principles are not in a position of equality. The threat to persons' basic interests posed by chronic severe poverty is neither random nor remote. Chronic severe poverty presents an ongoing threat to the basic interests of members of a particular group. Members of this group are, from the outset, precluded from the opportunity to lead a minimally decent life and stand to suffer drastic harm (such as their own or their children's death), unless they are helped. For these individuals, the cost they can be expected to incur through general acceptance of less demanding principles under which agents are not under a duty of beneficence to help them is extremely severe (it is the cost of likely premature death or some other drastic harm), and they do not stand to benefit from these less demanding principles. Their objections to less demanding principles of aid under which they are not helped are therefore likely to be so strong that they outweigh the objections by individuals giving aid to all but hugely demanding principles. This indicates, then, that a Kantian contractualist account of the moral principles governing obligations of aid that arise in the context of chronic severe poverty will be vastly more demanding than those that arise in the context of random emergencies.

As I have argued, the fulfillment of the basic human right to subsistence is a requirement of minimal justice. If this right were to be fulfilled, then (setting aside the cases of certain severe disabilities and so on) persons' basic interests would generally be threatened only in the context of emergency situations. Moreover, our prevalent moral thinking holds that obligations to protect persons' basic interests in emergencies are highly stringent, because of the drastic harm the victims stand to suffer if they are not helped. As I noted earlier, Singer offers a plausible analysis of the rationale behind such obligations, grounded on the severity of the harm the person stands to suffer if he is not helped and the smallness of the cost to the agent of giving the help.

The prevalent view of these obligations as being only moderately demanding implicitly assumes that such emergencies are rare. However, as I have argued, the reasons that underlie the stringent obligations to give help in emergencies equally underlie obligations to help those whose basic interests are threatened by chronic severe poverty, although this threat to persons' basic interests is continuous and on a vast scale. This difference in scale in no way undermines the stringency of our obligations to aid the severely poor. Furthermore, insofar as chronic severe poverty poses an ongoing threat to members of a particular group, I have argued that the moral principles that underlie obligations of aid toward those suffering such poverty are even more demanding than those that arise in the context of random emergencies.

If the role of justice is to ensure an equitable resolution of competing interests then it is reasonable to expect that when the status quo is fundamentally unjust, the conflict between the agent's interest in not being burdened by onerous obligations of aid, and the interest of the individuals in dire straits in being helped, cannot be resolved. If the status quo were just, persons' basic interests would be protected against standard threats, and each person would have a reasonable chance of leading a decent life. Persons' basic interests would be threatened only in the context of rare and random emergency situations. The obligation to give aid in such an emergency would plausibly not require the sacrifice of the agent's core interests, and because emergencies would arise only rarely, this obligation would not involve a cumulative cost. In such circumstances, therefore, obligations toward those in severe need would not be very demanding.

In contrast, when the human right to subsistence has not been realized, then for those who lack minimally adequate access to subsistence or lack a realistic chance of earning a subsistence income, the existing status quo is deeply unacceptable. From the outset they face an ongoing threat to their most basic interests. In the case of each of these individuals whom individual agents are in a position to help, the severity of the harm they stand to suffer if they are not helped grounds a reason to help them that is as urgent as the reason to prevent death or extreme suffering in a random emergency, and insofar as their plight is not random, this reason is even stronger.

Notes

I am grateful to Thomas Pogge and Leif Wenar for their very helpful comments on previous drafts.

1. Peter Singer, "Famine, Affluence, and Morality," in William Aiken and Hugh LaFollette, eds., *World Hunger and Moral Obligation* (Englewood Cliffs, N.J.: Prentice-Hall, 1977), pp. 22–36. His argument is further explored and developed in *The Life You Can Save* (London: Picador, 2009).

2. For a perspicuous discussion of this see Allen Buchanan, "Justice and Charity," *Ethics* 97 (1987), 558–575.

3. I am following Cullity's forceful conception of such obligations, as discussed in Garrett Cullity, *The Moral Demands of Affluence* (Oxford: Oxford University Press, 2004).

4. For a discussion of the crucial causal role played by global as well as domestic social institutions in the high level of chronic severe poverty, see Thomas Pogge, *World Poverty and Human Rights: Cosmopolitan Responsibilities and Reforms* (Cambridge: Polity Press, 2002).

5. For a compelling defense of this claim, see Henry Shue, *Basic Rights: Subsistence, Affluence, and U.S. Foreign Policy*, 2nd ed. (Princeton, N.J.: Princeton University Press, 1980). For a defense of Shue's argument against some recent critiques, see Elizabeth Ashford, "The Alleged Dichotomy Between Positive and Negative Rights and Duties," in Charles Beitz and Robert Goodin, eds., *Global Basic Rights* (Oxford: Oxford University Press, 2009), pp. 92–112.

6. I am setting aside the issue of obligations to aid those who are responsible for their own plight. This issue has very little relevance to the issue of positive obligations toward those suffering chronic severe poverty, given they generally lack any realistic opportunity to earn a subsistence income (and, moreover, largely comprise children).

7. I have argued elsewhere that obligations of justice may be also be imperfect before just social institutions are in place that have specified and allocated them, but that, in virtue of their being obligations of justice corresponding to a right, they ought to be made perfect. There is a requirement of justice to set up an institutional framework to articulate and coordinate agents' individual obligations of justice to ensure the fulfillment of the right.

8. Jeremy Waldron, *Liberal Rights* (Cambridge: Cambridge University Press, 1993), pp. 15–16.

9. Elizabeth Ashford, "The Duties Imposed by the Human Right to Basic Necessities," in Thomas Pogge, ed., *UNESCO Volume I: Freedom from Poverty as a Human Right* (Oxford: Oxford University Press, 2007), pp. 183–218.

10. On many prominent Kantian contractualist accounts of justice (including John Rawls's), obligations of justice are grounded in relations of reciprocity. However, justice as reciprocity is not an adequate foundation for the duties that correspond to human rights, given that human rights are held by every person simply by virtue of being a person, regardless of whether they are fellow members of a reciprocal scheme. A Kantian contractualist account of the duties of justice imposed by human rights is therefore more plausibly grounded directly on the universal moral status of persons as rational autonomous agents. For a forceful defense of this, see, for example, Allen Buchanan, "Justice as Reciprocity Versus Subject-Centered Justice," *Philosophy and Public Affairs* 19 (1990), pp. 227–252, and Allen Buchanan, *Justice, Legitimacy, and Self-Determination* (Oxford: Oxford University Press 2004).

11. Pogge, *World Poverty and Human Rights*, p. 46–48.

12. See, for example, Shaohua Chen and Martin Ravillon, "The Developing World Is Poorer Than We Thought, But No Less Successful in the Fight Against Poverty," Policy Research Working Paper 4003 (Washington, D.C., World Bank Development Research Group, August 2008), go.worldbank.org/45FS30HBF0; Thomas Pogge, "Developing Morally Plausible Indices of Poverty and Gender Equity: A Research Program," in Alison Jaggar, ed., *Global Gender Justice*, special issue of *Philosophical Topics* 37 (2009), pp. 199–221.

13. Rawls, of course, sets aside the issue of duties of justice owed to the severely disabled, given his conception of justice as grounded in relations of reciprocity.

14. I am following T. M. Scanlon's formulation of Kantian contractualism, as he presents it in *What We Owe to Each Other* (Cambridge, Mass.: Harvard University Press, 1998), but my argument is not dependent on this formulation.

15. I am leaving open the question of what other basic human rights there might be. Following J. S. Mill and Henry Shue, I take the rights to subsistence and to physical security to be of paramount importance in protecting persons' essential interests, and so to be among the class of basic human rights.

16. This account of the distinction between obligations of justice and beneficence is compatible with the utilitarian claim that obligations of justice are a special category of obligations of beneficence. On Mill's view, for example, obligations of justice, which correspond to rights and are justifiably enforced, are marked out because of their role in protecting persons' most essential interests. Nonutilitarian accounts of justice, by contrast, often take obligations of justice to have a fundamentally different grounding than duties of beneficence. See, for example, Philippa Foot, "Utilitarianism and the Virtues," *Mind* 94 (1985), pp. 196–209.

17. Singer, "Famine, Affluence, and Morality," p. 28.

18. Ibid., p. 22.

19. Ibid., p. 28.

20. Singer, *Practical Ethics*, 2nd ed. (New York: Cambridge University Press, 1993), p. 245.

21. Singer, *The Life You Can Save*, p. 15.

22. Andrew Kuper, for example, argues along these lines in "More Than Charity: Cosmopolitan Alternatives to the 'Singer Solution'," *Ethics & International Affairs* 16 (2002), p. 111.

23. Singer emphasizes this implication of his argument in "Poverty, Facts, and Political Philosophies: Response to 'More Than Charity'," *Ethics & International Affairs* 16 (2002), p. 123.

24. Liam Murphy, "Institutions and the Demands of Justice," *Philosophy and Public Affairs* 27 (Autumn 1998), pp. 251–291.

25. This claim, of course, relies on the empirical assumption that at least some forms of aid are effective, which is beyond the scope of this essay to defend. For a forceful defense of it, see, for example, Garrett Cullity, *The Moral Demands of Affluence*, chap. 3, and Thomas Pogge, *World Poverty and Human Rights*, chap. 1, sect. II. The effectiveness of the positive duty of aid would clearly be vastly greater if it were fulfilled in conjunction with the negative duty not to support global social institutions that encourage and facilitate the exercise of nondemocratic power in poorer countries (and this negative duty is the primary subject of Pogge's book).

26. Peter Unger, *Living High and Letting Die* (New York: Oxford University Press, 1996).

27. Liam Murphy, *Moral Demands in Nonideal Theory* (New York: Oxford University Press, 2000).

28. Ibid., p. 67.

29. Pogge, *World Poverty and Human Rights*, p. 2.

30. For a longer discussion of this, see Elizabeth Ashford, "The Demandingness of Scanlon's Contractualism," *Ethics* 113 (January 2003), pp. 273–302.

31. Rahul Kumar, "Defending the Moral Moderate: Contractualism and Common Sense," *Philosophy and Public Affairs* 28 (Autumn 1999), pp. 275–309.

3

How International Nongovernmental Organizations Should Act

Thomas Pogge

We inhabit this world with large numbers of people who are very badly off through no fault of their own. The official statistics are overwhelming: 1,020 million people (more than ever before) are chronically undernourished,[1] 884 million lack access to safe drinking water,[2] 2,500 million lack access to improved sanitation,[3] 2,000 million lack access to essential medicines,[4] 924 million lack adequate shelter,[5] 1,600 million lack electricity,[6] 796 million adults are illiterate,[7] 218 million children are child laborers,[8] and 1,400 million consume less per month than could be bought in the United States for $38 in 2005.[9] Roughly one third of all human deaths, 18 million annually, are the result of poverty-related causes, straightforwardly preventable through better nutrition, safe drinking water, cheap rehydration packs, vaccines, antibiotics, and other medicines.[10] People of color, females, and the very young are heavily overrepresented among the global poor, and hence also among those suffering the staggering effects of severe poverty.[11]

The people appearing in these statistics live in distant, underdeveloped countries. Some of us in the rich countries care about and seek to improve their circumstances. However, it is difficult to do this on one's own, so we cooperate with others. We can do this politically, trying to get our governments and corporations to do less harm and more good in poor countries. We can also do this by supporting international nongovernmental organizations (INGOs) that offer to pool our contributions and make such funds effective toward human rights, development, and humanitarian goals.

Not enough of us act in either of these ways. The costs and opportunity costs of a full-fledged effort to eradicate severe poverty and its attendant medical and educational deficits worldwide might amount to some $300 billion annually—at least initially, because costs would decrease dramatically in future years.[12] This amount is affordable, even if it came from just the most affluent countries containing about 16% of the world's population. The gross national incomes of these countries sum to about $42 trillion,[13] 140 times larger than the cost of eradicating severe poverty.

But $300 billion annually is a huge amount relative to the roughly $28 billion the rich countries actually spend each year to protect the global poor: about $15.5 billion in official development assistance for basic social services[14] and about $12.6 billion (0.03% of gross national income) through INGOs.[15]

International nongovernmental organizations face difficult moral decisions about how to spend their funds. In the world as it is, with massive human deprivation and little money to reduce it, any decisions an INGO makes is likely to affect many lives severely. To put it bluntly, an INGO must often make decisions that will certainly lead to many deaths, because spending one's limited funds on trying to protect some persons is tantamount to leaving others to their fate. This is an awesome responsibility.

Contributors also face such awesome choices. Some INGOs are wasteful and corrupt, and contributions to them may then prevent no serious harm at all. And even when I am pretty sure that my contribution to one INGO will enable it to prevent deaths, it is clear that there are other INGOs for which the same is true. Different INGOs prevent different deaths. By contributing to one rather than another, I am, then, indirectly deciding who will live and who will die. Obviously, spreading my contribution over all effective INGOs is no solution, because each will then receive much less than if I had given my whole contribution to it alone.

International nongovernmental organizations can realize large economies of scale, because they deliberate and deliver for many. Choosing an INGO to do this for them, contributors are giving with a triple trust. We trust that the INGO has developed carefully formulated moral priorities governing how the collected money should be spent. We trust that this INGO has procured the information and inventive talent it needs to implement the priorities well through the funding of specific projects. And we trust that this INGO is funding the chosen projects efficiently. Although we can check up on any INGO in various ways, there remains a large element of trust that most contributors cannot eliminate at reasonable cost.

The trust of contributors saddles INGO staff with a second responsibility: They must not let their contributors down by setting the wrong moral priorities, by funding infeasible or counterproductive projects, or by frittering money away through carelessness and corruption. This responsibility cannot be discharged by ensuring that contributors never learn that their trust has been abused and their funds wasted. As a contributor, I care about averting serious harm. To be sure, I feel better believing that my contribution has succeeded than believing it has failed. Still, my objective is to avert serious harm—not merely to believe that I have done so. Whether an INGO lives up to its contributors' trust depends, then, solely on whether it *actually* makes their contributions effective through morally important projects.

Fortunately, the two responsibilities largely coincide in content. An INGO that fulfills its triple task well does no wrong either to its contributors or to the poor and oppressed abroad—even though it can protect only a small fraction of the latter.

The remainder of this chapter offers some thoughts on the first task of INGOs: developing moral priorities governing how the entrusted money should be spent. These thoughts fall short of clear-cut answers. They merely try to assemble the more important moral considerations that must inform any full-blown answer to the question of moral priorities. In investigating this question, let us bear two points in mind: (1) reflections on the first task are not wholly separable from the other two and (2) predictions about what an INGO can do and how cost-effectively it can do it are relevant to what moral priorities it should set. Furthermore, an INGO is not merely an actor in its own right; it is also an agent and trustee for its contributors. It must then reflect not merely on its own moral responsibilities, but also on its contributors' moral responsibilities, which these contributors entrust it with discharging.

FOUR BASIC COUNTERS

Let us begin with four moral considerations that may seem obvious but still need clarification.

(A) *Other things (including cost) being equal, it is morally more important to protect a person from greater serious harm than from lesser.*

The key concept in this proposition is that of serious harm. In the current context, I propose to define *harm* as shortfalls persons suffer in their health, civic status (civil and political rights, respect within their community), or standard of living relative to the ordinary needs and requirements of human beings. This rough definition has three noteworthy features:

1. It is sufficientarian in its suggestion of some threshold of minimal sufficiency to which shortfalls are relative. Those living at or above this threshold suffer no *serious* harm at all. To save words, I use *harm* in the sense of *serious harm* from now on.
2. By focusing on the basic needs of persons, the definition takes account of the decreasing marginal significance of resources (such as medical care, civil rights, education, and money).
3. The definition recognizes as harm any shortfalls, irrespective of cause. Thus, severe poverty is harm regardless of whether it is the result of a drought, a person's social status as a bonded laborer, or her own earlier recklessness. Harm caused in the last way is morally less important; the "other things being equal" clause allows for this.

To illustrate the first two features, suppose that some planned INGO project in India would add 100 rupees (Rs.) per month to someone's income. Feature (1) suggests that this addition may be morally insignificant because the relevant person's standard of living is already minimally adequate. She is suffering no harm from poverty as it is, and the project thus would not protect her from harm (although it may, of course, protect others). Feature (2) suggests that greater income deficits constitute *disproportionately* greater harm. Thus, an Indian subsisting on Rs. 200 per month below a minimally adequate standard of living is, other things being equal, suffering *more* than twice the harm of someone living only Rs. 100 per month below a minimally adequate standard of living. Thus, an extra Rs. 100 per month for someone living Rs. 200 per month below a minimally adequate standard of living protects her from greater harm than it would if she lived only Rs. 100 per month below minimal sufficiency. Put in general terms, incremental resources generally are morally more important the less its recipients have. What matters morally is not the project's impact on persons' resources, but its impact on their standard of living, on their ability to meet their basic human needs.

The further specification of proposition (A) confronts three main issues. One is what should count as harm and what weight should be attached to harm of different types. The development and defense of a suitable harm metric is evidently a complex task. I bypass this task here for reasons of space.

Another issue is to what extent *effects* should be taken into account. When a child suffers severe malnutrition, her mental and physical development is stunted, and this imposes additional harm on her throughout her life. It seems evident that such effects should count; preventing that child's malnutrition also prevents her suffering this later harm. The focus should be, then, on the overall harm reduction accomplished for the child's life as a whole.

But if effects are counted in this way, then protecting those with greater life expectancy will often be morally more important than protecting those with lesser life expectancy. Even lifesaving efforts, it would seem, should then generally be focused on younger people insofar as death would impose on them a greater loss. Although widely accepted within the medical profession, these implications may seem problematic to some who are also attracted to the view that the whole future of any one person has the same moral import as the whole future of any other person, regardless of how much time each is expected to have left to live.

The last issue concerns disagreements between those threatened by harm and those seeking to protect them (INGOs and their contributors) about what is to count as harm and how to count it. A woman may believe that cliterodectomy is normal and necessary, no more harmful than the extraction of a rotten tooth, or that the subordination of women in the household and in the public sphere is holy and good. We may believe that women are harmed by their subordination and also by being indoctrinated to believe that this subordination isn't harmful to them. If so, do we have moral reason to protect that woman from harm she does not recognize as such? A man may believe that he would suffer much greater harm by failing to fulfill an expensive religious duty than by being undernourished. We may believe the opposite. If so, do we have more moral reason to enable him to fulfill his supposed religious duty or to enable him to buy food? Would it not be paternalistic to impose our own notion of harm on those whom we are seeking to protect?

(B) *Other things (including cost) being equal, it is morally more important to protect persons from harm the more such harm they would otherwise be suffering.*

Given how I have conceived harm—in terms of the ordinary needs and requirements of human beings—(B) is independent of (A) in that the decreasing marginal significance of resources is already incorporated into the conception of harm. This conception already takes account of the fact that extra income of Rs. 60 per month has as much of an impact on the standard of living of the typical extremely poor Indian as, say, Rs. 100 per month of extra income has on the standard of living of the typical merely poor Indian. Proposition (B) thus holds that—quite apart from taking account of the decreasing marginal significance of resources—we should prioritize those who are worse off (defined in terms of harm).

The point is straightforward in cases in which the decreasing marginal significance of resources plays no role. Thus, consider an INGO that supplies poor households with a smart fuel-efficient stove that greatly reduces hazardous indoor air pollution and time spent gathering firewood. With nowhere near enough stoves for all poor households, the INGO must choose whether to supply the stoves to one rural area inhabited by extremely poor people or to another less-poor area. People in both groups would realize equal harm reductions (gains in life expectancy, health, and so forth), and even the less-poor people could never afford to buy such a stove on their own. Even though the two groups thus do not differ in terms of achievable harm reduction, proposition (B) directs the INGO to decide in favor of the extremely poor.

One might fix this point terminologically by drawing a distinction between the *magnitude* and the *moral value*, or *moral importance*, of any harm reduction. Although an extra Rs. 60 per month (a smart stove) is no more significant to a typical extremely poor person than an extra Rs. 100 per month (a smart stove) is to a merely poor one (the harm reductions achieved are the same), the former gain is still morally more important than the latter (the harm reduction it achieves is of greater moral value).

Proposition (B) holds, then, that the harm reduction achieved for one person may be both *smaller* and yet also *morally more valuable* than the harm reduction achieved for another. This can happen when the former person is exposed to greater overall harm than the latter. Insofar as scarce resources force INGOs to choose between such achievements, (B) directs them to prefer a smaller but morally more valuable harm reduction for one person over a larger but less valuable harm reduction for another. Equivalently, I will say that INGOs should aim for the greater *harm protection*, defined as reflecting the moral importance (moral value) of harm reductions rather than their magnitude.

The further specification of proposition (B) confronts three main issues, roughly parallel to those encountered in the specification of (A). One is about how the moral value of a harm reduction depends on how badly off its beneficiary is.[16] As in (A), INGOs should aim to achieve as much harm reduction as possible for those exposed to the greatest harm. They must also integrate the two maximands by specifying the moral importance of any harm reduction an INGO project might achieve for some particular person as a function of the magnitude of this harm reduction and the level of overall harm suffered by the person to be protected. This might be done symmetrically, weighing each factor equally; or asymmetrically, giving more weight to either factor. There is much room for reasonable disagreement about how strongly those who are worse off should be prioritized. Different INGOs will fix this priority at different levels. Each particular INGO, however, can meaningfully compare candidate projects only if it chooses a unique level, using the same constant for assessing the impact of all its candidate projects on the individuals they affect.

A further issue faced in the specification of proposition (B) is how much of persons' lives we should consider for determining how badly off they are. At one extreme, one might attend to their current situation only—that only harms suffered now are relevant. At the other, one could take into account their entire past and estimated future, their life as a whole—the fact that people have, years ago, suffered through a horrible drought would strengthen one's reasons to combat malaria among them rather than elsewhere.

(C) *Other things (including cost) being equal, it is morally more important to achieve some given harm protection for more persons than for fewer. Here, aggregate harm protection is a linear function of the number of persons protected. Generally, the moral value of several harm reductions is the sum of their moral values.*

Proposition (C) makes three progressively stronger claims. Its first and weakest claim is ordinal: Other things being equal, if $n > m$, then achieving some harm protection for n persons has more moral value than achieving the same harm protection for m persons. The second, stronger claim is cardinal: Other things being equal, achieving some harm protection for n persons has n/m times as much moral value than achieving the same harm protection for m persons. The third, strongest claim extends this additive aggregation of moral values to nonequivalent harm protections.

Accepting the strongest claim of proposition (C) means that the moral value or importance of a project is the sum of the moral values of the harm reductions this project achieves for the individuals it affects.

(D) *Other things (including harm protection) being equal, an INGO should choose cheaper candidate projects over more expensive ones. More specifically, the choice-worthiness of candidate projects is inversely proportional to their cost.*

This is motivated by the thought that any INGO's resources are scarce relative to the morally important projects it might undertake. Any INGO should prefer to implement cheaper projects, because it can then achieve more of what is morally important.

Taking all four propositions together, the moral principle governing INGO conduct can then, at first approximation, be formulated as follows:

(ABCD) *Other things being equal, an INGO should choose among candidate projects on the basis of the cost-effectiveness of each project, defined as its moral value divided by its cost. Here, a project's moral value is the harm protection it achieves—that is, the sum of the moral values of the harm reductions (and increases) this project would bring about for the individual persons it affects.*

This principle is underspecified in various ways—with regard to its notion of harm as well as with regard to its "other things being equal" clause. I devote most of the remainder of this essay to the exploration of this clause—that is, to the question: What other factors come into play to affect the balance of reasons bearing on the ranking of candidate projects?

Distributive Fairness

One significant factor that may render other things unequal is the factor of distributive fairness. Many INGO managers are strongly committed to a particular ideal of fairness across countries: They think it unfair to spend more resources on protecting people in some countries than on protecting people in other countries merely because resources can be employed more cost-effectively in the former than in the latter. They believe that as long as resources can achieve *some* harm protection in a country, a fair share thereof should be allocated to this country even if the same resources could achieve much more elsewhere.

This commitment to distributive fairness among those who are working on harm reduction abroad manifests itself in the real world. International nongovernmental organizations and other relevant (governmental and intergovernmental) agencies would work very differently if they did not have this commitment. They would then concentrate the limited funds available for this purpose on locales that offer the most favorable environments for the cost-effective reduction of severe poverty. Some years ago, Collier and Dollar argued that these countries were, in order, Ethiopia, Uganda, and India.[17] They estimated that—even excluding India and Bangladesh—a poverty-efficient reallocation of existing aid among all countries would reduce the average cost of lifelong poverty protection from $2,650 per person to $1,387 per person and would thus make it possible to save 19.1 million rather than only 10 million people from poverty.[18] Such a reallocation would completely exclude several dozen poor countries where aid is inefficient, and would raise aid to other countries where the cost of lasting protection from poverty is as low as $600 per person (Ethiopia) or $1,000 (Uganda) per person.[19]

Details aside, Collier and Dollar are surely right: The existing allocation of funds for harm reduction efforts is highly inefficient, and concentrating on a few countries would greatly increase what these funds achieve by way of poverty eradication. Although there is much to dispute in their rough calculations, they do provide a real-world context for discussing the proposed distributive fairness constraint. Is it morally more important to protect an additional 9.1 million people from a life in poverty by concentrating our efforts on where we can be most cost-effective? Or is it morally more important to allocate scarce resources fairly across all countries in which poor people live?

It seems obvious to me that we should here decide against the proposed distributive fairness constraint and in favor of protecting more people. I recognize that if we concentrate on a few countries, we will do nothing to protect many very badly off people who, through no fault of their own, live elsewhere. However, if we spread our efforts fairly over all poor countries, then we will do nothing to protect even more people who are just as badly off and just as free of fault in their fate. *Any* conceivable allocation of available resources will leave many people exposed to a life of severe deprivation—people who ought to be protected. If we cannot fully protect everyone, then we should at least achieve as much as possible.

To make this choice more concrete, imagine an INGO that, with its limited resources, can either build two wells in Ethiopia, providing safe drinking water to 5,000, or else build one well in Chad, providing safe drinking water to 1,000. The former project would protect many more people, but the latter would achieve a fairer distribution of INGO resources across countries because other funds have already been allocated to projects in Ethiopia. If we choose the former project, we can justify to the 1,000 Chadians our neglect of their plight by pointing to the disparity in numbers. However, how could we justify to the 5,000 Ethiopians our neglect of their plight if we chose the latter project? How could we explain to them that we find protecting them less important than protecting 1,000 Chadians who are no worse off than they are?

We would say that these funds should go to a project in Chad because other funds have already been allocated to projects in Ethiopia whereas no funds have yet been allocated anywhere in Chad. But is this a good reason? Our interlocutors can respond: "The projects elsewhere in Ethiopia do nothing to protect *us*. So why should they affect the decision? We happen to live in the same country as people now protected by other projects. Why should this count against us? Why are we so much less worthy of protection than we would be if our province were a separate country?"

Consider a hypothetical emergency rescue on the high seas. A large cruise ship has sunk in very cold waters and we are trying to save some of the scattered survivors by pulling them aboard our smaller vessel before they die in the icy waters. The passengers and crew of the cruise ship are nationals of many countries. If we simply try to save as many as possible, these countries would not be fairly represented among the rescued (according to whatever standard the advocates of a distributive fairness constraint care to specify). May we aim for fair representation of countries, then, even if this would make our rescue efforts less cost-effective and would thus lead to our saving fewer people? If the answer is negative, why must not INGOs, too, display fairness across *individuals*—giving equal weight to the interests of each and hence protecting as many as possible—at the expense of fairness across countries? The insistence on distributive fairness across countries goes against common commitments to the equal worth of all human beings, to the idea that we should treat all *persons* with equal concern irrespective of their nationality.

The advocates of distributive fairness across groups also face another problem: What about groups defined in terms of features other than nationality? If the allocation of resources must be fair across *countries*, must it then not also be fair across provinces, counties, religious denominations, generations, sexes, settlements of different sizes, and so forth? Affirmative answers add ever more—possibly inconsistent—fairness constraints, each of which will tend to reduce the cost-effectiveness of our harm protection efforts. Negative answers provoke the charge of inconsistency: What is so special about nationality? Why should we have to treat nationalities fairly, but not the other groupings mentioned?

Before concluding that the concern for fairness across groups must be set aside in deference to the very weighty concern to maximize harm protection, let us consider two special cases that are more problematic.

Imagine an acute famine emergency. An INGO is bringing in food, but, given its limited resources, it cannot ensure everyone's survival. No one can survive on a fair share of the available food. So, if some are to survive, the INGO must distribute its limited food supply selectively. But how to select? Consider two options. The INGO might select hungry persons at random up to the point where their minimal food requirements equal the available food supply. Alternatively, the INGO might opt for selection rules that maximize the expected number of survivors. Such rules would, in general terms, favor those whose minimal food requirements are smallest. They would, in particular, favor persons with more efficient metabolisms, children over adults, and women over men. How should the INGO staff proceed in such a horrifying situation?

In response to such questions, it is sometimes said that the INGO staff "should not play God." I find this idea unhelpful, because I cannot see what is supposed to follow from it. The decision about which distribution rule to use is ineluctably ours. The situation imposes this awesome choice on us, and we cannot evade the responsibility. Even if we run a lottery and even if we flee the scene, leaving desperate people to fight over the food we leave behind, we are still making a decision that determines who will live and who will die. We *must* face the question: How do we distribute the food?

Facing this question, I think we ought to apply optimizing selection rules to the situation. We ought to protect 20 men and 65 women, for example, if doing so enables 85 people to survive instead of the 80 that would survive if we chose to protect equal numbers of men and women.

This general rejection of distributive fairness constraints seems least plausible in cases in which the fact that some people are harder to protect is a result of injustice suffered by these very people. Thus, consider the decision that may be faced by an INGO constructing wells to ensure access to safe drinking water. Suppose this INGO normally rejects distributive fairness and builds wells only in urban areas, where population density is high, rather than in rural areas, where the same well would serve fewer people. But suppose further that the INGO operates in a country where the members of some despised minority religion are barred from living in urban areas (where their beliefs might "set a bad example") and are thus forced to inhabit isolated rural areas. In this context, one may well be inclined to reject the optimizing policy because it would, in effect, systematically aggravate the unjust disadvantage imposed on the members of the minority religion.

To see how much support this case can give to the idea of distributive fairness constraints, we must strip away at least two impurities. The case as described may evoke the thought that the members of the religious minority, suffering disdain and discrimination, are really worse off than the urban dwellers who would gain access to safe drinking water if the wells were built there. Insofar as this is true, propositions (A) and (B) already provide countervailing reasons that may tip the scales in favor of constructing the wells in minority areas. The case as described may also evoke the thought that those urban dwellers share in the disdain of, and collaborate in the discrimination against, the religious minority. This consideration might shift the balance of reasons against them, but for reasons of desert that have nothing to do with distributive fairness. To present the case as supporting distributive fairness constraints, let us then construct it by envisioning another equally despised religious minority, this one living in urban ghettos—a minority that is just as badly off, but does not share the widespread disdain others inflict on the first religious minority. Should our INGO here follow the optimizing policy and construct wells in the urban ghettos (where they will protect many members of the second minority) or should our INGO construct wells also in rural areas (where they will protect members of the first minority) even if this substantially reduces the overall number of people gaining access to safe drinking water? In the case so described, I do not find it difficult to endorse, for all the reasons discussed earlier, the first option at the expense of the suggested fairness constraints.

I do not believe that the arguments I have presented settle the matter conclusively. However, they do convince me, for now, that the proposed ideals of distributive fairness should not constrain the straightforward application of (ABCD). The "other things being equal" clause in this principle should not be read as permitting departures from cost-effectiveness for the sake of achieving an equalization of chances among needy individuals or a proportionate distribution of harm reduction efforts across countries or other collectivities.

FURTHER CONSIDERATIONS

Without claim to completeness, this section addresses five additional issues relevant to the proper specification of (ABCD).

Extinction and Diversity

(ABCD) conceives the moral value of any project in individualistic terms: as the sum of the moral values of the harm reductions (and increases) this project would bring about for the individual persons it affects. It may thereby leave out significant moral concerns. Suppose, for instance, that the cost-effective allocation of funds would exclude a certain region (the Amazon, say) in which certain nations or cultures are threatened with extinction. One may well think that when the last members of such a nation are killed or forced out of their ancestral lands, the moral loss is greater than the harm suffered by these individuals.

One may invoke the value of diversity to explain these intuitions in a way that fits the individualist paradigm: All human beings lose when the biological and cultural diversity of humankind is diminished. However, it is hard to establish that this loss to individuals can shift the balance of reasons away from, say, saving the lives of 5,000 starving Ethiopians toward saving the lives of 500 Amazon natives. Thus, it would seem that to accommodate those intuitions, normative individualism would have to be relaxed somewhat to make room for the realization that not every morally serious loss is harm suffered by individual human beings. The demise or demoralization of a nation with its own culture (language, religion, shared way of life) can be a serious loss in itself, over and above any harm this event involves for the nation's last members.

Risk and Uncertainty

Projects may differ in terms of how much visibility they afford. With some projects, moral value and cost are clearly predictable, but with other projects there are significant risks or even uncertainties. Let me briefly outline the latter distinction. A decision involves risk insofar as the decision maker does not know what will happen but can make reliable assumptions about the possible outcomes and their probabilities. A decision involves uncertainty insofar as the decision maker cannot make reliable assumptions about the probabilities associated with various outcomes or even about what the possible outcomes are. The distinction between decisions under risk and decisions under uncertainty is scalar—a matter of degree. For instance, one may know the value ("payoff") of one possible outcome and that its probability is between 40% and 45%, and the value of another outcome and that its probability is between 35% and 50%, but be ignorant of what would happen if neither of these outcomes came about. In this case, there is some uncertainty associated with the first two outcomes (their exact likelihood is unknown), and much uncertainty about other possible outcomes, because their exact probabilities and even their values are unknown.

To cope with risk, the standard method would estimate the moral value of a chancy project as its *probability-weighted expected moral value*. Insofar as the realized value of a project depends on chancy factors, different outcomes are possible. In this case, one estimates for each outcome its probability and the moral value the project would then realize. The probability-weighted expected moral value of the project is then calculated as the sum of these products (probability times conditional value). Likewise for risks regarding cost: Here one estimates the cost of a chancy project as its *probability-weighted expected cost*. Insofar as a project's cost depends on chancy factors, different outcomes are possible. In this case, one estimates for each outcome its probability and what the project would then cost. The probability-weighted expected cost of the project is then calculated as the sum of these products (probability times conditional cost). A chancy project's cost-effectiveness (*ex ante*) is then estimated as before—by dividing its (probability-weighted expected) moral value by its (probability-weighted expected) cost.

Is this a morally plausible way to assess chancy projects? Is it plausible, for instance, to assign equal moral value to (1) a 10% chance of saving 1,000 lives and (2) a 100% chance of saving 100 lives? Egalitarians may respond that (1) should be preferred, because it spreads survival prospects more evenly. Although this is true in a sense, I find the *ex ante* sense in which it is true morally irrelevant. In the long run, both strategies save equal numbers of lives. And the fact that, under (1), many additional people were the objects of failed harm protection attempts—this fact is of no value to these people. What other moral value could it have?

Others think that (2) should be preferred. They may feel that, taking a gamble, (1) expresses disrespect for human life—a feeling I find hard to understand. Or, familiar with financial markets, they may feel that some risk premium should be levied on (1). In the financial world, such a risk premium is deemed appropriate because of the decreasing marginal utility of money. But there is no decreasing marginal value of human lives saved.

Lacking compelling reasons for departing, in either direction, from an equal assignment of moral value, I conclude, then, regarding decision making under risk, that the cost-effectiveness of a chancy project should be understood to be its cost-effectiveness *ex ante*, calculated by dividing its probability-weighted expected moral value by its probability-weighted expected cost.

Coping with uncertainty is considerably harder. Some theorists have argued that uncertainty calls for a conservative response, one that gives great weight to the worst conceivable outcome. The most conservative strategy here is the so-called *maximin rule*.[20] "Maximin" is short for the Latin "*maximum minimorum*," meaning highest minimum. The maximin rule instructs agents to choose the option that is associated with the best worst-case scenario. But this rule seems plainly too conservative here. To see this, consider a case like this: An INGO has a truck with perishable food in a region where starvation is widespread. The food is enough to protect up to 800 people from premature death (keeping them alive until harvest time, say). One option is to drive the food to a township in the east, where it would certainly protect 200 people from imminent starvation. The other option is to drive it west, where the food may save 800 people in a larger town. Although it is known that the township in the east is reachable by truck, information about whether the town in the west can be so reached is unavailable. Trying the route west will consume the available fuel and, should the truck not get through, the food will protect no one.

In this sort of case, I think one should reason as follows: If the town in the west is reachable, then going west would save 600 more starving people than going east. If the town in the west is not reachable, then going east would save 200 more people than going west would. Given the uncertainty, these two conditionals are symmetrically placed. There is only one factor that can break the symmetry: the larger number of people protected. Therefore, the truck should proceed toward the town in the west.

In the real world, the uncertainty about probabilities is typically less total than in this example. Some rough estimates are normally possible concerning the likelihoods of some of the outcomes. In the real world, however, there are often other sources of uncertainty, because agents may not even have a complete understanding of all possible outcomes. Each of the two projects in the example might be helped or hindered in myriad ways, and it is impossible to anticipate all these possibilities, let alone to attach rough probabilities to them. Still, the overall principle that should guide INGOs in coping with risk and uncertainty is clear enough. An INGO should incorporate risk and uncertainty into its decision making in such a way as to maximize its expected long-run cost-effectiveness. Put more generally:

> (ABCD*) *Other things being equal, an INGO should govern its decision making about candidate projects by such rules and procedures as are expected to maximize its long-run cost-effectiveness, defined as the expected aggregate moral*

value of the projects it undertakes divided by the expected aggregate cost of these projects. Here, aggregate moral value, or harm protection, is the sum of the moral values of the harm reductions (and increases) these projects bring about for the individual persons they affect.

Fund-raising

The projects an INGO undertakes have a feedback effect on its fund-raising success. And this INGO may then face complex choices between intrinsically more cost-effective projects on one hand and more donor-enticing projects on the other.

Consider the decision between two projects, each of which would cost $2 million to implement. Project G has an estimated moral value of 9,000, whereas project H has an estimated moral value of only 3,000. (Project G might save 9,000 children from death by starvation, for instance, whereas project H would save 3,000 children from such a death.) One might then say that project G's *intrinsic cost-effectiveness* (9,000/2, score of 4,500) is three times as great as the intrinsic cost-effectiveness of project H (3,000/2, score of 1,500).

However, project H would be conducted in a current "hotspot" and therefore would draw a lot more media attention. This, in turn, would trigger extra contributions, which would reduce the "true" cost of project H, or so one might think. Suppose the fund-raising experts predict that project H would raise incoming contributions by $1.5 million, whereas project G—conducted in some remote location—would raise incoming contributions by only $200,000. If this is the situation, then one might say that the "true" cost-effectiveness of project G is 9,000/1.8 (score of 5,000) and that the "true" cost-effectiveness of project H is 3,000/0.5 (score of 6,000).

Which of the two methods of assessing the cost and cost-effectiveness of projects—intrinsic versus "true"—is correct? The answer, I believe, is *neither*. Focusing on intrinsic cost-effectiveness—perhaps on the grounds that the concern with fund-raising is profane or that the responsibility for how much money is received by an INGO rests solely with its potential contributors—unacceptably ignores the gain in harm protection that additional funds would make possible.

To appreciate why focusing on "true" cost-effectiveness is likewise unacceptable, one needs to draw a further distinction with regard to the additional contributions that projects may trigger. One needs to distinguish between additional contributions that constitute merely a redirection from one INGO to another and additional contributions that increase the sum total of funds received by all relevant INGOs. To mark this distinction, let us say that an INGO's projects may attract both *substitutional* and *accretive* contributions. In the former case, one INGO is substituted for another as recipient of part of the overall pool of relevant contributions. In the latter case, this whole pool is enlarged.

This distinction may be unfamiliar because it has little significance in the business world, where talk of cost-effectiveness has its main home. When deciding whether to run an advertising campaign, a firm will assess the cost of the campaign against its expected benefits in terms of additional business and earnings. In considering these benefits, the firm need not care whether it is benefiting by taking business away from its competitors or by increasing overall demand. If anything, it will slightly prefer taking business away from competitors because this will have a greater impact on its market share and will also weaken its competitors in absolute terms. A firm has no reason to want its peers to be successful and effective in the pursuit of their goals.

The distinction has great significance, however, in the INGO world, where many INGOs pursue the *same* goals. Many INGOs, for instance, seek to protect children from hunger and malnutrition. Each such INGO has vastly more moral reason to be concerned that children be protected than it has reason to be concerned that such protection be provided by *itself* rather than by one of its peers.

To illustrate the point, consider two INGOs with such a common goal and assume that $INGO_1$ tends to favor projects like G, whereas $INGO_2$ tends to favor projects like H. Insofar as the pool of contributions is fixed, the result will be that the cost-effectiveness of the two INGOs, considered as a team, will gradually decline. This is so because the diverse project policies of the two organizations will divert contributions from $INGO_1$ to $INGO_2$. This has the effect that more and more of the projects they initiate will be type-H projects initiated by $INGO_2$, rather than type-G projects initiated by $INGO_1$. By diverting funding from $INGO_1$ to itself, $INGO_2$ is reducing the cost-effectiveness of these contributions by two thirds (because type-G projects are three times as cost-effective as type-H projects).

Seeing how its funding is drying up, $INGO_1$ can follow $INGO_2$'s example by likewise switching its activities toward projects of type H. Doing so may help $INGO_1$ stem the decline in its funding. However, it will also accelerate the overall drift from type-G to type-H projects. Whether $INGO_1$ makes the switch, over time, ever more of the money raised by the two INGOs will go to projects of type H rather than to projects of type G. Furthermore, on the assumption of a fixed pool of contributions, this is a disaster, rendering these contributions much less cost-effective in terms of harm protection than they would be if devoted to projects of type G.[21]

Insofar as high-profile projects will bring in contributions that would not otherwise have been made, the shift to type-H projects may be desirable, as is illustrated by the "true" cost-effectiveness calculation conducted earlier. A key to deciding between projects G and H, then, is an empirical estimate about the extent to which new funds raised through projects G and H are substitutional or accretive.

The correct way of calculating the cost and cost-effectiveness of projects takes account of new funds, which the candidate projects would attract, only insofar as these are accretive. In the numerical example provided earlier, INGOs should choose type-H projects over type-G projects only if the new funds the former would raise are almost entirely accretive. This is based on the assumption that an INGO should aim for harm protection in general, regardless of how much thereof it itself achieves.

This discussion of fund-raising illustrates a somewhat more general point. An INGO can pursue an *agent-relative* goal, defined in terms of the moral value *it* realizes, or the corresponding *agent-neutral* goal, defined in terms of the moral value *all INGOs together* realize. As the example has shown, pursuit of the former goal may well detract from achievement of the latter by worsening the allocation of funds within and among INGOs.

In addition, pursuit of the agent-relative goal is also *directly collectively self-defeating*.[22] Each INGO does worse, even in terms of this goal, if all INGOs successfully pursue it than it would do if all INGOs successfully pursued the agent-neutral goal instead. An INGO seeking to maximize the moral value it itself realizes will favor type-H projects over type-G projects. Others must follow suit or be driven out of the business of harm protection. When all INGOs focus their resources on type-H projects, however, each will realize less moral value than it would realize if all INGOs focused their resources on type-G projects.

Because the agent-neutral goal is morally more plausible and because the agent-relative goal is directly collectively self-defeating, INGOs ought to be committed to the agent-neutral goal and should therefore understand *cost* in (ABCD*) in the sense of *correct cost*.

But what should any *one* INGO do if other INGOs are "defecting" to the agent-relative goal? Should it stick to the agent-neutral goal, accepting the consequent reduction in its funding? Should it likewise defect, accepting the consequent reduction in global INGO effectiveness? Or should it try to raise the issue with other INGOs and the contributing public?

Deontological Concerns: Discriminating Contributors

My discussion thus far of moral priorities for INGOs has resulted in a broadly consequentialist conception. To be sure, this conception is not consequentialist in the traditional sense. It does not instruct us simply to maximize the good, defined as harm reduction, but instead gives greater weight to protecting from harm those who are worse off (proposition [B]). Some theorists hold that this prioritarian element suffices to render a moral conception recognizably deontological.[23] In my view, however, a conception that instructs us to maximize some *weighted* aggregate (weighted in favor of those worse off, in this case) is still broadly consequentialist; it merely conceives morally relevant consequences a little differently. This is a terminological squabble among philosophers that need not detain us. I mention it only to flag that I now discuss more significantly deontological concerns.

Thus far I have argued that INGOs ought to focus their resources on the projects that are most cost-effective. This claim implies that INGOs ought to discriminate in favor of badly off people who can be cheaply protected from harm and thus against badly off people whom it would be expensive to protect. I have accepted this implication as plausible; such discrimination is not morally offensive in any way insofar as it is driven entirely by the concern to protect as many badly off people as possible (proposition [C]).

But now consider this complication. Suppose the affluent people giving money to INGOs are mostly white and somewhat racist. Projects that protect from harm badly off white people elicit much greater gains in accretive contributions per dollar expended than alternative projects that protect from harm equally badly off persons of color. (Judging by the public responses to the crises in Rwanda and Kosovo, this supposition is anything but unrealistic.) To illustrate the difficulty, consider the choice between two projects. Project K is targeted at badly off whites and project L is targeted at badly off blacks. Ignoring feedback effects on fund-raising, project L is considerably more cost-effective (in the intrinsic sense). Because project K would produce much greater gains in accretive contributions, however, project K is considerably more cost-effective on (what I have argued is) the correct understanding of cost-effectiveness. Given all that has been said thus far, then, the INGO ought to implement type-K projects over type-L projects. Is this plausible?

One may be tempted to try to avoid this hard question by pointing out, correctly, that the attitudes of affluent people are subject to change. An INGO might engage in a publicity campaign designed to foster sentiments of identification and solidarity also with badly off people of color. This is true enough, but it does not answer the difficulty. Any such publicity campaign diverts funds that could have been expended on harm protection projects. To be sure, this diversion can be justified—when it would increase the harm protection all INGOs achieve in the long run, for instance, by increasing the willingness to support type-L projects, by winning accretive contributions through improved INGO reputation, and by reducing the sense of exclusion and humiliation among poor blacks abroad. Still, such diversion would often be unjustified. Therefore, if correct cost-effectiveness is what matters, then an INGO faced with a situation like the one described often ought to leave the racist attitudes of its contributors alone and focus its resources on projects of type K. Does this show that the focus on correct cost-effectiveness needs to be modified?

There are essentially five responses to this difficulty. The first argues that there is nothing morally wrong with contributor racism or, more generally, with contributors directing their harm reduction efforts toward projects of their choice. It is *their* money, after all, and, just as they may freely decide what movies to watch or whom to go out with, so they are equally free, morally, to decide which good causes to support. I disagree with this first response on two counts. As the next subsection brings out,

I believe that, in the world as it is, our moral reasons to support efforts at harm protection are not exclusively positive (in the sense of positive duties). Rather, our contributions are morally required by more stringent duties arising from our material involvement in the production of harm. Moreover, even if we had only positive moral reasons to contribute to INGOs, it would still be morally odious to favor some badly off people merely because of their skin color. The stronger such favoritism, the more offensive it is morally.

The second response argues that contributor racism is indeed regrettable, but that there is nothing morally questionable about an INGO taking account of such contributor racism as an empirical fact in its effort to optimize its harm protection strategy. Again, I cannot share this response. To be sure, the INGO is intending to do the best it can toward realizing moral value and has no sympathy for the racism of its contributors. Still, it implements this racism, and this is morally offensive even when done in the service of a good cause.

The third response argues that it is indeed morally offensive for an INGO to implement contributor racism, but that this significant reason for favoring type-L projects is usually overwhelmed in our world by the great moral importance of achieving harm protection. The reason against allowing oneself to implement racism can then be permitted to tip the scale only when competing projects are, as far as can be estimated, close in cost-effectiveness correctly assessed. If one project is much superior in this respect, like project L is superior to project K, then the superior project ought to be chosen, albeit with a sense that one is thereby participating in a wrong done to those whom project K would have protected. I find this the most plausible response.

The fourth response argues that the concerns of combating racist attitudes among contributors and of not allowing oneself to become an instrument of racism have enough weight to affect the balance of moral reasons even with many early deaths at stake on the other side. This moral reason must then be traded off against the others. Thus, it may well be that we ought stand up for the principle that all children matter equally and save 10 black children from death by starvation, even if focusing on white children would have generated accretive contributions that would have enabled us to save more. This response also strikes me as having some appeal, although I do not know how one can answer the question how many extra deaths this "standing up for principle" can justify. What is the correct exchange rate between racism spurned and additional lives saved? As this exchange rate is increased so that standing up for principle becomes really costly in terms of harm protection, this response quickly becomes implausible to me.

The fifth response, in absolutist deontological fashion, gives overriding priority to the antiracist principle. When it comes to factors such as sex and skin color, we must simply ignore accretive contributions and focus solely on the *intrinsic* cost-effectiveness of projects. If following this criterion diminishes, even greatly, the harm protection we can achieve, then we must simply accept this diminution. In view of the huge difference our choice of harm protection strategy makes in terms of severe human suffering, I find this response unacceptable. The next subsection implicitly undermines one main source of its appeal—the deontological idea that one should not wrong some people to help others. Whatever the merits of this idea (it is implausible when understood as an absolute constraint), its relevance in this world is severely limited because most of what we, through INGOs, do to protect people in the poor countries is morally required from us not merely under the label of help or positive duty, but also as mitigation of wrongs from which we profit and in the production of which we participate.

Deontological Concerns: Material Involvement

The discussion so far suggests a broadly consequentialist approach, roughly: The greater the harm protection we can achieve, the more reason we have to achieve it. This suggestion is fine as long as other things are presumed to be equal. One pivotal factor that may not be equal, however, is how we, the INGO and its contributors, are causally related to the harm in question. We normally think of INGOs as fulfilling a merely *positive* moral responsibility to prevent or to mitigate harm suffered by others. International nongovernmental organizations may, however, also fulfill a *negative* moral responsibility not to cause harm.

It is often foreseeable that candidate INGO projects would harm innocent people. It may be foreseeable, for example, that warring factions will rob some of the resources we might dispatch into some volatile region and will then use them to inflict further violence. By fueling the fighting, these projects would thus cause harm. In such cases, the unmodified (ABCD*) may still be a plausible guiding principle, provided the available evidence does not allow us to identify any persons for whom the project's expected moral value is negative. But often we do have such evidence. We know which armed group is able and disposed to loot our resources, and we know who its intended victims are. In such cases, the ordinary cost-effectiveness reasons against choosing this project (see "Distributive Fairness") are enhanced by a negative moral responsibility not to add to the (risk of) harm suffered by such potential victims.

Another category of moral reasons is to prevent or to mitigate harm that one otherwise will have caused or have participated in causing. Such *intermediate* moral reasons can be relevant to INGO work in special cases in which INGO staff have—wrongfully, negligently, or even innocently—set in motion a train of events that threatens to harm innocent people. In such cases, the INGO's moral reason to protect them from these harms is more stringent than it would be if this INGO had not been materially involved in causing this threat.

The persistence of severe poverty in many poor countries is partly the result of the design of the global institutional order that foreseeably (re)produces vastly more poverty than would be reasonably avoidable. Had the rich countries pursued a different path of globalization during the past 20 years, the problem of severe poverty would be a fraction of its current size. Insofar as we citizens of rich countries (through our governments) participate in, or profit from, the imposition of this unjust order, we are materially involved in most of the harm human beings are suffering worldwide. International nongovernmental organizations and their contributors therefore rarely face actual hard choices between morally *less* valuable harm reductions that we have *intermediate* moral reasons to achieve and morally *more* valuable harm reductions that we have only *positive* moral reason to achieve.

Only a small fraction of the citizens of the rich countries are willing to contribute to averting such harm. Their contributions are nowhere near sufficient to avert all the harm that the citizens of the rich countries have intermediate moral duties to avert. In the context of this grievous injustice, we should, for the most part, direct our grossly insufficient contributions for maximum effect: toward the most cost-effective harm protection projects. Reflection on intermediate moral duties thus greatly increases the strength of our moral reasons to achieve cost-effective harm protection without justifying significant departures from (ABCD*).

Discussions of this essay suggest that most readers will sharply disagree with some of my conclusions. Fortunately, they also suggest that we all have a great deal to learn from a careful elaboration of, and engagement with, this view.

Notes

This chapter is an abbreviated and updated version of my "Moral Priorities for International Human Rights NGOs," in Daniel A. Bell and Jean-Marc Coicaud, eds., *Ethics in Action: The Ethical Challenges of International Human Rights Nongovernmental Organizations* (Tokyo: United Nations University Press, 2007), pp. 218–256. Many thanks to Matt Peterson and Leif Wenar for their help in adapting and revising it.

1. Food and Agriculture Organization, "1.02 Billion People Hungry," June 19, 2009, www.fao.org/news/story/en/item/20568/icode/ (accessed June 26, 2009).

2. World Health Organization, UNICEF, *Progress on Drinking Water and Sanitation: Special Focus on Sanitation* (New York and Geneva: UNICEF and World Health Organization, 2008), www.who.int/water_sanitation_health/monitoring/jmp2008/en/index.html, p. 30.

3. Ibid., p. 13.

4. Fogarty International Center for Advanced Study in the Health Sciences, *Strategic Plan: Fiscal Years 2000–2003* (Bethesda, Md.: National Institutes of Health, n.d.), www.fic.nih.gov/about/plan/exec_summary.htm.

5. United Nations-Habitat, *The Challenge of Slums: Global Report on Human Settlements 2003* (London: Earthscan, 2003), p. vi.

6. United Nations-Habitat, "Urban Energy," www.unhabitat.org/content.asp?c id=2884&catid=356&typeid=24&subMenuId=0 (July 24, 2010).

7. UNESCO Institute for Statistics, "Literacy Topic," December 1, 2008, www.uis.unesco.org/ev.php?URL_ID=6401&URL_DO=DO_TOPIC& URL_SECTION=201.

8. See International Labour Office, *The End of Child Labour: Within Reach* (Geneva: International Labour Office, 2006), p. 6.

9. This is the World Bank's official poverty line, most recently redefined in terms of daily consumption, the local cost of which has the same purchasing power as $1.25 had in the United States in 2005. See Shaohua Chen and Martin Ravallion, "The Developing World Is Poorer Than We Thought, But No Less Successful in the Fight against Poverty," World Bank Policy Research Working Paper WPS 4703 (Washington, D.C., World Bank Development Research Group, 2008), pp. 10, 44; econ.worldbank.org/docsearch.

10. World Health Organization, *Global Burden of Disease: 2004 Update* (Geneva: WHO, 2008), table A1, pp. 54–59, www.who.int/healthinfo/global_ burden_disease/2004_report_update/en/index.html.

11. UNICEF, *The State of the World's Children 2008* (New York: UNICEF, 2008), p. iii; United Nations Development Programme, *Human Development Report 2003* (New York: Oxford University Press, 2003), pp. 310–330; United Nations Research Institute for Social Development, *Gender Equality: Striving for Justice in an Unequal World* (Geneva: UNRISD/UN Publications, 2005); Social Watch, *Unkept Promises* (Montevideo: Instituto del Tercer Mundo, 2005), www. socialwatch.org/node/10021.

12. Thomas Pogge, *World Poverty and Human Rights: Cosmopolitan Responsibilities and Reforms*, 2nd ed. (Cambridge: Polity Press, 2008), chap. 8.

13. Or 73% of world income. See World Bank, *World Development Report 2010* (Washington, D.C.: World Bank, 2010), p. 379, go.worldbank.org/BKLQ 9DSDU0.

14. See millenniumindicators.un.org/unsd/mdg/SeriesDetail.aspx?srid=592& crid=. The latest figures currently available are for 2008.

15. United Nations Development Programme, *Human Development Report 2003*, p. 290, hdr.undp.org/en/reports/global/hdr2003.

16. Compare Derek Parfit, "Equality or Priority," in Matthew Clayton and Andrew Williams, eds., *The Ideal of Equality* (Houndmills: Macmillan, 2000), pp. 81–125, and John Broome, "Equality Versus Priority: A Useful Distinction," 2002, users.ox.ac.uk/~sfop0060/.

17. Paul Collier and David Dollar, "Aid Allocation and Poverty Reduction," *European Economic Review* 46 (2002), pp. 1475–1500, 1488.

18. Ibid., p. 1497.

19. Ibid., pp. 1488 and 1490.

20. For example, John Rawls, *A Theory of Justice* (Cambridge, Mass.: Harvard University Press, 1999 [1971]), pp. 132–135.

21. For the claim that something like this is actually happening, pursuant to what he calls the "humanitarian Gresham's Law," see Alex de Waal, *Famine Crimes: Politics and the Disaster Relief Industry in Africa* (Bloomington: Indiana University Press, 1998), pp. 138–143.

22. See Derek Parfit, *Reasons and Persons* (Oxford: Oxford University Press, 1984), chap. 4.

23. An example is John Rawls, *A Theory of Justice*, pp. 22–23 and 26.

4

The Valmont Effect
The Warm-Glow Theory of Philanthropy

Jon Elster

Why do people give to charitable causes? In the case of donations to victims of a tsunami and similar causes, the answer might seem obvious: They give to alleviate suffering and poverty. This motivation is an *altruistic* one. In this chapter, I discuss another answer that, for two distinct reasons, has acquired some prominence in recent literature: People give to experience the "warm glow" from giving. This motivation is an egocentric one (as I argue later, the warm-glow motivation is not the only egocentric reason for donations). One reason why this answer is plausible is that the assumption of altruistic motivations seems to predict much lower levels of giving than we actually observe, whereas the egocentric assumption may be more consistent with the observed facts. Another is that brain imaging seems to provide direct evidence for the egocentric assumption, by showing that certain reward centers in the brain are activated when people make decisions to donate. Altruistic and egocentric motivations both differ from the egoistic motivations associated with the model of *Homo economicus*. In one application of that model, Stark argues that remittances by migrants to their home country are motivated by their self-interest in preventing other workers in the home country, who would be rivals on the labor market in the new country, from emigrating.[1] The account is flawed, however, because it neglects the free-rider problem among the donors.[2] As we shall see, it has been argued that the free-rider objection can also be made to the altruistic account. By contrast, the warm-glow account has the advantage of not creating a free-rider problem.

As another term for *the warm-glow effect*, we might use *the Valmont effect*. In *Dangerous Liaisons*, the Vicomte de Valmont initially engages in charitable behavior for the purely selfish motive of seducing the présidente de Tourvel. Knowing that one of her agents is following him to observe his behavior, he seeks out a poor family whose property is about to be taken from them to pay for tax arrears:

I summon the tax collector. And, giving in to my generous compassion, I nobly part with fifty-six livres, for which paltry sum five human beings were being reduced to straw and poverty. After this simple little action you may imagine what a chorus of blessings echoed all around me...In the midst of the blessings from this family, I looked not unlike a hero in the final act of a drama. You will not forget that my faithful spy was there in the crowd. My aim was accomplished...After all, I am very pleased with my idea. I have no doubt that this woman is worth making a great effort for. One day this will count for something in her eyes.[3]

In his further reflection on his experience, Valmont also discovers the intrinsic pleasure of doing good. When the family members kneel before him to express their thanks, he discovers a strange sensation: "I shall confess to a momentary weakness. My eyes filled with tears and I felt within me an involuntary but delightful emotion. I am astonished at the *pleasure one feels at doing good*. And I should be tempted to believe that those whom we call virtuous do not have so much merit as we are led to believe" (emphasis added).[4]

This is the Valmont effect. We may note for future reference that the production of the effect did not enter into the conscious motivation of his action.

I shall now proceed as follows. In the following section I explain why the altruism-based explanations fell out of fashion, and argue that the objections that brought about its demise are, to some extent, the result of the artificial character of the economic modeling of altruism. In the third section I consider a range of egocentric motivations that might enter into the explanation of behavior that has a material cost for the agent. The final section of the chapter offers some concluding comments on the irrational nature of (some) warm-glow-motivated actions.

NASH ALTRUISM

Forty years ago, several writers noticed the fact that for a *community of altruists, the welfare of a recipient is a public good*.[5] If philanthropist A relieves the need of recipient C, thereby moving the latter to a higher level of welfare, the fact of decreasing marginal utility of consumption implies that the good that philanthropist B can do with his money is reduced, and hence he will donate less. To illustrate the mechanism behind this statement, I shall use an ultrasimple two-person model, easily extended to the general n-person case. By "easily extended," I mean that the payoff structures will be similar, *not* that the choices will be the same.

Assume two altruists A and B, and potential recipient C. Each altruist has an initial monetary endowment of M, whereas C has nothing. The inclusive utility of each altruist is equal to the consumption utility he derives from his own income and k times the consumption utility C derives from his income ($0 < k < 1$). C is assumed to be an egoist. A and

B do not derive utility from each other's income. The consumption utility is assumed to be the square root of income, thus ensuring decreasing marginal utility. We assume, somewhat artificially, that each altruist has the choice of transferring either X or Y to C ($2Y < X$). We may then ask the following question: Are there numerical values for X, Y, M, and k such that (i) a single altruist would donate X whereas (ii) each of two altruists would donate Y? In this case, moving from a situation with one altruist to a situation with two altruists would make the beneficiary of altruism worse off.

Condition (i) holds if

$$(M - X)^{1/2} + kX^{1/2} > (M - Y)^{1/2} + kY^{1/2} \quad (1)$$

The basic intuition is simple. Because of the decreasing marginal utility of money, a transfer will produce a greater increase in the consumption utility of the recipient than the decrease it will produce in the consumption utility of the donor, at least if the transfer is relatively small compared with M. This effect is offset by the fact that the value the altruist places on C's utility is discounted by a factor of k. The inequality will be satisfied if the first effect dominates the second.

To examine condition (ii), we have to take account of the strategic interaction between the two altruists:

B Gives		
	X	Y
A Gives	$(M - X)^{1/2} + k(2X)^{1/2}$	$(M - X)^{1/2} + k(X + Y)^{1/2}$
	$(M - Y)^{1/2} + k(X + Y)^{1/2}$	$(M - Y)^{1/2} + k(2Y)^{1/2}$

The four cells give the payoffs of A. Because the game is completely symmetrical (assume that A and B are identical twins), any conclusion we reach for A will also apply to B. Sufficient conditions for case (ii) to obtain exist if A would prefer to give Y regardless of the action taken by B:

$$(M - Y)^{1/2} + k(X + Y)^{1/2} > (M - X)^{1/2} + k(2X)^{1/2} \quad (2)$$
$$(M - Y)^{1/2} + k(2Y)^{1/2} > (M - X)^{1/2} + k(X + Y)^{1/2} \quad (3)$$

Inequality (2) states that A would prefer to give Y if B gives X and, inequality (3), that he would also prefer to give Y if B gives Y. It is easily seen that inequalities (1), (2), and (3) all obtain for the following parameter values $k = \frac{1}{2}$, $M = 10$, $X = 3$, $Y = 1$. For these values, the following "diagonal" inequality also obtains

$$(M - X)^{1/2} + k(2X)^{1/2} > (M - Y)^{1/2} + k(2Y)^{1/2} \quad (4)$$

Inequalities (2), (3), and (4) imply the existence of a Prisoner's Dilemma between the two altruists. Although each would rather that both give much than that both give little, each prefers to give little regardless of what the other does. Low donations are a *dominant strategy*, yielding the outcome in the lower right-hand cell of the previous table. As with many other instances of the Prisoner's Dilemma, the cause of the suboptimal outcome lies in a positive externality. By alleviating the need of the recipient, each philanthropist is also reducing the incentive for the other philanthropist to alleviate the need. Crucially, this conclusion turns on the assumption that each donor is aware of the existence and the motivations of the other. In a two-person case, this may be a reasonable assumption. In a society with tens or hundreds of millions of potential donors, it is wildly unrealistic.

In my example, the existence of a Prisoner's Dilemma is robust, in the sense that it does not depend on the artificial assumption that the donors are constrained to choose between the two amounts X and Y. Even when they are free to choose how much to give, optimizing behavior yields a Pareto–suboptimal Nash equilibrium, defined as the levels of donation that are optimal against each other. (In this case, though, the agents do not have a dominant strategy.) In contrast, the seemingly absurd result that the recipient is worse off with two altruists than with one is not robust in this sense. If they are free to choose, the two altruists will donate amounts that make the recipient better off than he would be with a single uncon-strained altruist.[6] One might perhaps find real-world situations in which the assumption is satisfied, but until one is found, the result is mainly a curiosum.

One response to the dilemma is to try to turn the public good into a private one. As is well known from the field of philanthropy, charitable organizations often try to turn the recipients of giving into an exclusive target for the donor. In traditional societies, as Kolm notes, each family had "its poor."[7] Today, the slogan "adopt a child" has, and may be partially motivated by, the effect of ensuring that the donor's effort does not create an externality for other altruists. The appeal by universities to alumni may be motivated by the same idea. Although externalities will also exist among alumni from the same university, they will be weaker than in unre-stricted giving.

Given inequality (4), it is also possible to escape the Pareto–suboptimal outcome in a Prisoner's Dilemma if individuals "choose along the diagonal" from the upper left-hand cell to the lower right-hand cell of the table. Although some scholars seem to claim that this framing of the issue could be individually rational,[8] their arguments have not convinced me. The fol-lowing two mechanisms seem more interesting.

First, the two individuals (or more relevantly, a large group of individ-uals in an n-person Prisoner's Dilemma) might vote for a law that forces everybody to donate generously. Some forms of taxation may indeed be seen as a collective commitment to philanthropy in the face of a free-rider temptation. Whether that dangerous phrase, "may be seen as," should be taken to refer to the motive for adopting taxes or to the effect of taxes is an open question. In other cases, however, there is no doubt that taxation has been a self-conscious response to the fact that individual efforts would cause a suboptimal provision of public goods. In one sense, however, this is only to move the problem one step back. Assume, as a stylized fact, that, during elections, votes are determined in part by the taxation policies of the parties. Because the very act of voting may be seen as a donation by the voter to society, why would citizens bother to vote? One response, as we shall see, is to appeal to a Valmont effect.

Second, magical thinking may cause individuals to act as if they were choosing along the diagonal. If A and B are indeed identical twins, each of them may be tempted to think that whatever she does, her twin will do as well. Many of us will have had the following experience. When we sit at home on a Saturday evening, watching a telethon on TV, a person soliciting a contribution rings the doorbell. Our first impulse may be to turn him away, but then a second thought occurs: "What if everyone did that? I can afford to give and, if not me, who?" And so we end up giving, as if our act could, magically, induce others to follow suit. Under same circumstances, this choice may be the result of something like the categorical imperative, but in other cases an explanation in terms of magical thinking or self-deception is more plausible. Voting, for instance, may be induced by the thought that: "If I vote, others like me are also likely to turn out."[9]

Although much alleviation of need and suffering is indeed funded through taxation, modern Western societies also have substantial numbers of individuals who donate their money or their time to charitable and philanthropic purposes. Because economists are loathe to explain their behavior in terms of irrational mechanisms such as magical thinking, they tend to look for a way of explaining it in terms of rational optimizing. Ideally, I believe, they would like to provide an explanation in terms of *rational egoism*. They might, for instance, try to explain philanthropy in terms of social norms, and social norms in terms of self-interest, by stipulating that people donate to good causes to avoid the sanctions that their peers would impose on them if they did not give. As I have argued elsewhere,[10] this explanation fatally fails to explain why rational self-interest would make others punish the nondonors. More obviously, it fails to explain anonymous donations. Although religious believers might donate anonymously, believing that God will see them and that they will be rewarded by salvation, this belief is actually inconsistent with most religious doctrines (you cannot force the hand of God). If donors are rational, they should understand this fact. In any case, there are presumably many nonreligious anonymous donors.

Most economists would agree, I believe, that egoism is an insufficient explanation of philanthropic behavior. Two convergent pressures then lead them to seek the explanation in egocentric rather than in altruistic motivations.

First, there is an empirical pressure: Nash altruism, in which each citizen donates an amount that is optimal given the donations of everybody else, would induce very low levels of giving. In the words of Andreoni, one can deduce from the assumption of rational equilibrium behavior that "in large economies virtually no one gives to the public good, hence making the Red Cross, the Salvation Army, and American Public Broadcasting logical impossibilities."[11] If donations are motivated by the fact that they are good for the donor rather than for the recipients, they produce a private good rather than a public good. Because the donor internalizes all the benefits from his gift, there is no collective action problem.

Second, more conjecturally, there is a psychological pressure. Economists might prefer the egocentric assumption to the altruistic one on the non-scientific ground of wanting to appear as hardnosed and realistic. As Robert Frank observes: "The flint-eyed researcher fears no greater humiliation than to have called some action altruistic, only to have a more sophisticated colleague later demonstrate that it was self-serving."[12] If the sophisticated colleague cannot show that the action was self-serving in the strict sense of promoting the material interest of the agent, he might still be able to score a point by showing that it was egocentric, for instance by producing a warm glow.

A succinct statement of the warm-glow effect in the context of a public good experiment, in which each member of a group had the opportunity to benefit other members, is that "the *act* of contributing, independent of how much it increases group payoffs, increases a subject's utility by a fixed amount."[13] Psychologically, this seems implausible. Because the warm glow is supposed to come from doing good, it is presumably enhanced by doing more good rather than less. A donation that's *known to be pointless* cannot produce a warm glow any more than a *costless donation* can. The greater the benefit to others and the greater the cost to oneself, the warmer the glow. In practice, and perhaps in principle, it would be hard to distinguish between the enhanced welfare of others as the *altruistic goal* of the donor and its role as a *condition for achieving his egocentric goal*. In the regression equation of Palfrey and Prisbrey, which uses as variables the egoistic cost to the agent, his egocentric benefits, and his altruistic benefits, the last is found to be "not significantly different from zero."[14] My reaction to their claim is one of frank disbelief, not because I can identify any error in their analysis, but because this is not how human beings are and behave. Even if they ultimately care only about a warm glow, they cannot get it unless they believe that they do good for others, and the more good they believe they do, the warmer the glow.

As further evidence of the lack of intellectual sophistication by economists in this field, one may cite the following argument that Andreoni makes for his theory: "the fact that people do get a joy from giving is such a natural observation as to be nearly beyond question."[15] Yes, but as the neuroeconomists know, getting pleasure from doing X and going X for the sake of the pleasure are two entirely different things.[16] To repeat, the confusion between getting to heaven as a result of good works and doing good works in order to get to heaven is not only an intellectual fallacy, but also an instance of the sin of simony.

Because the point is fundamental, it may be worthwhile mentioning that it has a venerable ancestry. Thus, in *On the Happy Life*, Seneca affirms the following:

> In the first place, even though virtue is sure to bestow pleasure, it is not for this reason that virtue is sought; for it is not this, but something more than this that she bestows, nor does she labor for this, but her labor, while directed toward something else, achieves this also. As in a ploughed field, which has been broken up for corn, some flowers will spring up here and there, yet it was not for these poor little plants, although they may please the eye, that so much toil was expended—the sower had a different purpose, these were superadded—just so pleasure is neither the cause nor the reward of virtue, but its by-product, and we do not accept virtue because she delights us, but if we accept her, she also delights us.[17]

Being neither an economist, a neuroscientist, or an expert on philanthropy, I am unable to propose a positive theory of why people donate to good causes. They probably have all sorts of reasons, in proportions and combinations that may defy precise analysis. The operation of social norms—giving because one is observed by others—is relatively uncontroversial. That of "quasi-moral norms"[18]—giving because one observes others giving—also seems plausible, especially perhaps in the wake of natural disasters. I would not exclude irrational phenomena such as magical thinking, but evidence might be hard to find. Targeted altruism (for example, "adopt a child") is observed in many contexts. Donations to the Salvation Army or to the Red Cross may be expressions of untargeted altruism, because *many donors do not go through the Nash equilibrium reasoning any more than most voters bother with the paradox of voting.* Warm-glow motivations probably also have a role to play, although for the reasons indicated earlier, they may be hard to separate from altruism. It may also be hard to distinguish from what I shall call *the agency effect.*

VARIETIES OF EGOCENTRIC MOTIVATIONS

The warm-glow effect is only one kind of egocentric motivation. It falls in the category of *internal egocentricity*, in which the agent is performing, as it were, for an inner audience. In addition, agents may *seek the approval of an external audience*. Often, we perform an action because we want to be praised for acting on an other-benefiting intention. When Louis XVI's First Minister Necker renounced on being paid for his services, even his adoring daughter Mme. de Staël acknowledged that he acted "for love of admiration."[19] In his case, he sought approval quite independently of any further effects it might have on the furthering of his aims. In contrast, when Valmont sought the admiration of the présidente de Tourvel, it was a means of seducing her, not an end in itself.

We may also act to *avoid the blame* of an external audience, once again independently of any further effects, As Aristotle said, "Shame is the imagination of disgrace, in which we shrink from the disgrace itself and *not from its consequences*" (emphasis added).[20] Just as being the object of admiration is intrinsically pleasant, being the object of contempt is intrinsically painful. Both motivations may be at work in philanthropy. Many donors want to make sure that their gifts are publicized so that they can attract approval for their generosity.[21] There is also evidence that in certain elite circles where philanthropy is de rigueur, people donate to avoid the disapproval of their peers.[22]

A similar duality may exist for the inner audience: I may seek either to gain its approval or to avoid its disapproval. As I understand the "warm-glow" literature, it is exclusively concerned with the former. However, if I donate to charity to be able to pat myself on the back, might I not also do so to avoid having to slap myself in the face? Might charitable contributions be performed to alleviate my guilt rather than to enhance my pride? I return to some aspects of that question in the final section of this chapter. Here, let me simply note the distinction between pride enhancement and guilt alleviation as *effects* of an action and their role as motives for action.

The *neuroscience of altruism and egocentricity* has taken off during the past several years.[23] I shall consider the studies by de Quervain et al., Moll et al., and Harbaugh, Mayr, and Burghart.[24] The explananda in these papers vary: altruistic punishment in the first, donations or refusals to donate to various causes in the second, and voluntary versus mandatory contributions to public goods in the third. Although all deal with warm-glow effects, only the second and the third are directly relevant for the question of egocentricity. I believe, however, that an analysis of the first will illuminate the latter two.

The topic of de Quervain et al. is altruistic punishment,[25] a topic that is doubly removed from philanthropy strictly speaking. First, the behaviors they study produce only an indirect benefit for people other than the agent. When A punishes B for B's unfair behavior toward A, B will behave more fairly toward some C in the future. Second, the benefit for C is unintended and unforeseen. A's goal is simply to take revenge *at some cost and no tangible benefits to himself*.

Here is a plausible real-life example of the behavior. Referring to vagrants in the French countryside in the time of the French Revolution, Georges Lefebvre writes:

> All these travelers, even if they were not beggars in the proper meaning of the term, would even so stop at a farmhouse and ask for food and a bed for the night. They were not turned away, any more than genuine beggars were. This was not due to charity or to good nature: the farmer cursed furiously behind their back.... The farmers were afraid. Afraid of a direct attack, naturally, but even more afraid of anonymous vengeance, trees and fences mysteriously cut down, cattle mutilated and, worst of all, fire.[26]

The reason why these punishments can be said to be objectively altruistic is that they *benefit future vagrants*, at some cost or risk to the person who carries them out and who might be caught doing so. Thompson provides another historical example.[27]

An important aspect of the study by de Quervain et al. is the following: Having identified a warm glow (the activation of reward centers in the brain) in the process of deciding whether to punish someone who had failed to return profits on an investment in a Trust Game, they ask whether this effect was *incidental* or *motivating*. In their words: "One interpretation is that a higher punishment could have induced stronger feelings of satisfaction, which suggests that stronger punishment causes stronger caudate activation. Alternatively, subjects who expected higher satisfaction from punishing a defector could have been willing to invest more money in punishment."[28] They decide in favor of the second interpretation, because, among the subjects who punish maximally in a "costless condition," those whose reward centers are most highly activated in that condition also punish more severely (at greater cost to the target and to themselves) in the "costly condition." Because they get more of a kick from punishing, they are willing to spend more on it, thus supporting the second hypothesis.

Hence, not only is revenge "sweet as honey," to use Homer's phrase, but, as when we eat honey, we take revenge *for the sake of* the sweetness. Thus, the study provides a warm-glow *explanation of behavior*, not merely a warm-glow *effect of behavior*. This distinction will be crucial in what follows. To place it in a broader perspective, it is the same as a distinction alluded to earlier, between salvation as the motivation for and salvation as the effect of charitable donations.

Before I proceed to the other studies, let me note that it would be interesting to see the work on altruistic punishment extended to third-party punishment.[29] When we find A punishing B for unfair treatment of C (assumed to be a stranger to A), are the same reward centers activated? If they are, is the effect incidental or motivating? Intuitively, it may seem less plausible that the punishing agent would act for the sake of a warm glow when he is the impersonal agent of justice, as it were, than that he would do so when he seeks personal revenge. In second-party punishment (revenge), what matters to A is not merely that B be punished, but that he be *punished* by A and that B *know* that A punished him.[30] In third-party punishment, it might seem that what matters is that B be punished and not that A be the punisher. Intuition suggests that A should not care whether A punishes B for B's unfair treatment of C or whether the punishment is carried out by a fourth agent D (or by C). The warm-glow effect should be the same in both cases—the pleasure from seeing justice done. But of course intuition might be wrong. Because it is known that reward centers are more highly activated when subjects obtain a monetary reward by pressing a button to get it than when the same reward is dropped in their lap,[31] the same might be true when the reward is justice being done. We may think of this as an *agency effect*. Conjecturally, the distinction between the warm-glow effect and the agency effect may be related to the distinction between liking and wanting proposed by Kent Berridge.[32]

Despite its title, the study by Moll et al. addresses ideological stances rather than charity.[33] Subjects were given the option of donating to or refusing to donate to various causes, including abortion, a children's hunger fund, the death penalty, euthanasia, nuclear power, and war. (The full set of 64 causes used in the experiment is not given in the article by Moll et al. or in the online supplementary information.) Of these, only the children's hunger fund counts as an object of philanthropy in the usual sense. Donations or refusals to donate could be costly or costless. Although it seems hard to imagine that anyone would pay for not increasing the endowment of a children's hunger fund, refusals make sense in the other, more ideological issues. The experiment also included choices involving monetary reward only, with no impact on the causes. The authors find that "donating to societal causes recruited two types of [neural] reward systems, [one that] also was involved in pure monetary rewards and [one that] was specific for donations and plays key roles in social attachment and affiliative reward mechanisms in humans and other animals."[34]

It seems quite plausible, on intuitive grounds, that people might derive pleasure from the decision to prevent an increase of the endowment for a cause they abhor, such as euthanasia or abortion. This would, however, merely provide a warm-glow *effect*. Unlike de Quervain et al., the authors do not propose a warm-glow *explanation* of the choices.[35] When referring to the findings of Andreoni[36] as "compatible" with their findings, they do in fact refer only to a warm-glow "effect."[37] Unless I have misread their study, it does not support the egocentric theory of philanthropy, in part because philanthropy is not the focus of the study, but mainly because the authors do not go beyond the warm-glow effect to argue for a warm-glow explanation.

The study by Harbaugh, Mayr, and Burghart addresses mandatory versus voluntary contributions to public goods, specifically to a local food bank.[38] They find, importantly, that mandatory transfers from a subject's endowment to a cause (a form of taxation) "can produce activation in specific brain areas that have been tied to concrete individualistic rewards."[39] Being taxed (for a purpose you approve) makes you feel good. They also find that activation of these areas as well as reported satisfaction were "higher for voluntary than for mandatory transfers *after controlling for payoffs*" (emphasis added).[40] They infer that "this choice-related benefit is consistent with a warm-glow motive for giving."[41] Hence, "both pure altruism and warm glow are important motives for charitable giving."[42] As noted by Fehr, one can move from correlation to causation "by using neural activity in one treatment to predict choice behavior in another."[43] In Quervain et al., the activity in the costless condition is used to predict choices in the costly condition.[44] In Harbaugh, Mayr, and Burghart, activity in the mandatory condition is used to predict choices in the voluntary condition.[45]

Harbaugh, Mayr, and Burghart observe, however, that the greater activation of reward centers in the voluntary condition might also be the result of what I called the *agency effect*.[46] It is important, I believe, to distinguish this phenomenon from the warm-glow effect. In the usual interpretation of the "kick" from *doing good*, it involves a desire to *feel good* about oneself (the warm glow from punishment differs in this respect). Thus, it has been claimed that when people express willingness to sacrifice their money for an environmental cause they do so to "purchase moral satisfaction,"[47] and that when they vote "sociotropically" rather than selfishly they do so to "enhance their self-image"[48] at little cost to themselves. In my terminology, they act egocentrically. Yet nobody could achieve a better self-image from pressing a button to get money compared with having it dropped into one's lap. True, working for a reward may add a feeling of desert and entitlement to the reward itself, but pressing a button is not a form of entitlement-conferring work.

Not being a specialist in these matters, I remain somewhat agnostic. De Quervain et al. seem to provide good evidence for a warm-glow explanation of revenge behavior, but do not address the issue of charitable donations.[49] Harbaugh, Mayr, and Burghart do address this issue, but it seems that an agency-effect explanation of their findings might be sufficient.[50] In the concluding section I shall assume, however, that some apparently altruistic actions are explained by the anticipation of a warm glow, and try to draw some further implications from that assumption.

ACTING TO GET THE WARM GLOW REQUIRES SELF-DECEPTION

Despite the advances of behavioral economics, many economists and political scientists remain under the sway of the model of *Homo economicus*. The assumption that agents are *rational* and *self-interested* is both parsimonious and capable of yielding sharp predictions. Yet when the predictions of the model fail, as they often do, something has to give. Generally speaking, the natural reaction to an explanatory failure is to try to explain the observed facts by departing as little as possible from the original model. In the case that concerns me here, the smallest deviation from *rational egoism* might seem to be that of *rational egocentricity*. In this model, the utility function of the typical agent would include her own material benefit and the degree to which she can think of herself as a moral agent. As in other cases, there would be a trade-off between these aims: She might be willing to sacrifice some material welfare to get the warm glow from the enhanced self-image.

Warm-glow theorists of philanthropy and similar unselfish actions (voting, preserving the environment, and so on) do not seem to realize that this small adjustment to the model, *substituting egocentricity for egoism*, requires another and more radical one: *substituting irrationality for rationality.* This substitution is required by what I take to be a conceptual truth: One cannot derive a warm glow from an action unless the agent believes that the action was performed at least in part to benefit others. *An egocentric agent who performs for the inner audience has to believe that she is altruistic.* An agent who performed "good actions" with the sole *conscious end* of enhancing her self-image could not achieve that aim, any more than one can enhance one's self-image by paying another person to praise oneself.

According to this analysis, some egocentric motivations require self-deception, which is a paradigm of irrationality. This conclusion does not apply to revenge behavior. It is perfectly coherent to desire revenge in anticipation of and for the sake of the pleasure one will derive from it. The idea that revenge is a dish that is best served cold implies, in fact, a forward-looking hedonic calculus of this kind. By contrast, warm-glow explanations of charitable donations necessarily require self-deception.

The same argument applies to the suggestion offered by Andreoni that people "feel relieved from guilt when they become a giver."[51] This may indeed be an effect of giving, but for the relief from guilt to provide an explanation of the donations, more is needed. In my opinion, the idea of consciously choosing to donate as a rational means to guilt alleviation is conceptually incoherent. Assume, for instance, that one offered the agent a cheaper means to the same end, in the form of a low-cost anti-guilt pill. Because a rational person would always choose the less costly means to a given end, he would take it. As I have argued elsewhere,[52] however, a person who felt guilty about not giving would also feel guilty about taking the pill. To explain behavior, the guilt-relieving aim could not be a conscious one.

I conclude by exploring some complications of this basic picture. As with other-related reputation, self-reputation may be sought either for its intrinsic or for its instrumental value. The desire to see oneself as not merely self-interested is an intrinsic motivation. The desire to see oneself as having a strong willpower may be either an intrinsic or an instrumental one. The desire, finally, to believe that one is in good health is a purely instrumental one. To realize any one of these desires, an individual may take action to make the target beliefs more credible. In the three cases I just mentioned, this might take the form of donating money, abstaining from an opportunistic sexual encounter, or working hard on some test that is supposed to be diagnostic of good health.

Let me begin with the last case, which is illustrated in a classic experiment by Quattrone and Tversky.[53] The subjects were first asked to hold their hands in cold water until they could no longer tolerate the pain. Next, they were induced to believe that the length of time they could keep their hand in the water was a good predictor (for subjects in one condition) of a long life expectancy or (for subjects in a different condition) of a short life expectancy. Finally, they were asked to do the cold-water test again. Subjects who had been told that tolerance to cold water predicted a long (short) life kept their hands in the water for a longer (shorter) period than in the first test. Although the *output utility* of the action was negative (for subjects in the first condition the pain was almost intolerable), this effect was more than offset by its positive diagnostic utility—that is, by the utility the subjects derived from their belief in a long life expectancy.

As interpreted by Quattrone and Tversky, these findings imply that the subjects were deceiving themselves. This is not the garden-variety form of self-deception in which people simply adopt the belief they would like to be true, but a two-step operation in which they act to produce confirming evidence for the belief. It would seem that the same mechanism operates in the person who donates to charity to prove to himself that he has an altruistic character, or the person who abstains from taking a drink before noon to prove to himself that he does not have an alcoholic disposition. Because the acts in question were undertaken only for their diagnostic value, they do not—assuming rationality—have any.

Drazen Prelec and Ronit Bodner have, however, challenged this conclusion in recent articles.[54] One can perhaps summarize their argument by saying that when taking actions for their diagnostic value, people are engaged in *motivated self-discovery*. Hence, they argue, actions taken to bolster self-reputation may be perfectly rational (and provide genuine information), rather than self-deceptive. Bootstrapping can work.

For an example, suppose I would like to believe myself to be altruistic rather than selfish. Although I do not know exactly where I am located on the altruism scale, I have a subjective probability distribution over the positions on the scale. My initial endowment of self-esteem equals the expectation of this distribution. I then take an action (for example, donating to charity) that generates both outcome utility and diagnostic utility. The latter is the difference between the expectation of self-esteem based on the new distribution that is conditional on having taken that action, and the expectation that corresponds to the initial endowment.

> Where does this [new] distribution come from? The simplest assumption, though perhaps not the most accurate one psychologically, is that inferences are *true*, which means that the revised distribution [. . .] is consistent with maximization of both components of total utility. What does this mean psychologically? It means that the decision maker is fully aware that he or she is partly motivated by the desire to get good news.[55]

The central claim is that such rational self-signaling can induce a new distribution that makes the person better off overall. Even if the outcome utility component of the reward should fall, diagnostic utility may increase to offset it. Moreover, even though "the diagnostic value of an action is properly discounted for the presence of diagnostic motivation,"[56] *the discounting does not drive the value all the way to zero*. Given an underlying character trait of altruism, an action chosen for the purpose of revealing its strength will reflect not only my desire to see myself as altruistic, *but also the strength of the trait.* A very selfish person would not be willing to invest a lot in building a self-reputation as an altruist. Knowing this fact, a rational agent will see a generous contribution as an indicator of an altruistic character. (Here I assume that the disposition is fixed and *revealed* by behavior rather than, as Aristotle argued, *shaped* by behavior.)

At the same time, the agent will know that his contribution is deceptively high, in the following sense. Let us distinguish between a *concern for disinterestedness* (an egocentric desire for self-reputation) and a *disinterested concern* for other people's welfare (altruism). Harry has both concerns, but Jane has only the latter. The strength of their altruism is the same. Although Harry will donate more than Jane, he cannot rationally infer that his altruism is stronger than hers because he knows that part of his contribution is a result of his desire to strengthen his self-reputation.

In contrast, in self-deceptive self-signaling "you generously give yourself *full* credit for doing the good thing, even when part of the motive was precisely to get the credit" (emphasis added).[57] In other words, a self-deceptive Harry would conclude that he was more altruistic than Jane. Bodner and Prelec refer to this inference as a "face-value interpretation" of the behavior.[58] As they write, "A person [such as Jane, in my example] whose actions were made innocent of their diagnostic implications would be justified in maintaining face-value inferences. Diagnostic utility would be experienced as an unintentional by-product of choice, not something that can consciously affect choice."[59] For someone like Harry to maintain that inference would, however, be self-deceptive.

The questionable part of this argument is obviously the assumption that people have enough information about themselves to make true inferences about their dispositions from their behavior. How can they know, however, that second-level self-deception is not at work? In fact, Jane has an incentive to believe that she does not care about the diagnostic implications of her behavior, because that belief will enable her to infer a strongly altruistic character from relatively small donations.[60] We may, therefore, give the last word to Kant:

> It is absolutely impossible by means of experience to make out with complete certainty a single case in which the maxim of an action otherwise in conformity with duty rested simply on moral grounds and on the representation of one's duty. It is indeed sometimes the case that with the keenest self-examination we find nothing besides the moral ground of duty that could have been powerful enough to move us to this or that good action and to so great a sacrifice; but from this it cannot be inferred with certainty that no covert impulse of self-love, under the mere pretense of that idea, was not actually the real determining cause of the will; for we like to flatter ourselves by falsely attributing to ourselves a nobler motive, whereas in fact we can never, even by the most strenuous self-examination, get entirely behind our covert incentives, since, when moral worth is at issue, what counts is not actions, which one sees, but those inner principles of actions that one does not see.[61]

Notes

The author is grateful to Ernst Fehr for helpful guidance in preparing this article, to Aanund Hylland for technical assistance, and for comments by Jakob Elster and Thomas Pogge on an earlier draft.

1. Oded Stark, *Altruism and Beyond* (Cambridge: Cambridge University Press, 1995), chap. 4.

2. Hillel Rapoport and Frederic Docquier, "The Economics of Migrants' Remittances," in Serge-Christophe Kolm and Jean Mercier Ythier, eds., *Handbook of the Economics of Giving, Altruism and Reciprocity* (Amsterdam: North-Holland, 2006), pp. 1135–1195, 1149.

3. Pierre Choderlos de Laclos, *Les liaisons dangereuses* (1782), Letter XXI.

4. Ibid.

5. Serge-Christophe Kolm, "The Optimal Production of Social Justice," in Julius Margolis and Henri Guitton, eds., *Public Economics* (London: Macmillan, 1969); Harold Hochman and James Rodgers, "Pareto Optimal Redistribution," *American Economic Review* 59 (1969), pp. 542–557.

6. Thanks to Aanund Hylland for pointing this out to me.

7. Serge-Christophe Kolm, *La bonne économie* (Paris: Presses Universitaires de France, 1984), pp. 79–80.

8. Susan Hurley, *Natural Reasons* (New York: Oxford University Press, 1992); Michael Bacharach, *Beyond Individual Choice* (Princeton, N.J.: Princeton University Press, 2006).

9. George A. Quattrone and Amos Tversky, "Self-Deception and the Voters' Illusion," *Journal of Personality and Social Psychology* 46 (1984), pp. 237–248.

10. Jon Elster, "Social Norms and Economic Theory," *Journal of Economic Perspectives* 3 (1989), pp. 99–117.

11. James Andreoni, "Impure Altruism and Donations to Public Goods: A Theory of Warm-Glow Giving," *Economic Journal* 100 (1989), p. 465.

12. Robert Frank, *Passions within Reason* (New York: Norton, 1998), p. 21.

13. Thomas R. Palfrey and Jeffery E. Prisbrey, "Anomalous Behavior in Public Goods Experiments: How Much and Why?" *American Economic Review* 87 (1997), p. 830.

14. Ibid.

15. James Andreoni, "Philanthropy," in Serge-Christophe Kolm and Jean Mercier Ythier, eds., *Handbook of the Economics of Giving, Altruism and Reciprocity* (Amsterdam: North-Holland, 2006), p. 1220, note 16.

16. Dominique J.-F. de Quervain et al., "The Neural Basis of Altruistic Punishment," *Science* 305 (2004), pp. 1254–1258.

17. Seneca, *On the Happy Life*, sects. 9.1 and 9.2.

18. Jon Elster, *Explaining Social Behavior* (Cambridge: Cambridge University Press, 2007), Ch. 4.

19. Germaine de Staël, *Considérations sur la Révolution Française* (Paris: Tallandier, 2000), p. 104.

20. Aristotle, *Rhetoric*, p. 1384a.

21. Erik Schokkaert, "The Empirical Analysis of Transfer Motives," in Serge-Christophe Kolm and Jean Mercier Ythier, eds., *Handbook of the Economics of Giving, Altruism and Reciprocity* (Amsterdam: North-Holland, 2006), p. 161.

22. Eric Posner, *Law and Social Norms* (Cambridge, Mass.: Harvard University Press, 2007), p. 61.

23. For a survey, see Ulrich Mayr, William T. Harbaugh, and Dharol Tankersley, "Neuroeconomics of Charitable Giving and Philanthropy," in Paul W. Glimcher et al., eds., *Neuroeconomics: Decision Making and the Brain* (London: Elsevier, 2008), pp. 303–320.

24. De Quervain et al., "The Neural Basis"; Jorge Moll et al., "Human Fronto-mesolimbic Networks Guide Decisions about Charitable Donations," *Proceedings of the National Academy of Sciences* 103 (2006), 15623–15628; William Harbaugh, Ulrich Mayr, and Daniel Burghart, "Neural Responses to Taxation and Voluntary Giving Reveal Motives for Charitable Donations," *Science* 316 (2007), pp. 1622–1625.

25. De Quervain et al., "The Neural Basis."

26. Georges Lefebvre, *The Great Fear of 1789* (New York: Schocken, 1973), p. 17.

27. Edward Palmer Thompson, "The Moral Economy of the English Crowd in the Eighteenth Century," *Past and Present* 40 (1971), pp. 76–136.

28. Quervain, "The Neural Basis," p. 1257.

29. Ernst Fehr and Urs Fischbacher, "Third-Party Punishment and Social Norms," *Evolution and Human Behavior* 25 (2004), pp. 63–87.

30. Adam Smith, *The Theory of Moral Sentiments* (Oxford: Oxford University Press, 1976), p. 69.

31. Caroline F. Zink et al., "Human Striatal Responses to Monetary Reward Depend on Saliency," *Neuron* 42 (2004), pp. 509–517.

32. Kent C. Berridge, "Wanting and Liking: Observations from the Neuroscience and Psychology Laboratory," *Inquiry* 52 (2009), 378–398.

33. Moll et al., "Human Fronto-mesolimbic Networks."

34. Moll et al., "Human Fronto-mesolimbic Networks," p. 1624.

35. De Quervain et al., "The Neural Basis."

36. Andreoni, "Impure Altruism."

37. Moll et al., "Human Fronto-mesolimbic Networks," p. 1624.

38. Harbaugh et al., "Neural Responses."

39. Ibid., p. 1623.

40. Ibid., p. 1624.

41. Ibid.

42. Ibid.

43. Ernst Fehr, "Social Preferences and the Brain," in Paul Glimcher et al., eds., *Neuroeconomics: Decision Making and the Brain* (London: Elsevier, 2009), pp. 215–232, 226.

44. De Quervain et al., "The Neural Basis."

45. Harbaugh et al., "Neural Responses."

46. Ibid.

47. Daniel Kahneman and Jack Knetsch, "Valuing Public Goods: The Purchase of Moral Satisfaction?" *Journal of Environmental Economics and Management* 22 (1992), pp. 57–70.

48. Bryan Caplan, *The Myth of the Rational Voter* (Princeton, N.J.: Princeton University Press, 2007), p. 151.

49. De Quervain et al., "The Neural Basis."

50. Harbaugh et al., "Neural Responses."

51. Andreoni, "Philanthropy," p. 1220.

52. Jon Elster, *Alchemies of the Mind* (Cambridge: Cambridge University Press, 1999), p. 302.

53. Quattrone and Tversky, "Self-Deception."

54. Drazen Prelec and Ronit Bodner, "Self-Signaling and Self-Control," in George Loewenstein, Daniel Read, and Roy F. Baumeister, eds., *Time and Decision* (New York: Russell Sage, 2003), pp. 277–298; Ronit Bodner and Drazen Prelec, "Self-Signaling and Diagnostic Utility in Everyday Decision Making," in Isabelle Brocas and Juan Carillo, eds., *The Psychology of Economic Decisions* (New York: Oxford University Press, 2003), pp. 105–123.

55. Prelec and Bodner, "Self-Signaling and Self-Control," p. 283.

56. Ibid.

57. Ibid., p. 294.

58. Bodner and Prelec, "Self-Signaling and Diagnostic Utility," p. 109.

59. Ibid.

60. Jon Elster, *Le désintéressement* (Paris: Seuil, 2009), p. 355.

61. Immanuel Kant, "Groundwork of the Metaphysics of Morals," in Mary J. Gregor, ed., *Practical Philosophy/Immanuel Kant* (Cambridge: Cambridge University Press, 1996), pp. 61–62.

5

Aiding the World's Poor

New Challenges for Donor States

Roger C. Riddell

Providing aid is a complex issue, not least when it is governments that provide it. In Peter Singer's view, "we have no obligation to assist countries whose governments have policies that make our aid ineffective."[1] However, what is "ineffective aid?" And how much aid might one allow to be ineffective to remove, from Singer's perspective, the obligation of rich governments to provide it? Ten percent, half of it, or more? If only, say, 30% of aid really helps those who receive it—providing hundreds if not thousands of people with the resources and opportunities to be productively employed to enable them to earn sufficient adequately to feed, clothe, and house their families—then should we stop providing this aid because other aid to the government of a country fails to achieve its purpose?

The impact and effectiveness of aid is problematic because the core challenge and basic dilemma in aiding the poor is that most of the poorest people live in the poorest countries; those in which the prospects for aid to work well are often the least good. In broad terms, the evidence suggests that aid will work well when provided to countries committed to and capable of using aid funds efficiently and effectively, with transparent systems, and where those making decisions and spending the money are accountable to their own citizens. Yet, the countries that need aid tend to be characterized by a combination of severe skills shortages, fragile state and parliamentary institutions, inadequate legal systems, weak regulatory systems, underdeveloped and weak markets vulnerable to manipulation by powerful interest groups, operating without the benefits of a free press, and a strong civil society able to monitor public spending. In addition, a significant and growing proportion of the poorest countries suffer from conflict and civil unrest, providing a turbulent, unpredictable, and even more difficult environment in which to try to make aid work effectively. These are precisely the factors that are likely to undermine and reduce the impact of aid. If the basis for providing aid is an assurance that the funds will be used to maximum effect, then aid should be steered toward countries such the United Kingdom, Norway, or Sweden.[2]

It is against the backdrop of this core dilemma of giving aid that this chapter considers some key challenges, including key *new* challenges that face donor states when providing foreign aid.

AID AND EMERGENCIES

One growing challenge facing donors has been the rising number of disasters affecting the world—a central issue for the world's poor, as it is judged that around 90% of those affected by disasters are among the world's poorest and most marginalized people. During the first 50 years of the past century, there were fewer than 50 major global natural disasters; by 1980, the number had risen to more than 200, and by the early years of this century, to more than 400.[3] The continued effects of climate change are likely to reinforce this upward trend, resulting in even more deaths and even more people directly affected by disasters. What has this increase in emergencies meant for aid flows?

Historically, a clear distinction has been made between humanitarian or emergency aid, on the one hand, and development aid, on the other. The general public's engagement with the world of aid is predominantly through the media, whose focus has overwhelmingly and increasingly been on emergencies and disasters. Consistently and repeatedly throughout recent decades, the public response to a growing number of national appeals for emergency aid (not only in the United Kingdom but worldwide) has been one of increasing donations, with the 2004 Boxing Day tsunami appeals breaking all previous records. This public response has been mirrored in the rising contribution that official aid donors—governments—have made to the growing number of emergencies.

However, despite this response, there still remains a large gap between the amount of money needed to respond adequately to all emergencies and the amount of emergency aid actually provided. This fact is not widely known because the media focus on a small number of "high-profile" emergencies, a number of which tend not only to be well-funded, but sometimes "overfunded." In contrast, most other appeals remain substantially underfunded. For instance, during the 8-year period to 2007, only 85% of the United Nation's best-funded appeals were fully met, falling to a derisory 32% for the worst-funded appeals, resulting in more than one quarter of the highest priority needs of those suffering from emergencies remaining unmet.[4]

Most people believe that if ever there is an obligation to assist the distant needy, then it applies with most force when disasters strike, and when external assistance is urgently and clearly needed. However, the moral issues are more complex.

THE RELATIVE IMPORTANCE OF EMERGENCY
VERSUS DEVELOPMENT AID

Against the background of blanket media coverage of high-profile emergencies, it is not surprising that it is widely believed that emergency or humanitarian aid is the most important type of aid provided and that the work of nongovernmental aid agencies, such as Oxfam, Christian Aid, Muslim Aid, WaterAid, and many others, comprises the major part of the global aid effort.

In sharp contrast, humanitarian aid comprises less than 15% of total global aid, and most of this is provided by governments and not by private donations.[5] Indeed, today, as in the past, the vast majority of foreign aid is raised by funds provided by rich-country governments, funding aid activities of governmental agencies, such as Britain's Department for International Development and intergovernmental agencies, and the World Bank's main aid arm, the International Development Association. Probably well less than a fifth of all aid is used by nongovernmental organizations for both their emergency and development work.[6]

A linked and probably far stronger belief among the public is that emergency aid is most urgently needed because it is this type of aid that is used to save lives. The figures, again, tell a different and more nuanced story. Many people die, directly or indirectly, as a result of emergencies, and the numbers have been increasing in recent times. In the decade to 2004, more than 900,000 people are estimated to have died in disasters, a 40% increase in the 640,000 killed the previous decade.[7] Likewise, the number of people affected by disasters has expanded even more rapidly from the 1960s onward, increasing from 100 million in the early 1980s, to 200 million by the early 1990s, and to more than 250 million people by the early decades of this century. There is also evidence of growing numbers of people requiring emergency food supplies, especially in Africa. In early 2006, the World Food Programme estimated it was trying to provide food for 40 million people, compared with 20 million people 10 years earlier.[8] Even without the 2004 Boxing Day tsunami, which is estimated to have caused the death of 230,000 people, the decade-to-decade increase in deaths would have been more than 50%.

However, when these figures are placed alongside the number of deaths occurring each year as a result of poverty—hunger, malnutrition, lack of shelter, disease caused by poor or inadequate water and sanitation, lack of basic medicines, or bed nets for those living in malarial areas, lack of access to primary health care, and low levels of immunization against killer diseases such as measles—they look very different. Each year, it is estimated that perhaps 18 million people die from these and other diseases of poverty.[9] When placed alongside the deaths from emergencies, the differences are startling: For every one person who dies in an emergency, between 150 and 200 people die from diseases of poverty. The vast majority of these deaths occur in the poorest 65 countries of the world, and are largely preventable. Although known, they pass largely unnoticed and are given little prominence in the press and media, in part because the numbers of poverty-related deaths are so large and the scale of the problem so huge that they are difficult to grasp, and in part because the regularity of these deaths means they are not considered to be "news." The annual number of deaths from poverty is equivalent to 100 average size jumbo jets (each carrying 500 passengers) crashing each day, leaving no survivors. Two hundred thirty thousand people are estimated to have died in the Asian tsunami and its aftermath; this number dies every 5 days from the extremes and diseases of poverty. On the basis of such figures, it would seem that an even higher share of total aid should be directed to reducing poverty than the current 85:15 split, even the 93:7 split of 30 years ago. In a very real sense, poverty ought to be perceived as an emergency.

What is the moral difference between a life needlessly lost, or easily saved, in an emergency and a life needlessly lost as a result of vulnerability to disease and death from extreme poverty or one saved by addressing the main factors that cause most extremely poor people to die prematurely? The question is important to the aid debate because of the way that the public perceives the obligation to assist, and the sorts of aid needed.

When an emergency strikes, especially when it receives a high media profile, the public response—across all donor countries—is to donate to appeals. This positive response occurs with little to no reference to concerns raised (in the media) about problems with emergency aid funds used in previous emergencies. Successive evaluations commonly report, for example, a mismatch between those who needed the aid and where it was allocated; aid wastage caused by the duplication of agencies' efforts, or poor-quality goods provided; "technical assistance" provided by those lacking the basic skills needed; aid never reaching those for whom it was intended; and aid arriving too late.

The sense that "something should be done" and emergency aid be provided always appears to "trump," or overshadow, concerns about the impact of previous emergency aid interventions. What this suggests is not that impact "doesn't matter," but rather that aid failures and inefficiencies are generally not perceived as providing the basis upon which the decision to give emergency aid rests.

We need, however, to be careful before leaping too quickly to the conclusion that it is aid that is the main factor that will bring about the outcomes upon which the moral obligation to respond are based.

DOES THE OBLIGATION TO HELP MEAN THAT THERE IS ALSO AN OBLIGATION TO PROVIDE AID?

Most aid donors believe most or at least a significant share of the aid they provide "works," and they place in the public domain examples of such successes to support this assertion. If most aid works and extreme poverty

persists, then more aid should help lift more people out of poverty—
hence the appeal by aid donors and supporters of aid for more aid to be
provided. For their part, rich states have been unanimous in recent years
in arguing that not enough aid is given, and almost all have said they need
to give more. Against this backdrop, it is easy to understand why the
public is led to believe not only that aid is needed in order for extreme
poverty to be reduced, but why it is also widely believed that aid is
necessary for development, that aid is the motor that drives development
and poverty reduction, and that, without aid, extreme poverty will not be
eliminated.

Aid's most vehement critics muster three sorts of arguments to counter
these views. One group argues that aid doesn't work, producing evidence
to prove this and going on to suggest that, because aid has not (ever)
worked in the past, it never will.[10] A second group argues that the process
of giving aid either directly or indirectly produces significant perverse
effects that eclipse any good that aid might achieve—for instance, by
fueling corruption, distorting markets, or reducing the incentive of recipients to use their own resources to fund expenditure, notably by raising
taxes.[11] A third group argues not merely that a discussion of aid, its needs
and its impact, is largely irrelevant, because extreme poverty and under-
development are either caused or perpetuated by an array of other far
more important factors and influences. Consequently, these critics suggest
that if you want to help the poor, then "look elsewhere."

One prominent writer from this school of thought is John Rawls, who
argues that well-ordered people have a duty to assist what he terms "burdened societies." But this duty only extends to the requirement of
assistance to help the societies to become "well ordered."[12] He conjectures
that "there is no society anywhere in the world, except for marginal
cases,"—he cites the case of arctic Eskimos—"with resources so scarce
that it could not, were it reasonably and rationally organized and governed, become well-ordered."[13] Another is Thomas Pogge. However, unlike
Rawls, Pogge does not believe the focus of attention should be on how
poor societies are organized. Rather, he argues, we should instead focus on
"the ways in which the affluent and their governments impose an international economic order that deprives the poor of their livelihood."[14]

Where does the truth lie to support these claims and counterclaims?
Five points summarize the main research findings. First, countries have
developed and reduced, if not eliminated, extreme poverty without (or
with very little) development aid. Likewise, countries in receipt of
significant amounts of aid over prolonged periods have experienced no
marked improvement in the incidence of poverty. Thus, in many ways, we
can assert that aid is not necessary for development and poverty reduction
to occur. Indeed, it is often factors other than aid that can and have made
a crucial difference to their development paths. This is not surprising
when one realizes that the share of aid in aid-recipient economies is really
quite low. Official aid accounts for less than 1% of the gross domestic

product (GDP) of all developing countries, only 5% of the GDP of sub-Saharan African countries, and less than 10% of the GDP of the world's 50 poorest countries.[15]

Second, however, there is both strong and consistent evidence of discrete aid projects achieving their immediate objectives. A recent review of this evidence came to the conclusion that, notwithstanding a range of biases in the studies conducted, upward of 75% of official aid projects achieved the core purpose for which the aid was provided. Schools were built, teachers were trained, and bed nets and antiretroviral drugs were delivered to those for whom they were intended. What is more, over time, project success rates have been increasing, although, unsurprisingly, success rates are among the lowest in many of the poorest and conflict-ridden countries, and project sustainability remains a problem.[16]

Third, there is also evidence to show that aid has often and increasingly made a difference at the sectoral level—notably, when provided in significant amounts and when focused on particular targets, such as providing resources for an expansion in school places, or training teachers, for funding immunization programs, or for expanding water and sanitation programs at the regional or national level.[17]

Fourth, and more crucial, we still have very little robust evidence to show the causal relationship between aggregate aid flows at the national level and their effect on the numbers of people living in poverty. The evidence we have is scanty and partial, and tends to show mixed results. Sometimes aid seems to have had an impact on poverty reduction (Uganda and Vietnam are good recent examples) and sometimes it hasn't (Zimbabwe), but oftentimes we don't know.[18] However, we should not be particularly surprised by this lack of evidence, because aid is only one factor among many influencing employment levels, growth rates, living standards, and poverty levels.

Fifth, we know increasingly more about the different factors that influence—help to accelerate and constrain—growth, development, and poverty reduction within different countries, and hence know more about the way that resources, including aid resources, can be used to help address constraints, plug gaps, and provide assistance to those who need it.[19]

What, then, does all this tell us about the need for aid and the ways that help ought to be provided? My own view is this. Although aid is certainly not necessary for development and poverty reduction to occur at all, it has helped and can help to reduce poverty faster than if aid had not been provided, both by helping to fill crucial resource gaps and by helping to address key systemic problems within poor countries—and there are many—that hold back "pro-poor" growth and development. However, aid is unlikely to have a tangible and long-lasting effect unless provided in conjunction with efforts to address a range of systemic and structural problems, and impediments outside the aid-recipient country and external to the "aid relationship." What this suggests, in turn, is a need for donor states and nongovernmental organizations to be more honest in explaining what aid can do, and might do, in ridding the world of extreme poverty, and its limitations.

But is aid *needed*? The answer is yes if it is provided in sufficient amounts to "make a difference," and if used in ways that address the major factors that impede the process of poverty reduction, both those directly affecting poor people and wider systemic constraints. Thus, there is a need for development aid if there is a need to prevent and to reduce faster the number of deaths caused by extreme poverty.

OTHER NEW CHALLENGES FOR DONOR STATES

What other contemporary challenges do donor states face in providing development aid that is targeted at the eradication of world poverty? Four are particularly important. These are (1) tensions between the moral obligation to help the poor and donor self-interest in the allocation of aid, (2) precisely how to provide aid for poverty reduction, (3) the multiplicity of official aid donors and requirements when giving aid, and (4) systemic problems arising from the voluntary nature of aid giving. I shall briefly examine each of these in turn.

The Moral Obligation to Help the Poor Versus Donor Interests in the Allocation of Aid

Historically, states have given aid to recipient countries for a variety of different motives. As already noted, moral philosophers have debated whether more rich individuals and more affluent states have a moral obligation to give aid. Perhaps not surprisingly, most major donors have decided that they do, indeed, provide aid for moral reasons, although they have tended to make stronger assertions in relation to humanitarian rather than development aid. However, the force of these assertions is diluted when set alongside other motives that influence the decisions of governments to give aid and how to allocate it. For most donor states, national security, the promotion of commercial interests, and short-term political objectives have all shaped decisions by governments about how much aid to give, whom to give it to, and for how long.

More than 40 years ago, Sweden's parliament authorized the state to provide aid for "no other motivation than moral duty and international solidarity."[20] Other Scandinavian and Nordic countries made similar statements, with the Finns and Norwegians going on to claim that their moral responsibility involved combating injustice and promoting development "wherever we can."[21] More recently, the United Kingdom stated that world poverty is "one of the greatest moral challenges we face," and "combating global poverty is . . . a moral obligation," and provides the grounding upon which their official aid programs are based.[22] In 2005, the members of the European Union signed the European Consensus on Development, agreeing that "combating poverty is a moral obligation."[23]

Although the United States has historically given greater prominence to national security concerns in articulating why it provides aid, it has also deployed the language of moral obligation to assist the world's poor. This view has been articulated most explicitly in relation to humanitarian aid. The U.S. government provides humanitarian assistance "solely on the basis of urgent need, reflecting the concern for saving lives and alleviating suffering, regardless of the character of their governments."[24] However, it has also been a justification for official development assistance provided by the United States. Indeed, President John Kennedy's view that the United States' aid program is based on moral obligation has been prominently displayed on the website of the main government aid agency, even during the recent Bush administration.

> Why, then, should the United States continue a foreign assistance program? The answer is that there is no escaping our obligation: our moral obligations as a wise leader and good neighbor in the interdependent community of free nations; our economic obligations as the wealthiest people in a world of largely poor people.... To fail to meet these obligations now would be disastrous.[25]

Over time, the main donor states have narrowed down the purpose for which they say they are providing aid, with poverty eradication becoming a more central purpose, and the commercial interest of the donors in particular becoming of far less importance. As the Cold War ended, there were great hopes that the national self-interest and short-term political motives for giving aid would become far less influential in the decisions states made about the allocation of their aid funds. However, these high expectations have not been met. To this day, national self-interest continues markedly to influence donor decisions of *whom* to aid. Two examples illustrate this. First, in recent years, only just over 40% of all official aid is channeled to the 63 poorest countries of the world in which well over 90% of the world's poorest people live.[26] Second, in 1999, among them, Afghanistan, Iraq, and Pakistan received less than 2% of total official aid. In 2005, 5 years later, these three countries accounted for 26% of all ODA, nearly a 30-fold increase. In that year, Iraq and Afghanistan were among the top 15 largest recipients for 17 of the largest 19 bilateral aid donors; 10 years earlier, neither of these countries had been in the top 15 of any major donor country.[27]

Because Afghanistan and Pakistan are among the poorest countries of the world, and child mortality rates in Iraq are among the highest in the world, there can be overlap between poverty-reducing and strategic goals and objectives in providing aid. The core problems that arise when short-term political interests enter the decision of which poor people and poor countries to assist are, first, the increased likelihood of a continued and major mismatch between aid needs and the allocation of ODA funds and, second, unpredictability and high levels of volatility in the flows of aid that are provided. The unpredictability and volatility of aid reduces even further aid's potential impact, because recipients are understandably reluctant to allocate aid to recurrent expenditures this year—such as to pay teachers' or nurses' salaries—when, next year, there is no knowing if aid will again be provided. A recent study of aid in Uganda revealed that aid levels have fluctuated (rose or fell) by 20% or more annually for the past 5 years.[28]

How Best to Provide Aid for Poverty Reduction

After rich states have decided who to give aid to, the next question is to determine precisely *how* that aid should be provided. Understandably, donors have been concerned that the aid provided be used for the purpose intended and that it should be effective, and they have usually sought to achieve these aims in two ways.

Predominantly, aid has been "parceled up" into a series of discrete stand-alone projects that they either manage themselves or over which they exert considerable power and influence. However, some aid has also been given to the recipient's finance ministry to boost total spending, or channeled to government ministries, departments, and institutions to boost specific areas of spending, such as health or education, or to help address skills gaps, strengthen institutions, or help enhance capacities. In providing aid in this way, most donors have applied an array of different specific conditions to the aid as a *quid pro quo* for the funds provided.

The balance between direct project aid and aid given to recipient government departments or institutions—known as *program aid*—has oscillated as fashions in giving aid have changed. Recent years have seen an increase in rhetoric about the merits of program aid, although, in practice, most aid is still given in project form, with the projects usually being designed by the donors and under their watchful eye. Public discourse talks of aid being "given by the rich to the poor." In contrast, to this day, most official aid is not actually given to recipients in the form of free cash that they can choose how to deploy. Almost all official aid is "tied," either formally and explicitly, or more loosely, to priorities established by the donors, and most is still provided as discrete stand-alone projects.

Four problems have arisen with this way of giving aid, providing new challenges to the way aid giving has traditionally been cast. The first is that providing aid in the form of stand-alone projects risks isolating them from the wider world and thus creating "islands of development." Indeed, because donor projects often suck in expertise and resources from the wider economy, they can have a perverse systemic effect on broader development efforts, as higher salaries paid by donors draw scarce skills away from key government posts. The second problem—seemingly obvious and, indeed, increasingly recognized—is that development is far more likely to occur if poverty reduction plans and policies are drawn up and implemented (in other words, "owned") by the recipient country. The more donors push their ideas, the less likely it is that policies are recipient owned, so that commitment to pursue such policies will be reduced. Third, and related, the presumption that donors know how best to promote development has been frequently proved to be wrong. The conditions donors have attached to their aid have often turned out to have led to outcomes that have undermined, rather than furthered, poverty reduction. Fourth, however, recipients have, in practice, often ignored some of the key conditions that donors have attached to their aid. In the majority of cases, this has not led to donors cutting off their aid, or even reducing it, confirming the view that conditionality is not a very effective way of influencing the way aid funds are spent.[29]

Another related issue concerns the link between the aid given and those living in extreme poverty. There is a long-standing and widely held view that if aid is to make a difference to poor people, then it needs to be given to poor people directly (perhaps as cash handouts) or at least be used for projects with a purpose that directly benefits particular groups of poor people. More recently, as what is termed the *rights-based approach* to development has moved more to center stage, there has additionally been growing support for the view that poor people themselves ought to be involved in decisions about how they might be helped—and aided— making them more the subjects of decisions about their own development rather than merely passive receivers of actions and activities decided by benevolent outsiders.

This thinking needs to be placed alongside analyses of the different factors found to make an impact on poverty reduction. There is extensive evidence that shows that a major way of reducing poverty is to pursue a range of initiatives that are not targeted specifically at poor people. Using aid to ensure particular (poor) people have access to education and health care, clean water, and sanitation will certainly enhance their well-being, expand their choices, and equip them with opportunities for productive employment. Yet, equally, poor people will benefit from initiatives that result in more rapid and sustainable wealth creation and an increase in the number of productive jobs. These cover a wide range of activities, such as building an efficient road network, developing modern communication and telecommunications systems, expanding the rule of law, strengthening the regulatory framework, encouraging the development of a free press, and so on. All have been found to have a significant impact on poverty reduction, and hence need to be considered as part of a package of ways in which aid might assist to accelerate the reduction of those living in extreme poverty.

Indeed, if a country fails to address the major structural, systemic, and institutional impediments to development—and if donors indirectly contribute to such failures by solely providing aid for projects directly aimed at helping particular groups of poor people meet specific and immediate short-term needs—it is quite probable that more people will remain in poverty for longer than if aid funds had been used to help address those impediments and move the economy to a more sustainable development path.

Aid and the Millennium Development Goals

This discussion provides the backdrop for discussing the way that the aid debate has recently been recast—namely, by linking aid giving to the Millennium Development Goals (MDGs). A major change in aid giving took place at the 2000 Millennium Summit Declaration when all nations committed themselves to ridding the world of extreme poverty. The commitment was formalized in eight (linked) MDGs, which were to form a new template against which the efforts of aid donors were to be refocused. The first and overarching MDG was the "eradication of poverty and hunger." Hence, aid was to be provided in the context of *externally* created goals and objectives, and judged against these.[30] However, 5 years later, in 2005, the main state donors agreed (in what has become known as the *Paris Declaration on Aid Effectiveness*)[31] and committed themselves to provide aid to recipients within the framework of development strategies and policies drawn up and implemented by the recipient countries themselves. Hence, aid was also to be provided in the context of *internally* created goals and objectives, and judged against these.

It could be argued that there is little or no conflict between these two approaches to giving aid, because all countries have signed up to the MDGs, so they provide the template on which all development strategies in aid-recipient countries need to be based from now on. The reality is both quite different and more complex.

From the donor side, a major problem has been that the main donors as a whole have failed to provide the additional funding they pledged would be forthcoming to achieve the MDGs.[32] Another problem is that the commitment to providing aid within the context of the MDGs has been decidedly mixed. Although some state donors, such as the United Kingdom, have used the MDGs to inform the allocation of their aid funds, others have not. Indeed, four out of the five main state donors—the United States, Japan, France, and Germany—who between them account for more than half of all official aid, do not allocate aid according to MDG criteria.

Second, although most aid-recipient countries signed the Millennium Summit Declaration, they did not play a prominent role in the creation of the MDGs, raising questions about their "ownership" of and commitment to the MDGs. It is not that poor countries do not want to rid their countries of poverty; the central issue is how best this might be done. Most aid-recipient countries have goals and objectives other than those encompassed by the MDGs. For instance, most are keen to expand secondary and tertiary education to be better placed to benefit from globalization, whereas the MDG education goals focus exclusively on primary/basic education. Not surprisingly, therefore, the majority of poor countries have not formally incorporated the MDGs into their development plans and planning frames. What is worrying is not so much that poor countries have not drawn up development plans that coincide with the MDGs, but that they haven't drawn up any development plans for themselves. Most continue to be lent on by donors to adopt policies and strategies either penned by or closely mirroring approaches developed by the main donors.

This has not stopped donors from allocating aid funds into initiatives that coincide with some MDG priorities. Although these have often led to immediate and tangible gains—such as more people in school, fewer children dying of malaria because of the distribution of more bed nets—they have also led to some perverse systemic effects. Donors have tended to channel aid into more "popular" areas or sectors, such as HIV/AIDS, and this has led both to an underfunding of other areas or goals and to systemic distortions. For example, donors have provided more money to health and education and less to water and sanitation. And in some countries, the popularity of HIV/AIDS has led to an underfunding of other health priorities. To illustrate this, a recent study of the health sector in Rwanda concluded that donor funding of HIV/AIDS projects had resulted in a lack of funds for primary health care services, undermining the Rwandan government's overall health strategy.[33] More recently, donors have begun to switch their aid to areas and activities that they believe are under-resourced or are not receiving sufficient attention. For instance, a number of donors, Britain among them, have, rather belatedly, decided that the best way to reduce poverty is to focus on activities that promote "pro-poor" growth.[34] This is leading to yet another switch of aid funds to achieve different purposes, this time to focus on wealth-creating and employment-enhancing activities, resulting in yet more volatility in aid flows and more uncertainty for recipient countries trying to plan public expenditures.

The Multiplicity of Official Aid Donors and Requirements When Giving Aid

Throughout the six decades that the governments of rich countries have provided aid, the number of official donors has steadily grown and now exceeds 200. At first sight, this appears to be beneficial for efforts to reduce world poverty, as more donors are likely to mean more aid extended to more (poor) recipients. The reality is quite different. Donor growth has become a significant and growing challenge to the efficiency of the official aid system—with most donors requiring and drawing up separate and different contracts with each recipient, with each recipient having to receive hundreds of fact-finding and assessment missions from different donors, and against the backdrop of the continued absence of a robust overall structure within which official aid funds are channeled. For example, during the 1960s, each recipient had to deal with about 12 donors. By 2005, the number had tripled to about 33. More than 100 different aid organizations are providing health sector aid.[35] In 1990, no single aid-recipient country had to interact with more than 40 individual donors. Today, almost 40 recipient countries have to deal with more than 26 separate donors.[36] In 1997, official aid was made up of around 20,000 discrete projects and programs, and linked donor–recipient interactions projects totaled around 20,000. Eight years later, the number has tripled to more than 60,000.[37]

Official donors are not only aware of the systemic problems of providing aid, but, in the 2005 Paris Declaration, they committed themselves to begin to address some of them. In particular, they agreed to work together more to harmonize their different (individual) aid efforts and to align them more closely with the plans and programs of aid-recipient governments. Some donors are now pooling their aid together, and some have agreed to reduce the number of recipients to whom they give aid. However, annual progress reports and those produced for the stock-taking follow-up meeting in Accra in 2008 concluded that "the pace of progress is too slow. Without further reform and faster action we will not meet our 2010 commitments and targets for improving."[38] What is more, some of the targets they have set themselves are not very ambitious. For example, in each aid-recipient country, instead of aid being channeled into recipient country systems, donors run, on average, 54 separately managed aid project implementation units. If the Paris Declaration targets are met, by the year 2010, the numbers would decrease, but would still leave, on average, 18 such donor-managed units in every aid-recipient country.[39]

Aid Volume, Aid Allocation, and the Voluntary Nature of Aid Giving

The final challenge to be highlighted focuses on the way that official aid funds are raised. The most immediate problem concerns the continuing gap between the total aid provided and the aid needed. However, underlying this immediate problem lies a more encompassing and fundamental problem: the voluntary nature of the aid-giving system.

The Prospects for Official Aid Flows

At a succession of recent world summits, all leading donor states pledged to provide increasing amounts of official aid until the target ratio of ODA to gross national income (GNI) reaches 0.7%, resulting in an increase in ODA of $50 billion a year, which is seen as critical to achieving the MDGs by 2015. Based on prevailing aid volumes, reaching this target would involve a more than doubling of ODA from the levels of ODA provided in the year 2000.

This process of donor aid pledging is nothing new. It has a long history. Successively during the 1970s, '80s, and '90s, donor states made almost identical pledges, aiming, for example in the 1970s, to double aid levels within 5 years. Perversely, the highest ODA-to-GNI ratios were achieved during the late 1960s, the years immediately prior to when the very first pledges to reach the 0.7% ratio were ever made.[40]

Even before the global financial and economic crisis, which became visible during mid 2008, the near-term prospects for official aid levels were not particularly promising. The ODA-to-GNI ratio climbed from 0.26% in 2004 to 0.33% in 2005, but then fell back to 0.28% in 2007, with (optimistic) simulated projections suggesting that, at best, the ratio might increase to 0.37% by the year 2010—bringing it back to the levels of the early 1970s. This would result in a funding gap of $34 billion.[41]

However, increasing levels of unemployment in donor economies and the need to focus government expenditure on maintaining levels of domestic demand are likely to put added pressure on donor states to reign in what are widely perceived to be low-priority expenditures, including the official aid program. By early 2009, Greece, Ireland, and Italy had already announced cutbacks in their aid expansion programs. The history of past problems provides some guidance to what might happen now. In particular, earlier economic crises in donor states resulted in significant contractions in aid programs of both large donors (Japan and the United States) and smaller ones (such as Italy), whereas the Nordic banking crisis of the early 1990s led to sharp short-term decreases, in real terms, in official aid provided by Norway (10%), Sweden (17%), and Finland (62%)—some of the most generous providers of aid.

What is more, it has become increasingly evident that the global crisis recession is likely to lower growth rates and exacerbate the problems of poverty in the poorest countries, resulting in even more assistance, including even more aid being needed if the (quite modest) MDG poverty reduction targets are to be met. Indeed, the World Bank has estimated that the crisis is likely to have resulted in the numbers living in poverty increasing by 46 million in 2009 alone,[42] whereas the International Monetary Fund judges that low-income countries will have required at least a further $225 billion in 2009 over and above their earlier financial resource needs.[43]

The implication is clear: If the driver for providing aid is to contribute to making substantial inroads into poverty reduction, then we are moving into an era when even more will be needed than has been promised when even those promises are not being met.

The Mismatch between Aid Needs, the Way That Aid Is Provided, and the Voluntary Nature of Aid Giving

At one level, it is understandable why the (small) amount of official aid provided by (rich) donors has been based on a share of the (large) amount of the total wealth created—namely, the ratio of official aid to GNI—because this is a proxy for the "ability to pay." However, two historical trends need to be highlighted. The first is that, notwithstanding recent increases in the ODA-to-GNI ratio, the share of wealth given as official

aid by the richest countries of the world remains lower than the levels
recorded during the 1970s and early 1960s, when the ODA-to-GNI ratio
peaked at 0.54%.[44] The second trend has been the massive widening of
the average "wealth gap" between rich and poor countries. Thus, although
in 1965 the average income per inhabitant in the main donor countries
was 22 times greater than in the poorest countries, by 2003 it was 65
times greater.[45] In other words, during the past 40 years, the richer countries could "afford" to provide an increasing share of their wealth as aid to
the poorest; in practice, they provided a decreasing share of that increased
wealth.

The problem with linking the provision of aid solely with the wealth
created in donor countries is that there is no necessary link between the
amount of aid provided by the rich and the amount of aid required by the
poor. Space does not permit a substantive discussion here of precisely
how much aid is needed and how one might go about trying to calculate
what that figure is, or might be. However, from the studies that have been
undertaken, albeit based on partial and often rather crude methods used,
there is little doubt that the amount of official aid currently provided falls
well short of the amount needed—both the amount required adequately
to respond to emergencies (discussed briefly earlier) and the amount of
development aid needed by the poorest countries to help them sharply
reduce the number of people living in extreme poverty.[46]

The basic reason why this gap persists is that official aid funds are
raised (and allocated) solely on the basis of the voluntary decisions made
separately by each and every official donor country. Pledges are made by
donor countries, often at international conferences, to provide a certain
amount of aid, and sometimes to provide a share of official aid to the
poorest countries. However, there is no mechanism in place to ensure
that these pledges result in the aggregate amount of aid promised being
given. Similarly, the total amount of aid provided to a particular recipient
comprises the cumulative total of aid funds that each donor individually
chooses to provide to that country. No direct and formal link is made
between the funds given and the amount required. To my knowledge, in
no recipient country do donors get together with individual recipient
countries to determine how much aid a recipient is able to use and
absorb efficiently, and to commit themselves as a group to providing the
overall aid needed—with each agency committing itself to provide a
share of the total.

The looseness of these arrangements becomes apparent when, or if,
individual donors fail to provide the aid they have already announced they
will give to a particular recipient country in the coming year. No donor
feels any obligation to help make up a shortfall in the total aid provided
when one of their number fails to provide the amount of aid it has
promised. Likewise, when donors as a whole fail to keep their promises to
provide aid to the level promised, no donor feels obliged to make up the

shortfall when one or more donors provide less than they pledged, and no institutional mechanisms or processes exist to address this problem.

If the history of official aid giving teaches us one lesson, it is that the current "system" of raising aid funds and allocating aid on the basis of individual voluntary decisions doesn't work. It provides a wholly inadequate basis for raising and allocating official aid funds. This remains among the most critical challenges facing donor states today, although it is rarely discussed.

Surprisingly, it is not a new challenge. Almost from the time when the current aid system was being formed, a succession of prominent people have called for a more rational system of raising and allocating official aid funds. For instance, the first report of the Independent Commission on International Development published in 1980, more widely known as the Brandt Commission, as it was headed by the former German Chancellor Willy Brandt, judged, more than 25 years ago, that even then the time had already passed when the world ought to be raising aid funds through some sort of automatic mechanism, and disbursing aid without the repeated interventions of governments.[47] Eleven years earlier in 1969, the very first international commission on aid, chaired by the former prime minister of Canada, Lester Pearson argued that official aid should be separated from and should have a separate identity from short-term political considerations, and that, although donors understandably had a keen interest in ensuring that the aid they provide was well spent, their interests should be "carefully limited and institutionalized."[48] A third prominent politician critical of the way the aid system subsequently evolved was none other than the person considered the founding father of the international aid system: U.S. President Harry Truman. In his 1949 presidential inaugural speech, Truman outlined the basis of the system under which he thought official aid ought to be provided. In his view, donors should provide aid by pooling their resources together, by coordinating their aid-giving efforts, rather than acting on their own, and by ensuring that the aid given would enable recipients to use it in the ways that *they* saw fit.[49]

The current financial crisis and linked global recession have stimulated a growing number of world leaders to begin to focus seriously on the urgent need for countries and economies to change the way they have attempted to manage and regulate their economies and financial systems—individually—replacing it with an overarching structure within which their individual actions are more closely coordinated, and countries will be required to take action to ensure systemic durability. This is clearly also an opportune moment for politicians in donor countries to reengage in discussions that will lead to their taking similar sorts of systemic action to address the core problems in the way they continue to provide aid to the poorest countries, for this has been "urgently needed" for at least the past 30 years.

CONCLUSION

One of the key messages of this chapter is that aiding the world's poor is a complex issue. If you agree that we in the rich world *have* a moral obligation to assist in the reduction and elimination of extreme poverty, and if you believe that aid can help to make a significant difference—and a careful analysis of the evidence suggests there is sufficient evidence to show that it can—this is merely the start of your ethical journey of analysis and assessment. This is because the beneficial effects of aid are by no means certain or automatic, and donors are faced with an array of choices, questions, and challenges to try to determine how those aid funds might best be used. Indeed, this chapter suggests that the gap between what aid achieves and what it might achieve remains wide. Those who believe there is an obligation to rid the world of extreme poverty need to be in the vanguard of those working to narrow that gap and to urge more radical reform. Although aid is not the answer to development, it has helped, and the potential for it do far more is great. To call for the abandonment of the whole aid enterprise is likely to result in more poor people than if the current system is reformed. This is more likely to happen if aid's champions focus less on its achievements and far more on the factors that continue to constrain and limit its current effectiveness.

Notes

1. Peter Singer, *Practical Ethics* (Cambridge: Cambridge University Press, 1993), p. 241.

2. For a discussion of the factors likely to contribute to or enhance the impact of aid see, for example, Paul Collier, *The Bottom Billion: Why the Poorest Countries Are Failing and What Can be Done About It* (Oxford: Oxford University Press, 2008); John Degnbol-Martinussen and Poul Engberg-Pedersen, *Aid: Understanding International Development Co-operation* (London: Zed Books, 2008); Matthew Lockwood, *The State They're In: An Agenda for International Action on Poverty in Africa* (Bourton-on-Dunsmore: Intermediate Technology Development Group, 2005); and Roger C. Riddell, *Does Foreign Aid Really Work?* (Oxford: Oxford University Press, 2008).

3. See "National Disasters 1900 to 2009," in EM-DAT: The International Disaster Database, www.emdat.be/natural-disasters-trends (accessed July 24, 2010).

4. Development Initiatives, *Global Humanitarian Assistance, 2007/2008* (Wells, Somerset: Development Initiatives, 2008) p. 25–26, www.goodhumanitariandonorship.org/documents/gha_2007_final_a4.pdf.

5. Riddell, *Foreign Aid*, p. 317.

6. Ibid.

7. International Federation of Red Cross and Red Crescent Societies, *World Disasters Report 2005* (Geneva: International Federation of Red Cross and Red Crescent Societies, 2005), annex 1, table 13.

8. Riddell, *Foreign Aid*, p. 314.

9. World Health Organization, *The Burden of Disease 2004 Update* (Geneva: World Health Organization, 2008), p. 54ff, www.who.int/healthinfo/global_burden_disease/GBD_report_2004update_AnnexA.pdf.

10. See, for example, Fred Erixon, *Aid and Development: Will It Work This Time?* (London: International Policy Network, 2005).

11. The leading scholar associated with this view is the late Professor Peter Bauer. See Peter Bauer, *Dissent on Development* (London: Weidenfeld and Nicolson, 1971). More recently, very similar arguments have been deployed by Dambisa Moyo, *Dead Aid: Why Aid Is Not Working and How There Is Another Way for Africa* (London: Allen Lane, 2009). Both, however, have argued in favor of humanitarian aid.

12. John Rawls, *The Law of Peoples* (Cambridge, Mass.: Harvard University Press, 2003), p. 37.

13. Rawls, *The Law of Peoples*, p. 108.

14. Thomas Pogge, *World Poverty and Human Rights* (Cambridge: Polity Press, 2002), p. 20–26.

15. United Nations Development Programme, *Human Development Report 2007/2008* (New York: Palgrave Macmillan, 2007), pp. 290–293, hdr.undp.org/en/reports/global/hdr2007–2008/.

16. Riddell, *Foreign Aid*, pp. 179–194.

17. Ibid., pp. 195–200.

18. See Raghuram G. Rajan and Arvind Subramanian, *What Undermines Aid's Impact on Growth?* International Monetary Fund Working Paper No. 126 (Washington, D.C.: International Monetary Fund, 2005), www.imf.org/external/pubs/ft/wp/2005/wp05126.pdf; David Roodman, *The Anarchy of Numbers: Aid, Development and Cross-Country Empirics*, Working Paper No. 32 (Washington, D.C.: Center for Global Development, 2007), www.cgdev.org/content/publications/detail/2745; and Riddell, *Foreign Aid*, pp. 213–222.

19. See Dani Rodrik, *Rethinking Growth Strategies*, WIDER annual lecture 8 (Helsinki: UNU-WIDER, 2006), http://www.wider.unu.edu/publications/annual-lectures/en_GB/AL8/_files/78091862539831929/default/annual-lecture-2004.pdf; and Dani Rodrik, Avarind Subramanian, and Francesco Trebbi, *Institutions Rule: The Primacy of Institutions Over Geography and Integration in Economic Development*, Working Paper 9305 (Cambridge, Mass.: National Bureau of Economic Research, 2002), ksghome.harvard.edu/~drodrik/institutionsrule,%205.0.pdf.

20. Christian Andersson, "Breaking Through," in Pierre Frühling, ed., *Swedish Development Aid in Perspective: Policies, Problems and Results Since 1952* (Stockholm: Almqvist and Wiksell International, 1986), pp. 27–44.

21. For Finland see "Finland's Development Co-operation," 2005, global.finland.fi/julkaisut/pdf/perusesite_en.pdf. For Norway, see report no. 35 to the Störting (2003–2004), "Fighting Poverty Together: A Comprehensive Development Policy" [summary], www.dep.no/ud/english/doc/white_paper/032131-030005/ind-bn.html.

22. Department for International Development, *Eliminating World Poverty: Making Governance Work for the Poor* (Norwich: The Stationery Office, 2006), p. ii, www.dfid.gov.uk/wp2006/whitepaper-printer-friendly.pdf.

23. European Union, *The European Consensus on Development* (Brussels, European Parliament, European Council and European Commission), p. 3, http://ec.europa.eu/development/icenter/repository/european_consensus_2005_en.pdf.

24. U.S. Agency for International Development, *US Foreign Aid: Meeting the Challenges of the Twenty-First Century* (Washington, D.C.: U.S. Agency for International Development, 2004), p. 20, www.usaid.gov/policy/pdabz3221.pdf.

25. See www.usaid.gov/about_usaid/usaidhist.html.

26. Riddell, *Foreign Aid*, pp. 78–80.

27. Organisation for Economic Cooperation and Development, *Development Cooperation Report 2006* (Paris: Organisation for Economic Cooperation and Development, 2007), statistical annex, table 32.

28. See Roger Riddell, Lawrence Bategeka, and Deep Basu Ray, *Measuring Impact: The Global and Irish Aid Programme: Study 7: The Uganda Case Study and Implications and Reflections Especially For Small Donors* (Dublin: Advisory Board for Irish Aid, 2007), pp. 1–4, www.abia.gov.ie/Uploads/Ugandacasestudy report.doc.

29. See Riddell, *Foreign Aid*, pp. 231–252.

30. The details of the MDGs can be found at the following United Nations website: www.undp.org/mdg/basics.shtml.

31. Organization for Economic Cooperation and Development, *Paris Declaration on Aid Effectiveness* (Paris: Organisation for Economic Cooperation and Development, 2005). The text of the Paris Declaration can be accessed at www.oecd.org/dataoecd/11/41/34428351.pdf.

32. MDG Gap Taskforce, *Delivering on the Global Partnership for Achieving the Millennium Development Goals* (New York: United Nations, 2008), www.un.org/esa/policy/mdggap/mdg8report_engw.pdf.

33. International Development Association, *Aid Architecture: An Overview of the Main Trends in Official Development Assistance Flows* (Washington, D.C.: International Development Association, February 2007), sitesources.worldbank.org/IDA/Resources/Seminar%20PDFs/73449–1172525976405/3492866–1172527584498/Aidarchitecture.pdf.

34. Department for International Development, *Growth: Building Jobs and Prosperity in Developing Countries* (London: Department for International Development, 2008), www.dfid.gov.uk/pubs/files/growth-policy-paper.pdf.

35. International Development Association, *Aid Architecture*, p. 19.

36. Organisation for Economic Cooperation and Development, *Development Cooperation Report 2009* (Paris: Organisation for Economic Cooperation and Development, 2009), p. 41, www.oecd.org/document/62/0,3343,en_2649_3372 1_42195902_1_1_1,00.html.

37. Organisation for Economic Cooperation and Development, *Development Cooperation Report*, p. 22.

38. Accra Agenda for Action, *Final Communiqué from the Third High-Level Forum on Aid Effectiveness* (Accra: Third High-Level Forum on Aid Effectiveness, 2008), p. 1. See www.oecd.org/dataoecd/58/16/41202012.pdf. For more detailed analysis of progress made, see Bernard Wood, Dorte Kabell, Nansozi Muwanga, and Francisco Sagasti, *Evaluation of the Paris Declaration (Phase 1)* (Koeg, Denmark: Kabell Konsulting, 2008), www.oecd.org/dataoecd/57/3/41136587.pdf.

39. Organisation for Economic Cooperation and Development, *Paris Declaration*, p. 9.

40. Riddell, *Foreign Aid*, pp. 21–49.

41. Organisation for Economic Cooperation and Development, *Development Cooperation Report*, pp. 57–58 and 104–105.

42. World Bank, *Swimming Against the Tide: How Developing Countries Are Coping with the Global Crisis* (Washington, D.C.: The World Bank, 2009), p. 9, siteresources.worldbank.org/NEWS/Resources/swimmingagainstthetide-march2009.pdf.

43. International Monetary Fund, *The Implications of the Global Financial Crisis for Low-Income Countries* (Washington, D.C.: International Monetary Fund, 2009), p. vii, www.imf.org/external/pubs/ft/books/2009/globalfin/globalfin.pdf.

44. Riddell, *Foreign Aid*, p. 22.

45. Ibid., pp. 126–128.

46. Ibid., pp. 122–125.

47. Willy Brandt, *North–South: A Programme for Survival:The Report of the Independent Commission on International Development* (London: Pan Books, 1980), p. 244.

48. Lester Pearson, *Partners in Development: Report of the Commission on International Development* (New York: Praeger, 1969), pp. 22 and 127.

49. President Truman's Inaugural Address can be found in full at www.trumanlibrary.org/whistlestop/50yr_archive/inagural20jan1949.htm.

6

Poverty Is No Pond

Challenges for the Affluent

Leif Wenar

> More than half the people of the world are living in conditions approaching misery. Their food is inadequate. They are victims of disease. Their economic life is primitive and stagnant. Their poverty is a handicap and a threat both to them and to more prosperous areas.
>
> For the first time in history, humanity possesses the knowledge and skill to relieve the suffering of these people.
>
> —Harry Truman, Inaugural Address, 1949

> More than a billion people struggle to live each day on less than many of us pay for a bottle of water. Nearly ten million children die each year from poverty-related causes.
>
> For the first time in history, it is within our reach to eradicate world poverty and the suffering it brings.
>
> —Peter Singer, *The Life You Can Save* (2009)

This chapter is for individuals who understand the overwhelming disaster of severe poverty abroad.[1] The magnitude of this disaster is assumed. To use Roger Riddell's analogy, the average number of deaths from poverty each day is equivalent to 100 jumbo jets, each carrying 500 people (mostly children), crashing with no survivors.[2] From a human perspective, severe poverty should be the top story in every newspaper, every newscast, and every news website, every day.

Morally alive individuals want to know how they should respond to the disaster of severe poverty. For nearly 40 years "The Singer Solution" has been the leading secular paradigm, explaining to affluent individuals (you are likely "affluent" in the relevant sense)[3] why they must act and what they must do. Peter Singer argues that affluent individuals are required to send a substantial amount of their income to nongovernmental organizations (NGOs). Singer, like the appeals for funds from the NGOs themselves, tells individuals that they can be confident that sending money to an NGO will save poor people's lives. Many individuals have accepted this framework as defining the moral situation that confronts them.

This chapter aims to maintain Singer's admirable focus on what individuals can do in response to the enormous tragedy of severe poverty. Most of the chapter examines facts well known by professionals about the complexities of foreign aid. The focus is on what these complexities mean for individuals—on what potential donors *can reasonably believe* will happen if they take action on aid. The conclusion will be that Singer's framework is not adequate to the realities of our situation. Those who feel the tremendous moral urgency of severe poverty must decide how to act without the confidence of knowing that their actions will help the poorest, and must accept that the action they take may not only help, but might also harm, poor people in other countries. Accepting these unfortunate realities will require a reexamination of our moral reasoning about poverty.

SINGER'S ORIGINAL ARGUMENT

Singer's 1972 argument is based on a moral principle, buttressed by an example, that is applied to affluent individuals using particular empirical premises, leading to a call to action. Singer's moral principle is this: "If it is in our power to prevent something bad from happening, without thereby sacrificing anything morally significant, we ought, morally, to do it."[4]

Singer prompts his readers to affirm this principle with the famous example of the child in the pond: "An application of this principle would be as follows: if I am walking past a shallow pond and see a child drowning in it, I ought to wade in and pull the child out. This will mean getting my clothes muddy, but this is insignificant, while the death of the child would presumably be a very bad thing."[5]

Those who believe they ought to save the child should endorse the moral principle. Singer next uses an empirical premise about aid effectiveness to argue that the principle imposes moral duties on affluent individuals with respect to those suffering from severe poverty (Singer's example of poverty was the Bengal famine of 1971): "Expert observers and supervisors, sent out by famine relief organizations or permanently stationed in famine prone areas, can direct our aid to a refugee in Bengal almost as effectively as we could get it to someone on our own block."[6]

If affluent individuals can direct their money effectively to poor individuals, then the moral principle requires them to do so, just as the passerby ought to sacrifice his clean shoes to save the child. In the article published in 1972, Singer did not specify how effective aid donations can be at saving lives overseas. Reprising his argument 25 years later, he indicated a range within which he was confident that a donation could save a life threatened by severe poverty:

We are all in that situation of the person passing the shallow pond: we can all save lives of people, both children and adults, who would otherwise die, and we can do so at a very small cost to us: the cost of a new CD, a shirt or a night out at a restaurant or concert, can mean the difference between life and death to more than one person somewhere in the world—and overseas aid agencies like Oxfam overcome the problem of acting at a distance.[7]

According to this passage, saving a life by giving to an aid agency like Oxfam is very cheap. Singer's examples are of the price of a CD, shirt, dinner, or concert, which can save "more than one person." This appears to put the cost of saving a life in the $5 to $50 range.

The moral principle directs individuals to save lives up to the point where they are giving up something morally significant. Because Singer's empirical premises imply that saving lives is cheap, his argument implies that "the whole way we look at moral issues—our moral conceptual scheme—needs to be altered, and with it, the way of life that has come to be taken for granted in our society."[8] Affluent individuals are morally required to give a good deal of their wealth and income to aid NGOs—much more than they tend to give now.

THE DONOR'S QUESTION

What affluent individuals need to know about aid is the answer to the Donor's Question:

> *The Donor's Question: How will each dollar I can give to aid, or each hour I can devote to campaigning for aid, affect the long-term well-being of people in other countries?*

Donors cannot expect a precise answer to this question. As with many complex issues, we must aim for informed, reasonable estimates. Our main aim in the next five sections is to assess what individuals can reasonably believe will happen when they give to or campaign for aid.

The Donor's Question distinguishes between sending money and campaigning. Singer's recommendation is that individuals should send money to an aid NGO, such as Oxfam, Care, or Save the Children. The other option (which Singer is less confident will be effective) is to campaign to pressure rich-country governments, or multilateral institutions such as the World Bank, to increase or improve their "official" aid.[9] We will consider both possible courses of action here: both sending money to an NGO and campaigning for official aid.

Another choice facing affluent individuals is whether they should support humanitarian aid or development aid (or both). Humanitarian aid aims at short-term benefits for those who receive it. Humanitarian aid includes immediate provision of food and shelter, dehydration relief, and medical attention (as in Singer's original case of the Bengali famine). Development aid aims to improve the well-being of the poor in the medium to long term, ideally enabling the poor to be self-sufficient.

Typical development projects include constructing dams to improve irri-
gation in Colombia, teaching basic reading skills to pastoralists in Kenya,
organizing a farmer's cooperative in Nepal, and running a microlending
program to help women start their own businesses in Malawi. Again, we
will consider both humanitarian and development aid here.

AID: THE BIG PICTURE

In the big picture, official aid flows are larger than private donations by a
ratio of around 6:1. The ratio of development aid to humanitarian aid is
about the same. The "typical" aid dollar is sent by a government or multilateral institution to fund development. Some aid is given to poor-country
governments for the purposes of expanding economic or social programs,
stimulating the country's growth, or strengthening institutional capacities.
Some aid is channeled to NGOs to fund the projects that they run.

The big picture of aid contains a large number of actors and initiatives. Official aid agencies like the United States Agency for International
Development (USAID) and the World Bank fund hundreds of bilateral
programs and individual programs and projects. There are also many
aid NGOs—between 20,000 and 40,000 by some estimates—with
1,000 NGOs in India alone registered to receive foreign funds.[10] Some
of these NGOs are giants like World Vision and Catholic Relief
Services—with budgets greater than the gross domestic products of
some poor countries—or the Bangladesh Rural Advancement Committee,
which provides health services for nearly two thirds of the country's
population. Other NGOs are tiny or single-focus organizations, devoted
to a particular region or a cause, like performing cataract surgery. In
2003 the president of the World Bank noted that in the previous
10 years 400,000 development projects had started, and that 80,000
were currently underway; these numbers have likely grown since then.

Individuals thus have many options for acting on aid. Many organizations will accept their donations, and there are many messages that cam-
paigners could convey to their governments and the multilateral
institutions. What affluent individuals need to know is what will happen
if they choose one of these options. Where can individuals get information
about the likely effects of the many courses of action open to them?

SOURCES OF INFORMATION FOR INDIVIDUALS

Promotional Materials and the Media

The most readily available sources of information are promotional materials from aid NGOs: newspaper advertisements, direct mailings, television commercials, and websites. These are unreliable sources of information.
Most of the materials that NGOs target at the public are prepared by

marketing professionals and are subject no effective independent over-sight. The information these materials tend to highlight—individual suc-cess stories, figures for total funds spent, pie charts showing percentages of budgets devoted to "projects" versus "administration"—are not the kinds of information needed to make judgments about how effective NGOs are in achieving their aims, much less about the larger impacts of their activities.[11] Promotional materials mostly present individuals with a "money shot": a carefully selected and portrayed moment where the NGO appears to help poor people. Most NGOs promote themselves primarily with these money shots plus slogans ("We Save the Children: Will You?"; "Save a Child's Life").[12] The purpose of these promotional materials is to raise revenue, not to provide accurate information about the overall effects of donating to the organization.

The media are the other readily available source for individuals about aid: both about bilateral and multilateral aid, and about NGO activities. Media stories are also unreliable sources of information about the effects of aid. Most stories portray dramatic crisis events (such as a famine), when reporters usually transmit the "numbers threatened" and "dollars needed" figures given to them by aid organizations. There is also an occasional "aid isn't working" story based on interviews with aid critics. Most mainstream journalists lack the expertise or resources to attempt overall evaluations of, for example, official British aid to Zambia, or Norwegian Church Aid's efforts to increase access to antiretroviral treatments in Laos.

The Expert Aid Literature

The most promising sources of information are aid experts: the hundreds of thousands of people who work for aid agencies and the thousands more who study what they do. Individuals can read the literature on aid written by experts, or can consult the experts directly (by, say, talking to someone in the development studies department of a local university). I will focus here on the aid literature, which reflects what one would hear directly from the experts.

Individuals who approach the empirical literature on aid will likely be struck by at least three of its features. First, the aid literature is gigantic and extremely diverse.[13] Second, despite its extent the literature rarely if ever takes up the Donor's Question. What affluent individuals need to know is how each dollar they can give, or each hour they can devote to campaigning, will affect the long-term well-being of people in other coun-tries. The experts who produce the empirical literature have generally not addressed this question in their work.

The third striking feature of the empirical aid literature is that it is highly contentious. There are a few statements about poverty and aid that are widely accepted among experts.[14] Yet almost everything else is dis-puted. This is perhaps not surprising given how highly charged aid is ideo-logically. However, what is remarkable in these debates is how deep the disagreements run about what methods are appropriate for assessing the data, and about what data are relevant for evaluating particular development strategies. Indeed, even the most commonly used World Bank statistics addressing elementary questions like how many poor people there are in the world have been strongly criticized by responsible academics as "neither meaningful nor reliable."[15] These disagreements lead to quite varied assessments of the specific and overall impacts of aid.

Radicals on aid suggest, for example, that aid is primarily a continuation of the Western imperialist project, or that most people living in severe poverty do not want to be "developed" out of it. Within the mainstream literature, aid experts can be divided (with no disrespect for their talents) between "believers" and "atheists." Believers such as Jeffrey Sachs argue that we know aid can do good and that we need more of it. They publish books with titles like *The End of Poverty: How We Can Make It Happen in Our Lifetimes*. Atheists such as William Easterly argue that we know that conventional aid will be mostly wasteful or harmful. Their books have titles such as *The White Man's Burden: Why the West's Efforts to Aid the Rest Have Done So Much Ill and So Little Good*.[16] This division between believers and atheists has been a feature of the literature on aid for decades, and can be found with respect both to official aid and NGO projects, and both to humanitarian and development aid.

The primary cause of the disagreement among experts about the effects of aid is the extraordinary complexity of the contexts in which aid efforts are attempted. As we will see, the political, social, and economic systems of the areas that receive aid are extremely complicated. These contexts differ from one another along several dimensions, and they are subject to different external forces. Areas where severe poverty exists are often quite different from those in the developed world (for example, they are often less democratic or more chaotic). These areas always contain many actors who have different agendas and varying abilities to pursue them. Powerful actors in these areas are often able to influence aid efforts so as to benefit themselves, which hinders the success of the efforts.

Moreover, the mechanisms for collecting basic data on what specific interventions do in poor countries are usually quite limited. And because aid is only one of many factors at work in these systems, it is hard to tease out of this data what specific effects aid is having over and against the influence of other factors. These complexities explain why intelligent, informed people of goodwill make such sharply divergent assessments of the main empirical question about aid: What happens when we do X?

The next section reviews some of the challenges for aid agencies generated by the complexities of the contexts in which aid is given. These challenges are widely discussed in the mainstream aid literature and bear directly on the question of what individuals can reasonably believe will happen if they donate to or campaign on aid.

Because discussions of the challenges of aid are usually taken up by aid critics, I'd like to make explicit and emphasize the position I'm taking in this chapter. All of the challenges I will summarize are well known to aid experts, and many agencies make major efforts to overcome them. These challenges are all "old news" to people in the aid business. This chapter will not take either a believer or an atheist position on aid effectiveness. After setting out these challenges *I will make no overall assessment whatsoever about whether aid of any type does more good than harm, or more harm than good. Nor does this chapter aim to discourage individuals in any way from acting to relieve poverty* by discussing the challenges of doing so. Rather, the intention (much in the spirit of Peter Singer) is to set out the best current understanding of the facts that define our situation so that individuals can make their own decisions about what they should do.

Finally, in case this needs saying, I assume that most individuals involved in aid seek a better world for the poor. One finds in the aid industry the normal range of human motivations, yet aid officials and certainly aid workers tend to be more concerned than most about reducing severe poverty. Workers in the field also sometimes undergo real hardships and show striking courage. Good intentions are not the issue: The Donor's Question is about effects.

CHALLENGES OF AID

There is an extremely complex causal nexus between affluent individuals and people living in extreme poverty. Some of this complexity exists within the internal structures of the governmental and nongovernmental organizations that are intermediate between the rich and the poor. Most of the complexity exists within the political, economic, and social contexts where the poor people live—within the poor countries, as these interact with the wider world. The forces that shape the fates of people in poor countries are just as numerous and intertwined as those in developed countries. Some of these forces are familiar; some are quite different.

These causal complexities generate a number of challenges for the success of aid initiatives. In the following paragraphs I have collected some of the challenges under seven headings. This list is not meant to be complete; and, again, there is no suggestion that these challenges are insuperable. Everyone in the aid business knows about these challenges, and many governments and agencies try to overcome them. The challenges, however, remain serious and persistent. They confront both humanitarian and development aid agencies, and both governments and NGOs.

Time, Management, and Coordination Challenges

In a humanitarian emergency such as an earthquake or a famine, aid must be provided quickly to be effective. Many governmental and nongovernmental agencies typically rush to provide aid, raising the risk that these efforts will duplicate each other, provide inappropriate or substandard aid, target those who do not need the aid, or leave gaps in coverage among those who do. In some emergencies such as the 2004 Asian tsunami, donors gave more money than could effectively be absorbed; in most other emergencies, funds have been insufficient.

In development it is the long duration of aid efforts that often poses challenges instead of their immediate urgency. For example, if a child who is infected with worms is given anthelminic drugs, her worms will clear. However, if that is all that happens, she will likely be reinfected with worms within a few months. Parasite eradication, as any successful poverty relief program, requires a long-term commitment. With major public health problems like hookworm, malaria, and HIV/AIDS, 10 or 15 years is a reasonable timescale for making significant progress. The more remote or transitory a recipient population is, the more difficult long-term engagement becomes.

Moreover, throughout the duration of a long project the setting can be expected to shift. Project managers will expect to confront economic or environmental changes, new directives from local government, new players who enter trying to capture project resources, or new attitudes toward the project and its staff among the project's intended beneficiaries. It is not uncommon for projects to face financial challenges as well—for example, when an NGO's funder fails to follow through on its commitment to provide resources during the implementation phase.

Nongovernmental organizations face distinctive management and coordination challenges. In most poor countries, state institutions are either quite weak, or they are strong and self-serving. Indeed most poor people in most poor countries remain poor at least in part because their political institutions are inefficient, venal, despotic, or absent altogether. Nongovernmental organizations join the effort to reduce poverty specifically because they perceive that domestic government ministries like health and education are not fulfilling their functions. Nongovernmental organizations, both in humanitarian and development aid, are "free-floating" agencies, with directors, managers, and front-line workers who take on tasks that domestic governments cannot or will not do.

Because aid NGOs are free floating, each is its own self-contained and self-defined "mini ministry." Some have a single-issue focus, like reproductive health or the environment. Others are church based and their missions may combine aid work with proselytizing. A number of NGOs employ front-line workers who are mostly young, short-term employees without experience of the area in which they will work. Many aid agencies come into a country from the outside, with a mission and managerial staff that are literally foreign. All these factors can make it difficult for NGOs to integrate their programs with government ministries, with recipient populations, and with the other NGOs working in-country. The lack of coordination mechanisms makes miscommunication and crossed purposes between different NGOs, and between NGOs and locals, a constant hazard. Like their official aid counterparts, some aid agencies also have a tendency to try to "plant a flag" on some area or problem and compete with other agencies regarding aid provision for it.

As for official aid, when multiple donors and ministries fail to coordinate, there is also considerable potential for waste, coverage gaps, and policy conflict. As a United Nations Development Programme report notes, at one point some 40 donors maintained 2,000 different aid projects in Tanzania.[17] The task of joining up these projects into a coherent, overall pro-poor strategy would be monumental, even if there were some agency that could take it on. Official donors often demand extensive reports from recipient governments, diverting civil servants away from the task of implementing programs. Official donors also often fail to deliver on promised aid, and other official donors typically feel no need to make up for these lost funds. This lack of coordination can make planning difficult even within better run poor-country bureaucracies.[18]

Participation

Most development planners face the general dilemma that projects must be sensitive to local skills and customs to ensure participation and thus success; yet the success of many projects also turns on effecting significant changes in the productive, political, or reproductive practices of those who are meant to participate. Asia and Africa are speckled with decaying infrastructure projects from earlier eras of development aid whose operation did not fit with the skills and customs of the local populations. Projects intended to resettle communities, or to empower marginalized groups, or to democratize local politics typically disrupt settled practices in ways that some intended participants naturally resist. When a project's success will depend on a change in gender or sexual relations—such as in female literacy or AIDS prevention projects—these kinds of difficulties with local "ownership" are intensified.

Official donors face participation challenges on a national scale parallel to those that project planners face on a local scale. Official donors often believe that they know what the domestic government should do to make aid work. However, they also know that effectiveness depends on domestic governments "owning" these initiatives. In the past official donors have grasped one horn of this dilemma by making future aid conditional on domestic governments carrying out certain directives. Yet domestic governments have often ignored these directives, and received more aid anyway, making conditionality approaches now less credible.

Resource Diversion

People in poor countries are, of course, just as rational and just as morally scrupulous as people in rich countries. Their political and economic situations are just as complex. One major difference between the situation of people in poor and rich countries is that state institutions in poor countries are usually far less effective. This general fact increases the potential for diversion of aid resources away from the intended beneficiaries.

If a development project is implemented through the ministries of the poor country, project funds and supplies may be diverted at the national, district, or local levels of governance. Aid, that is, may be captured by corruption, and more aid may stimulate more corruption. One study of Ugandan public education funding found that during a 4-year period public schools received only 10% of the grants intended for them; the rest was siphoned off by local officials.[19]

Aid NGOs often have to pay the poor-country government directly: either to get permission to carry out their projects or through paying local taxes. These payments from NGOs to poor governments can support the rule of authoritarian leaders, or they can feed corruption in the bureaucracy. Nongovernmental organizations must sometimes pay corrupt officials or warlords to get visas or to maintain their headquarters in the national capital, and must sometimes pay off or even employ criminals to carry out their projects in the field. These payments can enrich and legitimize groups that use their power in ways that exacerbate poverty. Those who exercise illegitimate power in a country are often glad to welcome aid agencies in, as bringing agencies into the country will increase their opportunities for patronage. And NGOs by definition have no official power of their own, which limits their ability to bargain with governments and criminals.

The dangers of resource diversion are especially clear in contexts of armed conflict. To gain access to the needy, humanitarian organizations may have to turn food aid over to a local army or militia. Combatants often steal food, blankets, or vehicles from aid agencies, either for their own use or to exchange for other supplies (including weapons). The presence of "free" food or medical care in some region may encourage combatants to continue fighting, or it may encourage them to drive unwanted minorities into refugee camps where the services are provided. The camps where humanitarian aid is provided may themselves also become loci of disease transmission, or (as during the Rwandan genocide) havens where refugee-soldiers can regroup and recruit in preparation for launching further attacks.

The risks of resource diversion illustrate what might be called the iron law of political economy. Resources tend to flow toward those that have more power; or, to put it the other way around, the less powerful people are, the harder it is to get resources to them. The richer, stronger, healthier, better armed, better fed, better educated, and better located people are, the more likely they are to capture benefits from any stream of resources.

Economic Effects

Famines of the kind that Singer discusses are caused more by a breakdown in political and economic institutions than by "natural" events like crop failures. As Amartya Sen has written, for good governments "famines are, in fact, so easy to prevent that it is amazing that they are allowed to occur at all."[20]

It is because famines happen in contexts of institutional failure that the insertion of resources from outside at times does not have its intended effects. For example, Ethiopia received significant food aid each year during the decade after the famine of the mid 1980s, normally equivalent to about 10% of its total food production. During this period, and despite the fact that there was enough food in-country to meet the nutritional needs of all Ethiopians, almost half of Ethiopian households remained food insecure. A significant amount of food was distributed through food relief projects, yet relatively little of this food reached those in need. Well-off districts were just as likely to receive the imported food as very poor districts, and, on average, less than 23% of food-insecure households received any food. Moreover, much of the food that was distributed to food-secure households ended up being resold on local markets, depressing food prices and diminishing incentives for domestic production, thus increasing food insecurity and stimulating another campaign for food aid the next year.

Aid can also have other counterproductive economic effects. Aid money is fungible, and official aid flows can free up money for the domestic government to pursue other ends. For example, aid funds can be shifted by a recipient government to build up its military. Pumping aid money into an economy can increase price inflation for basic goods, or it can raise the exchange rate of the country's currency so that export industries find it harder to do business (the "Dutch Disease"). Donations in kind from rich countries (like used clothing) can wipe out domestic manufacturing (for example, in apparel)—one of the traditional paths out of poverty for poor countries. Investing in training young people in areas like health can backfire if there are not enough jobs to be filled in the country or if such jobs pay more elsewhere (stimulating "brain drain").

Aid projects can also attract local employees whose skills would be more productively used somewhere else in the economy. In Kenya, a World Bank agricultural project paid staff 12 to 24 times as much as the pay of a senior economist in the Kenyan government.[21] In Kosovo, foreign aid agencies hired many local teachers and administrators to become translators and drivers. (The sheer number of these agencies in Kosovo also drove up the price of housing beyond what many locals could afford.)

Aggregation Effects

As the last example indicates, sometimes aid has unintended effects because of the *combination* of initiatives undertaken simultaneously in the same location. Aid projects can counteract each other's effects, even across the divide of humanitarian and development assistance. Providing free humanitarian relief aid to pastoralists, for example, can tempt the pastoralists to remain in the aid camps instead of returning to their traditional lands where development projects aim to increase their self-sufficiency.

Other unintended effects in this category echo the challenges of management described earlier. One study reports that "in a typical African country, some 30 official donors and several dozen international NGOs provide aid to over 1000 distinct projects and several hundred resident foreign experts....A higher level of total aid and higher donor fragmentation are associated with worsening bureaucratic quality in aid recipient governments."[22] Donors and NGOs are often more concerned to "move money" and to initiate projects than to consider how the aggregation of initiatives will affect recipient government efficacy and project quality.

Weakened Governance and Dependency

A long-standing concern about aid initiatives is that they may weaken the links between the developing country's government and its citizens. This concern is especially pronounced when donors bypass the government and provide "services" directly to the citizens. From the government's perspective, it becomes easier to ignore the poorest citizens in policy planning decisions when it is known that foreign-funded NGOs will step in to attempt to cover them. From the citizens' perspective, there is less reason to press for increased transparency, accountability, and democracy in their national and local governments when it is not these governments, but rather those NGOs, that are providing basic services to them. This concern is particularly urgent in the dozens of countries where foreign-funded NGOs provide a significant proportion of basic services.

Stories linking official aid and personal corruption of officials are legion in the aid industry. Also of concern is that officials may make aid money available to citizens only in return for political support. Official aid can foster a culture of rent seeking within a country, meaning that the way to get ahead is not to produce goods or services, but rather to make friends with ministers or to secure a lucrative post in the civil service as a base to pursue personal projects.

The fundamental concern about governance is that both official and nonofficial aid may break the social contract between government and the citizenry. Both the government and citizens may become more dependent on foreigners than on each other. Governments that receive a large portion of their budget from foreign donors become more concerned with keeping these donors happy than with maintaining the support of the public. Citizens who depend on foreign NGOs become less concerned to try to influence what they usually perceive as a distant and dysfunctional government.

Sociocultural Impacts

A final set of challenges regarding sociocultural impacts is often discussed in the expert aid literature and among aid workers. The concerns here tend to be expressed in personal rather than statistical terms, because the potential problems are difficult to measure scientifically.

Aid agencies must select people in the recipient countries to work with. Whoever they choose will often thereby gain resources, opportunities, and, perhaps most important, legitimacy. When rich foreign governments work with certain leaders, these leaders are legitimated in the public's eyes. When NGOs choose to work with the village elders, the elders (often the most conservative community members) gain power.

Similarly, when agencies move in to an area and classify recipients by their regional membership, race, ethnicity, or need, they may increase tensions between groups by reinforcing people's identification with or against those groups.[23] Even hiring translators can have unintended effects, as agencies are likely to be hiring locals whose foreign language abilities mark them out as privileged members of local elites. Aid can, in short, increase inequalities in wealth and power in poor countries, and exacerbate existing rivalries.

There are, finally, potential adverse sociocultural impacts when rich foreigners run projects in poor communities.[24] When aid workers in the field hire armed guards to protect their own property, it may send an implicit message that guns are needed for the good life. Even well-meaning aid workers can find it hard to interact with destitute people reliably and without condescension. And for the poor, there may be the simple daily frustration of seeing rich foreigners maintain a lifestyle (expensive vehicles, leisure and good food, travel abroad) that they and their families will never attain. Perhaps the best way to get a sense of these kinds of concerns is to imagine your own community as the object of aid projects run by foreigners who are very much wealthier than yourself and your neighbors.

TWO CONSEQUENCES OF COMPLEXITY

All these challenges have long been known to aid professionals, and the best aid donors (like the Scandinavian governments) and NGOs (such as Oxfam and Care) make concerted efforts to work around them. The best NGOs have, for example, permanent staff in-country who make regular contact with government ministries. The best agencies try to employ experienced local workers in both managerial and front-line jobs, and to engage with communities to discover what their needs really are and how their social systems function. The best agencies also use formal and informal mechanisms to coordinate their efforts with at least some of the other major agencies that work in the same regions. Nevertheless, all of these challenges—time, management, and coordination; participation; resource diversion; economic effects; aggregation effects; weakened governance and dependence; and sociocultural impacts—remain significant, and anyone working in aid will have stories ready to illustrate all of them.

Again, the aim of setting out these challenges is *not* to come to an overall assessment about whether aid of any sort does more good than harm, or more harm than good. The only aim is to spotlight the extremely complex causal nexus between affluent individuals and people living in extreme poverty. Two modest conclusions flow from these facts about causal complexity.

> 1. *It is likely that some aid will make some people in other countries worse off than they would have been, even in cases when the aid is beneficial overall (that is, even when, overall, it helps more than it harms).*

This follows from the challenges we have just seen. From the perspective of an individual living in poverty, a particular aid effort may harm more than it helps. The aid may strengthen the autocrats, corrupt bureaucrats, warlords, soldiers, or criminals that have power over that person. A humanitarian effort may draw the person away from their self-sustaining livelihood; a development project may draw them into acquiring skills for which there is no employment. Aid in aggregate may increase inflation, reduce employment, or weaken the provision of public services. Aid flowing into this person's country may delay needed political reforms, and make both the government and the citizens more responsive to foreigners than to each other. Aid may inflame economic inequalities or ethnic antagonisms in ways that are bad for this person, or that damage his or her self-esteem. And so on. Even assuming an aid project or official aid to a country helps overall, it may leave at least some people worse off than before.

The second conclusion flowing from the causal complexity of aid is this:

> 2. *It is very difficult for affluent individuals to make reliable estimates of the overall effects of their aid donations or campaigning.*

The Donor's Question is: How will each dollar I can give to aid, or each hour I can devote to campaigning for aid, affect the long-term well-being of people in other countries? As before, with such a question we must be satisfied with informed, reasonable estimates. The complexity of the causal nexus between donors and recipients, however, means that it is quite difficult to make such judgments.

EVALUATION AND CHECKING MECHANISMS

We have nearly completed our survey of the complexities of foreign aid. Yet it might appear that we have set the epistemological hurdle too high for aid. After all, many affluent individuals feel confident in donating to domestic (rich-country) organizations like charities supporting the homeless. And many feel confident that some of the taxes they pay to their own government will in part be used to help the poor within their own country. If individuals feel confident in their domestic, rich-country "aid efforts," can they not feel similarly confident about aid efforts abroad?

People differ in their assessments as to what extent the seven challenges presented here also apply to "aid" within rich countries (for example, conservatives are wary of "welfare dependency"; liberals worry about "the stigma of charity"). However one assesses those issues, individuals in developed countries should accept that their epistemological situation is worse regarding foreign action than regarding domestic action. It is much harder for individuals to have informed, reasonable views about aid abroad than about "aid" at home.

This is, in part, evident from what we have already seen. Unlike in the domestic case, aid abroad essentially involves very powerful foreigners coming into a poor country and either acting directly on the poor or trying to get them to change their ways. And the institutions in poor countries are typically much worse than in rich countries: Economies are more fragile, the political situation is more chaotic or more repressive, or both. Foreign aid is intrinsically harder than domestic "aid," and the environments in which it takes places are almost always less conducive to success.

There are also two reinforcing reasons for individuals to feel less confident about foreign aid than about "aid" in their own country. The first is that the expert mechanisms for evaluating the effects of foreign aid are poor sources of information on aid's overall effects. The second is that there are fewer means for keeping foreign aid on track. These are problems of evaluation and checking mechanisms.[25]

Aid Evaluation

Evaluation is its own professional specialization, with university-based training programs, departments within government ministries, a specialized literature, international conferences, and so on. The evaluation of policy reforms and individual projects undertaken within wealthy countries like the United States or the United Kingdom is a sophisticated, relatively well-resourced activity with a long history. Foreign aid evaluation is, in comparison, underfunded and very much in its infancy.

The evaluation of foreign aid projects and programs is the primary means by which the success of these programs is judged. Evaluation is, therefore, the major mechanism through which it could be known which aid agencies are effective and which types of projects work in which settings. Books on aid effectiveness like Cassen's classic *Does Aid Work?*[26] are based on these evaluations.

Those who examine the field of aid evaluation for the first time may be surprised by what they discover. Aid evaluation is, by its nature, difficult. Moreover aid evaluation is also done rarely, it is often done poorly, and it is often not analyzed systematically or fed back into planning. Furthermore, even if evaluation were perfectly successful, it would be of limited use in answering the Donor's Question. Here I focus on development evaluation at the project level, which is more sophisticated and better resourced than humanitarian evaluation.

Development projects are always difficult to assess. An evaluator must judge what effects a given intervention (like an AIDS education program or a microlending initiative) has had within a complex environment, and can only make these judgments by contrasting the current situation with the counterfactual situation in which the intervention was not made. The evaluator, that is, tries to measure the difference between "What happened when we did X this time?" and "What would have happened if we hadn't done X this time?" In all but rare cases, the evaluator must guess the answer to the second, counterfactual question. This is hard. The effects observed in the actual situation (increased condom use, decreased purchasing power) may have been caused by X, or they may have been caused by other factors in environment (for example, a news story about a celebrity's HIV infection, or an increase in inflation). Or the effects that X actually had may have been amplified or more than canceled out by nonproject causes. Teasing out the causation is inherently challenging. Moreover,

- In-depth, robust evaluations are rarely undertaken. Only a very small percentage of aid projects and programs are ever formally evaluated. Cracknell reports that the amount spent on evaluation by the American, Swedish, and British aid agencies and the World Bank in the 1990s ranged from 0.05% to 0.2% of the total budget.[27]

- Evaluation is often done poorly. Most of the project evaluations that are done are self-evaluations, carried out by those who have implemented the project. The remainder are done by consultants hired by the implementing agency, or by the staff of the evaluation department of a ministry or multilateral organization. One problem is that self-evaluators tend to lack training, whereas specialists often have limited familiarity with the country or region where the project is located. However, the most serious concern about the quality of evaluations is that they carry a systematic positive bias. Self-evaluators, consultants, ministries, and aid agencies have interests in evaluating projects that look more likely to succeed, and all have interests in more positive evaluations being filed. There are few quality control mechanisms to check the tendencies toward positive bias.

- Evaluations are often not analyzed systematically or fed back into planning. To do large-scale analyses aimed at answering the question "What happens when we do X?" one needs individual evaluations that have standardized parameters. Standardization across evaluations is often not sufficient to perform good meta-analyses. The great majority of agencies do not even attempt to do formal meta-analyses of their evaluations. Indeed, only a very few agencies systematically collect and disburse evaluation information within their organizations for the sake of future project planning. (Systematic release of evaluations to outsiders is even more rare.) The summary explanation for this lack of analysis and feedback is that decisions about future aid funding are not ordinarily based on proof of past effectiveness.

Most aid evaluations are currently neither good quality nor well used. This is particularly disappointing, because in aid it is often surprising what does *not* work. For example, a plausible project in Kenya tried replacing school textbooks with easier to understand flip charts.[28] One analysis of the evaluation data from the project found that the charts raised students' test scores by 20% of a standard deviation. A second analysis found only a 5% improvement. However, when the project was subjected to randomized evaluation (that is, compared to a control group), there was no evidence of improvement in test scores at all. The promising project didn't work; yet, the standard evaluations reported that it did.

The topic of randomized evaluations is important and leads to the main point about evaluations. Randomized evaluations are the coming thing in development, seen as "the gold standard" for determining what works. With randomized evaluations, there is no need to guess at the answer to the counterfactual question "What would have happened if we hadn't done X this time?" because the evaluator can look at the control group for the answer. Randomized evaluation is not a panacea (it is expensive, hard to "scale up," and judgment must still be used to assess how a particular type of project would transfer to other environments). However, it is a clear improvement over the current standard evaluation procedure.[29]

Nevertheless, even if all aid evaluations ever done had been of the quality of randomized evaluations—indeed, even if all projects ever implemented had been evaluated at this quality—the sum would be much less than what donors need to know. This is because evaluations primarily measure *success at meeting immediate objectives*. Evaluations almost never try to measure systematic effects of the type discussed in the list of seven challenges presented earlier. The evaluation of a clean water project will conclude that a new pump was installed at a certain cost. The evaluation of an antimalaria project will report that a certain number of bed nets were distributed and that a certain percentage can be expected to be in use. These evaluations will pronounce on project success based on this information; they will declare whether that aid "worked." Only rarely will the possible political, economic, social, and psychological effects of the project (on inflation, corruption, social tensions, self-image, and so forth) be described, and even more rarely will any attempt be made to measure any of these effects.

This is understandable: systematic effects are much more difficult to measure than immediate outcomes. Yet without information about systematic effects, donors cannot make reasonable guesses at the answer to their question. Even the best project evaluation is an "extreme close-up" of a particular cause–effect link. Donors need the big picture.

Riddell, a leading expert on aid effectiveness, says this about official donors and project evaluation in *Does Foreign Aid Really Work?*:

> What does the evidence tell us about the success of a project to help fill the wider objectives? The answer is that there is remarkably little evidence available which enables us to form judgments at either the sectoral level or economy wide. For decades donors never really thought it was necessary to address the wider impact of their projects: it was simply assumed that if the project was successful so are the wider impacts. In recent years, some donors have sought to fill these information gaps by commissioning studies and evaluations which examine the systemic relationships between aid inputs and wider outcomes. However, the dominant conclusion emerging is that there is still insufficient evidence for some judgments about the relationship between projects and wider outcomes, especially at the sectoral level and beyond.[30]

And however bad the epistemological situation is regarding official aid, the situation with respect to NGOs is worse:

> What is the overall impact of NGO development activity in particular countries? Regrettably there has always been and remains to this day an almost complete absence of data and information with which to assess the wider systemic impact of NGO development interventions and activities. Compared to the amount of money spent and ink spilt trying to analyze the impact of official aid at the country level and beyond, it is surprising that no rigorous attempt has been made to try to assess the overall effect of NGO activities in any aid-recipient country. Indeed neither has there been an attempt to aggregate the combined effects of all the major NGO interventions in a particular country, or even of a particular sub-sector where NGO contributions played a major role in the delivery of services, in order to try to develop a sense of the overall effect of all the different interventions in different sectors.[31]

Checking Mechanisms

The epistemological situation of an affluent individual *qua* foreign aid donor is much worse than that of the same individual *qua*, say, taxpayer. The quality and availability of data, and the quality and systematicity of analysis, is much better on initiatives undertaken within rich countries. Consider for example a major domestic U.S. public policy initiative like the Clinton–era reforms of welfare provision in the United States. The scope and depth of individual studies[32] and synthetic analyses[33] on the effects of this initiative are much better than almost anything in foreign aid. Regarding analysis (as everything else) the rich devote much greater resources to what goes on within their own borders.

Moreover, donors should worry more about the possible negative systematic effects of foreign aid. This is because the checking mechanisms for keeping aid on track are typically weaker in poor countries than in rich ones. If some policy or project in a rich country is having no effects, or unintended adverse effects, there are many mechanisms to detect and change this. Media reports, bureaucratic audits, academic scrutiny, and democratic voting are (relatively) effective checking mechanisms in developed nations. These mechanisms tend to be weak or absent with respect to aid abroad.

Take the checking mechanisms on aid NGOs for example. Aid NGOs are not run for profit, so are not accountable for providing good projects in the same way that businesses are held accountable through consumer choice for providing good products. Nor, of course, are aid NGOs accountable to any democratic electorate. And the checks that can constrain government ministries, such as bureaucratic oversight, media scrutiny, and academic study, in fact put quite weak corrective pressures on aid NGOs. These institutions are, first, almost always less robust within poor countries. Moreover, because NGOs are bringing money into a poor country (typically by implementing smaller, local projects), the government and the media in the poor country usually do not give NGO impacts serious scrutiny. Moreover, the wider effects of a development project in a poor country is not a subject on which the international media ordinarily focuses. There are currently few paths or incentives for NGOs to translate academic studies into changed behavior. External audits on aid NGOs cover only the basics of financial probity, without touching on the results of the NGOs' projects. And most aid agencies tend to abide by a "code of silence," instead of criticizing one another.

Because of the lack of checking mechanisms, aid NGOs are almost entirely unaccountable for the effects of their interventions. If a well-intentioned NGO project fails effectively to help the poor, or if it unintentionally aggravates poverty, the NGO will ordinarily face no sanctions that might pressure it to change what it is doing. This is particularly unfortunate, because, as we have seen, the nature of foreign aid and the weak institutional environment in poor countries make it more likely that aid efforts will go off track.

To sum up the last five sections, the two main points entailed by the surveys of aid are as follows:

1. It is likely that some aid will make some people in other countries worse off than they would have been, *even in cases when the aid is beneficial overall* (that is, even when, overall, it helps more than it harms).
2. It is very difficult for affluent individuals to make reliable estimates of the overall effects of their aid donations or campaigning.

Given the expert debates over aid, the challenges of aid, the deficiencies of aid evaluations, and the lack of checking mechanisms on aid agencies, affluent individuals might reasonably find themselves being neither believers nor atheists about aid's effects. A more honest position is agnosticism. With these points, let us return to Singer and the situation of affluent individuals.

SINGER'S *THE LIFE YOU CAN SAVE*

The Empirical Claims

Singer's 2009 book is in many ways continuous with his previous work on aid. Singer bases his argument on the same moral principle (if at low cost to yourself you can prevent something bad from happening, you ought to do so), the same example (rescuing the child in the pond), and the same call to action (the affluent should give much larger amounts to aid NGOs than they now do).

The main innovation in the book concerns the empirical premises. In his article published in 1972, Singer said that "a real expert assessment of the facts" about aid was not required to support his call to action, because it was not in dispute that aid is effective.[34] In contrast, in 2009 Singer devotes one quarter of his book to "the facts about aid," and a whole section to the empirical assessment of the question, "how much does it cost to save a life?" While the original article said that aid workers "can direct our aid to a refugee in Bengal almost as effectively as we could get it to someone on our own block," the book says: "It's difficult to calculate how much it costs to save or transform the life of someone who is extremely poor," and "working out the likely real-world consequences of aid is often more complicated than we thought."[35]

Singer's recent attention to the causal complexities of aid is welcome (as, of course, is his repeatedly drawing attention to the moral urgency of poverty). However the quality of the book's representation of the epistemological situation of affluent individuals is mixed. On the one hand, the book covers several of the points from the aid literature reviewed in the previous sections. For instance, Singer notes that the "percentage of budget spent on administration" figures advertised by NGOs are not useful, that importing food into poor countries can damage local farm production, that aid funds can cause "the Dutch Disease" and hinder the growth of pro-poor industries like apparel and food processing, and so on.

On the other hand, some stories that the book offers as evidence of aid's effectiveness bypass the complexities familiar to aid experts. For example, Singer presents as evidence of effectiveness what appears to be a verbal report from a rich friend that the friend believes his donations saved children's lives. And Singer says that a single positive remark made to him by one aid recipient during a brief Oxfam–sponsored visit to a project in India "surely demonstrates that the project was a success."[36] Overall, the book is a mixture of points from the expert literature, "extreme close-up" evaluations of project successes, and the kind of "money shots" one finds in NGO promotional materials.

For affluent individuals, the main interest of the book is Singer's final answer to the Donor's Question: "We have seen that much of the work done by charities is highly cost effective, and we can reasonably believe that the cost of saving a life to one of these charities is somewhere between \$200 and \$2000."[37] Singer here asserts that affluent donors can save a life that would not otherwise be saved by sending \$200 to \$2,000 to an aid NGO. This dollar range is (adjusting for inflation) around 30 times higher than the \$5 to \$50 range that Singer estimated in 1997. Donors will want to know how useful these figures are.

One major source for Singer's numbers comes from a fascinating organization in New York called GiveWell. GiveWell was formed in 2006 by two American hedge-fund managers in their mid 20s who wanted to donate some of their incomes to effective poverty relief. As Singer tells their story:

> [They] were astonished by how unprepared charities were for questions that went beyond... superficial and potentially misleading indicators of efficacy. Eventually, they realized something that seemed to them quite extraordinary: the reason they were not getting the information they wanted from the charities was that the charities themselves didn't have it. In most cases, neither the charities nor any independent agencies were doing the kind of rigorous evaluation of effectiveness that [their] background in investment management had led them to assume must be the basis of the decisions that major donors made before giving. If the information didn't exist, then both individual donors and major foundations were giving away huge sums with little idea what effects their gifts were having. How could hundreds of billions of dollars be spent without some evidence that the money is doing good?[38]

Given what we have seen earlier about aid NGOs, what these young Americans found is not so astonishing. What is remarkable, however, is that the hedge-fund managers decided to quit their jobs and form GiveWell, whose mission is to dig out the best-quality information available on "What does it cost to save a life?" and pass this information on to potential affluent donors. GiveWell now recommends specific NGOs and gives dollar figures on how much it costs to save a life, and Singer relies on these figures in his book.

Let us look closely at GiveWell's best case: the aid initiative they recommend which looks the least likely to produce unintended effects. This is a campaign by an NGO called PSI to sell insecticide-treated bed nets to poor people, primarily in Africa, with the aim of reducing malaria deaths. Give-Well estimates that donors can save a life that would not otherwise be saved through donations to PSI of between \$623 and \$2,367. GiveWell settles on \$820 as a reasonable estimate, and Singer reproduces these figures.[39]

For those who appreciate the challenges of aid, GiveWell's methodology offers a case study of why the figures given cannot provide a reasonable answer to the Donor's Question. GiveWell calculated its figures using only the following (PSI-supplied) data:

- Number of bed nets distributed
- Probability of bed nets being used
- Probability of nets saving a life if used
- Budget for the project

This is all the information on which the "cost of saving a life" figure is based. Is this enough information to answer the Donor's Question? Let's say you had given $820 to PSI in 2009. Could you be reasonably confident that the morally salient outcome of your giving was that you had saved a life that would not otherwise have been saved? We can draw on just a few of the challenges of aid listed in this chapter to show why the answer is, clearly, no. As always, the main confounding factors are the counterfactuals and unintended effects. This is apparent even just looking at PSI's best case—the country where it claims to be most cost-effective: Madagascar.[40]

- PSI is one of several organizations distributing bed nets in Madagascar, including UNICEF, various Red Cross affiliates, and the Madagascar Ministry of Health.[41] Most of the money for these efforts comes from official sources: the Global Fund to Fight AIDS, Tuberculosis and Malaria; the World Bank; USAID; and so on. This multiplicity of agents raises the first set of counterfactuals: If PSI had not distributed a bed net that was bought with your donation, would another aid agency have distributed that bed net anyway? And if your private donation had been absent, would the Global Fund or the World Bank have compensated for the deficit? (If that compensatory money was drawn away from other Global Fund projects, what different impacts would *those projects* have had? Or would the Global Fund's own donors have contributed more overall to make up for what you didn't give?)

- PSI is a "social marketing" organization. It sells highly subsidized bed nets instead of giving them away for free (as other NGOs and Madagascar's health ministry do). PSI does this in the belief that the poor are more likely to get and use nets that are sold on the market. However several top experts (including ones Singer relies on for positive studies on aid) have been extremely critical of social marketing.[42] Moreover, a randomized evaluation of social marketing in Kenya found that selling bed nets greatly reduces take-up of nets, does not get nets to those with greatest need, and does not lead to higher usage.[43] It could be that your donation to PSI in 2009 hindered malaria-fighting efforts compared with what another NGO would have done with your money.

- PSI does not publish a detailed budget (nor does any major aid NGO). Therefore, it is not possible to determine who ultimately received the money from your donation to PSI. Some proportion would have been spent on buying bed nets to sell on to the poor; yet some proportion of your donation might also have been diverted within Madagascar. In 2009 the president of Madagascar was overthrown with at least the acquiescence of the country's powerful military. He was accused by his critics of "massive corruption, nepotism, mismanagement and misuse of public resources."[44] It is possible that some of the money you gave to PSI might have been captured by and so empowered actors involved in the poor governance of Madagascar.

- Madagascar's Ministry of Health reports that it has distributed more than one million free bed nets since 2003, so it appears to be capable of distributing nets.[45] One might wonder why foreign NGOs like PSI are distributing bed nets in Madagascar at all. If the Malagasy government were wholly responsible for securing the basic health of the Malagasy people, would the people demand more from their own government?

These concerns alone preclude the GiveWell figures on PSI from providing a reasonable answer to the Donor's Question. And Singer's cost estimates in *The Life You Can Save* inherit these weaknesses.

Implications for "The Singer Solution"

Here, again, is the principle on which Singer bases his call to action on aid:

If it is in our power to prevent something bad from happening, without thereby sacrificing anything morally significant, we ought, morally, to do it.

The principle draws attention to only one kind of negative effect of our contributing to aid: that we ourselves may "sacrifice"—that we ourselves may have less disposable money or time. The principle does not mention the possibility that aid contributions may also lead to some poor people being made worse off than they would have been.[46] Yet, as the discussion here has emphasized, everyone in aid acknowledges the possibility that aid will harm as well as help.

Let me highlight this point. The question here is not whether we are *averse* to a risk of harming others. The issue is that Singer's principle does not acknowledge the *existence* of a risk of harming others. And the existence of risk typically changes our moral reasoning. When what we can do might harm others as well as help others, our judgments about what we are morally required to do are quite different than in situations described by Singer's principle. *The Life You Can Save* is a different book than *The Lives You Could Save or Endanger*.

Consider, for example, the impact on your thinking of this Singer–like passage from the GiveWell website—without and with the final bracketed sentence, which is my addition:

> **What do you get for your dollar:** ...Across the organization, we estimate that it costs PSI about $650–$1000 to save a life. These estimates do not include other benefits of PSI's activities, such as preventing unwanted pregnancies and reducing nonfatal malaria infections.[47] [These estimates also do not include possible risks of PSI's activities, such as encouraging corruption in poor-country governments and weakening incentives for poor-country governments to be accountable to their own citizens.]

Singer's principle, in focusing only on the possibility of helping and not on any risk of harming, cannot guide the reasoning of an affluent individual thinking about aid. Insofar as Singer's principle suggests that aid does not risk significant negative effects on the poor, it does not apply to our world. Similarly, NGOs' appeals for funds that say only *that you can help* without mentioning *that you might harm* also do not correctly capture the real situation that you are in when making your decisions.

You can confirm this yourself. You can get in touch with anyone who studies aid professionally—say, an academic in a local university's development studies department—and ask questions such as this:

- For any actual donation given since 1972 to any charity that Singer has recommended, is it possible to be reasonably sure that this donation led to at least one life being saved *and* that it did not contribute to any poor people being made significantly worse off through resource diversion, weakened governance, sociopolitical impacts, or other systematic effects?

- Right now, can one reasonably expect that the total impact of the activities of *any* specific NGO to which one could contribute *any* amount will be that poor people's lives will be saved without any poor people being made significantly worse off?

It will be surprising if one gets many—indeed any—positive responses.

Singer's principle does not capture the correct factual relationship between affluent and poor individuals. So this principle does not capture the moral relationship between them, and it cannot ground a call to action. You are not in a situation analogous to knowing that you can save a child drowning in a shallow pond. Closer is this: If you hand cash to a stranger he may—along with other strangers hired by other people—try to save some children who have fallen into a lake. However, it looks like these strangers can only get to the lake by pushing through a crowded rave on a pier with no railings.

THE CHALLENGES OF INDIVIDUAL ACTION

The human disaster of severe poverty, juxtaposed with the tremendous resources of the affluent, has for many years fired calls to action on aid, as in the quote from Harry Truman's Inaugural Address that leads off this essay. Yet if aid were easy, severe poverty could easily have been ended by now. This chapter has discussed some of the complexities of aid and its resulting challenges. Any responsible call to individual action on aid must acknowledge these challenges, and especially two morally salient facts: aid may cause harm, and the quality of information on aid's overall effects is very poor.

It is easier to say what aid experts should do in response to these facts. Aid experts should act to limit harm and to get better information to affluent individuals. So, for example:

- At least some of the experts who study aid professionally (like academics) should focus at least some of their work on researching better answers to the Donor's Question. Responding adequately to severe poverty abroad is one of the greatest moral challenges in affluent individuals' lives. Aid professionals so far are not helping them much. It is something of a scandal that the only people now willing publicly to hazard a partial answer to the Donor's Question have no professional expertise in aid—these are the people who run GiveWell.

- Official donors should reduce the potential for negative effects by, for example, coordinating aid to ensure more reliable flows and less strain on poor countries' bureaucracies. They should also spend resources on more and better evaluations, and especially on evaluations that attempt to measure systematic effects. They should also tie future funding allocations to NGOs much more tightly to proven past performance.

- All aid agencies that bring money into poor countries should be more transparent about where the money ends up. Ideally, published budgets would detail categories like taxes, rents, bribes, and security as well as thefts of equipment. Because individual agencies would be disadvantaged in fund-raising by increasing transparency unilaterally, agencies should work together to frame and implement a strong and credible code of practice for transparency.

Some of these reforms would draw resources away from implementing projects, and even together they would not be sufficient to overcome all the challenges of aid discussed here. Still, the challenges of aid should be addressed systematically, and making these kinds of reforms would be justified for the sake of improving aid and our understanding of its effects.

The appropriate responses of affluent individuals to the complexities of aid are less obvious and may vary according to individuals' circumstances. As things stand, individuals cannot find reasonable estimates to answer the Donor's Question. What, then, to do?

Some individuals may try to increase the quality of their information by finding one promising aid project and trying to get a sense of its overall impacts on the poor (this will likely require significant time in-country). Others may try, individually or together, to incentivize aid agencies to make reforms such as the ones just described. These options require significant commitment, and will take patience. Gone, certainly, is the confidence from Singer's earlier articles that anyone in a rich country can save a life (and do only that) simply by writing a check instead of going out on a Saturday night. This seems inevitable on any realistic view of aid.

One thing that all individuals can do right now, however, is to think carefully about their own attitudes toward harm and uncertainty. We have seen that Singer's moral principle does not apply to our situation in our world. Individuals can therefore test their own commitments to forms of moral reasoning that offer more apt guidance. Do you, for instance, want to endorse an "overall cost–benefit" or "maximum expected gain" principle such as the following:

> One should always act to try to prevent something bad from happening when, as far as one can tell, the aggregate benefits of doing so will be larger than the harms of doing so considering all of the individuals who will be affected.

There are well-known concerns about such aggregative principles. If one does not want to endorse this kind of principle, however, then some other that is sensitive to the possibility of harm and uncertainty (perhaps some deontological principle) must be chosen. The question of the framework one will use to orient one's responses to poverty is a live and crucial one after the simpler principles are put aside. Philosophers might volunteer their skills to be useful to their fellow reasoners here.

What affluent individuals faced with the challenges of aid should not do is to take either of two paths of avoidance. The first path is to deny the facts about aid. Many affluent individuals take pride in being morally good people. Many, and especially those who already give to aid organizations, see giving to aid organizations as one important thing that morally good people do. These people sometimes find facts about the possible harms and uncertainties of aid as threatening to their own self-image, and so close their eyes to these facts. These well-intentioned people should be gently reminded: Severe poverty is not about you. Its moral importance is much greater than that of affluent people maintaining a certain self-image. It is imperative for all of us to try to reduce severe poverty, which means always focusing our attention on the world as it is.

The second path of avoidance is the selfishness of uncertainty, or "the paralysis of analysis." Individuals may become overwhelmed by the challenges of aid, conclude that they can never know what aid will do, and give themselves over to pursuing their own concerns. This is also not an adequate response.

Singer's spirit is exactly right: Responding to severe poverty is more important than many other things one could do instead. Severe poverty is an enormous human disaster, and each affluent individual should continually search for *some* ways that he or she can help. Helping may mean using one's special skills, drawing on one's own or one's community's resources, gathering and sharing more and better information, investigating new antipoverty strategies that might work. Helping may mean spending one's own money and passing up chances for fun. Severe poverty is a moral catastrophe and, one way or another, responding to it will require our most valuable resource: the days of our lives.

Notes

Epigraph source: Peter Singer, *The Life You Can Save* (New York: Random House, 2009), back cover (the sentences quoted appear in reverse order in the original). Many thanks to Christian Barry, Patricia Illingworth, Holden Karnofsky, Cara Nine, Alice Obrecht, Thomas Pogge, Roger Riddell, Peter Singer, and Lesley Sherratt for discussions of these issues.

1. This chapter draws on Leif Wenar, "What We Owe to Distant Others," *Politics, Philosophy and Economics* 2 (2003), pp. 283–304; "Accountability in International Development Aid," *Ethics and International Affairs* 20 (2006), pp. 1–23; "The Basic Structure as Object: Institutions and Humanitarian Concern," in D. Weinstock, ed., *Global Justice, Global Institutions* (Calgary: University of Calgary Press, 2007), pp. 253–278. These articles contain extensive references to the aid literature. To save space, the references therein are not repeated here.

2. Riddell, this volume.

3. In this chapter the term *affluent* is used relative to global incomes and includes almost everyone living in a developed country. To illustrate this, Milanovic estimates that, in 1993, an American living on the average income of the bottom 10% of the American population was, in terms of income, better off than two thirds of the people in the world. Branko Milanovic, "True World Income Distribution, 1988 and 1993: First Calculations, Based on Household Surveys Alone," *Economic Journal* 112 (2002), pp. 51–59.

4. Peter Singer, "Famine, Affluence and Morality," *Philosophy & Public Affairs* 1 (1972), p. 231. This article contains another version of the principle, with "of comparable moral importance" replacing "morally significant." The discussion here applies to both versions of the principle. Singer's *The Life You Can Save* (2009, p. 15) deploys a principle more like the "comparable moral importance" version.

5. Singer, "Famine," p. 231.

6. Ibid., p. 232.

7. Peter Singer, "The Drowning Child and the Expanding Circle," *New Internationalist* April 1997.

8. Singer, "Famine," p. 230.

9. Singer, *The Life*, p. 114. Individuals may also consider other courses of action not discussed in this chapter, such as to campaign for policy changes (for example, lower domestic agricultural tariffs and subsidies) that have nothing to do with aid.

10. Roger Riddell, *Does Foreign Aid Really Work?* (Oxford: Oxford University Press, 2007), pp. 53–54.

11. For example, the pie charts showing budgetary percentages give little relevant information about the structure of an NGO's operations or the effectiveness of its projects. Many individuals would be surprised at what some NGOs count as a "project expense" as opposed to an "administrative expense" and, in any case, many poverty reduction projects would likely be more effective if a higher proportion of funds were spent on administration. For these reasons, neither NGO fiscal reports (which only detail budgetary percentages) nor most "charity rating websites" (which use budgetary percentages to rank various NGOs) are reliable sources of information about NGO effectiveness.

12. www.savethechildren.org.uk (accessed August 22, 2009).

13. One can get a sense of the literature by typing terms like *official development aid* and *NGO aid* into a search engine like Google Scholar.

14. For example, most (although not all) agree that severe poverty has decreased in both absolute and percentage terms during the past 30 years, that aid flows have been small during this period relative to global economic activity, that much aid has been given for geostrategic instead of poverty reduction reasons, and that some of the largest poverty reductions during this period (including the largest in human history—the reduction of poverty in China) were mostly not attributable to aid efforts.

15. Sanjay Reddy and Thomas Pogge, "How *Not* to Count the Poor" 6 (2005), www.socialanalysis.org. See the debate at www.ipc-undp.org/theme.do#Pov.

16. Jeffrey Sachs, *The End of Poverty: Economic Possibilities for Our Time* (New York: Penguin, 2005); and William Easterly, *The White Man's Burden: Why the West's Efforts to Aid the Rest Have Done So Much Ill and So Little Good* (New York: Penguin, 2006).

17. United Nations Development Programme, *Development Effectiveness Report* (New York: United Nations, 2003), p. 41.

18. Ales Bulir and A. Javier Hamann, "Volatility of Development Aid: From the Frying Pan into the Fire?" *World Development* 36 (2008), pp. 2048–2066.

19. Ritva Reinikka and Jakob Svensson, "Local Capture and the Political Economy of School Financing," *Quarterly Journal of Economics* 119 (2004), pp. 679–705.

20. Amartya Sen, *Development as Freedom* (Oxford: Oxford University Press, 1999), p. 175.

21. William Easterly, "Introduction," in William Easterly, ed., *Reinventing Foreign Aid* (Cambridge, Mass.: MIT Press, 2008), p. 28.

22. Easterly, *Reinventing Foreign Aid*, p. 32.

23. Mary B. Anderson, *Do No Harm* (Boulder, Colo.: Lynne Rienner, 1999), pp. 46–47.

24. Anderson, *Do No Harm*, pp. 55–66.

25. These topics are discussed more extensively in Wenar, "Accountability," and "The Basic Structure." These articles set out a proposal for an organization (an association of evaluation professionals) for increasing evaluation quality.

26. Robert Cassen, *Does Aid Work?* 2nd ed. (Oxford: Clarendon, 1994).

27. Basil Cracknell, *Evaluating Development Aid* (London: Sage, 2001), p. 88.

28. Esther Duflo and Michael Kremer, "The Use of Randomization in the Evaluation of Development Effectiveness," in William Easterly, ed., *Reinventing Foreign Aid* (Cambridge, Mass.: MIT Press, 2008), p. 102.

29. See www.povertyactionlab.org.

30. Riddell, *Does Foreign Aid*, p. 189.

31. Ibid., p. 266.

32. For example, Rebecca M. Blank, "Evaluating Welfare Reform in the United States," *Journal of Economic Literature* 40 (2002), pp. 1105–1166.

33. For example, Ron Haskins et al., "Welfare Reform: An Overview of Effects to Date," *Brookings Institution Policy Brief* 1 (Brookings Institution, Washington, D.C., January 2001).

34. Singer, "Famine," p. 242.

35. Singer, *The Life*, pp. 103, 124.

36. Ibid., pp. 82–84, 112; 98, 96.

37. Ibid., p. 103.

38. Ibid., p. 84

39. Ibid., p. 88.

40. PSI, "Cost Effectiveness Report 2006," p. 10, www.psi.org/research/documents/health_impact/psi_cost_effectiveness_2006.pdf.

41. "President's Malaria Needs Assessment, Madagascar 2007," www.usaid.gov/mg/bkg%20docs/needs_assessment_report_2007.pdf.

42. Jeffrey Sachs: "You can't expect people with no money to buy bed-nets. . . . Enough with social marketing!" And Michael Kremer, one of the pioneers of randomized evaluation: "'I have nothing against people who sell Perrier,' he says—'or those who buy it. Just don't think,' he adds pointedly, 'that selling Perrier will meet the water needs of the world's poor.'" Christopher Shea, "A Handout, Not a Hand Up," *Boston Globe* (November 11, 2007), www.boston.com/bostonglobe/ideas/articles/2007/11/11/a_handout_not_a_hand_up.

43. Jessica Cohen and Pascaline Dupas, *Free Distribution vs. Cost-Sharing: Evidence from a Malaria-Prevention Field Experiment in Kenya*, Brookings Institution Global Economy and Development Working Paper (Brookings Institution, Washington, D.C., 2007).

44. Bya Jerry Okungu, "People's Revolt Is the Only Answer to Africa's Despots, Says Ugandan Writer," *Senegambia News* [editorial] (March 27, 2009), www.senegambianews.com/article/Guest_Editorial/Guest_Editorial/Peoples_revolt_is_the_only_answer_to_Africas_despots_Says_Ugandan_Writer/18636.

45. "President's Malaria Needs Assessment," p. 18.

46. In *The Life You Can Save*, Singer mentions the possibility that aid can do harm (pp. 111, 115–117), but seems to downplay this at another point, at least for official aid (p. 121). Interestingly, in his 1972 article, Singer did mention that the "sacrifice" clause in his principle was meant to include "causing anything else comparably bad to happen, or doing something that is wrong in itself, or failing to promote some moral good" ("Famine," p. 231). Singer did not pick up on those possibilities there, and in the discussion of the principle in *The Life You Can Save* (pp. 15–19), the mention of these wider effects is dropped.

47. www.givewell.net/PSI (accessed June 1, 2009).

7

Ethics in Translation

Principles and Power in the Philanthropic Encounter

Alex de Waal

The encounter between modern philanthropy and the targets of its concern gives rise to odd juxtapositions. One aid worker writes:

> Southern Sudan is one of the lushest places on earth. It is a Garden of Eden watered by the Nile where visitors have the feeling that a casually discarded mango stone would sprout an orchard overnight. Strange then, that one of my first encounters with aid work in Africa was watching as a Hercules transporter plane rained sacks of sorghum into the fields of southern Sudan. Scores of children sat on termite mounds to watch the show, drawing the obvious conclusion; food does not come from the ground, it rains from the skies.[1]

Other Southern Sudanese children surmised that every white person owned his or her own airplane, or that building airstrips was the quickest route to gaining a share in this bizarre bounty.[2] It is a commonplace observation that humanitarian actions have unintended consequences and, similarly, every act of altruism has an iota, at least, of selfishness.[3] The concern of this essay is how ethics translate—the two senses of how philanthropic motivations become outcomes and how foreign humanitarian actors are understood by the objects of their benevolence.

The first half of the essay outlines the conceptual apparatus for addressing these questions, with a special focus upon the anthropological study of development programs and its younger siblings, the scrutiny of humanitarian efforts, human rights organizations, and peacemaking initiatives. The cases are drawn from Africa and, in the spirit of comparative ethnography, are illustrative rather than comprehensive.

Also in the anthropological tradition, I shrink from Weberian ideal types and, rather, focus on actual institutions and practices that may or may not promote human life and well-being, rights and dignity. Just as there is no ideal form of government (but democratic systems are among the least bad ones), there is no perfect humanitarian formula to be achieved (but today's actually existing humanitarianism is not doing too

133

badly, and is learning). The principles, institutions, and practices of humanitarianism, as with other forms of governance, are continually contested
and renewed: Those in power try to co-opt or manipulate them, whereas
their societal adversaries try to pull them in the opposite direction.
Political power is the main determinant of outcome. Nonetheless, the
principles themselves and the rules of institutions are important constraints on power and they can, at times, be important and autonomous
factors determining outcomes.

When humanitarians and public health officials state their ideals, equity
and an instrumental calculus of the public good tend to dominate. Private
philanthropy flourishes where political and economic liberalism are
underpinned by a sense of civic duty. As Amartya Sen has insisted, liberal
political principles, including freedom of expression and association, are
also handmaidens to effective public policy.[4] This mix of different ethical
calculi is no bad thing. As will become clear, I believe that there are clashes
of principles that are inherently irresolvable and that humanitarian outcomes are best served by moderation in ethical claims, so that differences
can, at least, be managed.

The second part of the essay applies the two senses of "translation" to
the case of Sudan. The rationale for this is not only my familiarity with 25
years of humanitarian efforts in the country, but also that Sudan has been
the locus of a succession of experiments in international engagement,
ranging from aid for development, through refugee relief, humanitarian
operations in wartime, and Islamist philanthropy,[5] to advocacy for military intervention in Darfur and United Nations (UN) Security Council
referral to the International Criminal Court.[6] The revolving of this carousel
of foreign efforts to "save" Sudanese obscures important continuities—
specifically, how external efforts are co-opted into Sudan's turbulent patrimonial system of governance. The essay concludes with some general
observations about the conflicts of rights and the local political constraints
on how international norms can develop.

THE COMPARATIVE ETHNOGRAPHY OF THE
PHILANTHROPIC ENCOUNTER

The anthropologist Conrad Reining[7] was the first to turn his analytical lens
away from the discipline's exclusive focus on remote or colonized people
to also include the foreign administrator within his ethnographic gaze.
Subsequently, a thriving subdiscipline of the anthropology of development
has emerged, including studies of how economic development, humanitarian relief, and human rights have been co-opted, subverted, or mistrans-
lated by the people variously labeled as beneficiaries and recipients, whom
the agents of philanthropy have generally seen as a blank canvas waiting to
be colored in. For the ethnographer, a strict definition of philanthropy is
less useful than a Catholic approach to the subject matter, including a host

of those who engage in African societies with the intention of promoting some desired social improvement, which brings no obvious material benefit to the agent of improvement beyond a salary and personal satisfaction. Hence, in this essay the terms *philanthropy, humanitarianism,* and *charity* are used more or less interchangeably.

James Ferguson's work on Lesotho[8] is a classic study of how the repeated "failure" of official development efforts in that country has served the purposes of the government's bureaucracy. "Development" has extended the government's administrative presence into areas of the country hitherto inaccessible and legitimized its intrusion into areas of people's lives previously regarded as private or subject to communal or kinship authority only. As with much of this literature, the writings of Michel Foucault lurk in the wings. The engagement of remote but ambitious institutions, whether national governments or multilateral institutions like the World Bank, follows a pattern in which people who are hitherto largely beyond the control of administrative order are brought within a framework of measurement, regulation, taxation, and statute law. These insights have fueled an incisive set of critiques of development practice, by Mark Hobart[9] and Arturo Escobar,[10] among others. What these critiques tend to overlook is the virtue in hypocrisy: Although the extension of bureaucratic control is associated with a transfer of power and new and more alien forms of corruption and patriarchy, the logic of bureaucracy has its own regulatory order that includes principles of order and law.

There are significant echoes from the parallel field of anthropological ecology, in which scholars in the field had already identified the ways in which official analyses and remedies could compound problems rather than promote solutions. Examples included the control of vectors of infection[11] and attempts to prevent environmental degradation.[12] A central insight from this literature is that farmers, herders, and gatherers using indigenous ecological knowledge and skills have often succeeded in managing fragile ecological systems with considerable success, both to preserve a productive and diverse environment and also to gain a sustainable livelihood.

Ferguson's combination of field ethnography and scrutiny of institutions has proved itself a productive model in adjacent fields. Prominent among these is the critical study of humanitarian activities—a field built up by a small British group of social scientists, among them Susanna Davies,[13] Mark Duffield,[14] David Keen,[15] Zoe Marriage,[16] and myself.[17] Beginning with the study of how rural people possessed the skills to survive periods of hardship and hunger—and were considerably more expert at this than foreign relief workers—the focus of interest rapidly shifted to how relief efforts operate in wartime "complex emergencies," often becoming enmeshed with the very structures of violence that reproduced hunger and deprivation. There is also a parallel group of scholar–practitioners in France, among them the late Francois Jean,[18] not unrelated to the distinctive brand of humanitarian action pioneered by Médecins Sans Frontières (MSF) and its founders.

The core ethical impulse in these writings is the same as with the critique of development—good intentions can have unintended and adverse consequences—but the scale and rapidity with which emergency interventions can harm as well as help has contributed a sharp edge to this writing. The principle "do no harm" has been recognized in humanitarian work as in medicine.[19] However, although moral concern has lent this scholarship a practical edge (for example, many of the writers mentioned have either worked with humanitarian agencies or have been prominent in reviews of humanitarian response in countries such as Rwanda and Sudan), it has also narrowed the field of vision. The question posed by the practitioner, "What do I do differently?" hangs over the researcher and writer. There is an implicit moral calculus, most starkly in terms of lives lost and saved, that keeps the scholar on constant guard. Might he or she be fostering indifference or cynicism and, as such, contributing to sins of omission as great as, or greater than, the operational errors of those in the field? The arena has further been colored by high-profile controversies over military intervention for humanitarian purposes and its younger sibling, the "responsibility to protect." This has had the unfortunate outcome that much of humanitarian scholarship remains framed by simplistic for-and-against debates, to the detriment of more detailed empirical study of the social products of relief interventions in affected societies.

Such a refertilization of humanitarian studies may well come from the results of applying a similar intellectual apparatus to questions about the functioning of human rights organizations, programs for HIV/AIDS, and local peace and reconciliation. The fact that these are relatively virgin territory for inquiry allows new questions to be posed. Frederic Schaffer's study of Senegal, tellingly entitled "Democracy in Translation,"[20] concludes that Senegalese prefer to see democracy as a fair sharing of benefits within a patrimonial system, rather than as a competitive political system guaranteed by civil and political rights. Harri Englund's ethnography of international efforts to support human rights and civil society and Malawi[21] takes this approach a stage further. Englund sets out to investigate how these efforts actually translate for Malawians, using his command of the vernacular. Official discourse on the topic is exclusively in English, and Englund found that among Malawians and foreigners alike, his interest in using the Chichewa language to discuss these issues was greeted with amusement. He notes:

> It is not obvious how new concepts and ideas associated with human rights and liberal democracy are to be translated into African languages. Moreover, I realized during my previous fieldwork projects that the Chichewa translation of human rights as "birth freedoms" (*ufulu wachibadwidwe*) presents an extremely narrow understanding of rights.[22]

He finds that for educated Malawians, working on human rights or civil society questions is a career path. Employment with international agencies or, for the more entrepreneurial, setting up a local nongovernmental orga-nization (NGO) that can solicit funds for projects, becomes a means of sustaining a livelihood and meeting a personal aspiration for modernity and connectedness. The funding mechanisms for civic education and human rights promotion tend to be short-term grants that are intended to "build capacity" and leave behind a sustainable and well-rooted civil society. In fact, without constant replenishment of external funds, almost all these initiatives would wither (the exception being church congrega-tions), and many of the Malawians active in this field move from one short-term grant to another, foraging for a livelihood among the ever-changing fruits on offer from foreign donors. Those funders' goal of "sus-tainability," to be achieved through short-term grants, contributes to achieving the reverse of their aim. However, democratization assistance does at least contribute to the livelihoods, activities, and connectedness of a subelite group that, although less influential than its patrons might hope, is nonetheless a force for civility.

Comparable themes emerge from the study of the functioning of inter-national support for civil society activities on HIV/AIDS. Stefan Elbe[23] has applied Foucault's concept of "governmentality" to the way in which the mechanisms for responding to the epidemic have been instrumental-ized in pursuit of extending the administration of life. In my own writing on this topic,[24] I have explored how the human rights principles adopted by international HIV/AIDS policy have fostered new forms of African civil society networking. In contrast to traditional international public health policies, which have sought to administer populations tightly, lim-iting individual rights in pursuit of disease control, the global HIV/AIDS response has followed the principle of epidemiological individualism and has emphasized liberal rights and responsibilities. There is much contro-versy over whether this has been an appropriate or effective public health response,[25] but it has undoubtedly contributed to the exceptional phenomenon of the response to a pandemic of a stigmatized communica-tive disease being associated with an *increase* in civil liberties rather than their repression. International HIV/AIDS institutions including UNAIDS and the Global Fund to Fight HIV/AIDS, Tuberculosis and Malaria have asked AIDS activists, including people living with HIV and AIDS, onto their boards, and no international AIDS conference can be held without giving a prominent platform to these individuals. The result has been that AIDS institutions and funds have supported an extraordinary civil society efflorescence across Africa that, in turn, has given influence and funds to individuals who would otherwise have been marginalized, stigmatized, discriminated against, or worse.

Local peace and reconciliation initiatives have been subjected to a more withering critique. Dave Eaton[26] on the Uganda–Kenya border reports on how efforts to foster peaceful relations and reconciliation among pastoralist groups, for decades locked into local conflicts, have not succeeded. Part of the reason for the failure is the shortcoming of the conventional analysis that armed conflicts are becoming more frequent and deadly as a result of the presumed proliferation of small arms and deepening stress on natural resources. Eaton demonstrates that raids have actually been declining and are unrelated to levels of natural resources, and that disarmament efforts are destabilizing because they tend to be lopsided, leaving one community disadvantaged with respect to its neighbors with whom it had previously enjoyed approximate parity of ownership of weapons, a situation that had served as a deterrent to raiding. Moreover, the visits of the peace support teams to the communities were themselves a source of instability, in part because of limited knowledge of the immediate political terrain and in part because aspiring local leaders used the opportunities presented by high-profile and well-resourced external organizations to campaign for political office. Unlike the human rights workers who are Englund's focus, these local elites have both the capability and readiness to use violence, making their empowerment a more hazardous enterprise, both practically and ethically.

In addition to the commonplace that we need to be interested in unanticipated outcomes, two major themes arise from this array of studies. One is the extent that international philanthropic engagement creates its own mechanisms of patronage, establishing privileged and protected sociopolitical spaces. National subelites use the opportunities presented by foreign funds, institutions, and networks to further particular interests and keep alive certain kinds of political and moral projects. In societies in which ideals of selfless professional service have all but vanished, international agencies create places of refuge for beleaguered individuals, typically those with a Western style or secular education who aspire to enlightened liberal ideals. Theirs is a project of extending power, or equally often, of protecting that power against the encroachment of more brutish forms of patrimonialism and political extremism. In the midst of war or state collapse, or simply economic austerity and retrenchment, the prospect of employment in an international NGO is a lifeline for members of an educated local elite. International agencies are (of necessity) mechanisms of patronage, but their patrimonialism can at least be emancipatory.

The second theme is the double standards exercised by the international agencies. Despite genuine efforts at inclusiveness and antiracism by these organizations and (especially) individuals within them, there is an entrenched discrimination in the value attached to international (mostly Western) and national staff. This is most clearly seen in the decisions made regarding who is evacuated in a crisis and who is left behind; whose death, injury, or kidnapping makes for an institutional crisis, and whose doesn't. Didier Fassin has eloquently expounded these gradients of valuing life in the case of MSF, one of the few agencies ready to conduct such debates in public.[27] National staff are acutely aware of their second-class citizenship within such organizations. Along with the local recipients of assistance, their assessment of the ethics of the intervening organization rests mostly on how the agency and its international staff members treat people as individual persons, rather than on the general moral principles in the agency's mission statement and strategic programming decisions.

A similar point emerges from Daniel A. Bell's study of the misunderstandings between Western and East Asian advocates of human rights. The clash between the two is less a matter of universal principles and more to do with the personal and institutional politics of how the universals are pursued. He writes, "What's problematic is the assumption that only U.S.-style political institutions can secure human rights."[28] Those within, or at the top of, these institutions, tend not to examine the ways in which institutional concerns have come to shape the agendas. Those outside the institutions, especially those without power to influence them, see the institutional practices first and the principles second, if at all.

Until recently, relatively little ethnography of philanthropy has examined clashes among principles and between the organizations that espouse them. Thus, differences of opinion and approach between, say, medical relief agencies and human rights organizations have garnered little attention. More has been written on the debates within agencies, such as the International Committee of the Red Cross (ICRC)[29] and MSF.[30] This is changing, as international engagement with wars and "complex emergencies" becomes ever more complex. Twenty years ago, just a handful of relief agencies (notably, the ICRC and MSF) were active in war zones. Now, many more are present, alongside multimandate UN missions that undertake peacekeeping, civilian protection and the promotion of human rights, peacemaking efforts, and the engagement of the International Criminal Court. The debate over humanitarian intervention has generated a small but important literature.[31] The potential clash between peace and justice has gained particular attention in the case of Northern Uganda[32] and Darfur.[33] The conflict between peacemaking and the threat of military intervention has also been noted.[34] The propensity of the UN Security Council to equip itself and other institutions with an ever-expanding armory of powerful if untried instruments without having first decided on a coordinated strategy with priority goals, runs the risk of these mechanisms running afoul of one another and the weapons themselves causing "friendly fire" casualties. The debates around these profound moral issues will doubtless provide material for a new generation of fascinating ethnographic and philosophical studies.

From the viewpoint of the host country professional employed by a philanthropic organization or the recipient of largesse, another dimension of particular interest is the question of the development and domestication of norms. Thomas Risse and Kathryn Sikkink have developed one of the few cogent models for how this might occur, given the skepticism and lack of good faith with which most national governments enter into engagement with human rights organizations.[35] According to the model, the repressive government moves from outright rejection of charges of violations to making tactical concessions in the hope of "buying off" its critics. In doing so, it may find itself "entrapped" in a process of opening up, compelled to engage in a moral dialogue with its critics, with results it cannot control. This in turn leads to the abusive government formally if reluctantly accepting human rights norms, albeit with little actual commitment to enforcing these promises, but through a process of "domestication" gradually "routinizing" the adherence to at least some norms.

The pattern that we see with Englund's human rights entrepreneurs in Malawi and the HIV/AIDS activists across the continent is a variant on the Risse and Sikkink model. Rather than the international human rights organizations engaging with a government as an external actor, they have intruded directly into the sociopolitical arena, becoming a patron of important domestic constituencies, whose members can move through a revolving door into and out of government office. The use of philanthropic sponsorship to promote political careers can be seen as the manipulation of external good intentions and charitable resources for narrow political gain. Alternatively, this form of patronage serves as an efficient mechanism for managing elite competition for power and the domestication of liberal and civic norms in the political arena. Without doubt the ethical standards of the erstwhile champions of human rights and civil society will slip as they move directly into political. But very probably, the standards of civic conduct and political liberalism overall are still elevated by this procedure. An incrementally more civil politics is the tribute that patrimonialism pays to external sponsorship of human rights.

CASE STUDY: SUDAN'S HUMANITARIAN CAROUSEL

Sudan is at once the locus of long-running and complicated civil wars and famines, a field for humanitarian experimentation, and also the site of pioneering social science research from the 1920s until the 1980s. Since then, pariah status and the decline of area studies have contributed dwindling scholarship on Sudan, dramatically lowering the bar on who qualifies as an "expert" on the country and thereby leaving it vulnerable to the moralizing of armchair pundits and other exercises in philanthropic adventurism.

Sudanese politics have long been unstable, with no government since independence able to secure a firm and lasting grip on power,[36] and characterized by extreme inequality between the center and peripheries. Since the late 1970s, intraelite instability and provincial frustrations have fomented a succession of crises in marginalized areas, several of which have become excessively long and bloody wars, in South Sudan and Darfur. The government has shown itself well able to initiate large-scale rural violence, usually by sponsoring proxy militia, but has a very limited capability to halt that violence after it has begun. The country is characterized by constant reshuffling of the political deck alongside persistent and little-changing patterns of turmoil, displacement, and bloodshed. It is a turbulent state.[37] Sudanese politics can equally be characterized as an alternation between occasional revolutionary episodes (in succession of leftist, nationalist, and Islamist character) and a recurrent political marketplace in which political allegiances are for sale to the highest bidder. In more stable periods, the government in Khartoum was the sole or dominant purchaser of loyalty, and provincial elites had nowhere else to turn for support, with the result that the provinces were neglected but stable, included on disadvantageous terms within the national patronage system. The entry of other bidders into the marketplace, including neighboring countries such as Ethiopia, Uganda, Libya, and Chad, and the international community, especially the United States, has allowed provincial elites to seek out other patrons and thus increase the price for their loyalty and the range of their political options.

Sudan's wars are neither strictly internal nor international. Although the Sudan government supports rebels operating in neighboring countries, those neighbors also function as sponsors of insurgency in Sudan.[38] Even when they are not actively funneling weapons and money to Sudanese rebel groups, the very fact that they are willing, in principle, to do so means that provincial leaders strategize accordingly. The leaders of the Southern-based rebellion, the Sudan People's Liberation Army (SPLA), shifted from enjoying the support of one neighboring country to another (getting backing from Ethiopia, Uganda, and Eritrea at different points), and during the brief periods when it lacked a powerful foreign sponsor, hanging on in the well-founded anticipation that it would indeed win a new patron (it got the backing of the United States).

This model of political functioning is relevant to humanitarian engagement, particularly insofar as the entry of international organizations into the political marketplace alters the political dynamics. Humanitarians function as dispensers of resources and employment, and create new patronage networks and new opportunities for subelites to pursue political strategies. From the beginnings of large-scale development and relief work in the 1970s, Sudanese politicians, administrators, and academics interpreted international agencies in these terms. The UN High Commissioner for Refugees and the international NGOs it supported were perceived as competitors of the Sudan government's Commission of Refugees.[39] The immense NGO-led efforts to reconstruct South Sudan after the peace agreement of 1972 that ended the first civil war resulted in foreign agencies providing most governmental services such as education, health, and clean water in large parts of South Sudan.[40] Equally important, international agencies provided employment and consultancies for a growing number of Sudanese professionals and academics. In earlier decades, college graduates would have followed a career track into the civil service and the professions, but government austerity measures and the fast-growing number of qualified individuals meant that there were no longer sufficient opportunities for them. In addition, during the 1980s, the growing "Islamization" of the governmental sphere meant that those with a secular education and liberal political views were unwelcome. Many were dismissed and few recruited. Employment with international agencies therefore provided a kind of internal refuge, a protected enclave where individuals unsympathetic to the repressive state and its Islamist project could find an income, a conducive working atmosphere among like-minded peers, a measure of protection against the arbitrary actions of government, and the opportunity for traveling abroad to attend conferences and thereby build up personal contacts that would enable them to pursue further studies or get ranking positions in the headquarters of international agencies. Meanwhile, the agencies' commitment to serving the people was a rebuff to the corruption and brutality of government. The very existence of these philanthropic organizations served as a standing reminder of a value set under threat of extinction.

For the critics of this kind of philanthropic encounter, it represented a retreat from accountability.[41] The alternative model they had in mind was one in which Sudanese citizens demanded essential services directly from their government and called it to account when the government failed. On several occasions in Sudanese history this had indeed happened, the classic example being the peaceful popular uprising of April 1985 that toppled the dictatorship of President Jaafar Nimeiri and ushered in a new era of elected parliamentary government, sadly short lived. One of the sparks for the demonstrations was the scandal of drought migrants arriving on the outskirts of the capital city, and the authorities refusing to recognize their distress and need for help. In a spirit of voluntarism, the citizens of Khartoum and its twin city Omdurman organized charitable relief and also protested official indifference, contributing to the mass demonstrations that brought down the government bloodlessly.[42] If such popular pressure to sustain a political contract to prevent famine could be sustained, then crises could be prevented, in line with the celebrated observation by Amartya Sen that democratic rights serve as a famine prevention measure.[43]

The most incisive criticism of the "political contract" model for famine prevention in Africa is that it misstates the nature of political accountability in most countries on the continent, which is achieved not through liberal institutions, but through patronage structures.[44] In urban areas, claims on the state can be made by government employees and city residents by virtue of proximity and the contractual relations they have with the government as employer and provider of essential services, but in rural areas such claims can only be made through the intermediary of elite representatives who have standing within the ruling hierarchy. Echoing Schaffer's study in Senegal,[45] the challenge is not to construct a Western or Indian model of competitive politics, but instead to create an inclusive patrimonialism in which all can stake their claim to a sufficient, if perhaps less than fair, share of national resources. Under the earlier critique of humanitarianism, the major problem was that international agencies helped locate famine creation and famine relief in technocratic and charitable spheres, thereby depoliticizing it and allowing repressive governments to escape their political responsibilities for prevention and response.

Under the revised critique, their function is to establish parallel networks of patronage beyond state control, thereby weakening the state and helping to create conditions for political conflict and turbulence. The role they play is akin to the sponsors of insurgency across Sudan's borders, except that it aspires to be civic and nonviolent.

There are exceptions to the pacific nature of this engagement. Foreign relief workers who have stayed long enough to become familiar with the Sudanese political scene sometimes take their stand of solidarity with their Sudanese colleagues and clients to the logical next step of providing dual-use technologies. During the long war in the South, a number of relief workers became so committed to the Southern cause, which they saw as fundamentally just, that they were prepared to turn a blind eye to the use of assistance to further the military ends of the SPLA.[46] The justification was that if the SPLA was unable to hold territory then the people would be at the mercy of government-backed forces, which had a terrible record for violating human rights. In the case of Darfur, the argument has not been for military assistance to the rebels but, rather, for international military intervention to protect civilians, a step aimed at curtailing Khartoum's powers or overthrowing the regime altogether. The Darfur rebels have assiduously courted the activist groups that advocate this course of action, anticipating that the outcome will be to their political benefit. The example that both have in mind is NATO's humanitarian intervention in Kosovo that removed Belgrade's political and military presence in the province.[47] The logic of international philanthropic patronage and protection, in circumstances in which the U.S. government has determined that Khartoum is responsible for genocide, does, indeed, lead inexorably to a foreign protectorate.

The Sudanese Islamists recognized this logic early on, although it was their own paranoid and repressive response that did most to elicit the international reaction that they were so determined to avoid. Beginning in the 1970s, they began to develop their own Islamist model of philanthropy.[48] Modeled in part on their secular or Christian rivals, and funded by money from the oil states of the Gulf, these agencies also drew upon specifically Islamic precepts.[49] Islamic charity is recognizably part of the same tradition as its Christian and Jewish cousins, but with some important variants. For example, there is no strictly enforced boundary between commerce and charity, a continuity that left some Islamic agencies susceptible to the lure of using their tax-exempt status for commercial advantage, but has also allowed for the development of distinctive forms of microcredit that have proved an effective poverty alleviation tool. In Bangladesh, the Grameen Bank and Bangladesh Rural Advancement Committee have turned Islamic–style, no-interest microloans into a major instrument for small-scale development, and Sudanese agencies have also experimented with similar schemes on a smaller scale. In addition, Islamic law and philosophy tends to collapse the distinction between personal ethics and public law, making charitable donations (the Islamic tithe, or *zakat*) a general obligation and the receipt of such assistance a matter of right for those deemed deserving. The blurring of this boundary, combined with the totalizing concepts of the Islamists' own project for social and political transformation under the rubric of the "comprehensive Call to God" (*da'awa al shamla*) meant that Islamist voluntarism became an integral part of a state-led effort at imposing hegemony through violence. Some Islamist humanitarian agencies became handmaidens to *jihad* during the early 1990s.[50] In turn, this onslaught prompted some Sudanese in the areas under assault to turn to militant Christianity and to demand comparable solidarity in the struggle from their foreign sympathizers.

By the mid 1990s, the Islamists' *jihad* failed and, in due course, the Islamist agencies active in the country, both national and international, reverted to the more familiar forms of relief assistance and constituency building. Most Islamic philanthropy has not only abandoned its grander sociopolitical ambitions (and thus become more like its secular counterpart), but has accommodated to the realities of the Sudanese political marketplace.

In the meantime, perhaps the most profound of the principles of Islamic charity has reasserted itself—namely, the principle of anonymous benefaction. Recalling that in Sudan, as in most Muslim and Arab societies, social relations including charitable donation are conducted on a face-to-face basis with an expectation of reciprocity, it is notable that true philanthropy in the Islamic tradition insists that the donation should be invisible and unacknowledged. The Prophet Mohamed demanded that not even one's left hand should be aware of the charitable act of one's right hand. With the bankruptcy of the Islamists' revolutionary project and the absence of any organized alternative, the public sphere has decayed into cynicism, corruption, and the naked politics of the political marketplace in which loyalties are auctioned to the highest bidder. In these circumstances, ethical actions are invisible but not nonexistent. There are innumerable conspiracies of solidarity, protected by a social code, that keep intact the social fabric at the level of individuals and families.

Sudan's politics are turbulent in the sense of constantly being in motion, with little sign of substantive long-term change. Much the same is true of the succession of experiments in international engagement, which are in ceaseless flux but still exhibit the same basic characteristics. Over time they have become co-opted into Sudan's unstable patrimonial system of governance. The international presence, which currently includes two immense international peacekeeping missions as well as numerous aid operations, cannot withdraw without abandoning a substantial constituency of clients, and yet it is not contributing to stability. It is not useful to speculate about the counterfactual "what if?" Might Sudan have been better off without such extravagant levels of international engagement? But it is instructive to conclude that the terms of philanthropic engagement in Sudan are set, not by the ethical principles of foreigners, but by the resilient realities of Sudanese politics and society, which invariably capture external institutions and subvert humanitarian intentions.

IMPLICATIONS

The philanthropic enterprise is an influential engagement in the affairs of poor and conflict-ridden societies. Ethical motives and principles comprise the starting point for a range of charitable, humanitarian, and related activities. However, for the societies that receive this largesse, the institutions and personal relationships of the aid givers are more immediately significant than the any philanthropic motives and principles.

Over time, however, we may see the acceptance and domestication of humanitarian norms, primarily because the humanitarian enterprise itself is an instrument of patronage and power, protecting and promoting an influential domestic constituency in the country in question. The key term in this assertion is *may*. The process depends on how this constituency is situated within national politics. In many African countries, it is seen as perfectly legitimate for political elites to circulate between government office and civil society organizations with foreign sponsorship, although tensions between the two roles are to be expected. In such cases we can expect an incremental, if uneven, adoption of human rights norms and philanthropic practices. There will inevitably be disappointment as former champions of civility and rights fail to live up to their promises, but that disappointment is itself testament to the upward recalibration of standards that accompanies the engagement on humanitarian practice and human rights norms.

In contrast, in deeply conflicted countries (such as Sudan), the scenario is much more troubled, in that the humanitarian patronage afforded to liberal and secular elites is seen (correctly) by a beleaguered government as a political threat. In this instance, the risks of philanthropic engagement are considerable, both for the society in general (it may entrench political polarization and conflict) and for those members of the dissident elite who seek out international humanitarian clientage (who may be vulnerable to a backlash).[51] And the prospects for the relatively harmonious process of norm development that can occur in more civic political contexts are much more uncertain. Instead, we may see intractable conflicts among norms, with polarized positions adopted by the custodians of diverse positions and acrimonious exchanges among them. In both directions, good intentions may be lost in translation, and attempts to manage irresolvable differences in a civil manner may fail.

Notes

1. Jeevan Vasagar, "Ending Africa's Cargo Cult," *Guardian Online* (July 24, 2006), www.guardian.co.uk/commentisfree/2006/jul/24/post249.

2. Ataul Karim, Mark Duffield, et al., OLS: *Operation Lifeline Sudan: A Review* (New York: UNICEF, July 1996).

3. Compare with Tony Vaux, *The Selfish Altruist: Relief Work in Famine and War* (London, Earthscan, 2003).

4. Amartya Sen, *Development as Freedom* (Oxford: Oxford University Press, 2001).

5. Alex de Waal, "Anthropology and the Aid Encounter," in Jeremy MacClancy, ed., *Exotic No More: Anthropology on the Front Lines* (London: University of Chicago Press, 2002), pp. 251–269.

6. Rebecca Hamilton and Chad Hazlett, "Not on Our Watch: The American Movement for Darfur," in Alex de Waal, ed., *War in Darfur and the Search for Peace* (Cambridge, Mass.: Harvard University Press, 2007), pp. 337–366.

7. Conrad Reining, *The Zande Scheme: An Anthropological Case Study of Economic Development in Africa* (Evanston, Ill.: Northwestern University Press, 1966).

8. James Ferguson, *The Anti-Politics Machine: Development, Depoliticization and Bureaucratic Power in Lesotho* (Minneapolis: University of Minnesota Press, 1990).

9. Mark Hobart, *An Anthropological Critique of Development: The Growth of Ignorance* (London: Routledge, 1993).

10. Arturo Escobar, *Encountering Development: The Making and Unmaking of the Third World* (Princeton, N.J.: Princeton University Press, 1994).

11. John Ford, *Role of Trypanosomiases in African Ecology: A Study of the Tsetse-Fly Problem* (Oxford: Clarendon Press, 1971).

12. Melissa Leach and Robin Mearns, *The Lie of the Land: Challenging Received Wisdom on the African Environment* (London: James Currey, 1996).

13. Susanna Davies, *Adaptable Livelihoods: Coping with Food Insecurity in the Malian Sahel* (London: Macmillan, 1996).

14. Mark Duffield, *Global Governance and the New Wars: The Merging of Development and Security* (London: Zed, 2001).

15. David Keen, *Complex Emergencies* (London: Polity, 2007).

16. Zoe Marriage, *Not Breaking the Rules, Not Playing the Game: International Assistance to Countries at War* (London: Hurst, 2006).

17. Alex de Waal, *Famine Crimes: Politics and the Disaster Relief Industry in Africa* (London: James Currey, 1997).

18. Francois Jean, *From Ethiopia to Chechnya: Reflections on Humanitarian Action, 1988–1999* (Paris: Médecins Sans Frontières, 2008).

19. Mary Anderson, *Do No Harm: How Aid Can Support Peace—Or War* (Boulder, Colo.: Lynne Reiner, 1999).

20. Frederic C. Schaffer, *Democracy in Translation: Understanding Politics in an Unfamiliar Culture* (Ithaca, N.Y.: Cornell University Press, 1998).

21. Harri Englund, *Prisoners of Freedom: Human Rights and the African Poor* (Berkeley: University of California Press, 2006).

22. Ibid., p. 22.

23. Stefan Elbe, *Virus Alert: Security, Governmentality and the Global AIDS Pandemic* (New York: Columbia University Press, 2009).

24. Alex de Waal, *AIDS and Power: Why There Is No Political Crisis—Yet* (London: Zed, 2006).

25. James Chin, *The AIDS Pandemic: The Collision of Epidemiology with Political Correctness* (London: Radcliffe, 2007).

26. Dave Eaton, "The Business of Peace: Raiding and Peace Work along the Kenya–Uganda Border," *African Affairs* 107 (2008), pp. 89–110 and 243–259. [two parts.]

27. Didier Fassin, "Humanitarianism as a Politics of Life," *Public Culture* 19 (2007), pp. 499–520.

28. Daniel A. Bell, *East Meets West: Human Rights and Democracy in East Asia* (Princeton, N.J.: Princeton University Press, 2000), p. 56.

29. Caroline Moorhead, *Dunant's Dream: War, Switzerland and the History of the Red Cross* (New York: Carroll and Graf, 1999).

30. Tim Allen and David Styan, "A Right to Interfere? Bernard Kouchner and the New Humanitarianism," *Journal of International Development* 12 (2000), pp. 825–842.

31. Jonathan Moore, ed., *Hard Choices: Moral Dilemmas in Humanitarian Intervention* (Oxford: Rowman and Littlefield, 1998).

32. Tim Allen, *Trial Justice: The International Criminal Court and the Lord's Resistance Army* (London: Zed, 2005).

33. Julie Flint and Alex de Waal, "Justice Off Course in Darfur," *Washington Post* (June 28, 2008), p. A15.

34. Alex de Waal, "Darfur and the Failure of the Responsibility to Protect," *International Affairs* 83 (2007), pp. 1039–1054.

35. Thomas Risse and Kathryn Sikkink, "The Socialization of International Human Rights Norms into Domestic Practices: Introduction," in Thomas Risse, Stephen Ropp, and Kathryn Sikkink, eds., *The Power of Human Rights: International Norms and Domestic Change* (Cambridge: Cambridge University Press, 1999), pp. 1–38.36.

36. Peter Woodward, *Sudan 1898–1989: The Unstable State* (London: Lester Crook, 1990).

37. Alex de Waal, "Sudan: The Turbulent State," in Alex de Waal, ed., *War in Darfur and the Search for Peace* (Cambridge, Mass.: Harvard University Press, 2007).

38. Alex de Waal, "The Politics of Destabilization in the Horn," in Alex de Waal, ed., *Islamism and Its Enemies in the Horn of Africa* (London: Hurst, 2005).

39. Ahmed Karadawi, *Refugee Policy in Sudan, 1967–1984* (London: Berghahn, 1999).

40. Terje Tvedt, *Angels of Mercy or Development Diplomats? NGOs and Foreign Aid* (London: James Currey, 1998).

41. African Rights, *Food and Power in Sudan: A Critique of Humanitarianism* (London: African Rights, 1997).

42. Ibid., chap. 3.

43. Sen, *Development as Freedom*.

44. Compare with de Waal, *AIDS and Power*, chap. 4; Schaffer, *Democracy in Translation*; Patrick Chabal and Jean-Pascal Daloz, *Africa Works: Disorder as Political Instrument* (London: James Currey, 1999).

45. Schaffer, *Democracy in Translation*.

46. African Rights, *Food and Power*, chap. 12.

47. Anthony Lake, Susan Rice, and Donald Payne, "We Saved Europeans; Why Not Africans?" *Washington Post* (October 2, 2006), p. A19.

48. M. A. Mohamed Salih, "Islamic NGOs in Africa: The Promise and Peril of Islamic Voluntarism," in Alex de Waal, ed., *Islamism and Its Enemies in the Horn of Africa* (London: Hurst, 2005), pp. 146–181.

49. Jonathan Benthall and Jerome Bellion-Jourdan, *The Charitable Crescent: Politics of Aid in the Muslim World* (London: IB Taurus, 2003).

50. Alex de Waal and A. H. Abdel Salam, "Islamism, State Power and *Jihad* in Sudan," in Alex de Waal, ed., *Islamism and Its Enemies in the Horn of Africa* (London: Hurst, 2005), pp. 70–113.

51. We can see a comparable, more dramatic variant of this in the African backlash against the International Criminal Court following the chief prosecutor's demand for an arrest warrant against Sudan's President Omar al Bashir.

8

Global Philanthropy and Global Governance

The Problematic Moral Legitimacy of the Relationship between Global Civil Society and the United Nations

Kenneth Anderson

Global philanthropy refers, in part, to organizations that undertake altruism across borders. Typically they are international nongovernmental organizations (NGOs) that operate transborder in the provision of goods and services, of one kind or another, to populations, of one kind or another, that lack or have little access to them. This is, however, in the abstract. The actual range of goods and services proffered by international NGOs is vast and variegated—from physical goods addressing basic material needs of food and shelter to highly abstract yet widely accepted propositions such as human rights or good governance. Global philanthropy can encompass (as a term) both the international NGOs that make such offerings as well as the funding organizations—sometimes private philanthropies such as charitable foundations, but also governments and public international organizations such as United Nations (UN) agencies.

This essay focuses on "private global philanthropy" as constituted by international NGOs. The question of global ethics that follows in this essay is: What are the ethical and political relationships between international NGOs, on the one hand, and public international organizations such as the UN, on the other? This essay is thus about global governance, and the proper ethical role of international NGOs with respect to global governance and the institutions that promote it, primarily public international organizations such as the UN. But we might start with a prior question: Why, in the first place, should one especially care about the question of global governance?

A contested issue of globalization is the question of whether, how, and to what extent an *economically* integrating world requires a *politically* integrated planet—a world that has a global law, regulation, and enforcement that transcends all lesser political authority and to which all other political entities must cede their sovereignty.[1] It is a very old debate and an ancient dream, the world unified in peace under a single universal law and a supreme lawgiver who will end the wars and feuds and injustices and material want of the world as a whole.[2] A federal world, a world under a global constitution—loosely configured of necessity, naturally, but nonetheless one in which global law is the distinct ordering hierarchy and to which the sovereignty of individual states must necessarily give way.

For many, a politically integrated world is morally and politically desirable on its own terms. It is historical progress as such. For others, the justification for political integration is simply a necessary corollary—as a matter of global welfare and justice—of economic integration. The fact of a world in which economies are coming together among economic actors such as multinational business enterprises that are able to act across national political borders gives, according to many, ever greater urgency to the building of what has been called *global governance.*

At the same time, the world since 1990 has seen the unprecedented growth of international NGOs and transborder social movements drawing in large numbers of people around the world.[3] Their place in this globalizing world has also posed questions, particularly as they take up political activities at the global, and not merely national, level. To take up global political activities presupposes global actors with which to have political intercourse. The influence, reach, presence, and power of these international NGOs have grown fantastically during the past two decades, and they pose questions about for whom they speak—on anyone's behalf other than their own? To whom are they accountable for the positions they advocate, and does it matter? Do they represent anyone other than themselves? Should states and international organizations pay any particular attention to them, and if so, why and how? These are political and legal issues; but they are also ethical issues with respect to international NGOs and their funders, and with respect to the moral account that is given of them and how they are framed as an intellectual and ideological matter.

The account that follows suggests that these two actors and issues—global governance, through institutions of the UN, and international NGOs and their global role—are deeply interlinked. What links them is the question of *legitimacy*—which is to say, the quality of a political order to be able to act with the broad and largely unquestioning support of its members. At stake in this debate over legitimacy, the UN, and international NGOs is the question of whether global governance—one overarching lawgiver for the planet, a constitution for the world—is a desirable or even possible thing, and whether, in this account of global governance, international NGOs, and transborder social movements more generally, have any special ethical role to play.

We proceed in several notional historical steps, walking through a deliberately stylized historical account of global governance and international

NGOs, focused on the period since 1990 and the end of the Cold War. The discussion is largely a descriptive sociological and political assertion of the evolution of the global discourse over the role of international NGOs, rather than specifically an ethical argument; the ethical argument is implied, of course, by the description of this political debate. The conclusion of this essay is an ethically skeptical one. It is skeptical, on the one hand, of the desirability of global governance as conceived by global elites, including those in international NGOs as well as in public international organizations. And it is especially skeptical, on the other, of the proposed ethical role for international NGOs on the global stage in promoting and legitimating global governance. Accountability, representativeness, and political intermediation—these are all ethical concepts as much as political or juridical, and this essay argues that international NGOs lack the capacity in each of the three to carry out the legitimation functions that the prevailing, prominent account of global governance gives them.

POST–COLD WAR AMBITIONS FOR THE UNITED NATIONS, NONGOVERNMENTAL ORGANIZATIONS, AND GLOBAL GOVERNANCE (1989–1996)

The opening provided by the end of the Cold War invited many people to believe that the world might enter a new period of global political coordination to match the economic globalization that was emerging during this period. It was a period of heady liberal internationalism—the belief that sovereign power politics could be overcome through a liberal version of international law, resulting in a benevolent and liberal global governance under a loose, but still federal, global law.[4] Leading international law scholars offered pronouncements that the era of truly sovereign states was over; they moreover offered these views to a certain extent as legal opinions that this was, or at least was in a legal sense, coming to be, true.[5]

These hopes and dreams were fostered, somewhat perversely, by the remarkably united front offered by countries around the world, through the UN and the Security Council, to the invasion, occupation, and sack of Kuwait by Saddam Hussein's Iraq. For once, it seemed, the leading countries came together—including Russia and the United States—to take concerted military action against Iraq. Even if the United States overwhelmingly took the military lead, it was supported by a very broad coalition of states and the Security Council. President George Bush (senior) excited a great many globally when, in the wake of this action, he described a "new world order" that apparently seemed to foreshadow global governance through the UN and genuine collective security.[6]

In retrospect, it is clear that different actors supported the collective military action against Iraq in Kuwait for very different reasons. Some did so because they were genuinely worried about Hussein's naked use of force to acquire an entire country as territory. Others joined because of

Hussein's genocidal (as Human Rights Watch concluded) human rights abuses within Iraq against the Kurds and others; their concern was fundamentally the internal political order under Hussein.[7] Still other states, particularly Middle Eastern states such as Saudi Arabia, looked at the conflict through the geopolitical aim of weakening Iraq. And still others supported the first Gulf War from the idealistic belief that this essentially unprecedented military exercise in collective security would lead to long-term global governance through the UN.

That was with respect to sovereign states and international organizations. Within a few years, however, those idealistic hopes for collective security were dashed—in large part by the outbreak of the Yugoslavia wars and, still later, the genocide in Rwanda. The international community proved unable to respond to provide collective security; Europe proved unable to provide security even within Europe, and the Yugoslavia wars came to a halt only when the United States, under the Clinton administration, decided finally that it had to intervene.[8] In lieu of collective security as such, the UN Security Council implemented a series of war crimes tribunals that aimed to provide after-the-fact justice, first for Yugoslavia and later for Rwanda. These were widely celebrated as the beginnings of an international criminal justice system but, critics noted, their origins were an *alternative* to actual intervention before or during the fact.[9] At the same time, however, during the early 1990s, international NGOs became ever more active in all these causes—human rights, international tribunals, agitation for sovereign states to act in the former Yugoslavia, and many more. Their activities at the UN became more active as well.

The cause that transformed the self-understanding of international NGOs during the 1990s was the international campaign to ban antipersonnel landmines.[10] By the late 1980s, humanitarian groups, particularly the International Committee of the Red Cross (ICRC), had begun to raise awareness of the damage being caused by the heavy and increasing use of landmines in conflicts around the world. The issue appealed to a wide variety of international NGOs from a surprising range of perspectives—human rights groups, environmentalists, humanitarian relief organizations, development NGOs, and more—and during the early 1990s, they came together to form a loose network, the International Campaign to Ban Landmines.[11] Taking advantage of the emerging technologies of the Internet—the cutting-edge communications technologies of the day, e-mail, and listservs—they forged an international campaign for a treaty that would ban use, production, stockpiling, and transfer. Initially rejected and, indeed, laughed off by leading states, the movement succeeded in forcing powerful states, including the United States and others, to take account of the movement.[12] The campaign eventually succeeded in enlisting Canada and several other important states, and eventually produced the Ottawa Convention banning landmines.[13]

The success of the NGO campaign against landmines did not go unnoticed by the UN, including eventual Secretary General Kofi Annan and his senior advisors. They had been looking for political mechanisms to strengthen the UN as an instrument, not merely of the member states of the UN or as a kind of negotiating table between sovereign states, but of independent global governance[14]—global governance conducted by the UN in its own name and as its own source of legitimacy and authority, beyond and, indeed, above that of individual nation states, no matter how powerful. One question of deep and abiding importance, however, was the fact that the UN lacked legitimacy as a democratic actor.[15] It had connections to member states, but the UN itself lacked any direct connection, in the sense of democratic legitimacy, with the "peoples" of the world, as stated in the preamble of the Charter.[16] The lack of a connection to people as such meant, by implication, that the legitimacy of the UN was merely through the member states—and, by further implication, that its legitimate activities and scope of authority were merely what the member states granted it. The highest goals of global governance, as far as the senior leadership of the UN general secretariat was concerned, however, was to transcend the reliance for authority and legitimacy upon the member states, to govern, at least in some important matters, directly in the name of the UN and by appeal to the "peoples" of the world.

And yet there is no direct election to the UN; it is structured as an association of member states. It is not a global parliament that is elected by its people(s); it is a meeting ground of states. The ideological problem—the legitimacy problem—for the UN leadership, in pursuit of the authority of genuinely global governance, was to find a source of legitimacy that did not run through the member states, and yet did not require something that seemed—and seems—quite implausible if not fantastic, global parliamentary elections.[17] The lesson of the NGO landmines campaign, to the UN leadership under Annan, was that international NGOs, which could be perhaps plausibly understood as groups of global citizens, could be asserted as "representatives" of the world's peoples for purposes of providing the UN with a form of quasi-democratic legitimacy, or at least a plausible connection to a global constituency that did not run through the member states.[18]

For their part, the NGOs were happy to see themselves in this role. Besides confirming their own "autovision" as the citizens of the world forcing themselves into the closed negotiating sessions of states, being treated by the institutional UN as the legitimate representatives of the world's peoples who, in turn, conferred legitimacy upon the UN and its claims to governance over the member states, gave considerable status and power institutionally. International NGOs were no longer merely unofficial players standing outside the doors of power, outside the rooms in which states made their agreements. They had, in effect, the backing of the UN leadership to seek a place at the negotiating tables themselves, armed with the claim that they had a special role as representatives of the world's peoples.[19] States, overall, were not pleased with this claim, but some—Canada, for example—tended to go along, particularly insofar as it might serve other state purposes, usually to diminish the power of the world's remaining superpower, in the traditional geopolitical habit of middling states.[20] And the precedent for NGOs joining in treaty negotiations was already on the table in the landmines campaign, although—quite distinct from most other treaty negotiations—it was, in the first place, sponsored as much by the NGOs themselves.

THE GOLDEN AGE OF SOCIAL AND POLITICAL THEORY OF NGOS: DREAMING OF "GLOBAL CIVIL SOCIETY" AS A PARTNER IN GLOBAL GOVERNANCE THROUGH THE UNITED NATIONS (1996–2000)

The institutional UN sought to elevate the UN's own intellectual and ideological claims to governance by treating NGOs as the locus of the legitimacy of the world's "peoples." The NGOs, for their part, elevated their own intellectual and ideological self-conception by treating themselves (and inviting the UN and the rest of the world to treat them), not merely as international NGOs, but as something mysteriously called *global civil society*. Why this special term and what was its special significance? Why shift from calling international NGOs by a plain, practical, descriptive term—nongovernmental organizations—to calling them by a term far more laden with ideological significance in social and political theory, the far more intellectually portentous, but also ideologically fraught, *global civil society?*[21]

The origins of the terminological shift lie in the effort by intellectuals and theorists of the landmines ban campaign to draw larger lessons—with respect to both future NGO activity in very different fields as well as the very conception of globalization and global governance—from the leading role played by NGOs themselves. The increasingly fawning overtures made to the NGO community during this period by their counterpart intellectuals and theorists within international organizations, the UN secretariat, and its so-called "modernizers"—those UN strategists who saw the transformation of the organization as dependent upon finding a source of legitimacy that would "go around" the member states directly to global populations and constituencies—also played a role. This was also the period, after all, in which the International Campaign to Ban Landmines and its coordinator, Jody Williams, won the 1997 Nobel Peace Prize over state officials, such as then Canadian foreign minister Lloyd Axworthy, who had thrown all the weight of Canada's worldwide diplomatic service behind the ban campaign and who might have thought that their efforts deserved equal recognition.[22]

As a theoretical matter, however, NGOs, merely as such, are what they are—just organizations consisting of interested individuals. Their motivations might be noble, altruistic, cosmopolitan, and so on, but they are, as a matter of political role, simply organizations that attempt to persuade international organizations, states, and others in authority to act. To act sometimes on the basis of NGO expertise and sometimes simply on the basis of their enthusiasm and ability to influence the national governments where they hold some level of political capital—which is to say, most strongly in the world's democratic states in which citizens' groups can make themselves heard and their influence felt.[23]

Expertise, even when genuine, and enthusiasm are not ordinarily considered sufficient to give one authority, however.[24] The moral authority of NGOs in the international arena had traditionally rested upon recognized expertise and effectiveness in their particular missions—the relief group, for example, whose acknowledged record in wartime humanitarian aid gave a certain practical as well moral authority to its views before international bodies in areas of its subject matter. The ICRC was always the model—careful, precise, never flamboyant, typically self-effacing, and, above all, *competent* in its areas of competence. But the ICRC, and international NGOs seeking to model their efforts at global public policy on its example, never sought to claim a role in governance as such.[25]

The success of the landmines ban campaign, however, including the resulting attention from senior leadership of international organizations, convinced theorists of the international NGO movement that it was something more than merely a collection of organizations speaking for themselves.[26] The intellectuals and theorists of the international NGO movement developed an ambitious political and social theory that reconceptualized international NGOs into something politically and ideologically suitable to serve as a partner to public international organizations—the UN—in the service of global governance. This reconceptualization drew upon an old political and social theory in Western intellectual tradition— the theory of civil society—and asserted it as a paradigm at the global level, as "global civil society."[27] The conventional account of global civil society—but also its unconventional, skeptical critique—runs approximately as follows.[28]

Economic globalization has taken place through innovations that have brought down the cost of transportation and, even more dramatically, communications across borders and over long distances.[29] This implies, in the view of many, a corresponding need for political globalization to address the many issues of coordination that arise when economic activities (in the broadest sense of movement of goods, services, capital, and labor) can shift increasingly freely around the world.[30] Political globalization can take either of two main forms, however: a minimalist form and a maximalist form.

The minimalist form says that globalization can be given such regulation as it requires by coordination of sovereign jurisdictions without, however, giving up the essential attribute of sovereignty[31]—a political community, without a political superior.[32] Cooperation and coordination among sovereigns, even entering various political arrangements that would provide for arbitration and rule making in matters as diverse as the environment or public health, can be robust, yet without ever conceding the fundamental attributes of sovereignty: Call this *robust multilateralism*.

The maximalist form says, on the contrary, that globalization requires instead an ultimately federal system in which sovereignty of individual nation states is given up in favor of a central locus of governance that can enforce behavior in the collective interest, rather than a situation of individual countries forever breaking the rules in their immediate self-interest, whether the matter at issue is economic or security or something else.[33] Maximalists ordinarily point to the UN as the forum that should gradually evolve from a forum for multilateral discussion and, sometimes, cooperation and coordination, into a true global government. The term *global governance* is currently favored over the more plain *global government* because, as it became clear throughout the 1990s that nation states were not interested in giving up their sovereignty as such to a global government, theorists of political globalization invented a new theory by which the UN would exercise "governance" without (somehow) actually being the "government."[34]

Even if one is persuaded by the maximalist global governance position (as I am not, but we will leave the objections aside for another day), one must *still* confront the question of legitimacy that, as seen, the UN's own theorists of global governance had to confront. For them, the international NGO movement could provide that legitimacy, the will of the peoples of the world, specifically *democratic* legitimacy, that otherwise seemed both necessary and lacking. But this role also corresponded nicely, in the view of other theorists of international NGOs and global social movements, with the concept of civil society in a domestic society.[35] "Civil society" (which has a very long and, more important, shifting lineage in Western political and social theory)[36] had come to mean, by the 1980s, as theorized especially by intellectuals of the new social movements and dissident writers in such movements as Poland's Solidarity, the "independent sector"[37]—social institutions that were neither the market nor the state, the NGOs, the social movements, citizens groups, religious organizations, some political but many not, which gave meaning and social texture to individuals' lives.[38]

In domestic, liberal democratic society, civil society organizations are free to advocate, organize, argue, debate, and cajole. Ultimately, however, political authorities are accountable *not* to civil society organizations, but instead to citizens who vote in the privacy of the voting booth. The legitimacy of the democratic system depends ultimately upon the free and unconstrained vote of the citizens. Civil society organizations are important to the free flow of information and debate and policy in society, but they are not the guarantor of its legitimacy. In particular, in a domestic democratic society, civil society is immensely important to the robust and intelligent functioning of democracy, especially representative democracy, but civil society is conceived as neither "representative" nor as a necessary political "intermediary" between government and the governed. The ballot box ensures this.[39] Legitimacy in a democracy is given by people raising their hands and voting, not by the presence of citizens or activist groups as civil society, however important they may be to articulating a society's politics.

In the conventional account, global civil society is offered as the global homologue of civil society in a settled domestic society. For several years, this analogy seemed unimpeachable; global civil society would act as civil society does in an ordinary domestic society. It would agitate, advocate, cajole, demand, organize, lobby, and do all the functions of organizations and social movements in a settled domestic society. But whatever else it might be, the UN is not a global democratic institution. Given that the international system—the UN system, the system of global governance— was palpably *not* democratic, then these international NGOs, recast as a matter of ideology as "global civil society," were likewise palpably not the organizations of civil society, at least in the meaning of that term within a domestic, liberal democratic society.

This democratic deficit on the part of the UN, and the corresponding democratic deficit on the part of the NGOs, did not matter much, as long as the aspirations of the players in the system—the governance ideologists of the UN system and their confreres among the international NGOs— did not extend to matters that, on the one hand, were of genuine global importance but, on the other, reached as a matter of governance and law "inside" states, societies, and regimes. The fact that the international system lacked specifically *democratic* legitimacy did not matter so much when the issues presented to the system were either narrowly technocratic or else were matters of mere multilateral negotiation among states, not claims for the UN to govern in its own name.[40]

By the mid 1990s, however, the aspirations of this global system were reaching beyond the legitimacy that could plausibly be said to attach to the earlier system. The UN was seeking to take on governance tasks that quite apparently required much greater legitimacy than the existing system had or could claim to possess, given the available sources of legitimacy—effective delegation from the member states. It was doing so as a strategy of a virtuous circle, leveraging up its legitimacy by leveraging up its governance activities to acquire more legitimacy, and so on, round and round. Moreover, it was *also* being assigned such tasks by powerful nation states (not infrequently including the United States) seeking to offload global obligations from their own shoulders on to it.[41]

Peacekeeping, peace enforcement, weapons of mass destruction anti-proliferation, human rights in an ever-expanding array with reach into individual sovereign states, the security problems of failed and failing states—these issues, especially as they reached inside states, were understood to require greater legitimacy than the multilateral system of member states the UN offered. This legitimacy, to legitimate such governance, required overcoming the so-called "democratic deficit"—a deficit also identified and much debated in the context of the European Union. Indeed, for numbers of global constitutionalists—global federalists of global governance located in European academic and policy centers—the European Union offered the way forward for the world. It had achieved, in the minds of its architects and civil servants, at any rate, democratic legitimacy without all the ordinary trappings of nation state democracy— and the same model could, with sufficient attention, be ramped up to the world as a whole.[42]

In that case, however, legitimacy that was close to democratic legitimacy—ballot box legitimacy—was required, and yet, at the planetary level, not really imaginable. Some dreamers dreamed (and still do) of a "planetary parliament" directly elected by populations around the world.[43] Most others (even many who are otherwise deeply committed to the political ideals of global governance in a globally federal system) accept that planetary democracy in that sense is meaningless and unachievable.[44] Among its many difficulties, it confuses the limits in space and population upon what can be genuinely called a "democracy" with the unlimited, potentially infinitely upwardly scalable networks of a common market.[45] The latter becomes more efficient the larger it becomes; the former breaks down. The world's great democratic societies are trade-offs (sometimes uneasy ones) between the political requirements of democracy, which counsels limits on size, and the economic blessings of an ever-larger common market. But in the search for legitimacy in a system that, imagined for the planet as a whole, is too large for ballot box legitimacy, but which proposes tasks for which the legitimacy is greater than what can be conveyed "upward" by member states to the UN as a multilateral exercise, what is available?

The NGOs, of course, are available. But in that case, the form of analogy with domestic civil society is *not* that of a liberal, democratic, domestic society, but instead one in which, necessarily, the NGOs act in the *absence* of the ballot box. They are therefore treated as a kind of ideological stand-in for democratic institutions. Why does this matter? It matters because under these conditions, this "global civil society" is treated by the international system, by the UN and its administrators and governors and ideologists, as representative and intermediaries of the "peoples of the world" who, however, do not otherwise have a direct vehicle for their expression, as they would in a genuine domestic democracy.[46]

Despite this seemingly enormous conceptual difficulty, this conventional account of global civil society, as the wholesome homologue of civil society in a settled domestic society—particularly in an era in which civil society and its virtues had been extensively theorized, discussed, and praised as a necessary pillar of liberal democratic society—attained tremendous influence. It figured in many speeches at the UN, by UN senior leaders such as Kofi Annan and his chief aides. Kofi Annan, after all, could not have been more explicit when, in 1999, he said that if the "global agenda is to be addressed, a partnership with civil society is not an option;

it is a necessity. I see a United Nations that recognizes...the nongovern-mental organizations' revolution." And NGOs, he added, will give "global civil society its rightful place as one of the pillars of the international community in the twenty-first century."[47]

Likewise, the concept of a global civil society–UN "partnership" figured in many speeches and activities of the world's leading international NGOs, as they celebrated the undeniable achievements of the landmines ban campaign and took from that experience the conviction that they were, indeed, representatives and intermediaries for the peoples of the world. *They*, global civil society, would "democratize" foreign policy and interna-tional relations and bring the peoples of the world into the rarified cham-bers of the UN. And *they*, global civil society, would contribute to the erosion of nation state sovereignty in favor of a progressive form of global governance that would have, at its core, a partnership between the institu-tional UN, as the seat of global governance, and global civil society, which would intermediate on behalf of and represent the world's peoples.

THE CRITIQUE AND THE REACTION AGAINST GLOBAL CIVIL SOCIETY: AFTER SEATTLE (1999–2000)

The critique was always implied in the conventional account. Democratic legitimacy matters. "Corporatist" (to use John Bolton's useful term) forms of intermediation and representation, by well-intentioned, well-positioned NGOs, even if genuine (a questionable assumption, as it turns out), are insufficient to yield the kind of legitimacy for global governance that they claim. Put another way, the UN and the international NGOs were locked in a sort of "lovers' embrace"—eyes only upon each other, each in pursuit of its own ideological goal, but each finding in the other the confirmation of itself and its own very special status. The UN sought to be the seat of global governance; and international NGOs, recast as global civil society, appeared to be able to give it the measure of legitimacy needed. The inter-national NGOs, recast and confirmed by the UN as being intermediaries and representatives of the peoples of the world, thereby had an unques-tioned seat at the table of power. Moreover, the NGOs had a place at the table that required less *actual* expertise and competence at some *actual* activity or mission than before, because, after all, the *representatives* of the world's peoples have a place at the table *because* they are representatives, not because of their technical skills or competences. It really was as though these two were lovers, each gratifying and confirming the other, eyes for each other and no one else, because—as far as each was concerned—each confirmed the worth of the other, without regard for the world beyond.

This love affair went on more or less unchallenged until an event that today (having now experienced 9/11, the Iraq war, the emergence of Al-Qaeda and transnational jihadist terrorism, and much else besides) seems rather quaint. The event was rioting by antiglobalization protestors that brought to a crashing halt to the World Trade Organization trade talks in Seattle, December 1999. Antiglobalization protestors (with the active, profound assistance and coordination, and moral and material support of global civil society) took to the streets and forced the trade talks to shut down. Very quickly, global business interests that had looked upon the global civil society movement with a sort of benign interest (seeing it in precisely the terms offered by it, as a sign of the maturation of a global society, a global demos) began to question precisely those aspects that made the claim of global civil society special: its representativeness and its claims to intermediate. However, it was not merely global business interests that looked with profound dismay at what the rioters and their supporters had wrought. The senior leadership of the UN, including Annan, saw this as a disastrous development, because, indeed, they genuinely saw free trade, if properly managed, as deeply in the interests of the world's poor.

Heretofore, boosters of the idea of global civil society and global governance (as long as it included free trade) such as the *Economist* began to raise serious questions about the elevated political and ideological claims that intellectually transformed international NGOs into global civil society.[48] The skepticism was easy enough to develop. All one had to ask was: Who do these groups actually speak for, anyway?[49] As David Rieff baldly put it: "So who elected the NGOs?"[50] Governments in the developing world—the democratic among them desperate for free trade—acidly noted that these groups purported to speak for peoples, but denied the legitimacy of their governments, even ones that had been democratically elected.[51] Journalist Sebastian Mallaby conducted a celebrated—and reviled—study of the membership of one supposed NGO in Uganda that claimed to have the legitimacy to prevent a dam project with the capacity to bring electricity to vast numbers of people. The NGO in Uganda turned out to have 25 inscribed members.[52]

The international NGOs, under attack and subjected to a wave of unfamiliar skepticism from the long-supportive Western elite press, began to back away from the most extravagant claims to represent peoples and populations—at least when dealing with journalists. The head of Greenpeace UK, for example, gave interviews in which he denied claiming legitimacy to represent anyone except the members of the group itself.[53] Many other organizations adopted the same tack.[54] Yet when it came to demanding, outside the venues of the press, privileges based on the exalted status of global civil society—places in the negotiations of treaties and agreements and so on—the demands remained fundamentally unchanged.

The institutional UN, for its part, reacted with uncertainty. On the one hand, the legitimating role envisioned for global civil society remained unchanged. What else was there to play it? On the other hand, Annan and his senior advisors, in the weeks and months after the Seattle debacle, remonstrated openly with global civil society. Annan, in particular, rather bravely—given that he had declared these groups to be his constituency—

gave multiple speeches directly to NGO conferences and congresses in 2000, telling them flatly that they were wrong about economic globalization and trade. The task before them, he said, was not to prevent globalization, but to make its fruits available to all—a plea to make globalization a positive sum, not a zero-sum game. "We must swim with the currents of our time," Annan said, in one of the most cogent speeches of his career, delivered to a 2000 Millennium Forum of global civil society organizations that, if not personally hostile to him, was broadly hostile to Annan's claim that the problem was not globalization as such, not free trade as such, not the development of global markets as such—it was, instead, to embrace those currents while yet ensuring that globalization not be a zero-sum game between haves and have-nots.[55]

Global civil society, it seemed, had overstated its claims and even politically overplayed its hand. The collapse of the Seattle World Trade Organization trade talks badly damaged the global civil society movement with otherwise broadly sympathetic corporate, business, and many, many government interests, as well as intellectuals and policy experts. It was seen as unruly, anarchic, undisciplined, and often willing to tolerate street violence and thuggish language against economic globalization. In some respects, the institutional UN pulled back from global civil society, feeling pressure from member states—particularly those of the developing world that had hoped for considerable concessions in the trade talks, eventually aiming, they hoped, at reform of the agricultural subsidies of the European Union and the United States that so hobbled the trade opportunities of poor countries.[56]

Yet to a large extent, global civil society continued to have a positive reception at the UN. This was particularly so of global civil society's most presentable, upper middle class, bourgeoisie emissaries—not the violent anarchists of the street, having a good time throwing stones at police and burning down the McDonald's, but instead the high-minded, respectful, respectable faces—those of large, serious, well-funded organizations in the human rights world, development, and humanitarian communities. Respectable—and yet few found their way in Seattle to condemning the violent agitators in the streets. A bit of the upper-middle-class romanticism about radicalism and violence, perhaps, but with them—alongside them as their guarantors and supporters—important foundations with coffers that could augment the apparently (to the international civil servants, anyway) always straitened budgets of UN activities.[57]

Global civil society (its glamour a bit faded as the bearer of global democratic legitimacy, but the only available suitor for the role) remained a "partner" to the UN, in Annan's parlance, while nonetheless receiving a distinctly chillier reception, because, for the UN, the underlying issue of legitimacy remained unchanged and its possible choices constrained. The institutional UN and its leadership—the "modernizers" in the secretary general's offices among the organization's senior executives—remained convinced that the UN-destined-for-global-governance *had* to find a way

around the limited and limiting legitimacy conferred narrowly and jeal-
ously by the member states, and reach directly to the populations of the
world as the UN's legitimating constituency. This became especially clear
in the discussions and arguments between the "traditionalists" and the
"modernizers" in the secretary general's offices in the policy run-up during the early 2000s to Kofi Annan's ill-starred UN Reform Summit in
2005. The UN and global civil society—lovers, still, but no longer out of a
sense of true love, each giving legitimacy and countenance to the other.
The intellectual high-water mark had been crossed, and critical intellectuals were mounting attacks upon the history and concept of the very
idea of global civil society, let alone that it might confer authority upon
the UN as the representative and intermediary of the world's peoples to
their global government.[58]

THE UNITED NATIONS' RETURN TO THE MEMBER STATES
(9/11 AND THE IRAQ WAR)

And then, September 11, 2001. In a moment, the whole debate over the
nature and status of global civil society within the global system seemed
childish and silly. A form of nonstate actor had made its presence known,
but its claims, demands, origins, ideologies, zealotries, and fanaticisms had
very little to do with the nonstate actors that made up global civil society.
Throwing a few stones at policemen and burning a McDonald's with the
police simply not bothering to take action—it all seemed like a form of
recreation for bored Western young people, a way for boys to impress girls
masquerading as a political cause—all quickly forgotten as Western
adolescent games when, instead, the Twin Towers came down. But even
serious, respectable NGOs also found that they no longer occupied
attention in the way they had even after the Seattle debacle. International
NGOs were suddenly swept off the board as political actors. Global civil
society, as an intellectual construct for conveying legitimacy, was suddenly
irrelevant. The nation state was back. If the UN wanted to have a role to
play, it would pay attention to nation states and, above all, to the Security
Council.[59]

    As for the NGOs, well, they could be the camp followers of the nation
states as the Western alliance went to war, or they could stay home. Or
they could issue press releases and studies and reports and statements, as
they preferred or not, but they were no longer at the center of attention.
It was as though global civil society had been, for the UN, a lovely but
temporary dalliance with a mistress; but when reality intruded, the lover
rushed back to his wife, and so the attentions of the UN leadership
returned to the Security Council. This was so even though some of the
leading NGOs, in the human rights field especially, found their work more
in the public eye than ever, as the war on terror began to unfold after
9/11. The run-up to the Iraq war that began in 2003 emphasized even

more the preeminence of nation states and the central importance of the Security Council, especially for the UN senior leadership.[60] When the questions of war and peace were on the table in ways that involved directly the world's great powers, then the NGOs and global civil society seemed small beer, indeed. This was so despite the efforts of global civil society to mobilize large numbers of people in protests against the Iraq war in many countries.[61]

However, the response to the war on terror and the Iraq war illustrated, as well, something that everyone had always known to be true, but that was always glossed over by the apparently politically neutral language of global civil society: Although, in principle, institutions of civil society can include a wide variety of political orientations and, in democratic societies, do, in fact the meaning of the term in the international community is reserved for politically "progressive" organizations, defined in broad terms as a left-wing politics and an orientation toward global governance over merely democratic sovereign governance.[62] The legion academic literature on global civil society largely assumes that it is about the left-wing Human Rights Watch and Greenpeace, not the prolife efforts of the evangelical Christian and Catholic churches, and that it is committed to precisely what the institutional UN sought from it—an *a priori* commitment to the idea of global governance, a preference for the international over the merely national.

The covert narrowness of the received view, however, its politically constrained but apparently neutral view, was exposed not by the presence of some dissident international NGOs that defied the consensus—the National Rifle Association and its global affiliates, for example.[63] It was exposed, instead, by the emergence of transnational nonstate actors of great power and, as it turned out, dismayingly wide appeal in the Muslim world, at least for a time, that owed nothing intellectually or politically to the concept of civil society in relation to the international system. Put another way, after a post–Cold War decade in which global governance was pursued by the UN and global civil society as "international law," it turned out that there *was* a growing form of transnational law, under the radar screen of global civil society and international organizations equally, but with far greater weight, impress, and consequence—and it turned out to be not international law as such, but *shari'a*.[64] One could plausibly argue that *shari'a* law has a considerable claim to be *the* genuine growth industry in transborder global law.

This should give pause, one might think, to democratic liberal progressives who somehow automatically favor the transborder over the merely national, the international and global over the merely parochial sovereignty of the nation state. Global law might indeed grow, but not necessarily a *liberal* one. The reason this does not appear to give concern to progressive forces of global civil society is simply that it, like the UN itself, has largely given up the dream of an international order based around liberal, secular, neutral principles that separate private belief from public conduct in the public square, and has instead embraced religious and ethnic communalism and multiculturalism, rather than the neutral liberalism of individual rights and liberties, as the ideal for managing conflicts among religious and ethnic communities.[65] A world in which the legitimacy of democratic nation states is systematically degraded in favor of a shallow cosmopolitanism, promoted by global civil society, academics, the media, and international institutions, and that, for the sake of the supposed abstract virtue of governance at the global level, is a world that *in fact* empowers simultaneously subnational and supranational religious and ethnic groups over liberal democracy.[66]

Why a world of transborder, "multiculturally managed" cousin loyalties, however, would be a better place—merely because it endorses "global" governance—than a liberal one based around individual human rights and democratic participation in religiously and ethnically neutral states is far from self-evident. Nonetheless, it appears to be what global civil society and the institutional UN have endorsed as the new global ethic in the wake of 9/11 and the Iraq war. Anyone doubting that proposition might take the opportunity to attend the sessions of the "reformed" UN Human Rights Council in Geneva and see how much of its agenda is devoted systematically to replacing liberal concepts of free expression with impeccably multiculturalist ideals of religious communalism, beginning with the proposition that no religion, or at least Islam, shall ever be offended by contrary speech.[67]

WHAT NEXT?

Global governance—as a federal world under the UN, as a global constitutional order, as a political project to correspond to economic globalization of goods, capital, and increasingly labor and services—is stalled. But it is stalled in a peculiar way. The UN is immobilized in a cul-de-sac in which it can neither move forward meaningfully toward that political goal nor give up that overarching political goal in favor of something more modest, achievable, or, frankly, useful, either. Its legitimacy is peculiarly linked to the vision of its glorious future as the seat of global governance, and it seemingly cannot get on with something more functionally important because then the limited legitimacy that it does have is *also* at stake. It is a little like the exiled queen who has lost everything—except the claim to the throne, which justifies everything else and yet precludes her from doing anything different other than being pretender to the throne.

There are, indeed, useful, functional, grayly technocratic things the UN might be doing very well, but that it finds difficult to undertake because, in a certain way, doing them would be beneath its dignity. Doing them would constitute an acknowledgment that the UN will never really be the Parliament of Man, at least not in the grand and glorious sense of global governance. And because of that commitment to the future, too, other actors are skeptical about entrusting the UN with anything they really care about—peacekeeping in some forsaken failed-state hellhole, yes; replacing the Internet Corporation for Assigned Names and Numbers with the UN to regulate the Internet, no—because they understand the deep tendencies of the organization to politicization of even apparently routine issues.[68]

Not surprisingly, the global civil society movement is caught in precisely the same cul-de-sac. It turns out to be both unable to confer the legitimacy that the UN's ideas of global governance require and is also not able to act as "representatives" and "intermediaries" for the peoples of the world, at least not compared with nation states. The more savvy among them have moved to a two-sided, uneasy strategy of publicly abandoning the intellectual pretensions of global civil society and appearing, publicly, to beat a retreat to just being NGOs again. Beat a retreat, that is, from making such grandiose claims of representativeness and gone back to asserting—rightly or wrongly, true or false—their expertise and competence as reasons why anyone should pay attention to them. At the same time, however, international NGOs build on earlier success in creating an atmosphere of "partnership" among global civil society, international institutions, and like-minded states (precisely the formulation drawn out of the success of the landmines campaign) to demand a "seat at the table." The old, and one might have thought, discredited, corporatist claim of representativeness and intermediation continues to operate within the more limited precincts of international organizations—not at the level of deliberations of the Security Council, but in the myriad lower level issues that are the natural fodder of interest groups that have found a way to ally themselves with the UN's institutional interests, and to call it "representativeness" when that suits and "expertise" when it does not.

The ideological argument over global civil society will presumably resonate in the academic and NGO literature for years to come. The model worked out in the 1990s for global civil society continues to operate, with some surface modifications. To accommodate to new sensitivities, the NGOs are no longer announced as "partners," but instead as "norm entrepreneurs" and "transnational advocacy networks." This new terminology tends to obscure what is the same—call it by these terms, and so seek to defang the problems of representation, intermediation, and corporatism, but the moving actor is *still* an ideologically conceived global civil society. The academic literature will thrill for some years yet to analyzing how global civil society is drawing new norms in the international market in ideas and so democratizing and opening the "international community." The academic activist–scholars have difficulty taking on board that this supposed "openness" is actually and essentially a *closed* legitimation circle between global civil society and international organizations. Calling it "entrepreneurship" obscures as much as it illuminates what is the overarching issue of the United Nations and the ideal of global governance—the ongoing, decades-long legitimation crisis.

In any case, however, the world at the time of this writing appears to be moving toward a multipolarity that raises a whole different set of issues, both practical and ethical, with respect to international NGOs, public international institutions, and global governance. What happens when it becomes clear that the superpower, although militarily still the superpower, does not have unlimited resources and powers to be able to impose its will on China or Russia, or on such "resource extraction authoritarian states" as Iran, Venezuela, Saudi Arabia, and so forth, at least within their own spheres of influence and local geographies? Whether that condition will continue to accelerate is unclear—shifts in oil prices, a United States that loses interest in offering a global security guarantee or even a North Atlantic Treaty Organization one, a China that fails to continue achieving legitimacy through growth and sets off serious internal unrest, and so forth—so many contingencies. Yet were this trend to continue, many will celebrate it as the advent of a more "equal," a more "just," a better world. Many will also likely come to regret it, were this truly to come to pass, at least if they also count themselves fans of global governance. Why?

A genuinely multipolar world is, as David Rieff has noted, not a cooperative world but, almost by definition, a competitive one.[69] In that kind of world, states are more important than they ever were when they were under the hegemony of the United States, and there is less room, not more, for cooperation. Competition is not limited to the issues of deep conflict—Georgia, the Taiwan straits—but spills over into seemingly unrelated matters, such as whether the authoritarians of the Security Council, Russia, and China will begin reflexively to oppose initiatives in parts of the world—failed states, for example, in which they have no deep interests, simply for the sake of putting pressure on initiatives sponsored by the rest. Hold up value on otherwise unrelated issues; countries at the UN, after all, thrive on it as a form of rent seeking. Global governance does not have a real place in this world, at least not global governance conceived in its "high church" sense as a federal world under the UN, with the Charter as its constitution. In place of governance, the UN becomes what, on a more realist view, it always was—*at best*, the talking shop of the nations.

One could argue, perhaps, that NGOs in such a world become more, rather than less, influential; but frankly, the opposite argument seems far more persuasive. Global civil society and global governance achieve their maximal ideological appeal and, indeed, political influence when the basic security of much of the planet is taken care of. And that guarantee— provided not by the UN, with the great powers in much greater conflict and (even without great power conflicts as such) free-rider problems endemic to the collective security system, but by a relatively benign hegemon that, in pursuit of its own very broadly conceived security interests, a combination of its ideals and interests—carries the burden of much of the industrialized world's security interests. The cause of global governance, and partnership with global civil society, looks much less attractive when security itself is an issue. Moral exhortation is a lovely but superfluous attribute when what is needed are the big battalions. The NGOs might want to consider prayer to Kant in the name of the categorical imperative, then, that the United States not lose interest or capacity or undertake a calculation of fundamental trade-offs regarding the costs of being the hegemon. The global order that the superpower underpins is the one in which the NGOs swim as fishes in the sea.[70]

It is less clear whether a competitive, multipolar world favors or disfavors global governance conceived as a more limited, more technocratic project. Jettisoning the grand political project of political representativeness and intermediation and legitimacy in any sense cannot hurt in such a world. The attempt to bring together technocrats rather than politicians, and seek only such legitimacy as is required to solve particular problems and presume only such legitimacy as is required for some particular, narrow task at hand seems much the best approach—especially in a competitive, multipolar world. There is much to recommend the narrow technocratic approach, *provided* (of course) that it never gets above itself and begins to believe that the legitimacy of technocrats for discrete, reasonably apolitical functions can somehow be built up into some ideologically, politically grander structure.

There *is* no grander structure. Coordination among democratic sovereigns in robust multilateralism is the most that can, and should, be sought in the way of political globalization. It does not satisfy the vast imaginations for those that only the grandiosity of the Parliament of Man can satisfy. It promotes the UN-of-Less-Visibility and not the UN-of-Rock-Stars. It is resolutely state-centric and sovereign. It does not give NGOs a special place in the global firmament and certainly grants them no special legitimating authority. It treats them as what they are: private philanthropists. It is not a bad thing to be; it is a good and necessary role in the world. However, their ethical status does not include representation or intermediation—something that ought to be understood within and without the UN; give up the love affair, because it finally damages both parties. Robust multilateralism, for its part, as a model of governance, at least, has the possibility of effectiveness in particular matters for particular people and particular places. Taken together, enough of them, they make up the globe. The ethics of global governance, in other words, ought finally to include the acknowledgment that although there are international NGOs, there is no global civil society.

Notes

1. See, for example, Dani Rodrik, "Governance of Economic Globalization," in Joseph S. Nye and John D. Donahue, eds., *Governance in a Globalizing World* (Washington, D.C.: Brookings, 2000), p. 347.

2. As old as Isaiah 2:4 or Alfred Lord Tennyson's *Locksley Hall* (1837) and its rhapsodizing of the Parliament of Man. For a discussion of the dream of global governance as platonic ideal, see Paul Kennedy, *The Parliament of Man: The Past, Present, and Future of the United Nations* (New York: Random House, 2006); for a

highly critical discussion of the ideal of global governance as found in Kennedy's book, see Kenneth Anderson, "El Pasado Como Prologo: El Futuro Glorioso y el Turbio Presente de las Naciones Unidas," *Revista de Libros* 143 (November 2008). English language download available at papers.ssrn.com/sol3/papers.cfm?abstract_id=1265833 (July 22, 2010).

3. See Margaret E. Keck and Kathryn Sikkink, *Activists beyond Borders: Advocacy Networks in International Politics* (Ithaca, N.Y.: Cornell University Press, 1998) for the best-known account from the 1990s.

4. I borrow Francis Fukuyama's useful definition in *After the Neocons: America at the Crossroads* (New Haven, Conn.: Yale University Press, 2006), p. 7.

5. Perhaps most famously, Columbia Law School international law scholar Louis Henkin noted: "For legal purposes at least, we might do well to relegate the term sovereignty to the shelf of history as a relic of an earlier era...[it] is not a necessary or appropriate external attribute for the abstraction called a state." Louis Henkin, *International Law: Politics and Values* (New York: Springer, 1995), pp. 9–10.

6. President George H. W. Bush, "Toward a New World Order," speech of September 11, 1990. See George Bush and Brent Scowcroft, *A World Transformed* (New York: Knopf, 1998).

7. Human Rights Watch/Middle East Watch, *Genocide in Iraq: The Anfal Campaign Against the Kurds* (New York: Human Rights Watch, 1993), www.hrw.org/reports/1993/iraqanfal (July 22, 2010). My own contribution to this research, as a field researcher for Human Rights Watch in Iraq in 1991, was published as *The Destruction of Koreme* (New York: Human Rights Watch, 1992). For the definitive account of the use of chemical weapons in Iraq, see Joost Hiltermann, *A Poisonous Affair: America, Iraq, and the Gassing of Halabja* (New York: Cambridge University Press, 2007). My review can be found in Kenneth Anderson, "America, Iraq, and Poison Gas," *Times Literary Supplement* (July 9, 2008), entertainment.timesonline.co.uk/tol/arts_and_entertainment/the_tls/article4302201.ece (July 22, 2010).

8. Derek Chollet and James Goldgeier provide a superb account of the Clinton administration's foreign policy in all these matters in their *America Between the Wars: 11/9 to 9/11* (New York: PublicAffairs, 2008).

9. See Kenneth Anderson, "Illiberal Tolerance: An Essay on the Fall of Yugoslavia and the Rise of Multiculturalism in the United States," *Virginia Journal of International Law* 33 (1993), pp. 385–431. The suggestion that post hoc tribunals were being offered as an alternative to actual action was not a message anyone wanted to hear at that time, as I discovered whenever I raised this among human rights groups, funding foundations, academics, or government officials.

10. I speak in this section from my personal experience as director of the Human Rights Watch Arms Division from the inception of the landmines ban campaign and the formation of the International Campaign to Ban Landmines.

11. For one of the early manifestos of the movement, see Kenneth Anderson, Stephen D. Goose, Monica Schurtman, and Eric Stover, eds., *Landmines: A Deadly Legacy* (New York: Human Rights Watch/Physicians for Human Rights, 1993). An encyclopedic volume in the beginning days of the campaign, it laid out the basic propositions behind a ban treaty as well as the role of a wide range of international NGOs in pursuing it.

12. The U.S. military's approach to landmines and the campaign—sympathetic to the general humanitarian goal, but convinced both that new technologies would solve the problem and that, in any case, the situation of international border-

guarding landmines were indispensable to the peace and security of the Korean peninsula—is discussed in Kenneth Anderson, "The Role of the United States Military Lawyer in Projecting a Vision of the Laws of War," *Chicago Journal of International Law* 4 (Fall 2003), pp. 445, 448–453.

13. For an account of the landmines campaign that argues both for the special role of NGOs, but also for the special role of Canada as facilitating the special role of NGOs, see Maxwell A. Cameron, Robert J. Lawson, and Brian W. Tomlin, eds., *Walk without Fear: The Global Movement to Ban Landmines* (Toronto: Oxford University Press, 1998), particularly chaps. 19–21.

14. This was the view of what came eventually to be known by political scientist and senior UN advisor John Ruggie's terminology—the *traditionalists* within the secretariat who saw the legitimacy and authority of the UN as a function of the member states, and the *modernizers* who saw the need to go beyond, or indeed around, the member states and reach directly to legitimacy with global populations, including through and intermediated by the international NGOs. This internal argument, within the secretariat, is discussed in James Traub, *The Best Intentions: Kofi Annan and the UN in the Era of American World Power* (New York: Farrar Strauss Giroux, 2006), p. 383.

15. The notion of legitimacy used in this essay is not intended to be a highly technical one, because the subject is too complicated of its own. It is used here in the loosely Weberian sense that "action, especially social action which involves a social relationship, may be guided by the belief in the existence of a legitimate order." Max Weber, *Economy and Society: An Outline of Interpretive Sociology*, edited by Guenther Roth and Claus Wittich. (Berkeley: University of California, 1978), vol. 1, p. 31. I do not commit myself here to any deeply technical sense of the term, and broadly speaking this essay subscribes to the generally understood idea of legitimacy as "widespread belief in a system of governing institutions. . . . Legitimacy denotes the positive evaluation and acceptance enjoyed by a system of power and its bearers." John Keane, *Public Life and Late Capitalism: Toward a Socialist Theory of Democracy* (Cambridge: Cambridge University Press, 1984), pp. 224–225. Specifically with regard to legitimacy and law in the contemporary United States, see the fine article by Alan Hyde, "The Concept of Legitimation in the Sociology of Law," *Wisconsin Law Review*, 1983, p. 379.

16. Indeed, the very term "peoples," as used in the Charter preamble, raises questions all its own, as distinguished from, for example, "We the people of the world."

17. There was, indeed, a movement, in part among academics and in part among activists, for a global parliament. Proposals for its composition were sometimes modeled on the European parliament and sometimes expressed the view that its membership should consist of . . . representatives of international NGOs. It was an idea that was given a veneer of public international respectability during the 1990s by appearing in a report of global "big names." Commission on Global Governance, *Our Global Neighborhood: Report of the Commission on Global Governance* (Oxford: Oxford University Press, 1995). Most theorists, however, even those of impeccable liberal internationalist persuasion, found this a bridge too far, then and now.

18. Annan's rhetoric on this theme became more rhapsodic and ever more attuned to adulation of the international NGOs to a crescendo in 1999 and 2000. The Seattle riots and collapse of the trade talks in 1999 created what might best be described as great cognitive dissonance for Annan in relation to the

international NGOs and new transborder social movements, and 9/11, as the text discusses later, was a game changer, as it were, in Annan's attentions.

19. This is explicitly Maxwell A. Cameron's argument in his essay "Democratization of Foreign Policy: The Ottawa Process as a Model," in *To Walk without Fear*, (New York: Oxford University Press, 1998), pp. 424–447, which appeared at the high-water mark of theorizing of international NGOs as the interlocutors of states and international organizations in a new form of "democratized" global governance in 1998.

20. As Eric Posner notes in *The Perils of Global Legalism* (Chicago: University of Chicago Press, 2009), pp. 62–64, the final results of the landmines movement might be as readily explainable by the traditional realist hypothesis that medium-size and middle-power states, such as Canada, in effect supported and brought the Ottawa Treaty about because, as with many other initiatives in international law, it supported their power positions by using rhetorical tools to bind the superpower. The NGOs were not irrelevant in this process, but it is mostly explainable by state-centric mechanisms, not some grand theory of international politics and law.

My own view, as an insider and academic of that process, is that the international campaign to ban landmines would not have achieved a widely accepted treaty—certainly not in so short a time—had the government of Canada not decided to make it Canada's foreign policy objective of the later 1990s. I do not slight the campaign in saying that Canada's decision essentially to turn its entire worldwide diplomatic apparatus over to the NGO campaign gave access and lines of communication that otherwise would have made the campaign perhaps one of those unending but never quite "closing" campaigns. Canada's actions, however, although compatible with its own vision of itself as the "moral" internationalist, are also compatible with what, in those years, was widely seen as the interests of middling powers to constrain the United States.

Moreover, the personal ambitions of Canada's foreign minister in those years, Lloyd Axworthy, to win the Nobel Peace Prize, cannot be ruled out. The competition for the Prize among the various "virtuecrats" (Axworthy, Jody Williams, and others) was ugly, at least to me, as someone by then serving as an advisor to a major donor to the landmines campaign and hence both close to the insider competition and yet removed from it; as someone who had moved up the philanthropic food chain from donee to donor, watching the participants distract themselves endlessly with fights over Nobel-prestige and philanthropic resources, all of which each major player believed was their due from a just god. The level of distraction they caused within the broader ban campaign were enough to persuade me that the merest hint of awarding some worthy cause the Prize is probably sufficient to derail it from its mission of goodness.

In any case, we must be clear on what the campaign achieved and did not achieve. The ban treaty has received adherence from a vast number of the world's states, in some cases almost certainly insincerely, but with surprisingly plain rejection by precisely those states that must contemplate fighting a serious war in which losing is a serious possibility—which is to say, among others, the United States, India, Pakistan, China, Taiwan, and all the Middle East—or states with serious issues for the defense of international borders in geographically flat lands, such as the Korean peninsula, where the unilateral removal of landmines could be as profoundly destabilizing as the introduction of deliverable nuclear weapons. It does not detract from the achievement of the treaty to note that it has received almost precisely the adherence that power theories would predict, but not more.

In treaty matters, as the economists teach us, what matters is behavior on the margin. The fact that Germany adheres to the treaty does not really matter because, as Afghanistan demonstrates, Germany does not intend ever to fight, whereas the fact that India does not adhere *does* matter. See Kenneth Anderson, "The Role of the United States Military Lawyer."

21. Among the voluminous literature on "global civil society," the source that stands out is the yearbook series: Helmut Anheier, Marlies Glasius, and Mary Kaldor, eds., *Global Civil Society* (London: Sage, successive years). The series features empirical as well as conceptual articles on global civil society.

22. See Jody Williams, Nobel Prize Speech, 1997, nobelprize.org/nobel_prizes/peace/laureates/1997/williams-lecture.html (July 22, 2010).

23. John Bolton provides a telling practical example of the way in which international NGOs operate in the quasi-alliance among international NGOs, sympathetic middling states, and UN bureaucrats in his description of the fights surrounding the UN's attempts to create a small arms and light weapons control treaty—an effort that, in the hands of gun control NGOs, quickly morphed from a useful attempt to control the rampant spread of light weapons from the arsenals of the former Soviet Union across Africa into a campaign to create an international treaty that would effectively seek an end run around handgun laws in individual states, and the United States in particular. That long-term campaign, and countercampaign, is ongoing, but Bolton, in his memoir of his time in the U.S. State Department and as U.S. ambassador to the UN, offers a revealing view of how NGOs pursued influence in the endless rounds of meetings—"wear the United States down until only its key issues are unresolved, declare it isolated, and then use the sleeplessness and frayed tempers of many late-night sessions to press us to 'join consensus' and avoid 'isolation.'" John Bolton, *Surrender Is Not an Option: Defending America at the United Nations and Abroad* (New York: Simon and Schuster, 2007), pp. 90–92, 91.

24. Martin Shapiro astutely observes (I draw here directly from Anne-Marie Slaughter's description in her superb *A New World Order* [Princeton, N.J.: Princeton University Press, 2004] pp. 9–10), however, that the shift from government to governance marks a "significant erosion of the boundaries separating what lies inside a government and its administration and what lies outside them" with one result being to advantage "experts and enthusiasts" as constituting the two groups outside government itself that have the strongest incentives to participate, as Slaughter notes, in governance. However, Shapiro says, "while the ticket to participation in governance is knowledge and/or passion, both knowledge and passion generate perspectives that are not those of the rest of us. Few of us would actually enjoy living in a Frank Lloyd Wright house." Martin Shapiro, "Administrative Law Unbounded: Reflections on Government and Governance," *Indiana Journal of Global Legal Studies* 8 (2001), p. 369.

25. The ICRC stands, however, in a position slightly different from that of any other international NGO. Indeed, in an important sense, the ICRC *does* have a limited, recognized, treaty-based role in governance in the laws of war. The 1949 Geneva Conventions give juridical recognition to the unique role of the ICRC in conveying neutral humanitarian aid and relief, in convening conferences and treaty negotiations in international humanitarian law, and in acting as the repository of sovereign accessions to the Geneva Conventions. In other words, when it comes to drafting international humanitarian law treaties, the ICRC *does* have a juridical seat at the table, and might well chair it. This privilege has been far from irrelevant

to the ICRC. Not surprisingly, it has been not entirely enthused about the barbarians at the gates, as it were, the hoi polloi of the NGO movement seeking to join negotiations on roughly the same terms. But the ICRC claims to a role in the "governance" of international humanitarian law have always been based on the assertion of its unique neutrality, not, as the text elaborates with respect to the general international NGO movement, representativeness and intermediation.

26. See Kenneth Anderson and Monica Schurtman, "The United Nations Response to the Crisis of Landmines in the Developing World," *Harvard International Law Journal* 36 (Spring 1995), pp. 359–371.

27. The leading statement was given by left-wing British political theorist John Keane, in his influential and impressive *Global Civil Society* (Cambridge: Cambridge University Press, 2003), which drew upon his theoretical work during the previous decade.

28. This is a version of the critical argument offered in Kenneth Anderson and David Rieff, "Global Civil Society: A Sceptical View," in Helmut Anheier, Marlies Glasius, Mary Kaldor, and Fiona Holland, eds., *Global Civil Society 2004/5* (London: Sage, 2005), pp. 26–39.

29. Although the specific facts are now out of date, the argument is as relevant as ever. See Alan Rugman, *The End of Globalization* (New York: Random House, 2000), who argued that much of what is understood as globalization is really the lowering of communications costs, and anything digitized that can be transmitted relying upon such technologies. Things that weigh, and hence have transportation costs associated with them, still have transaction costs of movement, and hence there is a noticeable tendency toward regionalization of such goods.

30. For an excellent introduction to the social theory of globalization, see Malcolm Waters, *Globalization*, 2nd ed. (New York: Routledge, 2001). Waters sets out the sociology relevant to the argument that economic globalization implies some form of political globalization.

31. The argument for coordination among sovereigns as the proper form of political globalization is laid out in Kenneth Anderson, "Squaring the Circle? Reconciling Sovereignty and Global Governance through Global Government Networks," *Harvard Law Review* 118 (February 2005), pp. 1255, 1260–1266. It is also what Francis Fukuyama calls for as the position of the United States after neoconservatism, in *After the Neocons*, pp. 155–180; likewise, Jeremy A. Rabkin, *The Case for Sovereignty: Why the World Should Welcome American Independence* (Washington, D.C.: AEI, 2004). Yet this position is not that far, in principle, from the global government networks approach offered by Anne-Marie Slaughter in *A New World Order*. Much of the difference has to do with where you think the process should, over the long run, wind up—as permanent multilateralism among sovereigns or some sort of gradually emerging, genuinely global governance.

32. Borrowing Lincoln's classic formulation; Abraham Lincoln, "Message to Congress in Special Session" (July 4, 1861).

33. The literature on this proposition is nearly endless. One formulation is Antonio F. Perez, "Who Killed Sovereignty: Or: Changing Norms Concerning Sovereignty in International Law," *Wisconsin International Law Journal* 14 (1996), p. 463. Perez, like many (including me) who started out enthusiastic about global governance and the supposed erosion of sovereignty, over the years has become much, much more cautious.

34. The conceptual machinery behind the terminological shift was given by Wolfgang H. Reinicke, *Global Public Policy: Governing without Government?* (Washington, D.C.: Brookings, 1998).

35. A useful introduction to the historical and contemporary uses of the term is found in John A. Hall, ed., *Civil Society: Theory, History, Comparison* (Cambridge: Polity Press, 1995).

36. See the outstanding work by Marvin B. Becker, *The Emergence of Civil Society in the Eighteenth Century: A Privileged Moment in the History of England, Scotland, and France* (Bloomington: Indiana University Press, 1994).

37. The archives of the critical theory journal, *Telos*, with its emphasis on critical European thought and social theory, especially from Eastern Europe, are vital sources in understanding the evolution of thinking around the concept of civil society as it emerged in the 1980s and '90s.

38. See, for example, Jean L. Cohen and Andrew Arato, *Civil Society and Political Theory* (Boston: MIT Press, 1992).

39. For a fascinating, nonscholarly account of the rise of the ballot box and the secret ballot, see Jill Lepore, "Rock, Scissors, Paper: Your Ballot or Your Life," *New Yorker* (October 13, 2008), p. 90.

40. There is, of course, another possibility altogether—that democratic legitimacy is a red herring that does not matter. On the contrary, on this view, it is merely a front argument from reactionary defenders of sovereignty. Legitimacy does not require democratic participation as such. This is approximately the radical Left view offered by global civil society activist and scholar Alison Van Rooy in *The Global Legitimacy Game: Civil Society, Globalization, and Protest* (New York: Palgrave Macmillan, 2004).

41. For example, see Derek Chollet and James Goldgeier (*America Between the Wars*, pp. 272–275) on the United States seeking to find ways to utilize the UN against terrorism and other issues during the Clinton years.

42. See, for example, Erika de Wet, "The International Constitutional Order," *International and Comparative Law Quarterly* 55 (January 2006), pp. 51–76, particularly the footnotes thereto. Much of this is challenged, with an equally engrossing set of footnotes, in Ernest A. Young, "The Trouble With Global Constitutionalism," *Texas International Law Journal* 38 (2003), p. 527.

43. See, for example, Richard Falk and Andrew Strauss, "Toward Global Parliament," *Foreign Affairs* (January–February 2001), papers.ssrn.com/sol3/papers.cfm?abstract_id=1130417 (July 22, 2010).

44. Anne-Marie Slaughter, for example: "Yet world government is both infeasible and undesirable. The size and scope of such a government presents an unavoidable and dangerous threat to individual liberty. Further, the diversity of the peoples to be governed makes it almost impossible to conceive of a global demos. No form of democracy within the current global repertoire seems capable of overcoming these obstacles" (Slaughter, *A New World Order*, p. 8).

45. Researchers into democracy have noted size and population constraints; smaller along both dimensions makes democracy easier and more likely. See Larry Diamond, *Developing Democracy* (Baltimore, Md.: Johns Hopkins, 1999), pp. 117–160.

46. For many, to be sure, and the NGOs not least among them, this is a feature, not a bug. It is the argument laid out by, for example, David Held and his co-authors in many books and articles—that legitimacy does not require democracy in the ballot box sense, and that legitimacy in the sense of consent can be got by many different mechanisms, including through intermediaries such as global civil society. See, for example, David Held, *Democracy and the Global Order* (Palo Alto, Calif.: Stanford University Press, 1995). See also Diane Otto, "Nongovernmental Organizations in the United Nations System: The

Emerging Role of International Civil Society," *Human Rights Quarterly* 18 (1996), pp. 107–141.

47. One example among a great many: Kofi Annan, "Secretary General Says 'Global People Power' Best Thing for the United Nations in Long Time," Secretary General to World Civil Society Conference (December 8, 1999), *M2 Presswire*, December 9, 1999.

48. For example, "Citizens' Groups: The Nongovernmental Order: Will NGOs Democratize, or Merely Disrupt, Global Governance?" *Economist* (December 11, 1999); "NGOs: Sins of the Secular Missionaries," *Economist* (January 29, 2000), pp. 25–27.

49. For example, the highly regarded policy scholar and former State Department official Thomas Carrothers ("Civil Society: Think Again," *Foreign Policy* [December 22, 1999]), pp. 18–19—and he was not even referring to global civil society, but to the limitations of what one could expect from civil society in newly emerging democracies in such places as Eastern Europe.

50. Rieff raised this charge (and not to wild applause, to say the least) at a conference on child–soldiers at American University Law School in a session I chaired on February 27, 1998, and then followed it up in his widely remarked "The False Dawn of Civil Society" (*The Nation* [February 22, 1999]), pp. 11–16. It was quickly picked up as a talking point by many critics of NGOs.

51. Fareed Zakaria, then managing editor of *Foreign Affairs*, found, after contacting 10 NGOs after the Seattle riots, that "most consisted of 'three people and a fax,'" and expressed the concern that rich world "governments will listen too much to the loud minority" of first world activists and "neglect the fears of the silent majority" in the developing world who would benefit from activities not considered virtuous by the NGOs of the developed world. Justin Marozzi, "Whose World Is It, Anyway?" *Spectator* (August 5, 2000), pp. 14–15.

52. Sebastian Mallaby, *The World's Banker: A Story of Failed States, Financial Crises, and the Wealth and Poverty of Nations* (London: Penguin Press, 2004), pp. 7–8. There is practically a cottage industry among NGO activists responding to Mallaby's charges regarding the situation of this Ugandan dam. See, for example, Lisa Jordan and Peter van Tuijl, eds., *NGO Accountability: Politics, Principles and Innovations* (London: Earthscan 2006), and (critically reviewing the forgoing) Kenneth Anderson, "What NGO Accountability Means—and Does Not Mean," *American Journal of International Law* 103 (January 2009), pp. 170–178.

53. Justin Marozzi, "Whose World Is It, Anyway?," p. 14, quoting Peter Melchett, executive director of Greenpeace UK: "Democratic governments are elected and have democratic legitimacy. Other organizations, such as Greenpeace, The Spectator and the Guardian, do not. We have the legitimacy of our market of who buys us or supports us. I don't claim any greater legitimacy than that, nor do I want it."

54. Alison Van Rooy collects and critiques some of this reaction in *The Global Legitimacy Game*, pp. 64–76.

55. Kofi Annan, Address to the Millennium Forum (May 22, 2000); see discussion in Kenneth Anderson, "Microcredit," *Yale Human Rights and Development Law Journal* 5 (2001), pp. 85, 112–115.

56. UN Deputy Secretary General Louise Frechette remarked in the weeks after the Seattle debacle, for example, that "governments often question nongovernmental organizations' (NGOs) representativeness." Louise Frechette, *M2 Presswire*, January 20, 2000.

57. Few of those private charitable donors, then or now, however, directly gave to the UN, cannily preferring to work in parallel partnership with it, and preferring their own mechanisms of accountability and efficiencies—a telling statement on even what UN boosters such as George Soros think of UN efficiency when it comes to committing their own funds.

58. Intellectuals including me. See, in particular, Kenneth Anderson, "The Ottawa Convention Banning Landmines, the Role of Nongovernmental Organizations, and the Idea of International Civil Society," *European Journal of International Law* 11 (2000), papers.ssrn.com/sol3/papers.cfm?abstract_id=233561 (July 22, 2010).

59. See James Traub, *The Best Intentions*, pp. 156–166.

60. Ibid., pp. 167–187.

61. Veteran peace activist, campaigner, and new social movements theorist Mary Kaldor makes the case for the global social movement against the Iraq war in her *Global Civil Society: An Answer to War* (London: Polity, 2003).

62. A point made long ago by David Rieff, "The False Dawn of Civil Society," *The Nation* (February 22, 1999), pp. 11–16.

63. This is one of the many reasons why the intense debate (in the United States, at least) over domestic gun control efforts under the guise of a UN small arms and light weapons treaty is so important. Among many other things, it is a demonstration of the essential nonneutrality of global civil society as a category in international politics. See David Kopel, Paul Gallant, and Joanne D. Eisen, "The Human Right of Self-Defense," *BYU Journal of Public Law* 22 (2008), p. 43.

64. See, for example, Olivier Roy, *Globalized Islam: The Search for a New Ummah* (New York: Columbia University Press, 2004) and Mark Steyn, *America Alone: The End of the World as We Know It* (New York: Regnery, 2007).

65. I offer more discussion of this in Kenneth Anderson, "Goodbye to All That? A Requiem for Neoconservatism," *American University International Law Review* 22 (2007), pp. 277, 315–319.

66. This being, in effect, the (very) short response to Peter Spiro, *Beyond Citizenship: American Identity after Globalization* (Oxford: Oxford University Press, 2007).

67. The indispensable source of information on a daily basis is UN Watch, at www.unwatch.org/site/c.bdKKISNqEmG/b.1277549/k.BF70/Home.htm (July 22, 2010). See also, Brett D. Schaefer, "Free Speech? Not at the U.N. Human Rights Council" (Washington, D.C.: Heritage, 2007), March 29, 2007, www.heritage.org/Press/Commentary/ed032907b.cfm (July 22, 1010). Even Human Rights Watch, which up until recently has acted as a semiembarrassed apologist for the Council (after having made the mistake of backing it in UN reform negotiations for no better reason, seemingly, than to stick it to John Bolton but, being Human Rights Watch, being unwilling and unable to admit any mistake), has recently begun cautiously criticizing the Council's assault on free expression.

68. See, for example, Jay P. Kesan and Andres J. Gallo, "Pondering the Politics of Private Procedures: The Case of ICANN," *I/S: A Journal of Law and Public Policy* 4 (2008), p. 345. This article is generally sympathetic to the idea of UN agency regulation, but it gives a scrupulously useful account of those who are not.

69. David Rieff, "Concerts and Silly Seasons," *Open Democracy* (February 23, 2007), www.opendemocracy.net/democracy-americanpower/concerts_4380.jsp (July 22, 2010). Here, Rieff is criticizing Michael Lind's idea of a "concert of

power." See Michael Lind, *The American Way of Strategy: US Foreign Policy and the American Way of Life* (Oxford: Oxford University Press, 2006), pp. 171–188.

70. I address these questions in blunt language in "The Past, Present, and Future of the United Nations: A Comment on Paul Kennedy's *The Parliament of Man*" (English language version of essay in the Revista de Libros, November 2008), papers.ssrn.com/sol3/papers.cfm?abstract_id=1265833 (July 22, 2010), and again in my "United Nations Collective Security and the United States Security Guarantee in an Age of Rising Multipolarity," *Chicago Journal of International Law* 10 (2009), p. 55.

9

Toward a Political Theory of Philanthropy

Rob Reich

The practice of philanthropy is as old as humanity. People have been giving away their money, property, and time to others for millennia.[1] What's novel about the contemporary practice of philanthropy is the availability of tax incentives to give money away. The charitable contributions deduction in the United States is less than 100 years old, created by the U.S. Congress in 1917 shortly after the institution of a system of federal income taxation in 1913. Similar incentives built into tax systems exist in most developed and many developing democracies.[2]

More generally, laws govern the creation of foundations and nonprofit organizations, and they spell out the rules under which these organizations may operate. Laws set up special tax exemptions for philanthropic and nonprofit organizations, and they frequently permit tax concessions for individual and corporate donations of money and property to qualifying nongovernmental organizations. In this sense, philanthropy is not an invention of the state, but ought to be viewed today as an artifact of the state; we can be certain that philanthropy would not have the form it currently does in the absence of the various laws that structure it and tax incentives that encourage it.

Contemporary practice, in which philanthropy is structured by a regulatory framework of incentives, is not the norm, but the historical anomaly. Previously, the state protected the liberty of people to make donations of money and property, but did not provide incentives for doing so. Two natural questions arise: Why have such incentives and what is their justification in a liberal democracy?

In fact, the historical practice of philanthropy is littered with instances in which the question that presented itself to the state was how vigorously it should *constrain* the liberty of people to give money away. Public influence obtained through private wealth might be injurious to the state for, by example, threatening the authority of the ruling class. In the *Discourses*, Machiavelli tells the following story about ancient Rome:

> The city of Rome was afflicted by a famine; and as the public magazines were insufficient to supply the deficiency of food, a citizen named Spurius

Melius, who was very rich for those times, resolved to lay in a private stock of grain and feed the people at his own expense. This liberality attracted crowds of people, and so won him the popular favor that the Senate, fearing the evil consequences that might arise from it, and for the purpose of putting an end to the evil before it should grow too great, created, expressly against Spurius, a Dictator, who had him put to death.[3]

The question about constraining the liberty of people to give money away remains with us today. We need only consider debates about estate taxation and campaign finance contributions to realize that the state may have good reasons—reasons founded on justice—to limit the liberty of people to give money away.

We might also point to the U.S. Constitution itself for evidence that in some specific circumstances people should not merely *not* receive a tax deduction for a charitable donation, but should be entirely forbidden from making the donation. The Appropriations Clause of the Constitution—"no money shall be drawn from the Treasury, but in Consequence of Appropriations made by law"[4]—or the so-called Power of the Purse, can be construed to prohibit private donations to federal agencies. Although the clause is invoked to limit what the executive branch can propose and do without congressional authority, it also appears to limit *any* financing of federal agencies except through congressional authorization. "As a consequence of the appropriations requirement," Kate Stith argues, "all 'production' of government must be pursuant to legislative authority, even where the additional production is financed with donations and thus appears costless to the Treasury."[5] To the best of my knowledge, this is indeed our current practice: If a U.S. citizen wishes to make a donation to a federal agency, absent congressional authorization to do so (as with the Smithsonian Institution or the Library of Congress), her only option is to write a check to the U.S. Treasury.

In the United States and elsewhere there have been, and continue to be, reasons to limit the liberty of people to give money away for charitable purposes. I recount these facts simply to show that current practice in the United States in not the historical norm and to convey how unusual, in some sense, current practice actually is.

What rules should govern private charity in a liberal democracy? Consider this simple framework to motivate the question. Assume, first, that there is a private property regime of some type. Assume, second, that there is some kind of income tax. Individuals have private property, in particular some income or wealth, and then they have been duly taxed on it. After being taxed, they have money or property they wish to give away for charitable purposes. What now?

The default position of a liberal democratic state regarding charitable giving, it seems to me, ought to be strict nonintervention: Individuals should possess the liberty to give their money or property away to whomever or whatever they please. Restrictions on that liberty, such as with estate taxation or campaign finance restrictions, stand in need of justification; the state bears the burden of showing why such restrictions are necessary or permissible, consistent with justice. In parallel form, I suggest that incentives for people to exercise their liberty to give their money away also stand in need of justification; the state bears the burden of showing why such incentives are desirable and consistent with justice.

This returns us to my original question: What is the justification for the current practice in the United States and elsewhere of providing tax incentives for citizens to make charitable contributions? Because the tax incentive constitutes a subsidy—the loss of federal tax revenue—it is no exaggeration to say that the United States and other countries currently subsidize the liberty of people to give money away, foregoing tax revenue for an activity that for millennia has gone unsubsidized by the state. The United States has the most generous subsidy structure. Charitable giving in 2008 exceeded $300 billion, costing the U.S. Treasury more than $50 billion in lost tax revenue. Why does the United States do this?

The remainder of this essay lays out and assesses three possible justifications for the existence of tax incentives for charitable giving.[6] I focus special attention on the incentive mechanism currently used in the United States and in many other countries: the charitable contributions deduction, a deduction of charitable gifts from a citizen's taxable income.[7] The first justification is that the deduction is necessary to account for the proper base of taxable income; the deduction, in other words, is no subsidy at all. The second justification is that the deduction efficiently stimulates the production of public goods and services that would otherwise be undersupplied by the state. The third justification links the incentive to the desirable effort to decentralize authority, to some degree, in the production of public goods and, in the process, to support a pluralistic civil society in a flourishing democracy. My references here are chiefly to the practice and regulatory framework of philanthropy in the United States, although I believe my analysis holds more generally for any liberal democracy.

TAX BASE RATIONALE

The first justification rejects entirely the claim that the deduction is a subsidy. The deduction constitutes, instead, the fair or appropriate way to treat the donor; deductibility is *intrinsic* to the tax system. First promulgated by William Andrews, the basic argument is that deducting charitable contributions is necessary to properly define an individual's taxable income.[8] If taxable income is construed, as according to the standard Haig-Simons definition, as personal consumption and wealth accumulation, then charitable donations ought not be included in a person's tax base. The reason is that charity cannot be equated with personal consumption, because charitable gifts redirect resources from private and preclusive consumption to public and nonpreclusive consumption. Andrews concludes that "a deduction should be allowed whenever money is expended

for anything other than personal consumption or accumulation."[9] Tax
scholar Boris Bittker offers a similar argument, concluding that charitable
donations ought not count as consumption because, in making a voluntary
donation, the donor is made worse off (with respect to others at the same
income who do not make a donation), relinquishing use of resources that
could have been directed to personal benefit.[10]

Unlike subsidy justifications, the tax base justification focuses on the
fair treatment of the donor; it does not inquire into the goods produced
with the donation or the efficiency with which these goods are produced.
There are four obvious criticisms to make of the tax base rationale.

First, and at the level of common sense, if a person has legitimate ownership of resources and can rightfully decide how to dispose of those
resources, then whatever a person decides to do with those resources—
spend it on luxury goods or give it to charity—is, by definition, tautologi-
cally, consumption. Some people have a taste for spending, others for
donating; each brings apparent satisfaction to the respective person.

Second, there are obvious benefits that some, perhaps many or even all,
donors receive in making a charitable contribution. Economist James
Andreoni has attempted to model and measure the motivation of receiving
a "warm glow" or psychological benefit in behaving altruistically.[11] In making a charitable contribution, the donor experiences pleasure in giving
and receives in return for the gift a "warm glow," consuming the benefit of
altruism. A warm glow might be nonpreclusive in that purchasing joy
through a charitable contribution does not diminish the ability of others
to do the same. However, a warm glow is undeniably private rather than
public. Altruism might also be construed as a scarce resource, anyway.
Other economists have demonstrated how much charitable giving, especially to elite institutions such as universities, hospitals, and cultural organizations, is motivated by status signaling.[12] Here the motivation to give is
not altruistic, but self-interested—to maintain position or to move up the
social hierarchy. Regardless of motive—altruistic or self-interested—there
are returns to the donor that make it impossible to describe donors as
engaging in behavior that is public and nonpreclusive or that necessarily
makes them worse off. We need not be incorrigible cynics to believe that
donors are purchasing something for themselves when they make a charitable contribution.

Third, Andrews's theory has perverse implications about the permissible recipients of charity according to current law in the United States
and elsewhere. If, for Andrews, anything that is not personal consumption
or accumulation should be deductible from the donor's tax base, then a
billionaire businessman's donation of a million dollars to Wal-Mart, a for-
profit company, to encourage its efforts in union busting, ought to be
deductible. (Assume the businessman holds no stock in Wal-Mart.)
Similarly, a donation to a foreign country or foreign charity where the
donor has no connection and is motivated simply, say, to alleviate poverty,
ought to be deductible. However, U.S. tax law—like the tax regimes of

most of other countries——excludes donations of both kinds. In the United States, to qualify for a deduction, charitable donations must be directed to a qualifying so-called 501(c)(3) nonprofit organization that is registered by the Internal Revenue Service.

Finally, and moving from theoretical conceptualization to empirical fact, even the briefest reflection on philanthropy in the real world reveals how donors quite frequently purchase with their charitable dollars rival and excludable goods for which they are among the primary consumers. Contributions to one's religious organization are an obvious example; churches provide club goods rather than public goods or, to put it differently, they are more like mutual benefit rather than public benefit organizations.[13] Charitable gifts to arts organizations for which one receives, in return, premium seats, special access, private tours, and so on, are another example. Charitable gifts to one's child's public school may also deliver improved educational opportunities or outcomes for one's child, not to mention boosting the value of one's house as a result of the fact that public school quality and real estate values are correlated.[14]

On top of these criticisms can be added still another that is more fundamental. I refer to the argument expounded by Thomas Nagel and Liam Murphy that the choice of a tax base cannot be assessed in the absence of the larger normative consideration of what constitutes social and economic justice.[15] The definition of taxable income is strictly instrumental on their view; the tax system is just a mechanism for pursuing larger social aims. "Since justice in taxation is not a matter of a fair distribution of tax burdens measured against a pretax baseline, it cannot be important in itself what pretax characteristics of taxpayers determine tax shares."[16] As a result, there is, for Nagel and Murphy, no such thing as intrinsic fairness of the tax system or tax base, but only taxation that is an instrument in realizing or pursuing the aims of a larger theory of social and economic justice.

Their argument is built on the claim that private property is a convention of the legal system. Property rights are not preinstitutional or prepolitical, but rather a consequence of a set of laws that form part of a broader theory of justice. Consequently, pretax income does not count automatically as a person's own money, and without the notion of a pretax baseline of income, there can be nothing intrinsic about the selection of a fair tax base.[17] It is nonsense, then, to argue that charitable contributions ought to be deducted from one's taxable income, because such deductions logically belong to the identification of the appropriate tax base.

I accept the Nagel and Murphy thesis, but will not attempt to defend it here except to note that, whatever its merits, it locates the argument on the appropriate intellectual terrain: argument about social and economic justice. No one deserves a tax break for a charitable contribution simply in virtue of some account of a person's tax base. Tax incentives for giving, if they are to be justified, find their justification in a larger account of social justice for which the tax system is just an instrument.

SUBSIDY RATIONALE

The more typical defense of the charitable contributions deduction—and one that does, even if sometimes only implicitly, take into account a broader theory of social and economic justice—is that the state accomplishes something of important social value by providing subsidies for people to be charitable. The state provides incentives for charity because it is believed that the incentives stimulate the production of something of greater social value than what the state could have produced on its own, had it not offered the incentives.

The subsidy therefore counts as a tax expenditure, the fiscal equivalent of a direct spending program.[18] When the state allows citizens to deduct their charitable contributions from their taxable income, the state foregoes tax revenue, which is to say that all taxpayers are affected. They are affected in (at least) two important ways. First, they stand to lose some portion of the benefit they receive from direct governmental expenditures. If every citizen gains some fraction of the total revenue of the federal budget, the loss of billions of dollars in tax revenue through the deduction lowers every citizen's fractional benefit. Second, citizens lose in democratic accountability, for the foregone funds are not accountable, or even traceable, in the way that direct government expenditures are. To give an obvious example, citizens can unelect their representatives if they are dissatisfied with the spending programs of the state; the Gates Foundation also has a domestic and global spending program, in part supported through tax subsidies, but its directors and trustees cannot be unelected.

Thus, the success of the subsidy rationale depends on whether the benefits brought about by the subsidy exceed the costs of the lost tax revenue. Consistent with the Nagel and Murphy thesis, the subsidy is but a mechanism for realizing larger social aims. If these aims are realized, then the subsidy may be defensible.

The subsidy rationale has been invoked in several U.S. Supreme Court decisions, lending the rationale some additional weight. "Both tax exemptions and tax deductibility are a form of subsidy that is administered through the tax system," noted the Court in 1983 in *Regan v. Taxation with Representation*.[19] The deduction has, moreover, been included in the annual federal tax expenditure budget issued by the U.S. government.

What's obvious about the subsidy rationale is that it shifts attention from the fair treatment of the donor to the recipient of the donation and the good that is done with the gift. Even so, the particular vehicle used in the United States to provide the subsidy—a deduction from taxable income— is vulnerable to powerful criticisms that keep a focus on fair treatment of the donor. First, the deduction is available only to itemizing taxpayers, a group that constitutes roughly 30% of all tax returns. The other 70% of taxpayers, although they may make substantial charitable contributions (as an absolute sum or percentage of income), are excluded because they take the standard deduction. Thus, the subsidy is capricious, for its availability depends on a characteristic—one's status as an itemizer—that has nothing whatsoever to do with the value of giving. If the subsidy is justified because it produces some social good, then why should two donors who make identical donations to identical organizations, ostensibly producing the identical social good, be treated differently by the tax code?

Second, in a system of progressive taxation, the deduction is tied by definition to marginal tax brackets. The richer you are, the less a charitable contribution actually costs you. The deduction functions as an increasingly greater subsidy and incentive with every higher step in the income tax bracket. Those at the highest tax bracket (35% in the United States in 2008) receive the largest deduction; those in the lowest tax bracket (10%) receive the lowest deduction. Scholars have dubbed this the "upside-down effect," the result of which is that, for charitable deductions, "the opportunity cost of virtue falls as one moves up the income scale."[20]

However, these concerns do not constitute criticism of the Nagel-Murphy thesis, for these are not criticisms of the subsidy rationale per se. They are criticisms of the mechanism, currently in use in the United States and in many other countries, to deliver the subsidy, the tax deduction. Reform of the subsidy mechanism could eliminate or mitigate the problems. For example, the deduction could be extended to all taxpayers regardless of itemizer status; or the deduction could be eliminated in favor of a partial or total tax credit; or the incentive could come, as in the United Kingdom, in the form of so-called "gift aid," where the states matches some portion of an individual's charitable donation to an eligible organization; and so on.

How, then, might we assess the subsidy rationale as a whole? One obvious way to evaluate the subsidy rationale, rather than just the subsidy mechanism currently in use, is to look to the social good the subsidy produces and the efficiency with which it is produced.

Supposing that the goods produced by charitable recipients were of social value, we might ask, for instance, whether the subsidy is so-called "treasury efficient." Does the subsidy shake off more in donations than it costs in federal tax revenue? If so, the subsidy is treasury efficient. Economists will then argue about the optimal rate of the subsidy, or how to stimulate the most giving for the least cost to the treasury. Empirical analyses of the tax deduction in the United States show that the deduction is indeed treasury efficient, although significantly less so than initially was thought.[21]

Although treasury efficiency assures us that the subsidy is not a mere reward for charitable giving that would occur even in the absence of the subsidy—a loss of federal revenue to produce something that would occur anyway—its success depends very much on the initial supposition that the goods produced by charitable recipients are of broad social value.

When we inquire into the social good produced by charitable donations, rather than focusing squarely on questions of treasury efficiency, three problems present themselves, at least in the U.S. context.

First, U.S. law permits a truly kaleidoscopic landscape of public charities to receive tax-deductible charitable contributions.[22] Some, and perhaps many, of the social goods produced by charities will be of no value whatsoever to certain citizens. Because churches are eligible to give tax deductions to donors (for example, congregants) for contributions, atheists are vicarious donors to churches through the tax subsidy. In contrast, Catholics are vicarious donors to Planned Parenthood and its support for abortion rights. Such examples are easily multiplied. The basic point is that the subsidy cannot be justified as a Pareto improvement, where some benefit and no one is made worse off.[23] At best, the subsidy is a Kaldor-Hicks improvement, where the gains for those who consume the particular social good produced by charity offset the losses to those with no interest in that social good.

However, relying on a Kaldor-Hicks improvement as the standard for justifying the subsidy rationale raises a second set of problems. For obvious reasons, the beneficiaries of a deduction are highly skewed toward upper income earners. Wealthier individuals donate more as an absolute amount (but not as a percentage of income) and receive a larger subsidy for giving (the upside-down effect) and claim, as a result, a staggeringly large share of the deduction. (Those making $200,000 and more received 30% of all deductions for charitable contributions; those making $75,000 and more claim more than 65% of all deductions.[24]) The result is a plutocratic bias in the subsidy, where the favored beneficiaries of the wealthy receive the lion's share of the subsidy.

The plutocratic bias is troubling, for systematic overattention to the interests and preferences of the wealthy against the interests and preferences of the middle class and poor seems a strange, indeed unjust, basis for social policy. However, the trouble might be undercut if the product of charitable giving were pure public goods, in the economic sense—namely, goods that are nonexcludable and nonrivalous. If wealthy people donate to create goods that no one can be prevented from enjoying and that one person's consumption does not reduce the amount available to others, then the plutocratic bias nevertheless redounds to the advantage of all citizens. However, the vast majority of public charities do not produce pure public goods. Hospitals and universities, for instance, together account for more than half the revenue of all nonprofit organizations in the United States. Both hospitals and universities can easily exclude persons who cannot pay for their services.

Leaving aside the strict conditions of pure public goods, the concern about plutocratic bias might be mitigated if the favored beneficiaries of the charitable givers, and the wealthy especially, were charities engaged in social welfare or services for the poor. At the very least, then, the effect of charitable giving would be, to some degree, redistributive. Unfortunately this is not the case, at least in the United States. And this is the third problem with the subsidy rationale. (See figures 9.1, 9.2, and 9.3.) More than half of all individual giving in the United States goes to religion, and none of this money goes to the faith-based charities associated with religious groups. Those offshoots of religious organizations have been counted in the relevant category of public/social benefit organizations, which receive less than 6% of all charitable giving.[25] If we focus squarely on the favored beneficiaries of the wealthy, we see that cultural organizations, hospitals, and universities are the usual recipients. Sometimes these gifts have redistributive benefits (for example, scholarships for the poor); sometimes not. The best economic analysis of the redistributional nature of the charitable sector concludes, optimistically I think, that "no overarching conclusions about distributional impact can be made" and that, although "in no subsector is there evidence that benefits are dramatically skewed away from the poor and toward the affluent," there is also evidence "that relatively few nonprofit institutions serve the poor as a primary clientele."[26]

One final point. Suppose, now, that charitable donations were redistributive in the sense that gifts from the relatively wealthy flowed to the relatively poor. Granting this, we may nevertheless not yet conclude that nonprofit organizations and foundations are in fact redistributive all things considered, because we must still account for the tax concessions to philanthropy and the counterfactual scenario in which the money flowing into nonprofit organizations and foundations would have been taxed and become public revenue. The relevant question is not merely, "Is philanthropy redistributive?" but rather, "Do philanthropic dollars flow more sharply downward than government spending does?" In order for the return, so to speak, on the public's investment in philanthropy to be worthwhile, philanthropy must do better than the state would do had it taxed the philanthropic assets.

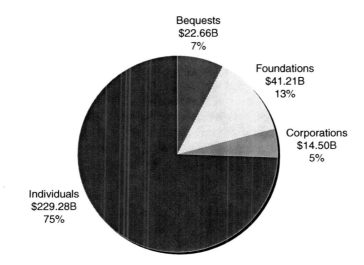

Figure 9.1 2008 U.S. Contributions: $307.65 billion by source of contribution.

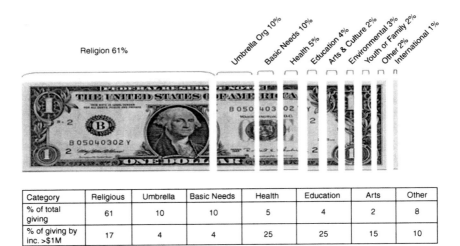

Category	Religious	Umbrella	Basic Needs	Health	Education	Arts	Other
% of total giving	61	10	10	5	4	2	8
% of giving by inc. >$1M	17	4	4	25	25	15	10

Figure 9.2 Donor Allocations.
Source: Center on Philanthropy, "Patterns of Household Charitable Giving," report prepared for Google Inc. (Center on Philanthropy, Indiana University, Indianapolis, Ind., 2007), www.philanthropy.iupui.edu/research/ giving%20focused%20on%20meeting%20needs%20of%20the%20poor%20july%202007.pdf, based on Center on Philanthropy's Panel Survey/Panel Survey of Income Dynamics 2005 data.

Answering this counterfactual question is difficult. We are forced to speculate about how the state might spend the tax revenue it could have collected if it hadn't extended the tax concessions to philanthropists for their gifts.[27] I will not make any such speculation here. Instead, I wish to note that anyone who seeks to ground the special tax treatment of philanthropy in the United States on the sector's redistributive outcomes must confront at least three reasons to be suspicious that any such redistribution actually occurs. There is the first and obvious difficulty that a motley assortment of nonprofit groups all qualify for 501(c)(3) status, puppet theaters and soup kitchens alike. There is the second difficulty that religious groups dominate as the beneficiaries of individual charitable dollars. And there is the third difficulty that the burden on the sector's advocate is to show not merely that philanthropy is redistributive, but also that it is more redistributive in its actions than would be the government. In short, we have some good *prima facie* reasons to doubt that philanthropy is redistributive in effect or eleemosynary in aim.

These problems once again target the mechanism in the United States and elsewhere to deliver the subsidy: the tax deduction. The plutocratic bias in the subsidy and the lack of redistribution could be altered by changing both the mechanism of the subsidy (change to a capped tax credit, for instance) and limiting the kinds of organizations that are

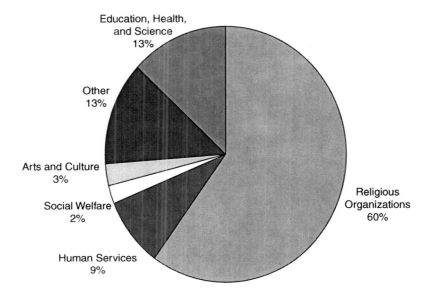

Figure 9.3 How Individuals Distribute Their Charitable Dollars.
Source: Rob Reich, "A Failure of Philanthropy: American Charity Shortchanges the Poor, and Public Policy Is Partly to Blame," *Stanford Social Innovation Review* (Winter 2005), pp. 24–33.

permitted to receive tax-deductible donations (eliminating churches and elite cultural organizations, for instance). Whatever the remedy, the expectation would be that the subsidy must still be *efficient*. To be justified, the subsidy must cost less to the treasury than it produces in social benefits.

I shall not explore these sorts of remedies here. Instead, I turn now to an alternative rationale that does not displace the subsidy rationale but drops the necessity that the subsidy be an efficient use of tax dollars in producing certain social goods.

PLURALISM RATIONALE

The pluralism rationale comes in several stripes and cannot be called a unified theory. The basic idea is that the tax incentive to make charitable donations should not be justified on the basis of assessing the discrete social goods, or outputs, of the various nonprofit organizations funded through these donations. Instead, the tax incentive is justified for its role in stimulating or enhancing the voice of citizens in the production of a diverse, decentralized, and pluralistic associational sector, which is in turn thought to be a bedrock of a flourishing liberal democracy. If nonprofit

organizations are the institutional face of associational life, then stimulating charitable donations to a wide array of nonprofits might amplify the
voice of citizens and enhance civil society to the overall benefit of liberal
democracy. Rather than focus on the matrix of goods produced by charitable organizations, the focus here is on the creation and sustenance of a
diverse slate of organizations themselves. The public good or social benefit
being produced is civil society itself, not the catalogue of public goods or
benefits produced by the roster of organizations that constitute civil
society.

Note that this is still a subsidy theory, but there is no necessary demand
that the subsidy be treasury efficient. Even if there is a net loss to the
treasury in the production of the social goods generated by nonprofit
organizations—if the state could more efficiently deliver these goods
itself—the pluralism rationale holds that the subsidy is nevertheless
worthwhile. Of course, there is no bias against the efficient production of
goods, but the pluralism rationale does not demand efficiency for the success of the argument. The state might justifiably forego tax revenue for
the sake of fostering citizen's voices and the sustenance of a pluralistic
associational sector.

Before elaborating the pluralism rationale in greater detail, consider a
few worries about the pluralism rationale. First, vigorous safeguarding of
liberty is typically thought to be the institutional guarantee for associational life. Is it really necessary to subsidize the exercise of liberty to produce a vibrant civil society? There was no charitable contributions tax
deduction when Tocqueville toured the United States, after all.

Second, the defender of the pluralism rationale has to answer to the
disturbing historical record about associational life throughout the past
century. It is no exaggeration to say that the rise of nonprofit organizations
in the United States and the use of the charitable contributions deduction
coincides with the *decline* of civic engagement and associational life,
at least if the Robert Putnam–inspired literature is to be believed. The
existence of professionally run nonprofit organizations may have contributed to the calcification of civil society.[28]

If U.S. taxpayers have spent hundreds of billions of dollars in tax expenditures to support charitable giving during the past generation, we might
ask whether this has stimulated an improvement in civil society that
would not have happened absent the subsidy. I do not hazard any such
guess here. Perhaps the decline in civic engagement and associational life
is less than it would have been in the absence of the subsidy. Whatever the
actual fact, the empirical case that the subsidy has improved civil society,
or lessened its decline, has (to my knowledge) not yet been made.

So what, then, is the case for the pluralism rationale in support of subsidizing charity or philanthropy? I believe the rationale has two main
ideas: decentralizing the process of producing social goods, and promoting
the pluralism of associational life and diminishing state orthodoxy in
defining its contours.

These ideas are captured in a U.S. Supreme Court opinion from Justice Lewis Powell, where he takes issue with the notion that the purpose of the nonprofit sector is to deliver or supplement services or social goods efficiently that the government would otherwise supply through direct expenditures. Powell rejects the view that

> the primary function of a tax-exempt organization is to act on behalf of the Government in carrying out governmentally approved policies. In my opinion, such a view of 501(c)(3) ignores the important role played by tax exemptions in encouraging diverse, indeed often sharply conflicting, activities and viewpoints. As Justice Brennan has observed, private, nonprofit groups receive tax exemptions because "each group contributes to the diversity of association, viewpoint, and enterprise essential to a vigorous, pluralistic society." Far from representing an effort to reinforce any perceived "common community conscience," the provision of tax exemptions to nonprofit groups is one indispensable means of limiting the influence of governmental orthodoxy on important areas of community life.[29]

In a diverse society, there will be heterogeneous preferences about what kinds of social goods to supply through direct expenditures of tax dollars. Democratic mechanisms for deciding how to allocate these dollars are, of course, one fundamental means of dealing with heterogeneous preferences. The preferences of the median voter assume a large, if not wholly determinative, role here. But another potentially important means is to decentralize the authority for deciding what kinds of social goods are produced and to permit, indeed to enhance, citizen voice in this process by providing a subsidy for that voice. Tax incentives for charitable giving represent, on this view, an effort to stimulate every citizen to cast his or her own preferences, in the form of dollars, about their favored social goods into civil society, where the resulting funding stream is partly private (from the donor) and partly public (from the tax subsidy).

The result is that citizen groups that cannot muster a majority consensus about a particular social good provision through the regular democratic political process will still have a tax-supported means to pursue their minority or eccentric goals. Associational rights would guarantee every citizen the liberty to join with others to pursue dissenting or conflicting visions of the public good or the production of social goods; the justification for subsidizing this liberty through tax incentives is to enhance or amplify every citizen's voice, stimulate their contributions to civil society, and assist minorities in overcoming the constraints of the median voter. Philanthropy becomes a means of voting for one's favored civil society projects with dollars partially private and partially public.[30]

Note, here, that concerns about the redistributive nature of charitable dollars have receded from view. When the justification for tax incentives for philanthropy run along the pluralist line, philanthropy is not, at least in the first instance, about assisting the poor or disadvantaged; it is, instead, about protecting and promoting a flourishing and pluralistic civil society.[31] If citizens should wish to fund nonprofit organizations that provide social services to the poor or disadvantaged, they can certainly do so, but these preferences would not be privileged against, say, preferences for cultural organizations such as museums or opera.

I believe this pluralism rationale has merit, and that it may indeed supply reason to subsidize the liberty of people to give their money away for charitable or philanthropic purposes. But however compelling the pluralism rationale may be, it cannot be said to sit behind the current design of tax-supported giving in most countries. Providing tax deductions for individuals who make charitable gifts does not honor the pluralism rationale but rather, I think, undermines and makes a mockery of it.

As described earlier, a tax deduction for charitable contributions, when there is a progressive income tax, establishes a plutocratic voice in the public policy. The deduction supplies a greater subsidy to the wealthy, who, of course, already are likely to possess a more powerful voice in the political arena without any subsidy whatsoever. If the tax incentive for charitable giving is designed as a deduction from taxable income, many people are denied voice entirely (because they do not itemize their deductions) and wealthier citizens claim far more of the subsidy than others. The consequence is a troubling plutocratic bias in

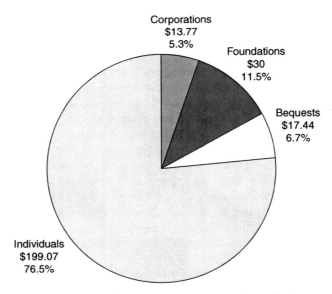

Figure 9.4 2005 Contributions: $260.28 billion by source of contributions.
Source: Melissa S. Brown, *Giving USA 2006: The Annual Report on Philanthropy for the Year 2005* (Glenview, Ill.: Giving USA Foundation, 2006).

the contours of civil society, systematically more nonprofits favored by the rich and fewer favored by the poor. We get not egalitarian citizen voice in civil society, but plutocratic citizen voice, underwritten and promoted by tax policy.

What kind of mechanism would better track the pluralism rationale? There are many options, but for the sake of illustration, consider two possible designs: first, a flat and capped nonrefundable tax credit for charitable donations. By offering an equivalent tax credit to all donors (say 25% of any donation) with the credit capped at some level (say $1,000), the mechanism avoids the upside-down structure of the deduction, offers an equal credit to all donors, and, of course, affords donors the liberty to continue to give money away after the cap has been reached, but no longer with any state subsidy to do so. Second, consider the practice of so-called "percentage philanthropy," which has arisen recently in several central and Eastern European countries. In Hungary, for instance, a law passed in 1996 permits citizens to allocate 1% of their income taxes to a qualifying nongovernmental organization. This is not a tax credit, as in the previous example, because Hungarian citizens do not pay less tax. Citizens redirect what would otherwise be state revenue in the form of income taxes to the civil society organizations of their choice. It must be said, however, that there is nothing in this latter scheme that deserves the description "charity" or "philanthropy," for the scheme redirects only tax dollars, not private dollars. Percentage philanthropy does not require any donation of an individual's own after-tax dollars.

CONCLUSION

Although people have engaged in philanthropy for millennia, the practice of giving money away has only recently become a tax-subsidized activity. Philanthropy is now embedded within a framework of public policies, usually centered on the tax regime, that structure its practice and alter its shape from what it would otherwise be without the state's intervention. Although nearly all liberal democracies have tax incentives for charitable donations, the justification for this practice is not well understood or theorized. I have canvassed three distinct justifications for providing tax incentives for philanthropy: a tax base rationale, a subsidy rationale, and a pluralism rationale. Although I find nothing to recommend the tax base rationale, the subsidy and pluralism rationales do offer potentially good reasons to support subsidies for philanthropy. Neither of these latter two justifications, however, provides support for the actual design of most tax-subsidized giving, where a wide array of eligible recipient organizations and a tax deduction for giving are the favored mechanisms. A political theory of philanthropy might offer a defense, or several distinct defenses, of state incentives for giving money away, but the current practice of state-supported philanthropy, especially in the United States, is indefensible.

Notes

1. For example, Paul Veyne's classic *Bread and Circuses* (New York: Viking Penguin, 1990) discusses the practice of *euergetism*—private liberality for public benefit—in ancient Rome; Maimonides codified eight different levels of charity during the 12th century.

2. For an overview of tax incentives for charitable giving across 21 countries, see Lester Salamon and Stefan Toepler, eds., *The International Guide to Nonprofit Law* (New York: Wiley, 1997).

3. Niccolo Machiavelli, *Discourses* (New York: The Modern Library, 1950), p. 493.

4. U.S. Constitution, Article I, § 9, Clause 7.

5. Kate Stith, "Congress' Power of the Purse," *Yale Law Journal* 1343 97 (1988), p. 1357. Stith notes that Congress has passed legislation to permit some federal agencies to receive private donations—among them, National Parks, the National Archive, the Library of Congress, and the Smithsonian. Despite the congressional authorization, Stith believes private funding to be of questionable constitutionality:

> "Where broad executive discretion is inherent in our constitutional scheme, the most questionable form of spending authority is open-ended authority to receive and spend donations and gifts. As long as the executive agency is prepared to accept the donation, Congress loses effective control over the contours of authorized government activity. Where a donor conditions a gift broadly—for instance, for the defense of the United States—the recipient federal agency is able to direct the supplemental funds to activities that might not have garnered congressional approval. Where the donor specifically conditions the gift—for instance, for defense in the Persian Gulf—the donor may effectively specify the objects of government expenditure. In either event, where Congress cannot significantly circumscribe an agency's purposes and powers, to allow the agency to spend all contributions would be to permit private power, subject only to executive discretion, to influence the contours of government and government policy." (pp. 1384–1385)

6. The taxonomy I develop here is neither original nor exhaustive. I have drawn from the literature on the charitable contributions deduction, which is large, unwieldy, and narrow, resting almost entirely within tax law and economics journals. What's remarkable about this literature is how little it engages with normative argumentation about justice. Most theories about the deductions, comments David Pozen, "lack a coherent normative basis." David Pozen, "Remapping the Charitable Deduction," *Connecticut Law Review* 39 (2006), p. 547. Pozen claims, not implausibly, that no justification is possible for the deduction as it currently exists in the United States.

7. Most countries use some kind of deduction scheme, including Australia, Germany, Japan, France, India, Spain, South Africa, Egypt, Mexico, The Netherlands, Russia, and Thailand. To the best of my knowledge, only Sweden provides no subsidy structure at all for charitable giving. The mechanism of an income tax deduction for a charitable donation works by creating a subsidy at the rate at which the donor is taxed. So a person who occupies the top tax bracket—currently 35% in the United States—would find that a $1,000 donation actually "cost" her only $650. The government effectively pays $350 of her donation, subtracting this amount from her tax burden. Similar incentives exist for the creation of private and family foundations, and for contributions to community founda-

tions, where donations and bequests to a foundation are deducted from estate and gift taxation. In permitting these tax incentives, federal and state treasuries forego tax revenue. Had there been no tax deduction on the $1,000 contribution, the state would have collected $350 in tax revenue.

8. William Andrews, "Personal Deductions in an Ideal Income Tax," *Harvard Law Review* 86 (1972), pp. 309–385.

9. Ibid., p. 325.

10. Boris Bittker, "Charitable Contributions: Tax Deductions or Matching Grants?" *Tax Law Review* 28 (1972), pp. 37–63.

11. James Andreoni, "Impure Altruism and Donations to Public Goods: A Theory of Warm-Glow Giving," *Economic Journal* 100 (1990), pp. 464–477.

12. Amihai Glazer and Kai Conrad, "A Signaling Explanation for Charity," *American Economic Review* 86 (1996), pp. 1019–1028; William Harbaugh, "Prestige Motive for Making Charitable Transfers," *American Economic Review* 88 (1998), pp. 277–282.

13. Some people mistakenly believe that gifts to religious organizations do in fact provide public goods, because many congregations are thought to provide extensive social services. The best available evidence about the use of donations to churches does not bear this out. Sociologist Robert Wuthnow, who writes admiringly of faith-based social service providers, observes that "the amount spent on local service activities is a relatively small proportion of total giving, probably on the order of 5 percent." Robert Wuthnow, *Saving America? Faith-Based Social Services and the Future of Civil Society* (Princeton, N.J.: Princeton University Press, 2004), p. 49.

14. For the deeply inequitable consequences of private giving to public schools, see the data in Rob Reich, "A Failure of Philanthropy: American Charity Shortchanges the Poor, and Public Policy Is Partly to Blame," *Stanford Social Innovation Review* (Winter 2005), pp. 24–33.

15. Thomas Nagel and Liam Murphy, *The Myth of Ownership: Taxes and Justice* (Oxford: Oxford University Press, 2002).

16. Ibid., p. 98.

17. "Since there are no property rights independent of the tax system, taxes cannot violate those rights. There is no prima facie objection to overcome, and the tax structure, which forms part of the definition of property rights, along with laws governing contract, gift, inheritance, and so forth, must be evaluated by reference to its effectiveness in promoting legitimate societal goals, including those of distributive justice" (ibid., pp. 58–59).

18. On the concept of a tax expenditure, see Stanley Surrey and Paul McDaniel, *Tax Expenditures* (Cambridge, Mass.: Harvard University Press, 1985).

19. *Regan v. Taxation with Representation*, 461 U.S. 540 (1983), p. 544.

20. Richard A. Musgrave and Peggy Musgrave, *Public Finance in Theory and Practice*, 4th ed. (New York: McGraw Hill, 1984), p. 348. The progressivity of an income tax code translates, perversely, into a regressive system of tax deductions: The wealthiest garner the largest tax advantages. Compounding this oddity is a variant of the objection offered earlier. Identical donations to identical recipients are treated differently by the state depending on the donor's income. A $500 donation by the person in the 35% bracket costs the person less than the same donation by the person in the 10% bracket. Because the same social good is ostensibly produced in both cases, the differential treatment appears totally arbitrary. The upside-down phenomenon is not specific to the tax deduction for

charitable donations, of course. Deductions, in general, massively favor the wealthy. In 1999, 50% of all tax deductions were claimed by the wealthiest decile of earners in the United States. (Source for statistics: calculations from Internal Revenue Service data.)

21. Newer studies that take long-term effects into account generally find lower price elasticities than earlier studies, ranging from 0.47 to 1.26, rather than 1.09 to 2.54. The decision to make a charitable donation is not made solely with reference to the availability of a deduction in any given year; people are likely to look to the years ahead and behind in deciding how much to give. Because previous studies focused on short-term effects of changes in tax incentives, they often exaggerated the impact of incentives. When tax benefits for charitable contributions decreased one year, short-term studies would document a significant decrease in giving for that year. However, these studies would miss the longer term reactions of donors, who would eventually increase their giving again once they became accustomed to the changes in tax incentives. Another development in recent studies is the use of panel studies as opposed to cross-sectional or time series samples. The panel data use information from the same group of individuals at successive points in time. See, for instance, Gerald Auten, Charles Clotfelter, and Holger Sieg, "Charitable Giving, Income, and Taxes: An Analysis of Panel Data," *American Economic Review* 92 (2002), pp. 371–382. The overall picture is that incentives are significantly less important than was initially thought. In explaining why people make charitable contributions, Evelyn Brody concludes: "Apparently tax considerations are not paramount. After all, philanthropy long preceded the enactment of the federal income tax, and no income-tax subsidy is available to the 70% of individual taxpayers who claim the standard deduction." Evelyn Brody, "Charities in Tax Reform: Threats to Subsidies Overt and Covert," *Tennessee Law Review* 66 (1999), p. 714.

22. U.S. law permits tax-deductible donations to organizations "operated exclusively for religious, charitable, scientific, testing for public safety, literary, or educational purposes, to foster national or international amateur sports competition, or for the prevention of cruelty to children or animals" (Internal Revenue Code Section 501(c)(3)). In 2008, not including churches or religious groups, these numbered in excess of 1.1 million organizations.

23. This is Mark Gergen's argument in "The Case for a Charitable Contributions Deduction," *Virginia Law Review* 74 (1988), pp. 1393–1450.

24. Calculations from Internal Revenue Service data.

25. Giving USA publishes an annual data book on charitable giving, from which I have drawn these figures. Recall, here, that donations to religion (in other words, to one's own congregation) do not fund more than trivial amounts of service provision; these donations predominantly fund operating expenses of the congregation (for example, utilities, salaries, facilities, and so forth). See note 13.

26. Charles Clotfelter, ed., *Who Benefits From the Nonprofit Sector?* (Chicago: University of Chicago Press, 1992), p. 22.

27. Western European governments have been historically more redistributive than the United States. The counterfactual question presented here has a correspondingly greater bite the more redistributive a government is with its taxpayers' dollars.

28. See Robert Putnam, *Bowling Alone* (New York: Simon & Schuster, 2001) and Theda Skocpol, *Diminished Democracy: From Membership to Management in American Civic Life* (Norman, Okla.: University of Oklahoma Press, 2004) on the rise of bureaucratic civil society.

29. *Bob Jones University v. United States*, 461 US 574 (1983). This case established that the Internal Revenue Service could revoke the tax-exempt status of an organization at odds with established public policy or an organization that fails to meet a public interest requirement in the statute that regulates nonprofit, tax-exempt 501(c)(3) organizations. Bob Jones University, a 501(c)(3) organization, had a policy that denied admission to applicants who were in interracial marriages or who advocated interracial dating or marriage. Powell's opinion concurred with the majority holding but disagreed with the rationale for revoking tax-exempt status as articulated by his fellow Justices, that tax-exempt organizations must "demonstrably serve and be in harmony with the public interest."

30. Saul Levmore nicely articulates this view, adding that the mechanism might also encourage volunteering for and oversight of nonprofits by "develop[ing] a sense of commitment to chosen charities." See Saul Levmore, *Taxes as Ballots*, *University of Chicago Law Review* 65 (1998), p. 406.

31. Liam Murphy and Thomas Nagel write, in *The Myth of Ownership*:

> The word charity suggests that [the charitable contribution] deduction is a means of decentralizing the process by which a community discharges its collective responsibility to alleviate the worst aspects of life at the bottom of the socioeconomic ladder. Since there is disagreement about what the exact nature of that responsibility is, and about which are the most efficient agencies, it is arguably a good idea for the state to subsidize individuals' contributions to agencies of their choice rather than itself making all the decisions about the use of public funds for this purpose. But even if that is so, the existing deduction cannot be defended on those grounds, because many currently deductible "charitable" contributions go to cultural and educational institutions that have nothing to do with the poor, the sick, or the handicapped. State funding of such institutions may or may not be desirable, but the argument would be very different, and "charity" is hardly the right word. (p. 127)

The pluralism rationale is an attempt to supply this "very different" argument.

10

Giving Back
Norms, Ethics, and Law in the Service of Philanthropy

Patricia Illingworth

There are many ways to increase giving. One widely used, although morally compromised strategy, involves appealing to people's emotions with what has aptly come to be called the "pornography of poverty." Providing people with tax deductions for their charitable contributions is another way to stimulate giving. Abundant social capital is also associated with increased giving and, unlike the pornography of poverty, is not fraught with moral compromises. Law, policy, and individual ethics provide countless opportunities to build (or destroy) social capital. In this essay, although I discuss the role of norms in cultivating social capital, I consider mainly two provisions in charitable tax law to show how an appreciation of social capital, in the context of these laws, could increase our stocks of social capital and increase giving. More specifically, I will argue (1) that limiting the charitable deduction to itemizers is likely to undermine social capital and giving, and (2) that law that prejudices global giving may adversely affect the cultivation of global social capital.

Currently, the Internal Revenue Code may discourage global giving through its water's edge policy, which states that to qualify as a charitable deduction for a taxpayer, the recipient of the donation must be created or organized in the United States.[1] I will argue that, because law not only reflects norms and values, but shapes them, such policies can undermine efforts to expand the scope of our moral world from a narrow, local, and domestic one to a global and cosmopolitan one.[2] I will also argue that this policy undermines the potential for global social capital, an important ingredient not only for giving, but for both international relations and cosmopolitan ethics. Although global giving has increased substantially in the recent past, largely because of the Gates Foundation, the expressive content of the water's edge policy in a global world is morally atavistic.

SOCIAL CAPITAL

The concept of social capital has a long history; yet, it is notoriously difficult to define, largely because it has been embraced by numerous disci-
plines, including economics, political science, public policy, and sociology,
to name a few. For ease of application, I simplify the definition. In general,
social capital has to do with the productive quality of social relations.[3]
According to Robert Putnam, it is both a public and a private good, one
that consists of the networks, norms, activities, and values, including trust,
that facilitate cooperative activity.[4] Putnam also observed a significant
decline in stocks of social capital in the United States.[5] More important,
when social capital is present, even those who do not contribute directly
to the reservoir of social capital can benefit from it.[6] In this sense it is not
a divisible good. Some of the social benefits associated with social capital
are poverty reduction, crime prevention, good health outcomes, and more
productive and honest business practices.

Trust is a crucial attitude for the creation of social capital. It has the
potential to transform self-interested and self-seeking actors into collaborators. Trust enables generalized reciprocity. In turn, generalized reciprocity takes interpersonal relations outside of a tit-for-tat exchange in
which people require an immediate return on their gifts. Generalized reciprocity consists of the willingness to give without demanding that others
reciprocate immediately or perhaps ever, but confident that others will
give, perhaps, to someone else altogether. Without trust, generalized reciprocity would be impossible, and without generalized reciprocity, there
would be little or no social capital.[7] This feature of social capital is
extremely important for philanthropy and I will have more to say about
it later in the chapter.

As with liberty, social capital is an enabler concept, valuable because of
what it enables. Liberty gives individuals the opportunity to satisfy their
conceptions of the good; social capital, and the social trust that accompanies it, gives them the wherewithal to work collaboratively with others
to enjoy the fruits that accompany cooperation with others. But also, as
with liberty, social capital can be used for bad. For example, people may
donate considerable amounts of money to hate groups, and some hate
groups, such as the Ku Klux Klan, have enormous amounts of social capital
at their disposal. This is the dark side of social capital. Another potential
dark side of social capital is its proclivity to develop most easily in homog-
enous and closely knit communities, sometimes giving rise to exclusivity.
Norms and networks that foster tolerance for diverse groups are especially valuable, because social capital that creates bridges between diverse
communities is a scarcer resource and is probably also good for global
social capital. Empirical research on these questions is just beginning to
be done.

For reasons that are not altogether clear, social interactions facilitate
trust and generalized reciprocity. Recent studies involving the "trust game"

suggest an interesting neurobiological explanation for trust, involving the peptide ocytocin (otherwise referred to as the *bonding peptide* and the *trust hormone*).[8] Study subjects were paid $10 for an hour and a half of their time. They were given an opportunity to share some, or all, of the money with another unknown subject who might or might not return some portion of the money to them. The money that was transferred was then tripled and added to the second subject's $10. The willingness of people to send money to the other person signaled their trust, and the willingness of recipients to send money back was a sign of their trustworthiness. The entrusted subjects sent money back and were also found to release increased amounts of ocytocin.[9] In fact, subjects with the highest ocytocin levels sent the most money back and, when the initiating subjects were given synthetic ocytocin, they were willing to share more of their money. The researchers believed that a social interaction in which giving is involved signals trust, creates positive feelings in the second subject, and stimulates trustworthy behavior. Consider the implications of this study for social capital.

The study involved a nonface-to-face interaction between two strangers, in which one gave the other money, trusting the other to reciprocate with money.[10] The act of giving created both trustworthy behavior and reciprocation. The reciprocation reinforces the first subject's trust, and the back-and-forth exchange exemplifies trust and cooperation. This suggests that giving is itself a mechanism that creates trust, and social capital. Interestingly, from the perspective of global social capital, it suggests that the trust that is essential for social capital does not need to be garnered from face-to-face interactions, but could be secured from other sorts of interactions in which people signal trust.[11] Still, some caution is in order, because even if subjects are willing to send strangers money, and to trust them, they may have presuppositions about who these strangers are. They may, for example, put the strangers in the class of "research subject just like me," minimizing difference while facilitating trust. Still, the study has interesting implications for both philanthropy and global social capital.

SOCIAL CAPITAL WITHOUT BORDERS

Given the potential for social capital to increase giving, global social capital could be a powerful mechanism for increasing global giving. Unfortunately, studies have shown that diversity is problematic for social capital.[12] Presumably some of the same problems that surface for social capital within diverse communities, such as universities, would also surface when the diversity is created by a global community. Although the research on social capital and diversity is at a nascent stage, Robert Putnam has some preliminary findings that include the observation that within ethnically diverse communities people engage in "hunkering"[13]:

Diversity does *not* produce "bad race relations" or ethnically defined group hostility....Rather, inhabitants of diverse communities tend to withdraw from collective life, to distrust their neighbors, regardless of the color of their skin, to withdraw even from close friends, to expect the worst from their community and its leaders, to volunteer less, give less to charity and work on community projects less often, to register to vote less, to agitate for social reform more, but have less faith that they can actually make a difference, and to huddle unhappily in front of the television....Diversity, at least in the short run, seems to bring out the turtle in all of us.[14]

Despite the tendency to hunker, the proliferation of international organizations suggests that although there is inadequate global social capital, there is some. Putnam's research on social capital suggests that social capital in diverse communities (and his research does not posit global diversity) may require refashioning social identities to embrace diversity.[15] To this end, people may need to locate their identities in larger, perhaps global communities. New social identities could focus on the norms of cosmopolitanism, or membership in the group that enjoys universal human rights. The challenge of reframing the norms that underlie our social identities could be undertaken by public philosophers, such as Thomas Pogge, who has already devoted considerable thought to our understanding of the "global citizen."[16] He has the following to say about citizenship in a cosmopolitan-informed world:

> Persons should be citizens of, and govern themselves through, a number of political units of various sizes, without any one political unit being dominant....And their political allegiance and loyalties should be widely dispersed over these units; neighborhood, town, country, province, state, region, and world at large. People should be politically at home in each of them, without converging upon any one of them as the lodestar of their political identify.[17]

For Pogge's global people to disperse political loyalties and allegiances more expansively, and to feel at home in each place, they would need varied and diffuse social capital. Generalized reciprocity would play a role in each of these social units. To counteract the inclination to hunker in the face of diversity, and difference, they made need help becoming global citizens. Social capital would come in handy, and generalized reciprocity would be important. Giving is the first step in the dance of generalized reciprocity, and norms and laws that facilitate giving in a global context would help Pogge's global people negotiate the challenges of transnational living.

SOCIAL CAPITAL AND PHILANTHROPY

Charitable giving is thought to increase as the stock of social capital increases people's regard for the generalized other. For Putnam, philanthropy is the result of social capital. "Social networks provide the channels through which we recruit one another for good deeds, and social networks foster norms of reciprocity that encourage attention to others' welfare."[18] Unfortunately, Putnam's studies also show that American philanthropic activity has steadily declined since 1961, about the same time that social capital began to decline.[19]

Putnam is not the only one to find that an increase in social capital is predictive of an increase in giving. Brown and Ferris found that both network-based social capital (the social capital that comes from social networks) and norm-based social capital (social capital derived from prosocial norms) were important for giving.[20] People with high levels of the latter were found to give more to secular causes and to volunteer more often whereas people with more network-based social capital were found to give more to religious and secular-based causes.[21] In the case of network-based social capital, people who are embedded in social networks are more likely to be asked to give, and they are more likely to give.

It would not be surprising, however, if philanthropy itself had the fortuitous consequence of fostering social capital. Generalized reciprocity is, according to Putnam, the cornerstone of social capital, and giving is at the heart of generalized reciprocity. Giving both reflects trust (that there will be reciprocation) and reinforces it when beneficiaries receive gifts and have their trust affirmed. To quote Putnam, "people who have received help are themselves more likely to help others, so that simple acts of kindness have a ripple effect. In short, giving, volunteering, and joining are mutually reinforcing and habit forming."[22] This insight is supported by studies that indicate that those who receive acts of kindness are more likely to help others, thus reinforcing giving and, indirectly, social capital. Philanthropy resembles generalized reciprocity insofar as the former like some instances of the latter constitute giving without expectation of reciprocation. If philanthropy is a form of generalized giving, and generalized giving is important for social trust and social capital, it may well be the case that philanthropy itself fosters social capital. This would explain the ripple effect, and the ocytocin studies in which the signal of trust created increased ocytocin and subsequent reciprocation. This would also make social capital extremely valuable, because not only is it associated with many goods, such as increased giving, but it is also self-generating, which makes it a relatively inexpensive mechanism for achieving these goods. If this analysis is correct, then by inducing greater philanthropy, we would also be increasing our stocks of social capital.

MAKING WAY FOR SOCIAL CAPITAL

Were we to take social capital into account in policy, ethics, and law, some of our assumptions about causation and responsibility may be challenged. In tort law, for example, causation is primarily analyzed in terms of "but for" causation; "but for" a particular action, a particular injury or harm would not have taken place.[23] This causal framework is better suited to individual events and actions than to collective ones. In fact, it asks the finder of fact to distinguish one event or action from all of the others that may play a causal role in an outcome. In contrast, the idea of social capital suggests that many things that we take to be the responsibility of one person or action are more accurately attributed to social relations—that is, to a collective. Even in the case of something as personal as health, social factors such as race, social class, gender, and social status can have powerful contributory, if not deterministic, effects. For example, Lisa Berkman found that the presence of social relationships improved health outcomes significantly[24] whereas Wilkenson[25] found that the presence of inequality in social relations led to worse health outcomes. For those wedded to a biological model of disease, this collective causal account is surprising, and requires a different approach to explaining, preventing, and treating disease.[26]

In the economic sphere, Herbert Simon made a similar point in his essay entitled, "A Basic Income for All." There he argues that an important source of the difference in incomes both within one society and between societies is the presence of and access to social capital. By "social capital," Simon has in mind "knowledge, and participation in kinship and other privileged social relations."[27] Peter Singer, in his essay in this volume, points this out as well. Thus, when we include social capital in our conceptual repertoire, it will often be more accurate to use "we" whereas we now use "I."

Rethinking the causal framework in this way would have implications for the giving norms that we endorse. Some people disavow a duty to give some of their wealth to others because they take sole causal responsibility for their personal wealth and goods. Furthermore, they believe they own their wealth *because* they have caused it (solely on their own) to come into existence. Social capital challenges that paradigm. It implies that many outcomes, including financial wherewithal, can be the result, not of individual talents, actions, and efforts, but of cooperative and collective actions and efforts. Considered from a fairness point of view, social capital-generated outcomes would "belong" to the collective. This point was made nicely by Simon and later echoed by Singer. Interestingly, the widely used expression "giving back to the community," used by donors to explain their giving and by fund-raisers to solicit it, may signal an appreciation for the role that social capital plays in personal fortunes, and of the normative implications of that fact for philanthropy.

CREATING AND INCREASING STOCKS OF SOCIAL CAPITAL: NORMS AND NETWORKS

Because, in the simplest terms, social capital consists of norms and networks, efforts to build it would ideally focus on both. From a practical point of view, it should not be difficult to increase our reservoir of social capital. In fact, many countries craft policy mindful of social capital (Australia, Ireland, and Canada, to name a few). People's access to networks and relationships could be improved, and pro-social capital norms could be created and disseminated. With respect to the first, local governments could create public spaces where people can mingle and interact. Law can be used to establish bridging social capital to enhance opportunities for people of diverse communities to interact with one another.[28] In the United States, the case of *Brown v. Board of Education* had the effect of integrating black and white students, and extending the networks of each to the other.[29] And *Goodrich v. Department of Public Health* did the same thing for gay couples when it legalized same-sex marriage in the state of Massachusetts.[30] Here, law creates new bonds of trust and reinforces existing ones, thus nurturing social capital. At a minimum, it delegitimizes separate treatment based on personal characteristics, thus paving the way for those previously excluded to be part of a broader and more diverse community.

Norms are also an important source of social capital. Most religions include norms of charitable giving and, in fact, giving to religious institutions constitutes a significant portion of charitable giving. Some norms encourage giving, such as the norm of "giving back," but they are few and far between, and there are many that discourage it. For many people, charity begins at home, and family comes first. Still others warn their children, "Don't talk to strangers."

To think about how to fashion prosocial norms, it will be helpful to think about the normative landscape. Frances Fukuyama has done a good job of mapping the norms that can foster social capital. According to him, there are two main types of norms: those based on hierarchy, such as the law, and those based on spontaneous and informal mechanisms. The rule-based norms of paying taxes by a certain date and voting on election day are examples of the former. Tipping a waitress, taking food to a sick neighbor, and giving candy to children on Halloween are good examples of the latter. These norms, both hierarchal and spontaneous, "bind communities together and are tightly enforced by them, sharply limiting the kind of choices people can make about their lives."[31] They govern social interaction and reduce transaction costs. For Fukuyama, some of the important factors that influence whether norms will surface in creating social capital are religion, formal laws, common law, tradition, biology, and the market.[32] Fukuyama's normative landscape suggests that some norms can be fashioned to serve the interests of social capital and philanthropy. Laws can be changed, tradition tinkered with, and biology reengineered by new technologies that redefine our humanity.

To this end, we could promote the norm inherent in generalized reciprocation. A community replete with social capital is one in which people are comfortable giving to others (without a demand for reciprocation), because they can be confident that, although they may not receive now, and from this beneficiary, they may be a beneficiary at some other time, or in some other way, and from some other person. People do not track who owes what to whom, because they trust their community members to take care of one another. Reciprocation is general, and in some cases may be purely hypothetical. Very often people who give to others are comforted with the thought that "he *would* do the same thing for me" and "he *would* if he could" without actually seeking or expecting reciprocation. And sometimes immediate reciprocation is regarded as positively inappropriate, as a crude effort to transform a "gift" into a consumer transaction. Timing can be everything in the dance of generalized reciprocity.

Generalized reciprocity has also been referred to as "paying forward": Instead of paying back to the benefactor a gift or kindness, the beneficiary pays forward. Because generalized reciprocation is neither tit-for-tat, nor necessarily between original benefactor and beneficiary, it can be an ideal way to understand philanthropic giving, in which gifts are given to people who cannot afford to reciprocate, such as donations to the global poor. People may give to the distant poor, and their neighbors reciprocate by bringing chicken soup to them when they are convalescing from an illness. When reciprocation is generalized, or conjectural, to use Putnam's term, there has to be a high degree of trust that others will reciprocate, because the benefactors may not themselves know of the reciprocation because they may not be the beneficiary. Regardless of whether they recognize it, fund-raisers rely on the idea that people may pay forward. The widespread practice of making a donation to a foundation or nongovernmental organization in another person's name may reflect the principle of generalized reciprocity. Consider an example: If I make a donation to Oxfam in my mother's name, out of appreciation for everything she has done for me, I would be paying forward. Anything we can do to diminish the influence of norms that emphasize *quid pro quo* exchanges, and replace them with generalized giving, and the norm of paying forward, will foster social capital.

Because trust facilitates generalized giving, norms that encourage it will also be helpful. Truth telling, promise keeping, personal integrity, fairness, and altruism identify values and principles that facilitate trust. If people can be counted on to tell the truth, then those with whom they interact can be confident of their trustworthiness. The same holds true for promise keeping. Personal integrity, understood as continuity in personal traits, allows people to predict the future behavior of those with whom they interact, thus enabling trust. Prosocial norms in which one person gives to another are conducive to building an environment in which trust can flow. Giving blood and bone marrow, giving up a seat to an elderly person, giving a lost wallet to the police, extending courtesies such as "excuse me" when one bumps into another, and giving up your place in a queue to someone in a rush are all examples of other- regarding norms. In contrast, leaving garbage on the street; failing to pick up after your dog; stealing parking spaces; or, as in my home town of Cambridge, Massachusetts, placing a chair where one has cleared off snow from a public parking place to signal ownership of the space show the opposite—

a firmly entrenched consideration of the interests of the self over those of others. Norms that focus on charity, such as "charity begins at home" build bonding social capital (social capital among closely knit communities), but do little to advance social capital that creates bridges among different groups. The latter and not the former would be helpful to Pogge's global people. Norms that are favorable to social capital can be created and sustained by local, state, and federal governments, employers, educational institutions, and, of course, individuals.

As Fukuyama states, law can be an important source of norms. Richard Pildes identifies several ways that law can affect social capital. It can destroy the social conditions that enable reciprocity, by destroying the social context that allows for social interaction and, in turn, trust. People need to interact to create social capital. Zoning laws can either facilitate social interaction or impede it.[33] The less densely populated a district, the more difficult social capital may be to acquire, simply because people interact less often. Law can also reflect the norm of reciprocity. According to Pildes, some law, such as the Takings Clause, reflects reciprocity by providing for compensation when there is a government taking. I will suggest later in the chapter that charitable tax law also exemplifies the principle of reciprocity. Such laws demonstrate government support for reciprocity over, for example, efficiency.[34] Pildes also mentions that law enforcement can destroy social capital by overriding social mechanisms for enforcing norms.[35] Laws that require publication of the names of "Johns," men who solicit prostitutes, are a case in point. Publishing their names may force their partners to take public action, perhaps to end an otherwise workable marriage. In this way, law can destroy the social mechanisms that prevail and sustain relationships.

Law has expressive content. It communicates a social meaning and fashions social norms. It reflects some norms, and shapes others. According to the expressive theory of law, in addition to controlling or facilitating conduct directly through contract, admonitions, and prohibitions, law serves an expressive function. Consider the following example: duty to rescue laws, although notably absent through much of the United States, echo the principle of generalized reciprocity, because they encourage the rescuer to help a stranger in distress. By communicating the importance of helping strangers in distress, these laws promote a pro-social norm that can foster social capital at the macro level. Whether duty to rescue laws would also be conducive to social capital at the micro level, depends on why individuals are reluctant to help strangers in the first place. There is quite a bit of speculation about this. Among social psychologists, however, there is a consensus that people don't render aid when others are present, because they don't know that it is their particular responsibility to do so. If this explanation of bystander nonintervention is correct, there is every reason to think that people would comply with the demands of duty to rescue laws willingly. If these laws are successful, they will also promote social capital at the micro level. They would not only ensure that people are helped, but also disseminate the important social norm that one ought to help strangers. By reaffirming this pro-social norm, these laws can encourage citizens to help one another, thus building trust and social capital.

Law can also take social capital into account as an interpretive mechanism in much the same way that it now takes liberty and market principles into account. Richard Daynard has identified a number of canons that the courts use in decision making. According to Daynard,

> [j]udicial decision-making canons are rules, largely implicit, that define the types of arguments appellate judges... actually make in the course of opinions explaining and justifying their decisions... some of the canons courts use to reach results antithetical to public health are (a) marketplace values (that is, law and economics analysis), enhancing consumer sovereignty as a legal desideratum..., (b) individual rights... in its perverse form, rights trump anything that is not a rights claim..., (c) strict constructionism, (d) judicial administration and (e) common sense.[36]

Just as law invokes canons of interpretation such as the principles of equality and liberty,[37] so it could consider the impact of a decision on our reservoir of social capital, and the ability of people to achieve their cooperative goals (namely, goals that take cooperation to achieve). In the remainder of this chapter, I can only begin to explain how law might be used to build social capital and, in turn, giving. Although I focus on a small part of charitable tax law, there are many laws that have the potential to create (and destroy) social capital. Nonetheless, because charitable law is about giving, it resonates with expressive content directly relevant to philanthropy. My analysis is largely illustrative and my conclusions, preliminary.

CHARITABLE DEDUCTION AND SOCIAL CAPITAL

In 1917, 4 years after the ratification of the 16th Amendment, Congress created the charitable deduction for donations to public charities and private foundations (religious, charitable, scientific, and the prevention of cruelty to children and animals). Since its inception, it has expanded in scope and amount.[38] Currently, in the United States, taxpayers who itemize are permitted to take a charitable deduction whereas nonitemizers are not.[39] According to Independent Sector, nonitemizers include low- to middle-income Americans, students, teachers, and bus drivers, for example, who often earn less than $50,000 a year, do not own their own home, and do not pay a mortgage. When the charitable deduction is applied to nonitemizers, it can make a difference in giving behavior.[40] In 1985, when for a short time nonitemizers could deduct 50% of their charitable contribution, they contributed $9.5 billion to charity. In comparison, in 1986, when they could deduct 100% of their contribution, they contributed $13.4 billion, about 40% more.

The reasons for the deduction are multifaceted and there is a myriad of controversy around it. When it was enacted, Congress provided the following justification, which has since become the standard account: "The exemption from taxation of money or property devoted to charitable and other purposes is based upon the theory that the government is compensated for the loss of revenue by its relief from financial burdens which would otherwise have to be met by appropriations from other public funds, and by the benefits resulting from the promotion of the general welfare."[41] As with Pildes's analysis of the Takings Clause, this explanation invokes a reciprocity consideration: Roughly, people who make charitable donations to advance the public good relieve the government of that particular responsibility, and the government reciprocates with a tax deduction. Here, law shows support for the norm of reciprocity.

Today, nonitemizers are unable to deduct their charitable contributions. Instead, their charitable contributions are captured in the standard deduction. The main reason for withholding the deduction from nonitemizers is an administrative one, the cost involved in monitoring many small donations. Some nonitemizers may donate more than assumed by the standard deduction whereas others may not have made any donations at all and incur an unjustified benefit. The value of reciprocation, which is at the heart of the charitable deduction for itemizers, seems to break down with nonitemizers. From the perspective of the expressive theory of law, the message communicated to nonitemizers may be that their gifts "don't count," perhaps because the gift is too small. Because the predominant legal rationale for the deduction is a reciprocity consideration, failure to extend it to nonitemizers may give rise to social distrust, at least when taxpayers have donated more than the standard deduction assumes. Thus, law can destroy social capital not only by what it does, but also by what it doesn't do. The fact that nonitemizers increased their charitable contributions by 40% in one year, from 1985 to 1986, following the increase in deductible amount, suggests that they are mindful of what the charitable deduction can mean for their giving plans and therefore may also be mindful of its expressive content.

Because the value of a donor's charitable deduction reflects the donor's marginal tax rate, the greater a person's income, the larger the absolute tax advantage for the same gift. So, those in the highest tax bracket would realize a greater tax advantage. If reciprocation were to follow a tit-for-tat principle, then the value of a gift should be the same for everyone, because it would be fixed by the gift itself. However, when reciprocation is generalized, it doesn't matter if some people realize a greater or lesser valued reciprocation. In addition, if we want to increase giving, and increased giving will both meet social needs and increase social capital, then increasing the value of the deduction for those who can give the most may be an important consideration. By the same token, if we want to decrease the relative value of the deduction for the affluent, that, too, would be consistent with a principle of generalized reciprocity.

If social capital were among our canons of interpretation, it could be implemented by considering the impact of excluding nonitemizers on generalized reciprocity. Looked at from this perspective, it probably doesn't matter how much money people give in absolute terms. If our interest is in furthering generalized reciprocity, it is important that people are engaged, participating in generalized giving, giving to others, creating social trust, and, thus, enabling cooperative activity. Excluding nonitemizers from the deduction may compromise generalized reciprocity and social capital. First, if nonitemizers do not receive a deduction for their donations, then the government may receive a benefit for which it does not reciprocate, perhaps contributing to social distrust. Second, taking a charitable tax deduction encourages people to keep track of how much or how little they give to others. There is some evidence that counting one's acts of kindness (and acts of giving would count) increases one's happiness, and that happy people become more kind with the counting.[42] Nonitemizers would not have this opportunity to count their kindnesses or to self-monitor their giving. Third, if we take social capital seriously, then extending the deduction to all taxpayers signals the government's approval of generalized giving and, in turn, social capital. Fourth, there appears to be something unfair about extending the deduction to itemizers while withholding it from nonitemizers. Although nonitemizers are free, in principle, to itemize, for many the cost and complexity of itemizing means that the option is but a fiction. Sometimes the costs, and administrative and legal hoops required to exercise a right are so burdensome that the right becomes virtually inaccessible.

If the causal analysis of social capital is accurate, then nonitemizers not only may not receive full credit for their specific charitable contributions, but they also would not receive credit for their contributions to the social capital that supports itemizers. Consider the following hypothetical example: If a nonitemizer neighbor walks the itemizer's dog while the itemizer is at a board meeting for a nonprofit, hasn't the nonitemizer also contributed to the philanthropic enterprise? Support of this kind is widespread, and especially so for the affluent, who have more social capital than the poor. So fairness considerations, combined with an appreciation of the casual role that social capital plays, suggests that nonitemizers ought to at least have their direct contributions recognized through a charitable deduction. Currently, the law fails to take advantage of an opportunity to promote social capital, and thus increase philanthropy.

The reasons the charitable deduction is important are less clear than that it is important. The Independent Sector refers to the impact that itemizing has on charitable giving as the *itemizer effect*. According to them, the itemizer effect influences how much households give in charitable contributions, an effect that holds true regardless of income, home ownership status, and other less significant household characteristics.[43] Because most people itemize to deduct home mortgage interest, they speculate that itemizers may give more because, as homeowners, they are more engaged in their communities, and their giving reflects this involvement. Put differently, itemizers may be more social capital rich.

However, there is another, more speculative factor, that may explain the itemizer effect. Just as duty to rescue laws tell the apathetic bystander to intervene and help the stranger in distress when responsibility to help is diffuse (bystander effect), so it may be that itemizing tells the apathetic donor to give. The more people are prompted to give, as they are when they itemize, and when they are embedded in social networks that ask them to give, the more often they give. With this explanation, itemizing functions as notice of the responsibility to give, in much the same way as norms and networks do in social capital-rich communities. "Prompts" of this sort can resolve any confusion or ambivalence about who should do what. When the state offers a charitable deduction to itemizers, it thereby informs them of their responsibility, encourages prosocial behavior, rewards the performance of the responsibility, and creates social trust and social capital. On this hypothesis, the itemizer effect amounts to an override of donor apathy by assigning responsibility for charity to individual taxpayers.

If itemizing does serve as a "prompt" to give, then we have good reason to expand the reach of the deduction to nonitemizers, because in doing so we would likely increase their giving. Even if this explanation of the itemizer effect turns out not to be accurate, or only a small part of the story, itemizing gives rise to increased giving, and excluding nonitemizers may undermine social capital. If lower income people give less because they don't have an opportunity to itemize, and giving fosters social capital, nonitemizers would also lose the personal benefits of increased social capital. This would be unfortunate, because people from lower socioeconomic groups already have less social capital than the affluent, and are not as well positioned to compensate for that financially (For example, they cannot afford to install a security system, but instead rely on neighborhood watch.) To secure the benefits of the charitable deduction, however, we need not abandon the standard deduction altogether, thus forfeiting its administrative benefits, but we could adjust it to reflect the additional charitable deduction.

In general, the charitable deduction seems to be a good way for society to increase both social capital and charitable contributions. Following the main thrust of the congressional justification for the deduction, it is based on principles of fairness and reciprocity—thus it reinforces social trust and social capital. The deduction acknowledges the importance of giving to others and signals state and community support for giving.

The fruitfulness of social capital for collaboration and cooperation is clear—the need for global collaboration to solve global deprivation is also clear. Currently, however, the Internal Revenue Code may undermine both global social capital and global giving through the water's edge policy. According to this policy, in order for an individual or corporation to deduct their charitable gift, the recipients must be "created or organized in the United States, any state, the District of Columbia, or any possession of the United States."[44] This same restriction does not exist under gift and estate tax deductions. Moreover, foreign charities are eligible to apply for exemption status. Because the laws are difficult and expensive for organizations in other countries to navigate, they rarely apply.[45] Therefore, there are countless charitable and not-for-profit organizations around the world to which Americans may want to donate money and that are worthy of those donations, but for which they would not receive a deduction, ranging from community centers for the elderly, fine art museums in Europe to remote Amazonian tribes seeking compensation for environmental harms. Some, but not all, of the restrictions can be circumvented by using intermediary organizations such as Oxfam. In any case, from the perspective of the expressive theory of law, the water's edge policy may communicate an unfortunate message about our global obligations. In a passage from the 1938 House Report, some of that message is explicit:

> The exemption from taxation of money or property devoted to charitable and other purposes is based upon the theory that Government is compensated for the loss of the revenue by its relief from financial burden which would otherwise have to be met by appropriations from public funds, and by the benefits resulting from the promotion of the general welfare. The United States derives no benefit from the gifts to foreign institutions, and the proposed limitation is consistent with the above theory.[46]

According to Congress, the water's edge policy has been adopted, not because foreign-based charities warrant special monitoring, but because the U.S. government has no duty toward these foreign organizations for which individual taxpayers could relieve government when they make charitable contributions to them. The last sentence in the previous passage mentions the need for a public benefit. More specifically, the requirement for public benefit goes as follows: "when the Government grants exemptions or allows deductions all taxpayers are affected; the very fact of the exemption or deduction for the donor means that all taxpayers can be said to be indirect and vicarious 'donors.' Charitable exemptions are justified because the exempt entity confers a public benefit."[47] In contrast, global giving is not regarded as a public benefit because it benefits people in other countries, and it would be unfair to compatriots (vicarious donors) because *they* forfeit the revenue. Although it is difficult to parse out the moral assumptions in this passage, implicit is the assumption that our primary obligation is to compatriots. If one believes that our obligations to others are not based on national affiliation, or on who stands to benefit, then this provision is morally disconcerting.

The Internal Revenue Code also requires that institutions that qualify for charitable deduction be consistent with public policy.[48] This requirement is nicely stated in *Bob Jones University v. The United States*, in which the Supreme Court held that there is a public policy requirement that charitable organizations must meet and that the Internal Revenue Service could revoke the charitable status of Bob Jones University because of its racist policies. According to the Court: "History buttresses logic to make clear that to warrant an exemption...an institution must...be in harmony with the public interest. The institution's purpose must not be so at odds with the common community conscience as to undermine any public benefits that might otherwise be conferred."[49] In addition, it is "long recognized in the law of trusts, that the purpose of a charitable trust may not be illegal or violate established public policy."[50]

There are a few lessons to be drawn from these passages. According to the legislative history, both reciprocity and public policy considerations are present in the justification of the deduction. That rationale also serves as grounds for the water's edge policy. Because, according to the standard explanation, the water's edge policy is based on the relief-of-government duty rationale, it is at risk of expressing the norm that neither the U.S. government nor its citizens have a duty to help people in other countries. It is also based on a now-outdated notion of global connections. Today, the United States and its citizens share many connections globally whereas in 1917, when Congress justified the water's edge policy, there were few. Because many Americans already believe that charity begins (and ends) at home, the expressive content of the policy may only reinforce a norm that already has a strong hold on our normative psyches. Were the United States to lift the water's edge policy and treat foreign-based charities in the same way domestic charities are treated, there is every reason to think that the former, like the latter, would be subject to the public policy requirement. If so, it would offer a considerable amount of protection against charities created in foreign countries that might be hostile to American interests.

Even if some of the practical impact of the policy would be mitigated through intermediary organizations, the water's edge policy still consists in morally problematic expressive content. It runs the risk of affirming the "charity begins at home" norm and undermining cosmopolitan ones. At the very least, the water's edge policy, combined with the standard explanation, implies that our obligations to the distant are not the same as our obligations to our compatriots, because with respect to the latter we stand to benefit whereas with respect to the former we do not benefit. Even if this claim were true in 1917, it is not true today in a global context, nor is it true for transpatriates such as Pogge's global people. If the charitable status of an organization were informed by cosmopolitan ethics, the relevant conception of community would be comprehensive enough to see how helping the distant benefits us all as part of one global community. Conceptually, social capital is notable because it contains no artificial boundary: The norms, values, and networks that can produce social capital are limited only by people themselves and what they can do and create, and not by national borders.

However, the water's edge policy does not consist of only morally disconcerting expressive content. Although American taxpayers are able to donate their charitable monies to exclusively international concerns through intermediary organizations, and to receive a deduction for those donations, not all the organizations to which they may want to donate money would fall under the umbrella of an intermediary organization, or have independent exemption status, including many that would meet the substantive requirements of social benefit and public policy. In effect, the water's edge policy circumscribes the foreign charities to which Americans might donate their charitable monies, and in this way discourages global giving, and may thereby increase the likelihood that they will donate to charities organized in the United States. This will be a greater hardship for some people than for others. Expatriates, for example, with emotional, cultural, and filial obligations to their native countries may be uniquely burdened. They may have specific charitable organizations to which they want to donate money. The water's edge policy reduces the charitable options of Pogge's global people to build loyalties and ties with many varied communities through gifting. It also reduces the various charitable venues that Americans might access to build ties and bonds to other communities, and in this way increases their stocks of trust and global social capital. Unable to deduct their gifts to the foreign charities of their choice, some Americans may not gift at all, or may find American charities where, from their perspective, their money may go further because of the deductibility of the gift.

Repealing the water's edge policy and placing global giving on an equal footing with domestic may result in some American money being diverted to foreign-based charities.[51] It would also give donors more freedom to send their charitable funds where they want, and it might induce greater overall giving as the deductible charitable options are enhanced. A substantial amount of international giving is through religious organizations, and presumably that would continue. Other significant amounts of money go to environmental issues, development, humanitarian relief, and human rights.[52]

More significantly, lifting the water's edge policy may create a new group of donors, those who, like Pogge's global people, have ties and loyalties with a number of political units and want to give to the communities where they have those ties. At the same time, this may create additional charitable giving with an increased dollar amount. Pogge's global people are more likely to want to give directly to organizations within these political units, and may be adept at doing so because they have established ties at the site of the charity. From the perspective of building global social capital, we could benefit from building and reinforcing these global ties. Regardless of how trustworthy an intermediary organization is, an arm's-length transaction through an intermediary organization is unlikely to produce as much global social capital as a network of multilayered personal relationships that transcend national boundaries. Social capital is primarily the stuff of individuals and not organizations (although organizations can facilitate interactions among people). In any case, regardless of where the charitable organization is based, to qualify for exemption it has to confer a social benefit and not a social harm, and it has to be consistent with the public policy of the United States, and not the Taliban!

It might be argued that the water's edge policy is desirable because it has the potential to reduce the risks of philanthropy-induced harms, such as those discussed by Leif Wenar, and at the same time to foster global social capital by making American donations especially visible.[53] It is not clear why charities that conform to the water's edge policy would be better equipped to mitigate philanthropy-induced harms than those that do not. Some foreign charities might well do a better job of serving their mission than American-created organizations. This might be so, for example, with respect to the environment and health care. Many philanthropy-related harms have occurred under the very watch of the water's edge policy. So, in and of itself, the water's edge policy is not a panacea against the harms caused by philanthropy, and intermediary organizations are not themselves immune from functioning as the source of those harms.

Alternatively, one might take the position that, although the rationale for the water's edge policy is problematic, the practical implications of the policy are good overall, because the policy provides the government with an opportunity to monitor foreign-based charities. Unfortunately, it isn't clear that these organizations, domestic or foreign, are carefully monitored. According to Wenar, "attending to the institutions that affect the long-term prospects of the poor, and working to improve how these institutions operate, will be a high priority for those whose real goal is to help alleviate severe poverty. For humanitarians, the basic structure of institutions must be a primary object of concern."[54] In addition, there are many domestic organizations, such as hospitals, that enjoy tax exempt status, and that don't deserve it, because they are profit oriented, and do little in the way of community benefit.[55] There are also many charities located on American soil, that enjoy exemption, and have had it suspended because of suspected terrorist activity. A partial list as of March 2009 includes the Al Haramain Islamic Foundation, located in Ashland, Oregon; Rabbi Meir Kahane Memorial Fund, Cedarhurst, New York; and the Islamic American Relief Agency, Columbia, Missouri.[56] Focusing our attention on the site of an organization's origin, as the water's edge policy does, may divert us from identifying mechanisms that will solve the problem regardless of where the organization is based.

Arguably, because Americans can donate money to international causes through intermediary organizations that will qualify for charitable exemption, they really are no worse off and are perhaps better off if they use an intermediary organization. It is certainly true that Americans can donate money to distant countries through U.S.-based charities. However, there are extra costs associated with using an intermediary organization, money that many people would rather go to feed the global poor.[57] And there are not American-based organizations for each and every international charitable purpose to which American taxpayers may want to give.

Reducing the number of international options Americans have to donate their money is overinclusive, insofar as it will primarily reduce giving to global charities that are worthy and that would satisfy the requirements of public benefit and public policy. However, it is also the wrong response to the problem of philanthropy-induced harms, because those harms (for the most part) have little to do with whether the charity is organized in the United States or elsewhere. Adequate mechanisms for monitoring charitable organizations regardless of where they are organized are needed.

If the United States were to lift its water's edge policy, it is possible that, in the spirit of generalized giving, other countries would follow suit. Although it is unlikely that the United States would receive money for poverty relief (nor should we), it might receive donations for medical research and the arts, for example. Thus, although some additional American funds may be sent outside the country, which would otherwise remain in the country, the United States might also receive an infusion of charitable monies from other countries that now have robust water's edge policies.

On January 27, 2009, in an important case, *Hein Persche v. Finanzamt Ludenscheid*,[58] the Court of Justice, the highest court in the European Union, found that Germany's water's edge policy (as well as that of some other Member States) was in violation of Article 56 of the European Commission Treaty,[59] at the heart of which was a concern for the free movement of capital. The Court reasoned, among other things, that if Germany (and other Member States) did not extend a tax deduction for gifts to other Member States, it would impede donations (capital) to those other Member States (the free flow of capital). In this case, Hein Pershe, a German citizen and taxpayer, had donated some toys and linens to a retirement home in Portugal, located close to where Mr. Pershe owned a residence. When Pershe claimed the deduction on his German taxes, it was denied by the Finanzamt, largely because the recipient of the gift was not established in Germany (Germany's water's edge policy). The Court of Justice had the following to say:

> The fact remains that where a body recognized as having charitable status in a Member State satisfies the requirements imposed for that purpose by another Member State and where its object is to promote the very same interests of the general public, so that it would be likely to be recognized as having charitable status in the latter Member State, which is a matter for the national authorities of that same Member State, including its courts, to determine, the authorities of that Member State cannot deny that body the right to equal treatment solely on the ground that it is not established in that Member State.[60]

There are a few points to be gleaned from this case. First, it is noteworthy that now states of the European Union are no longer permitted to preclude their taxpayers from deducting a donation to a charity in another member state solely because that charitable organization is established in another member state. In other words, taxpayers in Germany, as well as

other European Union countries, can make direct contributions to charities in a number of other member countries and deduct those donations.
Second, because the decision facilitates transnational giving, it furthers
the values inherent in cosmopolitan ethics. Third, the Court of Justice
also found that the need of a member state to "safeguard the effectiveness
of fiscal supervision" of distant charities was not an adequate justification
for maintaining a water's edge policy.[61] Thus, the cosmopolitan thrust of
the ruling is not overridden by either the need for monitoring or efficiency.
The Court of Justice acknowledged that donors may be required by their
tax authorities to provide evidence that the conditions of the deduction
are met. Presumably, then, foreign charities would decide whether they
are willing to provide that documentation prior to accepting the donation. Fourth, the Court appears to believe that the legal mechanisms available to countries and their tax authorities are adequate protection against
possible wrongdoing by charitable organizations or, at least, that the values
inherent in "the free movement of capital" are more important than any
threats posed by lifting the water's edge policy. Fifth, the Court's decision
provides an interesting model of the feasibility of a more open policy
toward global giving. More speculatively, if we were to think about the
law as a mechanism that can further global social justice, this decision can
serve as an important step toward that goal.[62] There are obviously many
differences between the United States and the European Union, but there
are also many similarities. Following the lead of the European Union, the
United States could set aside its water's edge policy and broaden its use of
the charitable tax exemption status, perhaps slowly, country by country,
beginning with some of the Organization for Economic Co-operation and
Development countries.

Hein Pershe shares some qualities with Pogge's global people, a citizen
in one country and a homeowner in another country, shifting wealth from
one to another, thus breaking down some of the political barriers between
each. Hein Pershe is not content simply to vacation in another country; he
has a home in Portugal and appears to have ties with the community.
Insofar as giving helps to create and cement cooperative connections and
relationships among people (recall the ocytocin study), law that discourages global giving—especially global giving that stems from those relationships—unduly burdens the ability of global people to build trust and
social capital, and to implement a cosmopolitan conception of the good.

Consider again the rationale for the water's edge policy. According to
the legislative history, people receive a tax deduction for charitable giving
because they have relieved the government of a responsibility that it would
otherwise have, and have conferred a social benefit. When people give to a
charity that is not "created or organized" in the United States, the water's
edge policy kicks in and they cannot deduct their contribution. Given
this, many people would simply choose not to make the donation, and
"professional donors" might simply ignore the possibility altogether,
focusing their charitable dollars where they know they can deduct them.
Others might seek out intermediary organizations that are created or orga-

nized in the United States and make their donation in that way. Still others, like Oprah, might create their own intermediary organization. There are not, of course, mediating organizations for every charitable concern that American taxpayers have. And many donors may want to give to particular charitable organizations, and not simply to charitable purposes. If the interests of intermediary organizations do not coincide with the donor's interests, the donor may find a domestic-based organization that will. But even if an intermediary organization can mitigate the impact of the water's edge policy, the rationale behind the policy will linger, will be invoked by courts, and will help to shape future law and norms. In the law, the outcome is important, but the rationale for law is also important. I have argued that both are problematic in the case of the water's edge policy.

Social capital is acquired through social interaction, including one-on-one interactions and individual engagement. To create global social capital, we would have to overcome some unique obstacles typically associated with social capital between diverse groups. In an ideal world, if we want to use global giving as a way to cultivate global social capital, we would, following Putnam's insights and Pogge's global people, encourage people to familiarize themselves with the peoples of other countries, perhaps cultivate a more expansive identity so that they see themselves as members of a wider world. As their affinity for other people grows, so, too, would their giving. Providing a charitable deduction would facilitate this process. Requiring an intermediary organization, on the other hand, could signal that charities that are not created or organized in the United States cannot be trusted, but require an intermediary. The more Americans travel, study, work, and marry abroad, the more they are likely to want to contribute directly to distant countries and to control where that money goes. As they learn more about the world, experience some of the deprivations of the world as deprivations of *their* global community, their desire to give globally is likely to grow, and, with that, social trust and global social capital. Withholding from them an opportunity to give directly to other communities will also reduce their opportunities to be fully engaged in the life of those communities. Unfortunately, the use of an intermediary organization can transform international giving into an arm's-length transaction, in which we are at risk of conveying a norm of "Donor Beware."

There are some good counterarguments. I have made a number of empirical claims about the impact of various laws on social capital and on taxpayers' beliefs. Although there are many studies about social capital, and some studies about social capital and philanthropy, there are no empirical studies to support some of the assertions about the impact of the law on social capital. On this matter, social capital is not alone, but in pretty good company. Many claims about the impact of law on privacy, equality, liberty, and the market do not have data to back them up. Nonetheless, the courts do not refuse to consider these empirical assertions in their determinations. Such studies could be done, and I believe they should be done. However, it would be a mistake to ignore the potential impact of the law on social capital and philanthropy, especially because liberty considerations also speak for doing so. In the case of nonitemizers, the liberty interests of taxpayers would be served by extending the deduction to them, and any double-dipping concerns could be remedied by adjusting the standard deduction downward. More expansive opportunities for global giving would also serve the liberty interests of American taxpayers, especially those who, like Pogge's global people, have cosmopolitan conceptions of the good. Although Pogge's global people may not, at this time, experience the restrictions imposed by the water's edge policy as restrictions on their liberty, this may be a relic of another time to be replaced with a more expansive conception of liberty that coincides with a global vision.

One might also object that there are so many ways that countries show preference for nationals, and the United States for its compatriots, that it is difficult to justify making an exception to that rule in the case of giving. Why giving, and not education, or health? Without actually agreeing to the principle that we should not expand our obligations in these other spheres, it is possible to distinguish giving. In the case of giving, the government has extended to citizens a considerable amount of autonomy with respect to whom they contribute money. In this way, the government furthers social engagement, civic mindedness, and social capital. Granted there are certain restrictions about what kinds of organizations are worthy of charity—for example, religion, but not cigar bars. Nonetheless, the charitable deduction encourages community engagement and it is paradoxical to discourage that self-determined engagement as people's vision of their community broadens.

My suggestions have been twofold. First, I suggested that a consideration of social capital should be included as one canon among others in the determination of charitable tax law. The courts might decide that the factual determination is not warranted, but that is different from not including it among the considerations. Second, I suggested that the law discussed in this chapter has expressive content that should be considered. Regrettably, there is no getting around the fact that determining the expressive content of any law is a speculative matter. Nonetheless, laws do have expressive content, and ignoring that content because there is no objective mechanism for identifying it would leave us vulnerable in a world in which people will act, or forebear from acting, at least in part, on the basis of the expressive content. To my mind, the expressive content of the water's edge policy is harmful in a world in which global connections are important and global tensions are high. Still, there are other considerations and other canons of interpretation to take into account. It is possible that, in determining whether to extend the deduction to nonitemizers and to modify the water's edge policy, these other considerations would outweigh the significance of those discussed here. This chapter should be understood as a contribution to that broader conversation.

In his book *The Life You Can Save*, Peter Singer devotes an entire chapter to "Creating a Culture of Giving." He is to be applauded for recognizing the significance of culture for philanthropy. However, creating a culture is a mammoth task that requires more than numerous individuals working independently committed to giving. It also requires a cohesive community in which the welfare of others is a primary concern; for that we need social trust and social capital, and we need it on a global scale. To create a *culture* of global giving, we must first have a global culture in which there is some social cohesion and in which people, such as Pogge's global people, with a cosmopolitan vision, trust and care for one another enough to want to give to others. Recall the earlier discussion of the ocytocin study in which signaling trust in a stranger creates trust. It might be that microfinancing is a successful mechanism not only for relieving global poverty, but also for creating global social capital. When people from rich countries lend money to people in poor countries for small business enterprises (solidarity groups), they signal their trust in these groups, create trust between the lender and borrower, rich country and poor country. A relationship is established. Microfinancing is enormously successful from both the perspective of lenders and borrowers.[63] Part of the reason for that success may have to do with the trust and social capital that are created. Requiring an intermediary organization to stand between the donor and the receiver of money that goes directly to foreign charities can convey the message that foreign-based charities need, especially, to be monitored, when the truth of the matter seems to be that *all* charities need to be carefully monitored, and we need to develop better mechanisms for doing so.[64] In a world in which parents still tell their children not to talk to strangers, and that charity begins at home, that suspicion could lead to hunkering, rather than a culture of global giving. Finally, it is helpful to think about the effect of law on global social capital, not from the perspective of an American donor sending money across a vast ocean, but from the perspective of Pogge's global people, individuals who have a conception of the good that includes creating trust and social relationships with many people in many places. Similarly, when considering the mechanisms available to stimulate global giving, it is important to consider them in comparison with the policy options most likely to be used for that purpose. Currently, the pornography of poverty stands out as a widely used marketing strategy for encouraging people to give globally. It is difficult to imagine that stereotyping the global poor with images of emaciated children covered with flies, and deceptive advertising about the specific children to receive American donations, is preferable to a transparent and relatively straightforward tax deduction that would also build global social capital.

Notes

This chapter has benefited enormously from the insightful comments of friends, colleagues, and collaborators. I am especially grateful to John Basl, Peter Berenson, Christopher Bosso, Peter Enrich, Lance Hopkins, Jung Lee, Hope Lewis, Thomas Pogge, Leif Wenar, and Daniel Wikler for their thoughtful comments. I am also grateful to Taran Nadler for outstanding assistance with research and manuscript preparation.

1. I.R.C. § 170(c)(2)(A) (2009).

2. Thomas Pogge, "Cosmopolitanism and Sovereignty" in Thom Brooks, ed., *The Global Justice Reader* (Oxford: Oxford University Press, 2008), pp. 51–72.

3. James Coleman, "Social Capital in the Creation of Human Capital," *American Journal of Sociology* 94 (1988), pp. 95–120.

4. Robert D. Putnam, *Bowling Alone: The Collapse and Revival of American Community* (New York: Simon & Schuster, 2000), pp. 20–21.

5. Ibid., pp. 49–64.

6. Ibid., p. 20.

7. Patricia M. L. Illingworth, *Trusting Medicine: The Moral Costs of Managed Care* (New York: Routledge, 2005), p. 93.

8. Paul J. Zack, "The Neurobiology of Trust," *Scientific American* 298 (2008), pp. 88–95.

9. Ibid., p. 90.

10. Ibid.

11. Robert D. Putnam, "E Pluribus Unum: Diversity and Community in the Twenty-first Century," *Scandinavian Political Studies* 30 (2007), p. 159.

12. Ibid., p. 137.

13. Ibid., p. 149.

14. Ibid., pp. 150–151.

15. Ibid., p. 150.

16. Thomas Pogge, "Cosmopolitanism and Sovereignty," p. 48.

17. Ibid., p. 58.

18. Putnam, *Bowling Alone*, p. 17.

19. Ibid., p. 123.

20. Eleanor Brown and James Ferris, "Social Capital and Philanthropy: An Analysis of the Impact of Social Capital on Individual Giving and Volunteering," *Nonprofit and Voluntary Sector Quarterly* 36 (2007), pp. 85–99, 94.

21. Ibid., p. 96.

22. Putnam, *Bowling Alone*, p. 122.

23. Page Keeton, *Prosser and Keeton on the Law of Torts* (St. Paul, Minn.: West Publishing Company, 1984), pp. 266–267.

24. Lisa Berkman, "The Role of Social Relations in Health Promotion" in Ichiro Kawachi and Bruce Kennedy, eds., *The Society and Population Health Reader: Income Inequality and Health* (New York: The New Press, 1999), p. 171.

25. Richard G. Wilkenson, "Social Relations, Hierarchy, and Health," in Ichiro Kawachi and Bruce Kennedy, eds., *The Society and Population Health Reader: Income Inequality and Health* (New York: The New Press, 1999), pp. 211–235.

26. Geoffrey Rose, "Sick Individuals and Sick Populations" in Patricia Illingworth and Wendy Parmet, eds., *Ethical Health Care* (Upper Saddle River, N.J.: Prentice Hall, 2006), p. 37.

27. Herbert Simon, "UBI and the Flat Tax," *Boston Review* (October/November, 2000), pp. 9–10.

28. National Economic and Social Forum, *The Policy Implications of Social Capital*, Forum Report No. 28 (Dublin: Government Publications, 2003).

29. *Brown v. Board of Education*, 347 U.S. 483 (1954).

30. *Goodrich v. Department of Public Health*, 798 N.E. 2d 941 (Mass 2003).

31. Francis Fukuyama, "Social Capital," in Lawrence E. Harrison and Samuel P. Huntington, eds., *Culture Matters* (New York: Basic Books, 2000), pp. 98–111.

32. Ibid., p. 106.

33. Richard Pildes, "The Destruction of Social Capital through Law," *The University of Pennsylvania Law Review* 144 (May 1996), p. 2055–2077.

34. Ibid., p. 2071.

35. Ibid., p. 2073.

36. Richard Daynard, "Regulating Tobacco: The Need for a Public Health Judicial Decision-Making Canon," *Journal of Law, Medicine and Ethics* 30 (2002), pp. 281–289.

37. Ibid.

38. David E. Pozen, "Remapping the Charitable Deduction," *Connecticut Law Review* 39 (December 2006), p. 537.

39. 26 U.S.C. § 170 (2008).

40. Independent Sector, *Deducting Generosity: The Effect of Charitable Tax Incentives on Giving* (Washington, D.C.: Independent Sector, 2003).

41. H.R. Rep. No 1860 75th Cong., 3d Sess. 19 (1938).

42. Keiko Otake et al., "Happy People Become Happier through Kindness: A Counting Kindnesses Intervention," *Journal of Happiness Studies* 7 (2006), pp. 361–375.

43. Independent Sector, *Deducting Generosity*, p. 27.

44. I.R.C. § 170(c)(2)(A) (2009).

45. David E. Pozen, "Remapping the Charitable Deduction," p. 537.

46. H.R. Rep. No 75–1860, 10–20 (1938).

47. *Bob Jones University v. United States*, 461 U.S. 574 (1983), p. 591.

48. I.R.C. 501(c)(3).

49. *Bob Jones University v. United States*, p. 592.

50. Ibid.

51. David E. Pozen, "Remapping the Charitable Deduction," pp. 578–579.

52. Ibid., p. 572.

53. Leif Wenar, "Poverty Is No Pond: Challenges for the Affluent," chap. 6, this volume.

54. Ibid.

55. *Utah County v. Intermountain Health Care, Inc.*, 709 P. 2d 275 (Utah 1985).

56. IRS, Suspensions Pursuant to Code Section 501(p) (2009).

57. David E. Pozen, "Remapping the Charitable Deduction," p. 578.

58. C-318/07, *Hein Persche v. Finanzamt*, 2009 E.C.J. 95 (2007).

59. Ibid.

60. Ibid., p. 8.

61. Ibid., p. 9.

62. I have in mind, here, a more globalized version of Ronald Dworkin's theory of the law as an institution that gradually moves toward a more just society, while maintaining respect for precedent and coherence in the law.

63. Muhammad Yunus and Alan Jolis, *Banker to the Poor: Micro Lending and the Battle against World Poverty* (New York: Public Affairs, 1999), pp. 235–243.

64. Leif Wenar, "The Basic Structure as Object: Institutions and Humanitarian Concern," *Global Justice, Global Institutions*, special issue of the *Canadian Journal of Philosophy* 31 (2007), pp. 253–278.

11

The Funder as Founder
Ethical Considerations of the Philanthropic Creation of Nonprofit Organizations

James Shulman

> It isn't every day that a respected private foundation decides to spend several hundred million dollars to create an entirely new academic institution. Clearly, they could have given the money to many excellent schools with a long record of success. Instead, they chose to start over with a clean slate and form a new institution.
>
> —Richard K. Miller, President,
> Franklin W. Olin College of Engineering

This essay explores the questions that might be asked as a donor or a foundation decides to create a new nonprofit organization rather than providing philanthropic support via an existing one. The creation of Olin College or any other of the examples considered in this essay might be thought of as generous impositions—ambitious exercises of power designed to effect positive change through the creation of a new organization. Although this essay explores the practical aspects of giving in this manner, the implications of the key decisions are essentially a matter of applied ethics, because philanthropy is subject to singularly few legal or social mechanisms of accountability. Given the significant investments needed to create and foster a new organization, as well as the impacts and dependencies that those new organizations can instigate, deliberation is important both before embarking on such a project and also along the way.

PHILANTHROPIC EFFECTIVENESS

To launch a new nonprofit institution inevitably uses a mode of philanthropy that has been categorized as "high-engagement philanthropy."[1] During the past decade, a good deal of debate about the practice of

philanthropy has centered on a specific "high-engagement" approach—
"venture philanthropy." Having drawn an explicit analogy to venture
capital investing, this school is generally characterized by grant makers
who make fewer grants, take an active interest in the enterprises being
funded, supply additional nonfinancial help (such as hiring consultants or
executive coaches), and rely upon (in ways that closely model the work-
ings of the business world) clear goals and metrics to define and gauge a
grantee's progress. These are clear practical tactics associated with this
approach; are there ethical implications associated with the venture
capital analogy?

Early-stage venture capital investors in the for-profit arena might fund
10 enterprises. They expect to break even on a few, lose the entire
investment on the majority, and earn significant outsized returns on one
or two. But the risk associated with such a bold strategy is not an ethical
one; it is an investment risk undertaken on behalf of investors who know
the rules of the game. The failure of a given investment or even an entire
fund means the loss of invested capital, defined and measured in a dispas-
sionate way. In philanthropic activity, losses and gains accrue to others
rather than to those who invest.

There are undoubtedly relevant parallels to the ways in which philanthropists—be they "venture philanthropists" or "old school"—"invest" in
nonprofit efforts, monitor those "investments," decide whether to follow
up on the original investment, and learn from what they have done. To a
certain degree, the venture capital lens for considering the support or
creation of new nonprofits is relevant, and, for this reason, I refer to that
mode of thinking throughout the essay—although it is important to note
that there are highly relevant differences between these sectors as well.
Measuring the "success" of a philanthropic investment depends greatly on
the complexity of the problem being addressed and the appropriate timetable for measuring results.

To a certain degree, venture philanthropy can be understood as a reaction to increasing frustration with an enterprise—philanthropy—that is
almost unique in the risk it runs of not being accountable to anyone. Joel
Fleishman notes that, although there are some structures that police egre-
gious mismanagement or ethical lapses on the part of foundations, few
forces prevent these important institutions from being "allowed to lan-
guish in self-protective insulation." However, the risks are not only those
associated with self-indulgence. Writing about the philanthropic practice
that fails to steward assets wisely, political scientist Rob Reich observes,
"had there not been tax concessions, [the wasted assets] would have been
the public's in terms of tax revenue. The wasting of philanthropic assets is
the wasting of assets that belong partially to the public."[2]

Of course, most grant makers take their responsibility seriously, feel
the burdens associated with this charge, and accurately remind us that
"giving money away well is not as easy as it might look."[3] But beyond
thoughtful self-policing, it is challenging to see how accountability

philanthropy will emerge. By placing more emphasis on the terms that go along with philanthropic support, venture philanthropy seeks to ensure effectiveness and accountability.

At the same time that such active philanthropy is being touted as the way to be effective, another school suggests a different approach. In surveying leaders of foundations, Jenni Mariano and Susan Verducci note how frequently grant makers and grantees acknowledge the importance of humility. One foundation leader whom they interviewed had some perspective on the best approach to respectful philanthropy:

> There is a natural tendency in a foundation to begin to think that all the wisdom and knowledge is lodged within it and that doing philanthropy is just a matter of going out and finding people who will support the answer the foundations have already reached.... The worst practice is when people use what appears to be philanthropy as a means of advancing, by the systematic use of money, their own agenda.[4]

If one of the varieties of a lack of accountability in philanthropy is hubris, might more active involvement of the donor (as espoused by venture philanthropy) or a foundation be the wrong answer? Calls for humble philanthropy suggest that the best sort of philanthropy identifies the most effective organizations, supports their work, and meddles as little as possible in directing them. This approach minimizes interference which a donor or foundation inevitably can only do from afar with limited operational knowledge and excess (and perhaps undue) influence.

It is likely that certain practices of venture philanthropy (such as planning/goal setting, good management practices, and definable aims) will help any organization function better. However, the impact of close involvement of the donor may add to—or detract from—an organization's effectiveness depending on a number of factors: the original formulation of what the founder's intentions were in creating the enterprise, mutual expectations about how the organization will deal with experimentation and change, the degree of ongoing support the organization and the founder foresee, and the donor's ability to be self-reflective about the asymmetric power relationship inevitably associated with being the source of financial resources. The effectiveness of the philanthropic involvement affects both the organization and cause being served.

PARTICULAR RISKS FOR THE FUNDER–FOUNDER

If one risk that philanthropists face is that their wealth and the concomitant flattery from the grant-seeking world diminish their ability to test their judgment about the most effective responses to societal needs, the funder–founder might face the most concentrated form of this risk. For, unlike the venture capitalist or venture philanthropist who reviews a proposal from an entrepreneur, the funder–founder has removed an additional layer of checks on the validity of the idea. In other words, the funder–founder is not responding to a story and weighing it in the context of the storyteller and other similar stories; the funder–founder *is* the storyteller. Many people are inclined (in their daily lives) to believe the stories they tell themselves; very few run the risk (as philanthropists do) of spending millions of tax-benefited dollars to try to make those stories come to life.

Nevertheless, although the danger of unreflective action on the part of wealthy individuals and foundations is high, it also would be risky to proclaim that no new ideas can rightfully emerge from those who either have amassed great wealth or steward great wealth and work assiduously to observe a sector closely. Philanthropies (like the best venture capital funds) are exposed to talented people with good ideas and, because of this vantage point, may well have a perspective gained from not being "too close to the ground." In this essay, I will consider a number of examples of the funder–founder and trace the path of institutions in formation to ask whether and how such active philanthropic creativity can effectively serve the public good. Eventually, the ultimate test of such creative and ambitious philanthropic action will be provided by how well such institutions transition from quixotic origins to carrying out their missions as accepted parts of the communities they serve.

CASES

The Nasher Sculpture Center

In October 2003, the Nasher Sculpture Center opened in downtown Dallas.[5] The building, designed by Renzo Piano with a garden by Peter Walker, was well received.[6] The collection, considered by some to be the most important private collection of modern sculpture in the world, had been the object of decades of courting on the part of the National Gallery of Art, Fine Arts Museum of San Francisco, the Guggenheim, and the Dallas Museum of Art. "Carter Brown [director of the National Gallery] became very interested," Ray Nasher noted in a 1997 interview. "We had many, many conversations...Tom Krens [director of the Guggenheim] was very interested. We had to think about it."[7] But in the end, Nasher chose to build his own museum.

Even that choice evolved during the 1990s from a sculpture garden that was to be funded by $15.6 million of city funds into a museum, garden, and education center (at a cost of more than $70 million) funded entirely by Nasher himself. Many great museums have been built by a single donor (including the Frick Collection, the Phillips Collection, the Kimbell, and the Isabella Stewart Gardner). The amassing of a great art collection grows out of passion, taste, and significant financial resources; and yet, these traits are not often correlated with a tendency to cede control. Notable exceptions from the past century can indeed be found in the gifts of Andrew Mellon's collection to found the National Gallery or the choice of Samuel H. Kress to distribute his 3,100 old-master paintings and other works to the new National Gallery of Art and to more than 70 museums from El Paso to Staten Island. Still, Kress's strategy is far from the norm, and the romancing of great private collections is a central activity for most museum directors today. In the end, some number of those collectors will choose, instead, to create a new and independent institution.

Four years after his museum opened, Ray Nasher died unexpectedly. Although the ultimate disposition of his estate has not been finalized, the Center will likely receive an amount that has been estimated to be $100 million. The Center (along with the Dallas Museum of Art and the Meyerson Symphony Center) form the core of an arts district that is touted in Dallas as "one of the strongest selling points we have as a city and one of the strongest assets we have as a community."[8]

Local Initiatives Support Corporation (LISC)

With a $5 million grant, matched by six corporations (Aetna, Arco, Continental Illinois Bank, International Harvester, Levi Strauss, and Prudential), the Ford Foundation created LISC in 1979. Its first executive director was Mike Sviridoff, who had played the leading role in generating the idea of LISC in his role as Ford's vice president for national affairs. The aim of LISC was to provide reliable information on the credit worthiness of potential borrowers, so that for-profit financial institutions could feel comfortable in lending money to community development corporations (CDCs) and other community groups in low-income urban and rural areas. In this way, private-sector funders could make more attractive investments by working with and through the local experts from the best CDCs.

The Local Initiatives Support Corporation has been a dramatic success. Its original goal of working with 100 CDCs in 5 years was easily surpassed. It worked very close to the ground. As Sviridoff noted in a 1984 interview: "The 'temperament of the 1980s' calls for less national and more local programming, less grand design and more 'closely targeted objectives,' less contention and more collaboration."[9] In 1985, 5 years after LISC was created, Sviridoff retired and was succeeded by Paul Grogan (who would go on to serve as president for 13 years). Today, it invests approximately $1 billion a year in affordable housing, retail space, and childcare centers in more than 30 offices around the country.

The impulse to take matters into one's own hands can happen (as with Ray Nasher) on the individual level, focused on the rarefied realm of a specific form of modern art, or on the other extreme, as in the creation of LISC by the Ford Foundation, where one of the largest institutions of philanthropy took on one of the most complicated and socially challenging issues (urban development). In any case, this technique of institution creation is undoubtedly ambitious; it is virtually impossible to be familiar with the terrain of nonprofit institutions and not recognize that any non-profit institution is difficult to sustain. Although both of these examples may well be success stories, this essay will describe how even these successes are complex and fraught with important decision points. Moreover, many other such projects (some of which are discussed later) fail. What factors need to be considered when a funder acts on an ambitious and creative vision?

PLANNING

Analysis

Most donors do some sort of planning before giving away money; often this analysis consists of listening to the story that a prospective grantee tells. Other analysis comes from conversations with people working in the field. Many donors (be they involved individuals like Nasher or involved program officers like Sviridoff) first spent time in the communities that they served and knew its customs, mores, and unfulfilled needs. Grant makers analyze the capacity of organizations to carry out projects based on their previous records of accomplishment. Whatever the initial mode of analysis, the first and most obvious questions for the funder–founder are: Why is a new venture needed and why is the donor the one to carry it out?

Is There a Need for a New Organization?

The nonprofit landscape is densely populated. What leads a funder to believe that existing institutional capacity is not adequate to address the need? The early-stage venture capitalist's first question of any potential new investment is: What is the headache for which your idea is the aspirin? In the case of Nasher, it seems that he came to believe that the particular medium upon which he focused (sculpture) was not fully appreciated (either by the public or by existing museums). "My hope," Nasher said in a 2003 interview, "is that [the Sculpture Center] really brings sculpture to the fore." Elsewhere, he noted, "You put a painting on the wall, and you get the illusion of depth. But my feeling is that a piece of sculpture is really 360 different works."[10] In the case of LISC, Sviridoff, knowing the CDC terrain from both his own experience and the analysis of existing Ford efforts, perceived that there was, in fact, a specific problem to be addressed:

> The problem...is to devise a way of selecting, without political pressures, community and neighborhood organizations that show real ability to launch substantial physical improvements....Delivering to these groups what government finds hard to deliver: the flexible technical assistance and investment and core support they need to draw more fully on government

resources and especially to attract new private-sector resources; and doing these things well enough in enough places to show that local groups in a wide range of deteriorating communities are worthy of long-term support from government and the private sector.[11]

The second question might be to ask why an already existing non-profit should not be supported to take on the problem, so that funders could avoid taking on the messy business of building institutions from scratch.

When the initial investments required to start new institutions are so high and when returns on social investment (be it money or time) impact the community, it is well worth asking whether a new institution is the right vehicle. An accomplished nonprofit executive, Bob Giannino-Racine, has expressed a concern with the proliferation of organizations involved in addressing very similar problems:

> Over the course of a six-month period, I'll probably meet with 10 or 15 young people who are in college or recently out of college, and many of them say that what they want to do then—or perhaps someday—is start their own nonprofit. Everybody wants to be the next social entrepreneur, the next Michelle Nunn [cofounder of the Hands On Network] or Wendy Kopp [founder of Teach for America]. In most cases, there are already groups working on "their" issue, but they're often not interested in learning about them. And that has big ramifications for the nonprofit sector, in part because we can have a really charismatic, inspiring young social entrepreneur who comes with an idea and there's almost a blind allegiance that often follows some of them, without any kind of needs assessment or accountability check.[12]

If funder–founders are acting on similar impulses, there should be cause for concern.

Such concern and the need for good analysis do not mean there is no place for new projects started by determined individuals who have seen the failings of other nonprofit efforts or those launched by funder–founders undertaken in response to perceived needs. Clayton Christenson notes that it is inevitable that new needs will spring up that extant organizations are not equipped to serve:

> Too much of the money available to address social needs is used to maintain the status quo, because it is given to organizations that are wedded to their current solutions, delivery models, and recipients. Many provide a relatively specific, sometimes sophisticated offering to a narrow range of people. While they may do a good and important job serving those people ... what's required is expanded support for organizations that are approaching social-sector problems in a fundamentally new way.[13]

The Frederick Olin Foundation saw such a need after years of hearing about what was wrong with the way that engineering was being taught. Its dramatic and experimental solution was to devote the Foundation's entire endowment to building a new undergraduate school of engineering, with radically different approaches to curriculum (no majors), faculty (no tenure), and tuition (full scholarships for all students, at least until 2021). The original LISC planning paper noted that change that is to be carried out via a new organization requires a willingness to ride out the risk and the period of skepticism that allows for the building of trust: "Identifying and cooperating in this way with community groups is a complex, often untidy, and unpredictable process. There are sure to be some disappointments, even failures. The risks are perhaps best assumed and the burdens mitigated by private philanthropic approaches, especially in the early stages."[14]

Whether it is in response to an underserved need, a belief that a new solution is needed to attack deep-seated problems (as LISC asserted), or an effort to proselytize about an underappreciated offering (such as Nasher felt was the case with modern sculpture), research about the most appropriate solution begins with recognition of the opportunity. What, then, should be asked as the funder–founder attempts to respond to the perceived need?

Creating Anew Rather Than Enlisting an Existing Organization to Carry Out the Idea

Within any realm of philanthropy, donors can choose to resist "meddling" with what they deem to be a well-functioning organization by providing such organizations with unrestricted support. Or, as is more often the norm, donors can designate support for the funding of a particular project. Most grant making follows the latter path, whereby the donor and the recipient strive to find if there is a match between the donor's vision and the directions of the supported organization. How should an inspired donor, having vetted an idea and explored the existing landscape of possible partners, justify moving from a philanthropic or consultative mode to an operating role? One example of a funder-created nonprofit that did not survive was Project 180, created by the Andrew W. Mellon Foundation in 1996 as "a strategy firm and development lab for projects, programs, and institutions that demonstrate market opportunity as well as the potential for significant social impact."[15] The new nonprofit was led by Rachel Newton Bellow, who left her post as Mellon's program officer for arts and culture to lead the new organization.

Project 180 was born because Bellow had become increasingly frustrated with putting "Band-Aids on gaping wounds," by making one-off, short-term grants to dozens of cultural organizations that, although enormously successful artistically, were struggling to survive economically. During the mid 1990s, she had spent a good deal of her focus on getting more deeply involved with institutions than the normal grant-making program officer would. For example, in 1995, she worked intensively with a troubled but promising enterprise—the Dia Art Foundation.[16] Bellow had worked with then-director Michael Govan and eventually awarded

Dia a $1 million grant that came with a requirement for the Dia board to match the grant 5:1, in effect offering Govan the leverage he needed to build an entirely new board able to respond to such a challenge. This activist grant-making strategy helped Govan succeed in changing a small and challenged institution into an internationally recognized and widely respected one. Bellow and the Mellon Foundation's analysis showed that no existing entity was doing this kind of active philanthropic work. However, the need that the new entity (Project 180) aimed to fill was not one that the community was ready to support, and the project closed after 3 years.

In the case of Project 180, the Mellon staff knew that they could not be effective consultants while acting as grant makers. The successful work that they accomplished as active grant makers was too active a role for a foundation, but what they learned in the end was that the intervening role absent the philanthropic leverage was not effective. The failure of Project 180 was, in part, a mistaken analysis of what the new "in-between" entity might be able to accomplish. The organizations that they sought to help really did need strategic consulting, but they couldn't afford to pay for it (absent philanthropic support). The Local Initiatives Support Corporation was formed because Ford could not play the operational role that it saw the community needing, but had more accurately identified a gap that could be filled. Funders who have been working in an area for an extended time might have not only a sense of what the field is seeking, but also a sense—borne from appraising their own "hits and misses"—of what sort of experimental approach might fill a gap.

The Significance of the Type of Organization Being Created

All types of institutions are not the same. Aside from highly unusual projects (such as the University of California's new campus at Merced or New York University's collaboration with the emirate of Abu Dhabi), few are as ambitious as Olin in seeking to create new institutions of higher education, given both the scale of physical infrastructure and the difficulty of *de novo* creation of culture, alumni, and history upon which such institutions depend.

Stand-alone institutions of various types are possible to create, as Ray Nasher learned, if one has focus and very significant startup capital. Notable examples of this mode in recent years include the Stowers Institute for Medical Research (created in 1994 with an initial gift of $50 million from Jim and Virginia Stowers, followed by subsequent investments on their part) and the Georgia Aquarium in Atlanta, launched with a $250 million gift from Home Depot cofounder Bernard Marcus. After its well-funded founding, it behooves the institution to fit in—an aquarium wants to become part of the tourist traffic (and hence offers, as the Georgia Aquarium does, combination ticket deals with other destinations). However, it also seeks to fit in by providing signals of being "like" a traditional institution. So, for example, the Stowers Institute notes on its website that "brilliant scientists...have given up positions at institutions like Harvard and the Howard Hughes Medical Institute to pursue their research at the Stowers Institute."[17] This kind of new institution may be driven by the donor's vision, but can assume the profile of a free-standing institution soon after its launch.

On the other end of the institutional spectrum is what we might consider "infrastructure light" agents of change. Much of the energy and focus of groups that practice venture philanthropy are aimed at organizations that harness the power of volunteers to address insufficiencies in existing (primarily government-funded) social services and K–12 programs. If the equity required for major capital expenditures (museums, aquariums, and medical research institutes) can run into the hundreds of millions of dollars, the equity required for building a new agent of social change among teachers, principals, or social service agencies is often "sweat equity"—the dedicated labor of passionate people. At this end of the spectrum, new institutions appear (and disappear) frequently. Those that survive can grow to significant national scale, but most of these organizations function at a comparatively modest level of operations.

A third kind of entity that a donor or a foundation might launch seeks neither the heavy footprint of the traditional institution nor the light capital footprint of the agencies led by new social entrepreneurs. These institutions are aimed to act as an intermediary institution that carries out the intentions of the donor via an operating entity. Doing so allows the new entity to live among the constituencies served, rather than at the more remote perspective of a funder. In the position paper that accompanied the launch of LISC, the authors wrote: "Experience shows the federal government finds it hard to select and work flexibly with the sensitive, creative, and tenacious local organizations that do the job of revitalization best. The government's ability to be selective is limited because it must accommodate to political pressure to spread resources evenly."[18] Although the authors wrote about the inability of the government to play the needed "close to the ground" role, the same could very well have been true about the role of grant makers like Ford, whose operating capacity and communications with potential grantees would be very different from the selection capacity of an intermediary like LISC. "Already interested in finding ways to broaden and strengthen this promising invention [CDCs], Ford decided to test the notion of a privately supported, free-standing, highly skilled 'intermediary,'" Sviridoff would later write.[19]

Intermediary organizations seek to carry out a range of functions that furthers the mission of their funder by being more enmeshed in the day-to-day needs of complex communities striving for change than a distant funder is likely to be able to be. Funding for this sort of activity—although different in scale from the capital required to build new

buildings—can be significant, because the donor's plan might be to provide some financial assistance alongside the other activities that the
intermediary might be charged to carry out. The Local Initiatives Support
Corporation received more than $90 million in funding from Ford during
the 1980s and '90s, although a significant percentage of these funds went,
not into LISC's operations, but were, in effect, regranted to the CDCs
that LISC selected. On the other hand, without such "regrantable" impact
funding, Project 180 found that it quickly became just another consultant. The successful intermediary venture lives somewhere between its
roots as a funder and the reality of operating on its own in the midst of the
complicated nonprofit ecosystem.

The vibrancy of this familial connection between the funder–founder
and the new entity is more important in such intermediary structures
than, perhaps, in the creation of institutions (like museums, institutes, or
aquariums) that are seeking to become quickly absorbed as part of the
"established" landscape. When Ray Nasher hired the chief curator of the
Fine Arts Museums of San Francisco, Steven Nash, to direct the Sculpture
Center, he took a decisive step in camouflaging the institution's place in
the established landscape. Nash, an expert on sculpture and a distinguished museum administrator, lent exactly the sort of practical expertise
a new institution would need. The goal of such new institutions is to
blend in as if they were always there—a gesture to earn acceptance rather
than to fill a structural gap in the landscape of offerings. However, for
LISC and Project 180, leadership came from the funder—Sviridoff left
his role as vice president of Ford and Bellow left one of the few comfortable jobs in the art world to start Project 180. Their willingness to share
in the risk—"to eat their own cooking," as investors say about those who
invest their own equity rather than just that of their investors—signals
commitment. Such commitment also ensures that the objectives of the
funder–founder are not merely conveyed to a management team, but are
also carried across the umbilical cord.

The idea having been analyzed, and the decision having been made
that a new institution of a particular type is needed, how can a funder
then vet the idea of the overall plan, knowing that the ideas of those with
accumulated wealth are often met with conscious or unconscious syco-
phancy? One way of getting past the limits of one's own thinking is by
testing the idea against others who have the freedom to be candid.

Syndication and Control

One of the junctures where the venture capital/venture philanthropy
analogy seems most apt concerns the sharing of risk. Risk of failure of an
early-stage entity in the for-profit world seems more analogous to the
risks inherent in startup nonprofits than when the analogy is pushed to
the question of "returns" on investment. Early-stage failure—be it based
on a bad initial thesis, a faulty analysis of the competitive landscape, an

erroneous confidence in the management team, or errors in resource allocation—is wasteful in both realms.

Harvard Business School professor Josh Lerner has written about
how syndication of venture capital deals—in other words, enlisting
other venture capital firms as co-investors in a deal, hedges the risk of
the investment, and not only by diluting one's own financial stake.
"Syndication...improves the due diligence process by letting venture
firms gather additional opinions on investment opportunities—and thus
reducing their risk even further."[20] Is it the case that, in the nonprofit
realm, a funder will get a much better read on the validity of an undertaking if others are invited to join in?

Looking back on Project 180, Rachel Newton Bellow notes: "By not
'shopping' the Project 180 concept to other foundations/investors, I
wasn't forced to respond to challenges around my key assumptions, to
hone and clarify the strategy, work out a realistic revenue model, think
through a staffing plan, etc."[21] Ford's efforts to syndicate the launch of
LISC produced just this sort of test. Moreover, the syndication of the deal
gave a degree of assurance to the corporations that were skittish of reper-
cussions if something went wrong while working in a troubled community.
If something went wrong, the backers knew that at least it had gone
through a process with others.

Ray Nasher, on the other hand, chose to retain sole control of his
project. The project became, throughout the course of the 1990s, more
and more his own. Nasher knew that working with the city meant being
exposed to its decisions. The city budget officer alerted Nasher that "if in
the next budget year, we're having budget problems, maintenance is one
of the first things I'll look to cut."[22] Nasher became increasingly wary (as
he negotiated with Dallas for the land and the support of what was then
envisioned only as an outdoor garden); he wanted nothing to do with a
building built by committee. "It would have taken 10 years if the [Dallas
Museum of Art] were to do it."[23]

Nasher wanted—and got—control. Although the reviews of the
building and the collection support Nasher's view that there was something
distinctive about what he was trying to do and how he decided to do it,
the Center was not able, in its early days, to attract significant outside philanthropy. Public records show that in 2005 and 2006, the Center received
an average of $111,000 per year in gifts, whereas the Dallas Museum of
Art received an average of $1,746,000.[24] "The notion of 'build it and they
will come' is one thing," notes Steven Nash, Nasher's first director, "but
the idea of 'build it and they will provide private philanthropy' is a lot
riskier."[25] Joint ownership after the fact is, apparently, harder to solicit.

Syndication allows for a "market test" of an idea in philanthropy, though
it comes at the "cost" of diluting the donor's control of the project. If the
project progresses, having others who care about "the baby" and are literally invested in its success may well help the young entity establish a more
secure place than if its funding is not diversified.

DECISIONS, AFTER FOUNDING, THAT AFFECT THE NEW ORGANIZATION AND THOSE WHOM IT SERVES

The Founder's Capital Planning

Building new institutions requires capital, most obviously for freestanding institutions. Launching an aquarium, museum, research center, or university unavoidably requires significant up-front capital expenditures right away, creating an ante that must be paid to enter the institution-building game. Such expenditures on construction are not onetime fees, because maintenance requirements are significant and (fortunately) fairly well understood. Roofs—probably even Renzo Piano's exquisitely engineered roof at the Nasher—will eventually leak. Capital expenditures will be required of any institution throughout the fullness of time and need to be part of the initial planning.

However, other categories of capital are needed, as well, that merit understanding before responsibly embarking on institution formation. One of them is that some intermediaries, such as LISC, will, in effect, regrant funds (as noted earlier) as part of what they do—standing in (albeit with local knowledge) for the original grant maker. There is another unusual challenge that encumbers those nonprofits that are not only capable of generating earned income, but also show some success in doing so. What enterprising nonprofits soon recognize is that, unlike their revenue-generating cousins from the for-profit realm, they have few opportunities to convert such success to the next stage or to invest in future growth. As William Ryan, Director of the nonprofit governance and accountability project at the Hauser Center at Harvard, notes, the successful nonprofit startup is at a disadvantage in the normal process of growth:

> Social enterprises aimed at self-sufficiency solve one type of capital problem, but generate another. A nonprofit that succeeds in offering a service in the market can gain the enormous benefit of unrestricted income.... But in order to develop the capacity and scale to reach that point of self-sufficiency, social enterprises, like any enterprise, normally require upfront or working capital.[26]

With no call upon capital markets (unlike the venture capital-backed firms that seek staged funding in progressive rounds, based on performance, and in exchange for equity in the firm), growing nonprofits have no way of investing in themselves. To the extent that a founder's plan anticipates market support for the entity, such further calls upon capital might be seen as an extension of the original founding decision. If, as was the case with Project 180, the project fails to show signs of earning the support of the market, the voice of the market should be respected and the experiment should probably be shut down, so that new philanthropic funds are not deployed to rescue risk capital that is not fulfilling its promise.[27]

In the case of LISC, however, the original programmatic success (of working with many more CDCs than the original plan had called for) bred new opportunities, but also operating challenges for the new organization. The Local Initiatives Support Corporation was not financially strong when Grogan took over in 1985. In 1986, Ford made a grant of $5.5 million to LISC to "expand the scope of its work and stimulate a stronger commitment to community development among its funding partners."[28] One strategy the new funds were to support was a Local Initiative Managed Assets Corporation that would purchase LISC loans and free up capital for new projects. Then, in 1988, Ford made another grant consisting of $4 million in general operating support and a $2 million program-related investment (a below-market loan) for use "as bridge financing for an equity investment fund dedicated to financing low-income housing."[29] Having demonstrated laudable success, LISC had identified new opportunities to maximize its impact. At these points of early achievement, a new organization is teetering on the edge of success while still tottering on the edge of failure, without any means to finance new opportunities for expansion. Like more established nonprofits, the new venture's leaders can become consumed by fund-raising.

This dilemma of fund-raising as a distraction will sound familiar to all nonprofits and could—in many ways—be read as a sign that a new nonprofit has established itself as having earned the dilemma of more established nonprofits. However, such a new entrant is unlikely to have the broader following of an established entity, and—as a result of the disruptive nature of its imposition on the established order—might not yet be able to make its way in a crowded and established philanthropic ecosystem. This would be true for any new entry, but the funder–founder's organization may have additional collegiality to build, given its creation in a "top-down" mode. Why would Dallas art patrons support Ray Nasher's pet project? Why would the Rockefeller Foundation buttress the Ford Foundation's well-funded success?

Planning for the support of the new entity in the early-growth capital stage is integral, because now the circle of risk has been widened. During the first stage, the risk was concentrated in the opportunity costs associated with the allocation of the philanthropic funds (and the societal subvention of these funds).[30] At the growth equity stage, it is likely that a dependency has implicated others in the ecosystem—the consumers of the nonprofit's services or the community that will be called upon to "pitch in" if the new institution stumbles. Local communities would have to take over for the founder; those dependent on the services provided will be left without alternative plans. Nancy Bissell, founder of the Primavera Foundation, which aids the homeless in Tucson, Arizona, describes the impact of cuts in all federal and state funding for all community-based residential behavioral health programs during the 1980s. Despite Primavera's success in converting an abandoned motel into a residence program for the homeless, and demonstrating that the homeless could contribute productively to urban renewal of blighted areas, all funding was cut off: "Those folks went back on the streets," Bissell remembers, "and I still see some of them around downtown. In the case of the closing of that particular program, the ones most affected were the clients, as we had only one paid staff person. I would say, though, that from a civic perspective, the whole community was diminished in a tangible way."[31] It is easy to see the irony of nonprofit success and the burden of the undertaking. The more successful the organization is, the more its circles of influence widen and the numbers of those who have a stake in its continued success multiply.

Continuity with the Founder: Stewardship of the New Entity

Good business planning (and well-planned follow-through) diminish the risk that the money could have been better utilized elsewhere. Aside from deputizing one of its own (as was the case with Bellow and Sviridoff), a founder's primary mechanism for steering a new nonprofit is its board of directors. What is the appropriate role for the founder in setting up a board for a new entity?

There is little unanimity on this point. From our vignettes, a range of directions can be seen. Nasher kept the Sculpture Center board close at hand, chairing it himself and populating its board (and the board of the foundation set up to support the Center) with friends and family. On the other hand, LISC's board did not include anyone from Ford. As former Ford Foundation President Susan Berresford noted, "Frank Thomas [her predecessor as president of Ford] had a strong policy of the foundation staying away from board seats on entities that it created. I think that it was related to his memory of his time at the Bedford-Stuyvesant Community Development fund where he never knew what to do with a consultant, an advisor, or a board member who represented funders—were they partners with whom he could honestly confide or were they outsiders with whom he could only share good news?"[32]

Defining the board and serving on it enables the funder–founder to monitor more closely its sizable investment and to understand its working more closely. Edward Skloot, former president of the Surdna Foundation, notes that, although they were aware of potential conflicts of interest, Surdna program officers can serve on boards of grantees: "Working in a foundation is hermetic....It's virtually impossible to know the financial and personnel situation of a grantee without being on the inside. With a board seat, an officer not only sees the difficulties up close, but has a chance to be directly helpful and head off major problems."[33]

When the funder creates the entity, both parties might benefit from this "up close" engagement, whereas board representation might also provide a way for the major investor to mind its investment in the manner of venture capitalists. The board will be (along with executive leadership) the vehicle that interprets the organization's mission, but, of course, interpreting is an act of definition. Once launched, the organization takes on—sooner or later, gradually or more suddenly—its own directions. The funder–founder can take a more hands-on or hands-off role in that definition, but should recognize that such definition needs to happen and will inevitably modify or reinterpret the original charge.

Stewardship of the fledgling project can take either form. Taking board seats ensures close tracking; long-term support (absent a board seat) may be based on the idea that the timetable for investment is very long term and understood by both sides. In that case, the institution starts off with a reservoir of trust that it is best positioned to make strategic decisions without interference—and without risking its founding relationship, as Susan Berresford argued:

> If a donor wants to ensure that all elderly people in the community get a flu shot before winter, a relatively targeted and short-term donor strategy makes sense. If the challenge is to create a brand-new and ultimately endowed organization to ensure the rights of a marginalized community, 10 to 20 years of donor engagement in institution building will probably be necessary. We looked at LISC or Vera or MDRC as 20-year investments and we planned our budget around those understood commitments.[34]

A plan for stewardship and for the funder's involvement is important, because whatever the original plan is, it will change. Evolution of the plan is natural; but so, too, is unexpected change.

Discontinuity Happens

"There is no such thing," Elizabeth Glassman, President of the Terra Foundation for American Art has concluded, "as the long reach from beyond the grave."[35] Having been hired to be the director of the Terra Museum in 2002, a museum created in 1980 by Daniel Terra for his collection of American art, she soon found herself working with Terra's widow, the board of directors, and—eventually—the attorney general of the state of Illinois to determine what direction the Foundation should take. Terra had built the museum; moved it into a downtown location in 1987; had opened another museum in Giverny, France; sponsored exhibitions; and had expressed an interest in Chicago cultural affairs. When he died in 1996 and his estate was finally settled, it remained unclear whether the museum should remain a museum, whether the commitment to Chicago was an essential part of the mission, and what the international program should or shouldn't be. The attorney general became involved because Terra's widow and two other board members were sued by other board members for attempting to move the museum from Chicago to Washington, DC. Today, much of the collection is on long-term loan and the Foundation is making its place as a grant maker devoted to the promotion of American art. However, the founder's death left the future unclear and led to a complicated revisioning.

New nonprofits, even the progeny of funder–founders, need to plan as best they can—from the beginning—to handle discontinuity. The more that all parties agree on the plan together upfront, the lower the risk that future discontinuity will either sink the effort or be used as an excuse for latent shortcomings. As Steven Nash puts it, "There is, of course, no way to tie down the mission over time. We got from Ray before he died a founder's vision statement—actual goals that he put down on paper. Will that document be the key 50 years from now? That's hard to say, but it certainly gives a different kind of guidance today than we would have had, given his sudden departure."[36]

Exit: Community Buy-In

Nasher's estate will apparently provide more than $100 million in endowment funds—the most powerful bulwark against challenges that any nonprofit might face. The Center reports that revenue from admissions at the Nasher decreased from $993,000 in 2004 to $495,000 in 2006. But as other challenges come, one decision—the decision to build the museum in downtown Dallas instead of at his house in the outskirts of Dallas—may well have been Nasher's most insightful decision.[37] By weaving the fate of the museum into the fabric of Dallas and the cultural district, Nasher avoided the isolationism that has made the 50-year history of the Barnes Foundation such a struggle—and such a burden upon public and private resources. Ambition and the desire to control every detail of the new institution served the building of the Sculpture Center well, especially with concomitant funding; however, the willingness of Nasher to let the center blend in—to lose itself—in Dallas's urban fabric signals a turn from singular ambition to community ownership that allows the founder a way out.

The arc of such a project begins with bold ambition—ambition on the part of a funder who presumes to know enough to bet on its own ability to effect change. If the venture is well planned, it begins to test itself against reality, against the needs of a community to see if its thesis was correct. Progress can be tracked, especially the signals of market feedback that are clear indicators of whether the offering is being welcomed as anticipated. Some other measures of success will inevitably be harder to see and harder to measure because of the time horizons and metric-resistant signs of progress toward mission-related goals. The time horizon needs to be sufficient (Olin College, for example, has pledged not to charge tuition until 2021) to allow the institution to build trust and for sentimental attachment to build for the new institution—a process that often does not materialize instantly in the nonprofit landscape. And as the new institution becomes less new and wins over its communities, the risks associated with the enterprise are now more widely shared.

Because of this shared risk, the risk tolerance probably needs to begin to be lower. Today's Olin students and faculty members are risk-taking pioneers. Risks in experiments are high, and many unknowns cannot be resolved because of the nature of pioneering. Although it is easy to see now how the original attendance projections for the Nasher may have been too aggressive, it was impossible to know with any certainty—and, one could argue, it was worth learning—how strong the public's appetite for sculpture exhibitions (as opposed to blockbuster painting exhibitions) would be.

If the turning point for the venture-funded entity is the initial public offering or the strategic sale, there is a somewhat analogous—but essentially different—turn for the funder–founder enterprise when it gains acceptance into the community fabric. The event is not marked by soaring stock prices and an opportunity for investors and management to cash out some part of their equity, but by a successful turn to gain the community's acceptance as a partner. As Michael Govan, formerly of the Dia Foundation and now director of the Los Angeles County Museum of Art, has put it, "Living people are great as collectors—they can make split-second decisions, they can follow their taste and build something very significant without a single committee. But all the things that they can't stand about institutions are going to be what sustains their collections after they die. Whether they like it or not, institutional characteristics (such as reaching consensus and building relationships with the community) are the things that are going to take care of their collections after they're gone."[38]

In all communities—for profit or nonprofit—building trust and gaining acceptance are pathways to success. For-profit success is measured by buying, whereas nonprofit success is often discernible as buy-in. Obviously, the successful management of spending and (where applicable) of revenue generation (be it from earned income or philanthropic support) represent very important measures of success. However, a new institution has to do more than survive financially (as is recognized in Olin's planning papers):

> The goal of becoming an asset to the community, a good neighbor and a partner with the local schools, requires an investment in long-term relationships in the community.... Olin College seeks to earn the respect of the citizens in the local community, as well as the Greater Boston area, by always taking the high road and providing an example of neighborhood sensitivity and community-mindedness in its actions.[39]

Humility demonstrates that the entity that was thrust into the community from "above" has "caught up" with the organizations that spring up—bottom up—from the needs of the community. This modest place demonstrates progress along the philanthropic arc, from a perch of perspective and power to an ambition of just fitting in and serving. In describing her movement from problem solving as a grant maker to attempting problem solving from within the landscape of the community, Rachel Bellow articulates the turn in the trajectory:

> Giving up power is the only way to get honesty in that transaction. You don't know what's going on in the transaction, and you don't know what goes on after the transaction. All you get are reports and flattery. The only way to get honesty is to correct the power inequities of the

relationship.... What you know and what you have to contribute from the foundation to that trajectory is a very, very small part and that's okay.[40]

Exit: Fitting In and Moving On

New nonprofits more firmly establish their place in the landscape when they are trusted and stable. Stability requires a number of demonstrations that the institution can live beyond the energy of its creation. This also means the organization must be able to transition away from the original leader, and in doing so become an independent and established institution. Michael Sviridoff handed LISC over to Paul Grogan in 1985 and the institution went through a major transformation (as Grogan recounts):

> It was the classic "person who follows the founder" story. We needed to raise other money and ended up emphasizing the banking and investment model more than the original emphasis on technical assistance. And, yes, that certainly led to some tense moments with Ford. But we knew that we needed them and, as I tried to say over the subsequent years, by changing the institution, we became a way for them to get things done that they wanted done. Sometimes people there would say, "Oh, LISC's gotten so big, you don't need us anymore," and I would counter that there were things which they wanted done that we could do better than any other mechanism—it was the mission that mattered, not the organizational size or structure, or even its origins.[41]

The evolution of LISC after its founding serves as a reminder that the equity being built is social impact, and that accrues, not to individuals in the organization, but rather to the community. At the appropriate time, weathering these changes or these struggles are signs that a new organization is now a dependable one.

How might an organization and its original funder plan for the funder to withdraw in such a way as to mitigate the risk that is now being shared across a dependent community? The best answer to this difficult challenge consists of having had an understanding from the start about roles, expectations, and transitions, and a willingness to accept and plan through change. As Berresford relates, in the context of one of the entities that Ford created during her years, the time came for a successful venture to wean itself from Ford funding, not because of its failure, but because of its success. The executive director resisted and argued that all would fall apart. "I told her that this was going to work. We had time, we could plan together, she was going to need to build an endowment and we would help. She was going to need some new board members, and we would work on that together. It turned out just fine."[42]

CONCLUSIONS

The ethical implications of creating a new entity are revealed only in how the work is carried out:

- Vetting an idea against community needs is essential to avoid philanthropic waste. Bringing in other funders from the beginning is one of the few mechanisms for vetting an idea. Although control is very enabling for the funder–founder and the new entity, sharing control brings in other counsel, wisdom, and ownership.
- There clearly are times when a new institution is the best solution to carry out change. Although there is risk, some experimentation for taking on complex social problems is needed.
- A funder–founder with real knowledge of a territory and a willingness to vet the idea thoroughly might be better suited to take risks than to try to steer existing institutions toward the effort.
- Institution building is a difficult and long-term proposition. Processes like constructing a building, creating an identity, and attracting a segment of the market to serve are the beginning, not the end, of the process.
- If the funder is depending on the new organization to carry out functions that it wants to foster, the new organization should be seen as a partner in accomplishing the founder's aims.
- Explicit long-term planning is the way to build levees against the unpredictable discontinuities that are always possible during the early course of institution building. Discontinuity may well still occur, but shared and explicit plans can provide a guiding text to which tomorrow's interpreters can refer.
- The widening circles of risk should be recognized. In the earliest days, acting as a funder–founder risks only capital. As the entity becomes a valued part of the life of a community, the risk becomes more widely shared.
- Weaving into the texture of a community is the great test of an organization created from "above." Because trust and respect are earned by service rather than by proclamations, the organization that can convert its top-down origin into an accepted place in the landscape has passed the most relevant market test—the market of trust. This challenge should not be underestimated, and it increases with the complexity of the problem being addressed and the number of actors whose trust and partnership need to be earned.
- Determining how and when the original relationship between the donor and the new organization has served its purpose will never be easy, because most nonprofits barely maintain operating equilibrium. However, planning that exit, together, can and should be accomplished in a way that is mindful of the questions and risks explored.

Our society is really just beginning to understand what it can and should expect from philanthropy. There will, alas, be ill-advised and careless acts of philanthropy that may be narcissistic, wasteful, and even damaging. But there also have been, and should be, bold strokes—chances taken by those who can afford to take them on behalf of people, institutions, and communities that are, by necessity and nature, more risk averse. Thinking through and nurturing these efforts is the only way of preventing the good ideas from ending up in the same category of wasteful philanthropy as the bad ideas that never should have gone forward in the first place.

Notes

I am grateful to the readers of various drafts (Rachel Bellow, Charlie Clotfelter, Jo Ellen Parker, Joel Fleishman, Mike McPherson, Angelica Rudenstine, Neil Rudenstine, Buzz Schmidt, Steven Schindler, Rachel Spiegel, and Gretchen Wagner) and to those interviewed (Susan Berresford, Rachel Bellow, Nancy Bissell, Elizabeth Glassman, Michael Govan, Paul Grogan, and Steven Nash) who were generous with their time and insights.

Epigraph source: www.olin.edu/about_olin/docs/inaugural_address.asp (July 23, 2010).

1. Terms that often blur in usage include *social entrepreneurship, venture philanthropy, high-engagement philanthropy*, and *high-impact philanthropy*. On the last two terms, see Venture Philanthropy Partners, *High Engagement Philanthropy: A Bridge to a More Effective Social Sector* (Washington, D.C.: Venture Philanthropy Partners, 2004), and Venture Philanthropy Partners, "Characteristics of High-Impact Programs: Leadership, Focus, Alignment, and Measurement," in Joel L. Fleishman, *The Foundation: A Great American Secret—How Private Wealth Is Changing the World* (New York: Public Affairs Books, 2007), chap. 11.

2. Fleishman, *The Foundation*, p. 339; and Rob Reich, "Philanthropy and Its Uneasy Relation to Equality," in William Damon and Susan Verducci, eds., *Taking Philanthropy Seriously* (Bloomington: Indiana University Press, 2006), pp. 27–49.

3. See the essay by Laura Horn and Howard Gardner, "The Lonely Profession," in William Damon and Susan Verducci, eds., *Taking Philanthropy Seriously* (Bloomington: Indiana University Press, 2006), pp. 77–94, about the strains brought about by isolation from the public and from other foundations, and from asking "how to claim some sense of professional accomplishment and competence without falsely taking credit for the generosity of some or for the work of others." The authors elucidate the struggle of good grant makers, concluding: "relying exclusively on exceptional individuals to find their own way in professional grantmaking is not a sustainable strategy for good work in philanthropy" (p. 93).

4. Jenni Menon Mariano and Susan Verducci, "Ethical Standards in Philanthropy," in William Damon and Susan Verducci, eds., *Taking Philanthropy Seriously* (Bloomington: Indiana University Press, 2006), p. 233.

5. The essay format provides insufficient space for full analysis, and these cases were chosen because their lessons resonate with other cases and experiences investigated in this research.

6. Witold Rybczynski, "Extreme Museum Makeover," April 27, 2005, www.slate.com. Other citations in this case are from Raymond Nasher, interview with Jim Lehrer, "Sharing Sculpture," *Online NewsHour* (October 20, 2003), www.pbs.org/newshour/bb/entertainment/july-dec03/sculpture_10-20.html (July 23, 2010); Robert Bliwise, "The Collector," *Duke Magazine* 89 (2003), www.dukemagazine.duke.edu/dukemag/issues/050603/collector1.html (July 23, 2010); Carol Vogel, "Coveted Sculptures Going to Dallas," *New York Times* (April 8, 1997), p. C9; Victoria L. Hicks, "An Arts Match Made in Dallas: New Sculpture

Center Required 20 Years of Careful Courting," *Dallas Morning News* (October 14, 2003), p. A1.

7. Hicks, "Arts Match Made in Dallas."

8. Phillip Jones, Chief Executive of the Dallas Convention & Visitors Bureau. Suzanne Marta, "Alliance Sees Arts District as a Destination," *Dallas Morning News* (July 18, 2007), p. 1D.

9. Alan Oser, "Nonprofit Realty Groups Getting More Private Help," *New York Times* (March 18, 1984), sect. 8, p. 7. Other key documents include Mitchell Sviridoff, "The Seeds of Urban Revival," *Public Interest* (Winter 1994), p. 114; and J. Scott Kohler, "Local Initiatives Support Corporation: Ford Foundation, 1979," Case 52, in Joel L. Fleishman, J. Scott Kohler, and Steven Schindler, *Casebook for the Foundation: A Great American Secret* (New York: Public Affairs, 2007), cspcs. sanford.duke.edu/sites/default/files/descriptive/local_initiatives_support_corporation.pdf (July 23, 2010), pp. 151–155.

10. Bliwise, "Collector."

11. Ford Foundation, *LISC: A Private–Public Venture for Community and Neighborhood Revitalization* (New York: Ford Foundation, May 1980), pp. 4–5.

12. *Chronicle of Philanthropy*, "Nonprofit Leaders and Experts Offer Their Predictions for 2008" (December 31, 2007), philanthropy.com/article/Nonprofit-LeadersExperts/62754 (July 26, 2010).

13. Clayton M. Christensen, Heiner Baumann, Rudy Ruggles, and Thomas M. Sadtler, "Disruptive Innovation for Social Change," *Harvard Business Review* 84 (2006), pp. 94–101.

14. Ford Foundation, *LISC*, p. 4.

15. Rachel Bellow, interview with the author.

16. Carol Vogel, "Inside Art," *New York Times* (June 23, 1995), p. 26.

17. www.stowers-institute.org/Public/Mission.asp. When Mitchell Wolfson established his museum in Miami, he called it the "Wolfsonian"—a decision to institutionalize the new entry in the same way that the Smithsonian was named after donor James Smithson.

18. Ford Foundation, *LISC*, p. 3. For the story of another ambitious but ultimately less successful attempt at setting up an intermediary organization to foster community development, see Prudence Brown's and Leila Fiester's "Hard Lessons about Philanthropy & Community Change from the Neighborhood Improvement Initiative," March 2007, www.hewlett.org/NR/rdonlyres/ 6D05A0B4-D15E-47FA-B62E-917741BB9E72/0/HewlettNIIReport.pdf (July 23, 2010). Commissioned by the Foundation to review the $20 milllion Neighborhood Improvement Initiative effort, the authors note that "Community change—that is, the development of neighborhood leaders, organizations, and networks so that they can support residents and link them to resources and opportunities, inside and outside the community—isn't for every foundation. Funders who are contemplating such investments need to seriously consider what capacities they have to play which kinds of role in the community change enterprise. Some will find the work too messy, politically charged, and/or hard to assess" (pp 56–57).

19. Sviridoff, "Seeds of Urban Revival," p. 94.

20. Paul A. Gompers and Josh Lerner, *The Money of Invention: How Venture Capital Creates New Wealth* (Cambridge, Mass.: Harvard Business School Press, 2001).

21. Interview with the author. For a review of other very successful Mellon Foundation creations from this same period (including JSTOR and the College and Beyond research project), see Fleishman, *The Foundation*, pp. 68–69.

22. Hicks, "Arts Match Made in Dallas."

23. Vogel, "Coveted Sculptures Going to Dallas."

24. These data are from searches at the Foundation Center's online directory.

25. Interview with the author.

26. William P. Ryan, *Nonprofit Capital: A Review of Problems and Strategies* (Washington, D.C.: The Rockefeller Foundation and Fannie Mae Foundation, 2001), p. 23.

27. See Venture Philanthropy Partners, *High Engagement Philanthropy*, p. 15: "[W]e are not advocating a completely democratic approach to allocation of funding. In fact, we stand on the side of a meritocracy, where only those organizations able—or likely—to demonstrate that they are delivering a quality service should have primary access to growth capital."

28. Ford Foundation, *Annual Report 1986* (New York: Ford Foundation, 1987), p. 2.

29. Ford Foundation, *Annual Report 1988* (New York: Ford Foundation, 1989), p. 3.

30. As Olin's President Miller noted, the funding that went into building the new college could have created or enhanced engineering programs at dozens of institutions around the country—and, indeed, Olin funding had, for 60 years, built and equipped engineering buildings at 57 campuses as diverse as Hampton, Worcester Polytechnic, and Johns Hopkins. After the Foundation decided in 1997 to devote all of its $460 million endowment to creating the new college, no more campuses received such buildings.

31. Interview with author.

32. Interview with author.

33. Edward Skloot, *Beyond the Money: Reflections on Philanthropy, the Nonprofit Sector and Civic Life, 1999–2006* (New York: The Surdna Foundation, 2007), pp. 91–92.

34. Interview with the author. See also Remarks by Susan V. Berresford, "Philanthropy: What's New, What's Not" (speech given at Duke University's Fuqua School of Business, February 6, 2007), www.fordfound.org/newsroom/speeches/192 (July 23, 2010).

35. Interview with the author.

36. Interview with the author.

37. Steven Nash, ed., *Nasher Sculpture Center Handbook* (Dallas: Nasher Sculpture Center, 2003), p. 11. The Dia's very successful Beacon, New York project faces very different long-term challenges than the Frick, sitting in the heart of Manhattan.

38. Interview with the author.

39. *Invention 2000*, vision statement, http://www.olin.edu/about_olin/history/invention2kf.aspx (July 23, 2010).

40. Rachel Bellow, "What's Next: Going Off-Road with the Arts as Venture Philanthropy," in *Grantmakers in the Arts: Proceedings from the 1999 Conference* (Seattle: Grantmakers in the Arts, 1999), http://s70362.gridserver.com/sites/default/files/Whats-Next.pdf, p. 11.

41. Interview with the author.

42. Interview with the author.

12

The Unfulfilled Promise
of Corporate Philanthropy

Thomas W. Dunfee

> Of every $1,000 spent in so-called charity today, it is probable
> that $950 is unwisely spent.
> —Andrew Carnegie

Corporate philanthropy involves a transfer of money, goods, or services by
a public for-profit organization based upon a significant social motive. In
the United States, the level of corporate philanthropy appears to have
averaged a little more than 1% of net profits for many decades. It typically
accounts for about 5% of total charity in the United States. In 2005, the
total amount given was around $14 billion. About a quarter of corporate
tax returns reflect deductions for charitable contributions.[1]

Although the amounts are nontrivial and the potential for improving
the social good is high, the practice of corporate philanthropy remains
distressingly opaque and shrouded in controversy. Critics on the right
charge that corporations are not proper agents for distributing charity, a
function that should be left to individual shareholders who are free to
disperse dividends and capital gains as they prefer. Critics on the left are
skeptical of corporate motives, believing that business strategies and
financial engineering goals dominate any desire to improve the social
good. This has led some to question whether the term *strategic philanthropy* is a classic oxymoron.[2] Aggregate data are imprecise, because
many firms either do not report their data to independent organizations
or only selectively disclose donations. More than a third of the top 150
firms in the Fortune 500 fail to disclose information about their giving
to the *Chronicle of Philanthropy*[3] whereas 60% of the S&P 500 failed to
provide data to *Business Week* when the respected publication initiated
an annual report on philanthropy, and even in the most recent report
the percentage responding stays well less than 50%. A visit to the website of virtually any major corporation will quickly make clear how difficult it is to obtain a comprehensive picture of a particular firm's
philanthropic activity.

Definitions concerning what falls within the domain of corporate philanthropy are uncertain in practice and, perhaps surprisingly, also in the
academic literature. The inability to define with precision what corporate
philanthropy includes creates measurement problems that make compar-
isons difficult. Should, for example, noncash distributions such as the
donation of drugs by pharmaceutical companies be counted and, if so,
how should the distributions be valued? Should they be valued at cost or
at a marked-up price? Similar issues arise in the treatment of employee
volunteer programs. How should employee time be valued? Does it make
a difference whether the employee is given credit by the firm for a
workday? The answers to these types of valuation questions can have a
major impact on reports of the level of corporate giving and in studies
seeking to compare activity across firms or industries.

The use of corporate foundations has an impact on assessments of philanthropy. Some corporations set up separate foundations funded directly
by distributions from the firm. This allows the business entity to time and
control the tax efficiency of its donations (it may give more in a highly
profitable year) while the foundation employs a professional staff to distribute resources in a manner attuned to donor need. Wal-Mart has the
largest corporate foundation. Corporate foundations accounted for about
$4 billion in 2005, which represented about 11% of all foundation giving.

Public reports of corporate philanthropy vary regarding the type of
activities included. Some firms appear to report only cash donations
whereas, at the other extreme, are corporations reporting a wide range of
social activity and initiatives. It appears that some firms fail to report publicly what they do. Some firms may present their information in a
self-serving way, overstating their actual contributions. The most reliable
source of information pertains to corporate foundations set up in the
United States who are required to file annual reports with the government.[4]
However, even those data are limited. The overall result is that the great
variety in the quality and quantity of data makes it virtually impossible to
come up with a hard comparison of relative levels of giving among firms.

Corporate philanthropy is characterized by extreme opacity and is
challenged by concerns about its legitimacy and efficiency concerns. In
response, this chapter will seek (1) to provide a working definition of
corporate philanthropy, (2) to resolve the question of legitimacy, (3) to
evaluate a claim that all corporations have an obligation to engage in philanthropy, (4) to highlight the all-important question of efficiency, and
(5) to suggest an orientation for decision makers that should enhance the
quality of corporate philanthropy.

A WORKING DEFINITION OF CORPORATE PHILANTHROPY

Corporate philanthropy is a special category or form of philanthropy. The
defining characteristic, of course, is that the philanthropic act is carried
out by a business corporation, ordinarily understood to be a for-profit

organization. The act itself involves a net transfer intended to create value for a donee. In contrast to ordinary market exchanges, a philanthropic act involves a desire to provide a social good. A much-debated issue is the prominence to be given to the altruistic, social benefit component of the donor's motivation.

Multiple motives underlie corporate giving programs. Even a single project may involve a variety of seemingly contradictory motives. For example, a firm may engage in philanthropy (1) to improve the general reputation of the company, (2) to induce customers to buy their products or services, (3) to smooth earnings, (4) to reduce taxes, (5) to improve their competitive position in the industry, (6) to motivate or attract employees, (7) to access important social networks, (8) to forestall regulation, (9) to insulate against negative public reaction to bad acts, and (10) to achieve a particular social goal. The Committee Encouraging Corporate Philanthropy provides annual reports of the results of surveys of slightly more than 100 large corporations. In their 2006 report, they described the results of a survey of motivations for giving. The allocation of a typical company was found to be 54% charitable, 35% strategic, and 11% commercial.[5] In a recent McKinsey Global Survey of chief executive officers (CEOs) and high-level executives, nearly 90% indicated that their firms seek business benefits from their philanthropy programs.[6]

Philanthropy may be a component of a business strategy. Social cause marketing involves creating an alignment between values of the company and those of customers. The assumption is that customers will try and then be loyal to the company's products and services because of the perceived commonality of values. Iconic academic consultant Michael Porter now advocates *strategic philanthropy* as a means by which firms can develop a competitive edge: "If systematically pursued in a way that maximizes the value created, context-focused philanthropy can offer companies a new set of competitive tools that well justifies the investment of resources. At the same time, it can unlock a vastly more powerful way to make the world a better place."[7] Evidence indicates that firms are indeed becoming more strategic in their approach to philanthropy.[8]

Philanthropy may be a component of financial engineering. Properly timed and framed, philanthropy may minimize tax liability or assist with earnings management. Deductions may be increased or reduced in a given year to smooth earnings. Deductions may be increased when a firm faces higher than usual taxes.

Agency problems may be associated with philanthropy. Corporate donations may be designed to fulfill the desire of the CEO or other top managers to be named to the boards of artistic or educational institutions. Membership on such boards brings prestige and social connections. Bartkus, Morris, and Seifert describe the claim that when Ross Johnson wanted to take RJR Nabisco private, he attempted to influence several key members of the board of directors by making large company donations to Duke University in their names.[9]

Suppose that a company were to make a large anonymous donation to the Red Cross. There is no public notice involving the donation. Assume further that the company does not even let its own staff or employees know. Instead, only a senior corporate official has knowledge of the gift. The company appears to receive no benefit, while at the same time there is a major social benefit. This would seem to be a case of pure social philanthropy. Presumably, there are very few cases like this in which a company has a purely altruistic motivation.

At the other extreme would be a company that decides the best way to introduce a new product (for example, a new shampoo) is by promising that it will make a small donation to the Red Cross for every bottle purchased. The action is taken at a time in which there has been a disaster that has created a significant blood shortage. Public support for the Red Cross as an institution is high. The shampoo donation program is designed by the marketing department is on their budget, and the success and continuation of the project will be determined solely on the basis of the sales of the new product. In this case the "philanthropy" is purely a business strategy in which any social motivation is purely instrumental.

Most cases of corporate philanthropy fall in between these two extremes. Social purposes and business strategies are liberally intermixed. In the case of mixed motives is there a decision rule capable of determining whether an action should be considered philanthropy? One might be tempted to try to quantify the relative importance of social versus business motives. Or one could try to develop a few heuristics that would signal the presence or lack of a sufficient philanthropic orientation. For example, the place where a philanthropy program is budgeted and housed might be quite revealing. A program developed and run by managers in a corporate responsibility office or by a corporate foundation might be identified as genuinely philanthropic. In contrast, a "philanthropy" program operated by a marketing unit might be suspect. Another approach could be to look at the ratio of the size of publicity expenditures compared with the size of the philanthropic donation. Firms spending a great deal on advertising, and publicizing relatively small donations would be considered to lack an appropriate motive.[10] Despite their intuitive appeal, the temptation to come up with hard formulas or heuristics for characterizing motive should be resisted on grounds of infeasibility.

Inherent in the nature of corporations is the fact that motives will be essentially opaque to outsiders.[11] Factors that might be used to identify motives can be manipulated. A firm engaging in a social cause marketing strategy has every incentive to make sure that its ersatz social motive is perceived by outsiders as genuine. There is simply no easy way for an outsider to determine "true" motives.[12] The task is further complicated by the inherent difficulty of attempting to ascribe a motive to an organization. People within the organization involved with a philanthropy program may each have different individual motives. The best that one can do in ascribing motives to an organization is to rely upon official organizational pronouncements.

A working solution is to take organizational statements of social motives at face value unless there is persuasive evidence to the contrary. The existence of a social motive can also be induced from the quality and nature of the philanthropic program. Although it can be assumed that almost all corporate philanthropy will involve some element of mixed motives, it will not be necessary to attempt the impossible by seeking to identify dominant submotives. Instead, one can just try to determine whether stated or derived social motives are significant in the sense that they are likely to confer a net increase in social good.

This approach results in the following working definition of corporate philanthropy: Corporate philanthropy involves a net transfer by a public, for-profit organization of money, goods, or services designed to confer a significant social good. Mixed motives are expected and are consistent with this definition, as long as an independent motive to confer a significant social good can be identified.

THE ERSATZ ISSUE: QUESTIONING THE LEGITIMACY OF CORPORATE PHILANTHROPY

Corporate philanthropy is ingrained in U.S. culture and is widely practiced and praised. At least a quarter of all firms engage in the practice with a bias toward greater involvement by larger firms. The Friedmanite claim that, in general, corporations should not engage in philanthropy has had little real-world impact.[13] One can imagine the chorus of concern and criticism that would greet an announcement from the Fortune 500 that they were going to adopt Friedman's ideas and stop all giving and social initiatives immediately. The protesting choir would be quite diverse. The ensemble of protesting choral sections would include university presidents, directors of museums and ballets, leaders of human services organizations, heads of major nongovernmental organizations (NGOs), politicians, heads of hospitals and medical research clinics, leaders of professional business associations, and even some investor-based groups.

Why has the Friedman view failed to have much impact? One explanation might be that philanthropy is so good for business that shareholders support it because they understand that it enhances long-term profitability. This win-win idea is an ever more popular idea as consultants push the concept of strategic philanthropy. Despite the general claims and arguments advanced in support of the win-win view,[14] hard evidence of a relationship between philanthropy and profits is hard to come by. Seifert, Morris, and Bartkus state that "there is little research evidence that giving has a positive effect on firm financial performance,"[15] noting that "the path coefficient between company size and relative corporate philanthropy was not significant in any model we tested."[16] Fisman, Heal, and Nair model corporate philanthropy and use economic databases to conclude that profits and philanthropy appear to be positively related only in industries with high advertising intensity and high levels of competition.[17]

Corporate philanthropy programs justified significantly on the basis of their contribution to the financial bottom line would have a hard time satisfying the rigorous standards typically followed when firms evaluate ordinary business investments. When firms make business investments, they are unlikely to rely on vague statements or projections about improved reputation or morale. Instead, they insist on the best available direct evidence concerning probable contributions to the bottom line or to a successful competitive strategy. They require hard data demonstrating that the business goals are being realized. A comparable approach doesn't appear to be possible for most types of corporate philanthropy. Meaningful "hard" numbers for the impact of philanthropic programs cannot be identified. End points cannot be specified with precision. Results are amorphous. So although advocates of corporate philanthropy may claim that there are business benefits, they cannot demonstrate the actual benefits in the same serious manner expected for a business investment.

If the business case is marginal at best, then why does the practice persist? One answer, supported by institutional theory in management and consistent with social contract-based approaches to business ethics, is that corporate philanthropy, at least in some markets and nations, is supported by influential business norms. Prophilanthropic norms are often reflected in peer pressure influencing individual executives and organizational management. Professional organizations such as the Business Roundtable support the practice. Chief executive officers interact socially in venues such as boards associated with educational and arts organizations in which corporate philanthropy is recognized and applauded. Galaskiewicz studied the Twin Cities of Minneapolis and St. Paul, famous for the 5% club that supports generous giving among major local firms, and concluded that socialites were critically important influencers of firm behavior.[18] Philanthropic actions provoke responses from competitors. Merck's much-praised development and distribution of a drug designed to combat the ravages of the affliction called river blindness was followed by other major pharmaceutical companies developing similar programs.

The business norm supporting philanthropy is clearly supported by key stakeholders and by broader society. Tax laws allow a deduction for charitable giving. The policy of granting a tax exemption can be seen as a direct subsidy of the practice because tax revenues decrease in response. In the United States, a National Corporate Philanthropy Day was initially promulgated jointly by the U.S. Secretary of Commerce, the governor of New York, and the mayor of New York City. The broad social norm found in many countries and cultures supports voluntary action by a corporation in support of a social good. Not only is such action seen as legitimate in and of itself, aggregate contributions are seen as a way by which business legitimates itself. John Manzoni, a senior executive at British Petroleum puts it as follows: "Part of the bargain, the social contract which allows companies to be as large as they are, is that they become engaged in the challenges the world faces, rather than dismissing them as someone else's problem."[19]

Today, when many argue that corporate philanthropy is fundamental to a company's license to operate, and the websites of more than 80% of the Fortune 500 explicitly describe social endeavors,[20] the time has come to declare the Friedmanite criticism officially moribund. However, even as its legitimacy is now unquestioned, serious issues remain concerning the effectiveness of corporate philanthropy in contributing to the social good.

CORPORATE OBLIGATIONS TO ENGAGE IN PHILANTHROPY

The conclusion that corporate philanthropy is a legitimate activity for a for-profit corporation based upon powerful supportive norms in business and society establishes that it is permissible for a firm to engage in social initiatives or philanthropy if it so chooses. But suppose, as is the case with the majority of U.S. corporations, a firm decides it will not take action designed to contribute directly to the social good. Instead, the firm focuses solely on its business activities while making no charitable contributions and eschewing all social initiatives. Can it be claimed that the firm has acted improperly, either in violation of an applicable ethical duty or in breach of a mandatory social norm?

Several caveats need to be recognized. First, there is a long-standing debate in the academic literature and in public venues concerning whether corporations have an obligation to engage in social responsibility. The definition of the term *social responsibility* is central to the argument. Some include an obligation to act in compliance with the law. Others include avoiding harms, such as endangering employees by unsafe working conditions or harming consumers by manufacturing or distributing dangerous products. The debate has produced problematic conflations of the quite separate dimensions of doing good versus avoiding causing harm. Although both are important, in certain circumstances they invoke very different types of considerations. To simplify the analysis and resulting claims, the focus in this chapter is solely on voluntary actions by corporations to improve the social good. Therefore, the arguments considered will be those relevant to contributions to social good consistent with the definition of corporate philanthropy put forth in this chapter.

A further distinction needs to be made between a narrow cash-based definition of corporate philanthropy and the broader range of potential corporate social initiatives. A claim that there is a duty to engage in old-style philanthropy of cash contributions or cash equivalents (for example, donation of goods) would, in effect, be proposing that firms must engage in these practices even though they have the ability to make a much greater contribution to the social good by use of other competencies. The analysis in this section focuses on the ability of firms to use a broad portfolio of strategies to enhance the social good.

Second, corporations are subject to legal constraints that may restrict their ability to engage in certain types of activities. A financial institution subjected to mandated capital requirements may not be able to divert funds toward discretionary charitable contributions. Third, any duty or obligation needs to be contingent on financial exigencies, because a company may be losing money, unable to honor contractual obligations to creditors, and so forth. Corporations have been criticized when they have continued substantial charitable contributions during periods in which they have announced sizable layoffs of employees justified by claims of financial necessity. US Airways made planes available during the period immediately after the displacement and devastation of Hurricane Katrina. At the same time, US Airways was struggling to avoid a complete financial collapse as it went into and then emerged from bankruptcy protection. A variety of stakeholders, including US Air employees, customers, and the general traveling public, might question the philanthropic act in these circumstances.

Any possible mandatory duty to engage in philanthropy would have to be contingent on financial capability, perhaps by limiting it to a percentage of profits above a certain threshold. It would also have to be consistent with legal constraints, although one can argue that public policy should be adjusted to recognize compelling normative duties. The arguments pro and con in relation to a mandatory corporate obligation can be quickly summarized.

In support of some form of contingent duty to engage in philanthropy are arguments based on interconnected notions of reciprocity, legitimacy, citizenship, efficiency, and extrapolation. The reciprocity argument is straightforward. Society provides the environment and background institutions that make it possible for business to thrive. In return for recognition of and protection of property rights, enforcement of contracts, and so on, business has an obligation to give back to society. This extends to every capable firm, because all firms enjoy the benefits of society. Free riders who fail to contribute take advantage of those who do, thus committing a double wrong.

The legitimacy argument is based on the recognition that it is important for corporations to be perceived as legitimate members of the societies in which they operate. Individual corporations or even entire industries that lose their status as legitimate members of society may be subjected to changed rules, making it far more difficult for the firms to achieve their business goals. One way to try to minimize reprisals is to maintain and maximize legitimacy through philanthropy. Altria (Phillip Morris) has been known as a major contributor to the arts for decades. When Goldman Sachs announced the $100 million program to provide business training to women in developing nations in March 2008, the *Financial Times* article noted that it came at a time when Goldman Sachs was making enormous profits during a period of economic downturn. The article noted: "Philanthropic work such as this tends to soften a bank's image."[21]

The citizenship arguments are based on a claim that corporations are citizens of a particular society having general duties similar to all citizens. The argument has been extended to the global level, where it is asserted that corporations as citizens of global society have special obligations to all humanity. In some cases, the argument is based upon reciprocity or legitimacy themes. In other cases, specific duties of citizens are identified (for example, an obligation to engage with and support stakeholders) and then are extrapolated to the corporate entity. The list of obligations may include a general duty of charity.

The efficiency argument is based on the assumption that there are circumstances in which businesses possess competencies creating a comparative advantage in contributing to the social good. Businesses control resources such as know-how, capital, staff, scarce goods, and so on. In certain circumstances, these resources enable business to make the best net contribution to the social good among all possible providers, including public-sector agencies and NGOs. For example, a corporation specializing in food services may be able to deliver better quality and a greater quantity of food to homeless individuals at a lower cost than can any other potential supplier. Because business in the aggregate may be seen to have significant comparative advantages in contributing to social welfare, the argument is made that it therefore follows that all businesses have an obligation to engage in philanthropy, making use of their unique capabilities.

Finally, if one recognizes a general duty of charity on the part of individuals, it may be possible to extrapolate that duty to the corporate entity that, in this context, is seen as a collective of individuals. Individuals don't lose their identities as obligation-bearing entities when they interact within organizations. Thus, if individuals are seen as having duties of charity, such obligations can be extended to the collectives in which the individuals choose to work.

Among key arguments against recognition of a mandatory duty on the part of corporations to engage in broadly defined philanthropy are those based upon property rights, public-/private-sector distinctions, competency issues, and economic efficiency. The property rights argument has several dimensions. The most basic is the idea that one who possesses goods or the means of delivering services has the right to determine their disposition subject to legal constraints. The owner has the right to choose how to allocate her property however she wishes. The belief of others that there is some form of duty is irrelevant; it is up to the owner to decide how to use her property.

The way in which corporations are organized is seen to strengthen the property rights argument. Conceptually the corporation is owned by the shareholders, who therefore are seen as the relevant decision makers for the disposition of assets. Milton Friedman famously argues that the best way to recognize this reality is for the firm to declare dividends or to enhance its market value so that shareholders can sell the stock.[22] Either way, the shareholder realizes assets that she can then dispose of as she wishes, including the option of making donations to charitable organizations. In the United States, tax laws encourage the use of appreciated stock in charitable contributions.

Agency issues are significant in corporate governance. Managers control the day-to-day disposition of corporate assets, and they may act to benefit themselves at the expense of shareholders. This issue is relevant to corporate philanthropy when managers benefit themselves personally by using corporate assets to create social initiatives or make charitable contributions. How this may be done is discussed more extensively in the next section. Agency theory emphasizes the right of owner/principals to control the disposition of their property. A mandatory duty imposed on agents to engage in philanthropy in a manner inconsistent with the owners' wishes would violate fundamental tenets of agency theory. Critics of corporate philanthropy see the phenomenon as a ruse often used by managers to benefit themselves at the expense of shareholders.

Friedman and others have argued for a clear separation between the roles of the public sector and the private sector.[23] Responding to social needs and improving social welfare are responsibilities of the public sector. Political systems determine how assets are to be distributed in the public sector. Friedman famously claims that the business of business is business. Managers should not preempt the public sector by making decisions concerning social welfare. When managers make social decisions, they interfere with the operation of the political system and they violate their role obligations.

Closely related to the role obligation argument is a claim that managers lack competency for dealing with social issues. Managers are selected because of their ability to generate profits by providing desired goods and services to buyers. They are not selected because of their ability to define social needs or to design programs to enhance the social good. Some might argue that the lack of competency is demonstrated in the current mishmash of corporate programs and the erratic way in which they have been implemented. Furthermore, when a firm engages in a wide variety of social initiatives—for example, developing special programs for local schools, supporting a local opera, or constructing low-cost housing—it is hard to claim that the relevant managers possess special competencies for all these diverse activities.

The economic argument holds that managers investing in social activities distort the efficient allocation of capital. Scarce investment dollars are being put to a second-best use. Presumably, managers would have made a business decision concerning how to invest the money now being used for philanthropy. Because they are responding to a mandatory duty to make charitable contributions, they interfere with the efficient operation of capital markets.

Many other arguments have been advanced in this long-standing debate. Perhaps one reason why the debate seems irresolvable is the incomparability of the types of arguments advanced. Some are based on consequential analysis of efficient outcomes, whereas others are based on normative or positional duties, or the existence of supportive social norms or public policy. In such a circumstance, weight should be given to long-standing norms and public policy. In the United States, although corporate philanthropy is permitted, even praised, it is not treated as mandatory and there have been few (if any) efforts to make pariahs of those firms (which happen to be the majority) that eschew the practice of corporate philanthropy.

Even though there haven't been legal actions or social movements supporting a mandatory obligation of corporate philanthropy, can evidence be found in market reactions to firms? That is, to reverse the way in which the issue is usually framed, is there evidence that the market punishes firms that purposely decline to engage in corporate philanthropy? If such firms underperform their philanthropic peers in capital markets over time, then one might be able to make the argument that investors in the collective believe that firms must engage in some form of philanthropy. Investors might prefer philanthropic firms because they believe that such firms are more likely to be profitable. Or they might treat their investment as a consumption function and, because they believe that firms do have a mandatory duty to be philanthropic, prefer to invest in firms that reflect their personal preferences. Either motivation could produce behavior that could have an impact on relative valuation in capital markets. For such an effect to be discernible in markets, there would have to be a substantial preponderance of investors who act with such motives. In fact, the studies conducted to date have failed to show any general positive correlation between philanthropy and financial performance, with a few narrow exceptions. On the other hand, engaging in philanthropy doesn't appear to hurt financial performance. So, on balance, the market appears to be neutral concerning the issue.[24]

Those advancing claims of a mandatory duty, particularly when the duty is at odds with long-standing practice and public policy, should have the burden of proof of establishing why a duty should be recognized that would require significant changes in behavior and attitudes. Although many of the pro arguments have appeal and some merit, so do many of the con arguments. At this point in time, one cannot identify a compelling case that would impose a mandatory duty of philanthropy on corporations.

THE FUNDAMENTAL ISSUE: THE EFFICIENCY
OF CORPORATE PHILANTHROPY

A serious issue, surprisingly little discussed, is whether the stakeholders of the current system of corporate philanthropy are being well served. As the quote from Andrew Carnegie at the beginning of the chapter reveals, the effectiveness of philanthropy is a long-standing concern. Many astute investors make very casual personal charitable donations, perhaps under the view that any net increase to the social good is sufficient. This attitude appears to be changing. In private philanthropy there is a growing interest in getting more value out of giving. Successful entrepreneurs seek to use the talents that brought business success and positioned them to be major philanthropists to ensure that their socially oriented investments are also successful. Similar issues abound in corporate philanthropy.

A major issue shared between individual and corporate philanthropy is the extent to which contributions benefit the least well off. The McKinsey Global Survey reported that companies were equally likely to fund culture/arts and health/social services.[25] A nontrivial amount of total philanthropy goes initially to elite institutions in the arts and education, whereas only about a 10th directly addresses basic human needs.[26] Emphasizing the fact that these donations are given favorable tax treatment, critics such as Reich argue that the net effect of the tax laws is to "increase inequality between the rich and the poor."[27] One may argue that funding elite institutions that then engage in programs such as tuition remission, medical research or even special art shows for underprivileged children indirectly provides support for basic human needs. Even so, there are genuine concerns that corporate philanthropy is not realizing its full potential for helping those in greatest need.

Some corporations focus on a select list of projects whereas others engage at a relatively small level with a large number of donees. Among the former are Intel, which indicates that its primary giving focus is on education, and Proctor & Gamble, which has indicated it will focus their charitable contributions on a single cause—assisting the development of children in need 11 years old and younger. In contrast to the tightly focused approach is Commerce Bank, a well-above-average corporate philanthropist in the aggregate, that reports on its website that it made 4,900 different contributions totaling $9 million (average, $1,837 per contribution) in 2006. The Commerce Bank website provides resources for applications for grants from community stakeholders. Other philanthropic projects involved partnering with Radio Disney to bring reading days for 10-year-olds at Florida branches, and giving American Dream scholarships to high school students and Hero Awards to community heroes. Many small community projects, when done well, may engage many local organizations and may leverage the corporate investment. On the other hand, they may be difficult to evaluate and can degenerate into a haphazard spraying of resources with little real impact.

Many firms have matching programs whereby they will match or enhance giving by their employees. This essentially involves delegating the selection of donees to employees. Such programs are pure cash philanthropy otherwise unconnected to the values or core competencies of the organization. The result of this strategy is to produce a large number of donees who receive small amounts of money. Employee matching programs are often adopted and operated on the assumption that they will enhance employee morale.

Mergers, privatizations, and other forms of corporate reorganization strike at the dependability of corporate philanthropy. Changes of ownership may result in a dependent donee being cut off. Texaco ended its long-time sponsorship of the Metropolitan Opera after merging with Chevron, and Mobil dropped Masterpiece Theater on PBS after merging with Exxon. The overall impact of mergers on philanthropy is unclear. A recent study of the banking industry indicated that the giving by major banks increased postmerger. There was, however, a change in donees because firms tended to give less to local organizations and, instead, emphasized national donees.[28]

Historically, concerns have been raised about CEOs and other senior executives having their firms give money to their own personally preferred charities. The 2007 McKinsey Global Survey found that the personal interests of the CEO and board members had, by far, the greatest weight in determining the focus of the corporation's philanthropy programs. There is potential for abuse when personal philanthropic preferences influence or control corporate philanthropy.

> [Consider the] infamous example of the $90 million donation from Occidental Petroleum Corporation to set up the Armand Hammer Museum of Art and Cultural Center. Hammer was the CEO of Occidental and the eponymous museum was established to display his personal art collection.... Minow speculates about cases where the seeming social purpose is secondary to a more pernicious motivation: a corporation donating money to the Olympics so that the chief executive will have the opportunity to be well treated at the events themselves; or a bank supporting a little league team whose players include the chief executive's child.[29]

When corporate philanthropy is dominated by CEO or board preferences, even business goals such as enhancing the reputation of the firm may be compromised. There is some evidence that the problems associated with undue influence by top management are being recognized in practice. As the philanthropic function has become more professionalized, it is thought that there is "relatively less interference from the top management team insisting on projects that coincide with their personal interests."[30]

Many philanthropic endeavors do not appear to be connected to the core competencies of the firm. GSK, Merck, Altria, and Bayer are among the many firms that make major contributions to the arts. Why global pharmaceuticals or tobacco companies as organizations would have special insights in this domain is not clear. Assuredly, senior managers at such firms have personal interests in the arts and may have sophisticated understandings relevant to arts management. However, that is not the same thing as a firm making direct use of its core competencies to achieve a social good. The expertise deriving from the core competencies of the global pharmaceutical firms in discovering, manufacturing, and delivering treatments would seem to hold far greater potential for enhancing the social good than would what are often one-off contributions to the arts. Many companies would appear to have core competencies that would provide a comparative advantage in responding to a particular need. A cell phone company could provide communications after a natural disaster. An express delivery firm may be able to deliver essential goods and medicines in areas of conflict. A food services firm could provide nutritious food for the hungry or homeless. The list of relevant corporate core competencies seems endless. A financial services fund can provide microcredit or support the design and delivery of social venture capital. Yet, too often, there appears to be a disconnect between major programs and firm core competencies. Wendy's supports adoption. Goldman Sachs has major environmental initiatives. On first impression, the connection to core competencies is not clear.[31]

The sum of these issues and challenges cause some to question the value of cash in particular and even the entire domain of corporate philanthropy. Nobel Peace Prize winner Mohammed Yunus is among those. He writes: "Sadly . . . very little of the cash so generously given ever gets all the way down to the very poor. There are too many 'professionals' ahead of them in line, highly skilled at diverting funds into their own pockets."[32] More fundamentally, the World Business Council for Sustainable Development, a global association of more than 200 major companies, directly challenges the value of socially motivated contributions. In a 2006 report, they state as follows: "If action to address such (social) issues is to be substantial and sustainable, it must also be profitable. Our major contribution to society will therefore come through our core business, rather than through our philanthropic programs."[33]

The efficiency of corporate philanthropy remains distressingly opaque. Corporations vary significantly in setting explicit goals, with very few providing hard numbers or criteria for evaluating the success of their initiatives. Most reporting online just provides descriptions of select activities. In addition, the total sums, although not known precisely, are not so large as to be a dominant tool for responding to social needs. On the other hand, corporate philanthropy involves significant sums. The absolute amount of corporate philanthropy is growing over the long term. When coupled with the special competencies of successful business firms, the scale of some of the largest firms, and the existence of comparative advantage in delivering certain social goods, there is a large value-added potential. The next section discusses strategies for improving the efficiency of corporate philanthropy.

IMPROVING CORPORATE PHILANTHROPY

There is a simple solution for the concern that some corporations treat philanthropy casually as an "add-on" activity, thereby failing to realize the full potential of their social investments. Firms should treat philanthropic investments in a manner relevantly similar to business investments in their selection, operation, and evaluation.

The selection of projects is paramount. Managers should begin by analyzing how the special competencies of the firm can be used to enhance a social good. The 2007 McKinsey Global Survey found that only a fifth of firms used "highest potential for social impact" as a major factor in selecting and focusing programs. This is problematic because firms often have resources providing them with comparative advantages over other potential providers of a social good. A firm with capacities in wireless technologies may be able to provide cell phone service or emergency access points in a developing or ravaged country that lacks such basic infrastructure. A firm with a highly educated workforce may be able to design and deliver educational programs within their areas of expertise. Ad agencies can support antismoking, responsible drinking, or driver safety information campaigns. The list is virtually infinite. The foundation of the strategy should be based upon aligning the firm's experience, knowledge, and business strengths with its philanthropic programs.

Having identified the relevant competencies of the firm, management then faces the difficult task of identifying the particular social good that the firm can provide. There appear to be fads among both individual and corporate donors who tend to follow others in favoring certain types of projects at a given point in time.[34] Some trends may play out at the industry level, as was the case of competitor imitation of the Merck river blindness project. Others represent more general trends. For example, the attack on the World Trade Center appears to have produced a trend involving corporations making highly visible donations in response to tragedies and natural disasters. Recent examples include corporate responses to the tsunami in Southeast Asia, earthquakes in Kasmir, and Hurricane Katrina in the United States. Billions were given in each instance, sometimes in a manner that raised questions about the overall efficiency of the process.[35] Surpluses of some items resulted whereas equally needy people in other parts of the world remained in need.

A major concern is the relatively low percentage of philanthropy that deals directly with human need, particularly the needs of the least well off. How might management deal with this dimension while selecting among projects? First, potential social projects connected to the core competencies of the firm need to be identified. Determine areas where a firm has a comparative advantage in contributing to the social good. After that is done, the next task would be to select the target beneficiaries of the project. Expecting management to identify the least-well-off potential donees at this point is unrealistic, even unfair. To begin with, identifying the least well off would be virtually impossible to accomplish, and the time and expense involved could detract from the amounts actually contributed. Furthermore, it could be unfair in the sense that a case could be made that a corporation should limit its selection process to considering those in need among its stakeholders, rather than the world as a whole.

Perhaps a more realistic way to approach the selection task would be to follow a two-step process. First managers would identify groups of potential projects and donees whom the firm could efficiently benefit through their existing resources and networks. Second, management would then consider the relative needs of the potential donees. This would not be an easy task. For example, Goldman Sachs might identify two projects that it might wish to support with substantial resources. One would be to buy up forest in Brazil and donate it to an environmental group to prevent deforestation and to protect indigenous peoples and wildlife. The other would involve starting a microcredit program in Brazil capable of providing capital and incentives enabling very poor people to become self-sufficient.

Whatever Goldman Sachs were to decide in such a case, there would likely be some advocates and NGOs that would be unhappy with the choice. Corporate charity always involves trade-offs and choices. It would be self-defeating and unfair to impose a normative standard recognizing corporate charity as legitimate only when there is unanimity among stakeholders that the best allocation has been made. Instead, the main point is for the philanthropic firm to engage in a serious evaluation of the quality and quantity of the social goods to be provided with due consideration of the expected benefits to the donees. Doing so should improve the overall quality of corporate philanthropy. Goldman Sachs could probably easily justify doing either one to their external constituencies. Applying the same type of serious analysis used in their business decision making should greatly enhance the social impact of their philanthropy.

When Hank Paulson, a noted environmentalist, was the chairman of Goldman Sachs, they championed the environment as their major focus. In 2008, Lloyd Blankfein, Paulson's successor, announced a $100 million "10,000 Women" campaign to provide training in business basics to women in developing countries. Goldman Sachs will work with universities and with NGOs to provide certificate programs providing education in accounting, marketing, and other business subjects.[36] Blankfein indicated that Goldman Sachs will use its resources and convening power to achieve the social goal of expanding the ranks of businesswomen around the world. The 10,000 Women project connects Goldman Sachs's competencies with a great social need. The project has the potential to increase economic activity in a context that should ultimately benefit many of the least well off through a resurgence of entrepreneurial activity. The most difficult issue with the new program is how it will be measured. Various "hard" measures might be used—for example, how many certificates have been granted or how much money has been spent on developing educational programs. However, these would fall short of the goal of measuring the overall social impact of the ambitious program. At the least, it would be helpful for investors and stakeholders to know how Goldman Sachs intends to measure whether the program turns out to be worth the $100 million investment.

One other factor should be considered at the very beginning of the selection process. I mention it here, rather than at the beginning of this section, because it is likely to apply to only a very few firms. Nonetheless, this factor, when it does apply, is critical from a normative perspective. Firm managers should determine whether their firm has a mandatory duty to devote its philanthropic resources to a particular need. I have argued that a mandatory duty exists in the following circumstances:

> Firms possessing a unique human catastrophe rescue competency have a moral obligation to devote substantial resources toward best efforts to aid the victims of the catastrophe. Unless financial exigency justifies a lower level of investment, they should devote, *at a minimum*, the largest sum of (1) their most recent year's investment in social initiatives, (2) their five-year average of investment in social initiatives, (3) their industry's average investment in social initiatives, or (4) the average investment in social initiatives by firms in their home nation. They may devote a portion of those resources to concurrent social initiatives only if there is an equally compelling rationale for such an investment.[37]

Only a few firms should be considered to have such a mandatory duty. A human catastrophe involves a devastating, overwhelming need. The harms involve current instances of severe physical injury, deprivation, or death on the part of many thousands. The firm must have the competency and capability to act to mitigate or alleviate the catastrophe. The key factor is that the firm must have a comparative advantage so that no other firm or entity would be more effective in responding. If a firm finds itself in this category then it should follow this principle, only giving to other donees if there is an equally compelling justification.

Finally, firms should be appropriately transparent about their philanthropy. It is ironic when firms that suggest one reason for their philanthropy is to build reputational capital and motivate consumers then fail to report their actions publicly and even oppose shareholder resolutions asking for more transparency. Transparency is essential in order for advocates of corporate philanthropy and other affected stakeholders to be able to determine the quality and effectiveness of corporate philanthropic programs.

Transparency is important even though it may result in criticisms and even opposition to certain programs. It appears to be the case that the proponents of some of the shareholder resolutions asking for the listing of donations to nonprofit organizations believe that shareholders or certain stakeholders will object to donations to controversial groups. In addition, bills have been introduced in the U.S. Congress (for example, H.R. 887, October 1999) that would require publicly held corporations to disclose total charitable contributions once a year, providing details for any contributions made to a nonprofit organization on which a company officer or director (or their spouse) serves. Again, the motive appears to be the hope that disclosure would result in a reduction in charitable contributions. However, the negative reactions to the proposed legislation, which never passed, is part of the evidence validating the presence of powerful pro-charity norms in the United States.

The case for more transparency is strong. The business model for philanthropy is based on the assumption that it will motivate existing employees, help in hiring, stimulate customers, and establish legitimacy in the community. Those objectives are much less likely to be realized when firms fail to disclose activities. Opaqueness regarding overall contributions may feed cynicism that what is disclosed is self-serving and incomplete. Lack of meaningful disclosure may also contribute to misperceptions on the part of the general public regarding the level of corporate engagement concerning social needs. For example, Bhattacharya and Sen note that "large swaths of consumers do not seem to be aware that by and large most companies engage in [corporate social responsibility] initiatives."[38]

Beyond the business case there is an even more compelling reason why firms should provide more disclosure of their philanthropic activities. In the account provided earlier, the norms supporting corporate interventions providing social goods were based on an expectation that firms could provide unique benefits to broader society. Delivery of unique benefits requires high-quality, meaningful social initiatives and creative philanthropy. The public should demand efficient philanthropy. To evaluate whether such a demand is being met, the public needs much more information about corporate philanthropy than is currently available. Information concerning the initial social goals for a program along with periodic reports on the progress of the programs are essential. Ideally, such information would be available in easily comparable form, with its validity ensured by a credible third party. That is one reason why firms should consider responding to the magazines and organizations that gather information and issue reports. In the interim, greater transparency, particularly on corporate websites, would represent a great advance.

CONCLUSION

Corporate philanthropy as it exists today has great unrealized potential to contribute to the social good. Although the motives driving corporate charity are mixed between business and altruistic motives, comparative advantages can leverage business interventions so that unique benefits are produced. Although a persuasive case cannot be developed for a mandatory duty of corporate philanthropy, it is clear that corporate social interventions are supported by powerful norms and public policy. These are reflected in the fact that a majority of the very largest firms engage in some form of philanthropy or social initiatives.

Unfortunately, the full potential for corporate philanthropy is not being realized through mismanagement, lack of focus, and agency issues. To enhance the effectiveness of corporate philanthropy, firms should treat their social investments in a manner relevantly similar to their business investments. That is, they should apply hard business criteria to the selection, operation, and evaluation of their philanthropic programs.

Firms possessing unique competencies to aid victims of a major human catastrophe have a constrained moral duty to use their resources toward that end. Greater transparency is essential for enabling corporate philanthropy to realize its unfulfilled promise for making unique contributions to the overall social good.

Notes

Epigraph source: Michael Schrage, "Charity Needs a Better Foundation," *Financial Times* (February 14, 2007), p. 15.

1. Carolyn Mathiasen, *2007 Background Report E: Charitable Contributions* (Institutional Shareholder Services, 2007), www.irrc.com.

2. Paul C. Godfrey, "The Relationship Between Corporate Philanthropy and Shareholder Wealth: A Risk Management Perspective," *Academy of Management Review* 30 (2005), p. 779.

3. Ailian Gan, "The Impact of Public Scrutiny on Corporate Philanthropy," *Journal of Business Ethics* 69 (2006), pp. 217–236.

4. Even for corporate foundations that file required reports there is uncertainty. A 2007 report of the National Committee for Responsive Philanthropy found that the reports of foundations associated with banks violated Internal Revenue Service rules, noting that the reports could not be externally verified. Furthermore, there was "a lack of standardization regarding what is included in the sector's definition of philanthropy." Rebecca Sherblom, *Banking on Philanthropy: Impact of Bank Mergers on Charitable Giving* (National Committee For Responsive Philanthropy, 2007).

5. Committee Encouraging Corporate Philanthropy, *Giving in Numbers: 2006 Edition* (New York: Committee Encouraging Corporate Philanthropy, 2006), p. 16.

6. McKinsey Global Survey, "The State of Corporate Philanthropy: A McKinsey Global Survey," *The McKinsey Quarterly* (January 2008), p. 3.

7. Michael E. Porter and Mark R. Kramer, "The Competitive Advantage of Corporate Philanthropy," *Harvard Business Review* (December 2002), p. 68.

8. David H. Saiia, Archie B. Carroll, and Ann K. Buchholtz, "Philanthropy as Strategy: When Corporate Charity 'Begins at Home,'" *Business & Society*, 42 (2003) pp. 169–201; Carol M. Sanchez, "Motives for Corporate Philanthropy in El Salvador: Altruism and Political Legitimacy," *Journal of Business Ethics* 27 (2002), pp. 363–375.

9. Barbara R. Bartkus, Sara A. Morris, and Bruce Seifert, "Governance and Corporate Philanthropy," *Business & Society* 41 (2002), p. 322.

10. I thank Ryan Berg for his comments in general and this point in particular.

11. A considerable amount has been written about attributing bad motives to organizations. See Godfrey for a recent account. Interestingly, little has been written about attributing good motives to corporations. In both cases, there are serious conceptual and practical issues relating to the manner in which complex organizations make and recognize decisions. Paul C. Godfrey, "The Relationship Between Corporate Philanthropy and Shareholder Wealth: A Risk Management Perspective," *Academy of Management Review* 30 (2005), pp. 777–798.

12. See the exchange between Godfrey and Bright for an example of the problems involved with coming up with an exogenous standard to determine the genuineness of intent. Bright suggests that one somehow identify a perception of

virtuous unconditionality, citing Merck's river blindness program as an example. Godfrey, in turn, takes Bright to task for "subjugation of the economic to the moral" (p. 755). David Bright, "Virtuousness Is Necessary for Genuineness in Corporate Philanthropy," *Academy of Management Review* 31 (2006), pp. 752–754; Paul C. Godfrey, "A Reply to Bright: Virtuousness and the Virtues of a Market," *Academy of Management Review* 31 (2006), pp. 754–756.

13. Milton Friedman, "The Social Responsibility of Business Is to Increase Its Profits," *New York Times Magazine* (September 13, 1970), pp. 32–33.

14. Porter and Kramer, "The Competitive Advantage"; Godfrey "The Relationship Between."

15. Bruce Seifert, Sara A. Morris, and Barbara R. Bartkus, "Having, Giving and Getting: Slack Resources, Corporate Philanthropy, and Firm Financial Performance," *Business & Society* 43 (2004), p. 137.

16. Ibid., p. 151.

17. Ray Fisman, Geoffrey Heal, and Vinay B. Nair, "A Model of Corporate Philanthropy," Working Paper (Columbia University, New York, 2007).

18. Joseph Galaskiewicz, "An Urban Grants Economy Revisited: Corporate Contributions in the Twin Cities, 1979–81, 1987–89," *Administrative Science Quarterly* 42 (1997), pp. 445–471.

19. World Business Council for Sustainable Development, *From Challenge to Opportunity: The Role of Business in Tomorrow's Society* (Geneva: World Business Council for Sustainable Development, 2006), p. 6, www.wbcsd.org.

20. C. B. Bhattacharya and Sankar Sen, "Doing Better at Doing Good: When, Why and How Consumers Respond to Corporate Social Initiatives," *California Management Review* 47 (2004), pp. 9–24.

21. Ben White, "Goldman in $100m Drive to Educate Women," *FT.com* (March 6, 2008), www.ft.com/cms/s/0/fefb1fd6-eb09-11dc-a5f4-0000779fd2ac.html?nclick_check=1.

22. Friedman, "The Social Responsibility."

23. Ibid.

24. Joshua D. Margolis and Hillary Anger Elfenbein, "Do Well by Doing Good? Don't Count on It," *Harvard Business Review* (January 2008).

25. McKinsey Global Survey, "The State of Philanthropy."

26. Stephanie Strom, "Big Gifts, Tax Breaks and a Debate on Charity," *New York Times* (September 6, 2007), p. A1.

27. Rob Reich, "A Failure of Philanthropy," *Stanford Social Innovation Review* 3 (2005), p. 26.

28. Sherblom, "Banking on Philanthropy."

29. Thomas W. Dunfee, "Do Firms with Unique Competencies for Rescuing Victims of Human Catastrophes Have Special Obligations?" *Business Ethics Quarterly* 16 (2006), p. 202.

30. Saiia, Carroll, and Buchholtz, "Philanthropy as Strategy," p. 176.

31. If, in general, firms were more transparent with their rationales for selecting given programs, it would allow stakeholders to appreciate how the programs connect to the firms. Lack of specifics feeds suspicions concerning the basis for selection, and gives emphasis to factors that may not be that relevant, such as the fact that the founder of Wendy's was adopted and the former head of Goldman Sachs is personally involved in major environmental NGOs.

32. Muhammad Yunus, "A Hand Up Doesn't Always Require a Handout," *Wall Street Journal* (October 14, 2006), p. 16.

33. World Business Council for Sustainable Development, *From Challenge to Opportunity*.

34. This is to be expected if, as is argued here, social norms are a major influence on philanthropy.

35. On the other hand, there appears to be a general impression that the response of corporations was more efficient than the interventions by the U.S. federal government.

36. White, "Goldman in $100m."

37. Dunfee, "Do Firms with Unique", p. 186.

38. Bhattacharya and Sen, "Doing Better at Doing Good," p. 14.

13

Philanthropy, Self-Interest, and Accountability

American Universities and Developing Countries

Devesh Kapur

Virginia Polytechnic Institute and State University and its Office of International Research, Education, and Development manage a research portfolio of more than $46 million in 44 countries around the world. Current research projects involve forestry and natural resource management, integrated pest management, sustainable agriculture, watershed management, and microenterprise development and higher education capacity-building projects in Haiti, Nepal, and Oman. Twelve full-time faculty and nine staff members support these efforts in partnership with more than 40 U.S. university partners and a similar number of developing country institutions.[1]

Virginia Polytechnic Institute and State University is just one example of the degree to which research universities in the United States are engaged in developing countries. The National Association of State Universities and Land-Grant Colleges (a voluntary, nonprofit association of public research universities and land-grant institutions) database of its members' international development projects exceeds 1,000.[2] Although there is no comparable database of private research universities, the total number of international development projects in which U.S. universities are currently engaged is likely to be double this figure. To put this number in perspective, the portfolio of ongoing international development-related projects by U.S. universities exceeds that of the World Bank.

Yet, although there is intense media and public scrutiny of the latter, there is virtually none of the former. American universities have long played a significant role in developing countries. They have trained developing country elites and technocrats, students and faculty, science and technology personnel. During the postwar era, American universities and academics conducted research on a wide range of problems facing poor countries, from specific agriculture products to the determinants of economic growth to the measurement of poverty.

The role of U.S. universities in developing countries has, if anything, expanded even more in recent years, and this trend appears to be the case of other developed countries as well. Global efforts to address health problems afflicting poor countries have led to a large expansion in the field of public health in U.S. universities, which have moved beyond research and training to university-led service delivery in poor countries. Faculty at U.S. universities are no longer simply advisors, but have official appointments in governments and play a more hands-on role as directors of emerging market firms that seek to signal their reputation by having faculty from marquee universities on their boards. U.S. universities are increasingly catering to the rising demand for quality higher education in developing countries by attracting the children of elites and by supplying education overseas.

There may be good reasons why there is little scrutiny of the involvement of universities in developing countries. First, universities engage in research, rather than projects that may directly impact the lives of many people. Second, universities are relatively open institutions with ostensibly strong internal mechanisms of checks and accountability.

Although these arguments are undoubtedly valid, they should not be overstated. In this chapter I examine the role of U.S. universities in developing countries and some difficult ethical and accountability issues that have not received much attention. I argue that it is not just that university researchers and research projects can and do impact people's lives in poor countries. University faculty engage in a range of private actions—from consulting to running their own firms to membership of company boards— based not only on their own personal capabilities, but also while leveraging the reputation of their universities. And universities—especially private research universities—are, in reality, not very transparent institutions (even the World Bank is more transparent). The vast majority of U.S. universities are nonprofits, and as with any nonprofit, they need financial resources to advance their mission; no money, no mission.[3] But a relentless pursuit of money can undermine the mission. This tension is inherent in any nonprofit, and universities are no exception. However, although academics have done a yeoman's job in examining the role of U.S. and foreign aid in developing countries, they have been much more circumspect in examining their own role and of universities in general. The academic community has tended to shine the light on other actors in international development, but rarely on itself. It is this lacuna that this essay addresses.

UNIVERSITY-BASED RESEARCH IN ECONOMIC DEVELOPMENT

Do academics play an important role in development? Although the precise degree is impossible to specify, it would stand to reason that they do at least to some extent, because the counterfactual—that they have no effect—would make it rather hard to justify the large sums spent on academic research related to development. If academics do have some effects—in particular, in countries and societies of which they are not a part—how should one think about their accountability? The very nature of the academic enterprise means that misguided notions of accountability could easily cast a pall on the free flow of ideas that are at the heart of the academic enterprise. In any case, the mechanisms and channels of academic influence on developing countries are so diffuse that accountability appears almost impossible to establish.

For decades, faculty from U.S. universities (as well as from other industrialized countries) have been advising developing countries. During the 1920s, Princeton University Professor Edwin Kemmerer played a role in Latin America; during the 1980s, it was Jeff Sachs from Harvard University.[4] Increasingly, especially after the 1960s, the role of U.S. universities in developing countries expanded from directly supplying advice (through faculty), to additional indirect mechanisms. The first mechanism was through the training of students who later joined international financial institutions (especially the International Monetary Fund [IMF] and World Bank), who in turn played a major role in shaping policies in developing countries. The second, and perhaps most important mechanism, has been the training of technocrats who returned to their countries in positions of responsibility, be it the "Berkeley Mafia" in the case of Indonesia, the "Chicago Boys" in the case of Chile, and a set of elite universities in the case of Mexico.[5] Greater influence also raises the case for greater scrutiny and accountability, whether from acts of omission or acts of commission.

A few examples illustrate the nature of the problem. During the 1960s, Harvard Advisory Services, drawing on expertise from academics at Harvard, the Massachusetts Institute of Technology (MIT), and Boston University, endorsed the development strategy of the then-military dictatorship in Pakistan "of betting on the strong." This strategy called for putting foreign aid-sourced investment resources in the dynamic Western half of the country (especially in the Punjab) rather than in the more populated Eastern province (East Bengal), which was perceived to lack economic dynamism. This further exacerbated the lopsided emphasis on West Pakistan, which already exercised disproportionate control over the key levers of the state. As one of the key academic actors involved in formulating the country's development strategy later rued, this development strategy contributed to building resentment in the larger and impoverished East Pakistan, leading eventually to a bloody civil war, military massacres, and the breakup of that country.[6]

Accountability in the case of acts of commission might seem more valid, but raises equally difficult—and delicate—questions. A recent example is the case of Harvard's advisory program in Russia, led by leading academics. The program, financed by the U.S. government, was meant to help set up a financial market infrastructure and create fair and open markets and the rule of law, which was deemed crucial to Russia's transition to market capitalism during the 1990s. The program collapsed in disgrace, resulting in a lawsuit filed by the U.S. government alleging that Harvard personnel used their positions and influence over Russian officials in those critical years in Russian history to advance their own and their spouses' private financial interests.

In 2004, U.S. District Judge Douglas P. Woodlock in the U.S. District Court for the District of Massachusetts granted the government's motions for summary judgment finding liability against Andrei Shleifer, Project Director and a professor in the economics department at Harvard, and Jonathan Hay, Project Manager, under the False Claims Act, and against Harvard University for breach of contract with USAID.[7] Judge Woodlock found that Harvard breached its contract with USAID by allowing Hay and Shleifer to profit from the program. However, he dismissed the charge that the university knowingly deceived the government. Subsequently, a jury found liability against Shleifer for violation of the conflict-of-interest policy in USAID's contracts with Harvard. Other than this narrow jury finding, the case did not reach the trial stage, but was settled in an out-of-court agreement in August 2005 (the text of the settlement is confidential).

At one level, one could argue that there was some accountability in the program because Harvard was required to pay $26.5 million to the U.S. government, and the faculty members involved paid $2 million, under a settlement reached in August 2005 (none of the defendants acknowledged any liability under the settlement).[8]

At another level, these examples demonstrate the asymmetry of accountability in international development. Even though the most severe damage from the failed Russian program was to Russia, there was no accountability to that country.[9] Equally troubling was the complete absence of any professional accountability. Academia, which protests vociferously if any of its privileges are threatened, was quite forgiving. Typical reactions were that the individuals were "great scholars" whose misconduct "was more likely incredible stupidity and carelessness...rather than anything deliberate."[10] Yet one would be hard put to find this as an explanatory variable in the countless regressions on governance and development. When it comes to developing-country officials, self-interest—the grabbing hand—is trotted out as an elegant parsimonious explanation, whereas complex human frailties such as stupidity and carelessness explain the behavior of "great scholars" and academic "stars."

Similarly, Yale University's International Institute for Corporate Governance was created to advise developing countries on "good governance." Instead, it suffered much embarrassment after its director was forced to resign following allegations of serious financial misconduct.[11]

One might argue that the first example merely illustrates that the road to hell is often paved with good intentions, rather than raising any issues of the accountability of academics in development, whereas the second did not directly affect developing countries. It does, however, raise the question whether the confidence with which some social scientists press for social engineering in other societies might be tempered if there were even a possibility of a loose form of accountability. In its complete absence, is there a danger of moral hazard?

Although academics have generated reams of debate and analysis on governance and accountability issues afflicting a range of organizations and actors engaged in poor countries, they have been markedly reluctant to examine their own accountability, whether they act directly in developing countries or indirectly through international organizations, especially the Bretton Woods institutions. Thus, although the Bretton Woods institutions have been much critiqued, the reality is that these institutions don't operate in an intellectual vacuum. There are deep links between elite U.S. universities and the Bretton Woods institutions, most manifest in the dominant ideas of these institutions. It should be emphasized that most of the ideas of these institutions are not generated within, but rather are brought in from outside—in particular, from the very same select institutions that are also the principal source of the human capital (the staff) of these institutions.[12] The World Bank and IMF are a gravy train of data on money for research on development, and academics have for long worked with these institutions as consultants and often as employees. The thick and steady two-way traffic between the Bretton Woods institutions and academia was a rarity during the first few decades of its existence. Subsequently, as research and analysis became more important for these institutions, a deep nexus developed (particularly in the research departments) with important agenda-setting consequences. Thus, if we believe that these institutions have failed or should be held more accountable for their actions, it is unclear why the very academic institutions that have been the source of their ideas, embodied in human capital or otherwise, have nothing to answer for. Of course, the essence of academia is to allow academics the space to be creative and innovative, and not to impose any conventional indicators of accountability on ideas per se. However, should this same standard apply when they serve on corporate boards and as advisors to governments, especially in other countries? It's a hard question to answer and I will revisit it in the Conclusion.

Indeed, for academics who are involved with the Bretton Woods institutions, there is only an upside. They have access to resources and a mechanism to implement their ideas, while at the same time maintaining their distance and independence if anything goes wrong. This reflects a more general problem in that social scientists can hardly ever be brought to admit that their opinion or advice was wrong. After all, even if what happened to people who acted upon the diagnosis or recommendation was disastrous, it can never be proved conclusively that things would not have turned out even worse had a different policy been adopted.[13] This is an important reason why the accountability of the Bretton Woods institutions has proved to be so difficult, but applies equally to academics who consult for and work with these institutions.

What is interesting is that, unlike the health and medical sciences, academics who write on issues that bear on the welfare of developing countries and try to influence these institutions in pushing those ideas are not required to be transparent about potential conflicts of interest. Consider the case of capital account liberalization, an issue area that was very important for rich countries in general and the United States in particular. The merits for developing countries were debatable in the 1990s and now, in retrospect, are even more debatable. Yet, academics pushing this line who were also consultants for Wall Street, with obvious interest in these issues, were never required to reveal any possible conflict of interest that might affect their policy positions. It might well be the case that an academic genuinely believes, based on research, that capital account liberalization—even if it serves the interest of large investment banks and the United States—might still also be in the self-interest of developing countries. After all, as the case with trade liberalization has shown, in many cases liberalization can be a positive-sum rather than a zero-sum game. However, if the same academic were also a consultant to Wall Street, there is at least a possibility of a conflict of interest. It does not stretch credulity to suggest that an academic strongly opposed to capital account liberalization is unlikely to be invited to a lucrative consultancy in Wall Street.[14]

Issues of the accountability of academics seem particularly germane when academics temporarily work in the Bretton Wood institutions and adopt practices counter to the most cherished values of academia. Consider the case of the debt crisis, which in retrospect was one of the severest afflictions that affected developing countries during the 20th century. Given the intensity of the crisis and its singular effects on these countries, research by the Bretton Woods institutions was of utmost priority. Nonetheless, the institutions squelched research on this sensitive subject. Although this might not be surprising (because the creditor nations did not want any case to be made for debt forgiveness), what is noteworthy, however, is that the key individuals making that decision had come from academia, and subsequently returned to academia. The cloak of protection of academia meant that there was simply no way they could be held accountable for their actions. Indeed, they were bestowed with accolades from their professional organizations, despite the violation of one of the most cherished values of academia: an openness to research. Many questions have been raised about the independence of the research of the Bretton Woods institutions. It is worth emphasizing that, in these institutions, the heads of research have not been career bureaucrats, but well-known academics who go in and out of these institutions and have not infrequently squelched research on issues crucial to the well-being of developing countries.[15]

The point is not about the content of an intellectual argument and the evidence brought to bear on that argument. The very nature of academic research means that the quality and content will be inherently debatable and contentious. Rather, it is about a banal reality that academia finds easy to believe of other actors but not of itself: People act on the basis of self-interest. One cannot claim both that human beings are guided by self-interest as a general rule and then suddenly take out academics as an exception to that rule. The fact is that the old belief (or myth) that intellectuals seek truth and politicians seek power, is one that may be open to the charge of being self-serving.[16]

More recently, U.S. business schools have become involved in developing countries (especially in so-called emerging markets) in a variety of ways, from lucrative executive education programs to faculty advising companies and even to serving as "independent" board members. Interestingly, business schools have weak ethical standards in this regard. Few institutions have strong conflict-of-interest policies or disclosure policies regarding a faculty member writing a case study or paper on a firm or nonprofit organization while serving on the board of a related firm (and being compensated). Faculty from elite business schools serve as independent directors, which has obvious signaling effects on the perception of corporate governance of the firm. Although business schools are only too eager to trumpet how extensively their faculty advise major corporations, they disavow them even when there are obvious failures of corporate governance in a firm where a faculty member has been serving as an independent director. One might assume that, because the reputational effects of a faculty member of a major business school serving as an independent director is especially greater in emerging markets (given the perceived weaker standards of corporate governance in those settings), these institutions might exercise greater diligence when faculty are involved in professional transgressions, especially in developing countries. However, this does not appear to be the case.

A recent massive corporate governance failure of one of India's largest information technology firms, Satyam, is a good example. The firm had two independent directors with Harvard affiliations (one at the Kennedy School and the other at the Business School). The firm's annual reports revealed that the Harvard Business School professor had received a remuneration of about $200,000 from Satyam as he was conducting customized leadership programs for its employees. He was also writing case studies of a nonprofit linked to the founders of the firm from which he was drawing a sizable remuneration.[17] Yet, when Harvard Business School was asked about the matter, it maintained that it had nothing to do with the faculty member's actions while serving on the boards of Indian companies. "The situation you describe would have nothing to do with Harvard University or Harvard Business School [HBS] as institutions. The HBS faculty is involved with companies as individuals."[18]

WHEN UNIVERSITY RESEARCH BECOMES PROPRIETARY

The passage of the Bayh-Dole Act was seen as a game-changing legislation that would significantly strengthen university–industry linkages, increase technology transfer, and provide substantial revenue sources to research universities. It was not surprising, therefore, that U.S. research universities strongly supported the Bayh-Dole Act, while downplaying the inherent tension between the revenue goals from the monopoly resulting from patents and licensing agreements and the "open knowledge as a public good" purposes of a university.[19] It is not just that partnerships with industry can undermine the independence of a university's research, or that the possibility of substantial pecuniary gains are likely to reshape focus areas of research, it is the very idea of the university as knowledge commons that is at stake: "Proprietary knowledge...is in principle antithetical to the openness in sharing knowledge that is at the heart of the university's mission."[20] By making knowledge exclusive, patents limit access to new ideas and raise the cost of innovation for other researchers, lowering their ability to innovate.[21]

In principle, universities are more willing to license the research tools they develop freely to other public-sector institutions in contrast to commercial firms. In practice, however, in the aftermath of the Bayh-Dole Act, universities sometimes grant exclusive licenses to companies who then refuse to sublicense any rights or that impose onerous terms on sublicensees. Recent research suggests that public institutions may issue such exclusive licenses with alarming frequency, even when the tools are useful primarily for diseases prevalent in developing countries. For example, a recent map of patents relevant to the development of a malaria vaccine found that only 8 of the 27 "moderate to high-priority" patent families that were originally filed by public entities remain available for licensing from that entity.[22] A review conducted by the National Institutes of Health concluded that universities have sought just about every kind of clause in research tool licenses to which they themselves have objected, including publication restrictions, rights in or the option to license future discoveries, and prohibition on transfer to other institutions or scientists.[23]

More important for our purposes, the broader societal effects—in particular, any implications for poor countries—were simply not part of the thinking as universities began to take advantage of the Bayh-Dole Act. These issues became apparent when, following federal government financing of AIDS research, several U.S. universities patented drug discoveries that were then licensed to major pharmaceutical companies for substantial fees running into the hundreds of millions of dollars.[24] With millions of lives at stake in poor countries without the financial means to pay for the very high cost of these drugs under patent, the role of universities became a source of controversy.

By way of illustration, the University of Minnesota licensed the AIDS drug Ziagento to GlaxoSmithKline. Activists accused the licensee of the university's patent of profiting from too-high sale prices of the drug in Africa and urged the university to push for the sale of less expensive versions of the drug. The university's position was that it had no control over the pricing and that the revenue supported its rescue mission, including more AIDS research.[25] The "revenue good—licensing of drug patents—

prevailed over the mission good of making drugs available to poor countries at low prices."[26]

The antiretroviral d4T was discovered by a Yale pharmacology professor,
William Prusoff, in the early 1990s and shortly afterward was licensed to
Bristol-Myers Squibb, which made $443 million on sales in 2002. Yale
earned $40 million annually in license fees.[27] In 2001, Doctors Without
Borders and Yale students organized and pressed Yale and Bristol-Myers
Squibb for "patent relief," allowing for the sale of generics in Africa. Although
Yale refused to make its contract with Bristol-Myers public (there is little
transparency in these contracts), the two did assent to "patent relief." As a
result, the price of d4T in South Africa decreased 96% (from more than
$1,600 per patient per year to $55 per patient per year) by late 2003.

The outcome of Emory's sale of its royalty rights of the antiretroviral
Emtriva (emtricitabine, FTC) to Gilead for $525 million in 2005 has (at
the time of this writing) not been as positive. Although Emory could have
used this sale to negotiate conditions about Gilead's licensing, registra-
tion, and patenting practices, it did not, leaving global access to Emtriva
unresolved. Thus, although Emtriva is recommended by the World Health
Organization as a safer and more effective alternative to 3TC in its first-
and second-line AIDS treatment guidelines, its prohibitively high price
makes it largely unavailable across the developing world. As a result of
activist pressure, Gilead has made the drug more accessible, but it is still
not widely available in poor countries.

These examples led the World Health Organization to call on "public
research institutions and universities in developed countries" to "seriously
consider initiatives designed to ensure that access to [research and
development] outputs relevant to the health concerns of developing
countries and to products derived therefrom are facilitated through
appropriate licensing policies and practices."[28]

There is no comprehensive data on the overall ownership position of
universities in current pharmaceutical technologies, but the aforemen-
tioned trends in research and development and patenting suggest their
ownership share is both substantial and increasing. In recent years, universities have obtained U.S. patent rights in a number of key pharmaceutical
products (table 13.1).

The tradition of open scientific practice in universities faces increasing
pressure from their patenting and commercialization activities. In principle, universities profess that the main purpose of their patent and
licensing policies is the advancement of the public good. However, their
technology transfer offices are judged by the revenue they earn, not by
their contributions to health, particularly global health. When, for
example, a university technology transfer office negotiates with a private
pharmaceutical firm over licensure rights to a university-owned patent,
such as an antiretroviral drug for treating AIDS, there is a conflict between
the school's desire to maximize revenue from its license on the one hand
and the greater public good that would result from the dissemination of

Table 13.1 Some Important Drug Patents Held by U.S. Universities

Type	Drug	U.S. University
Antiretrovirals	d4T	Yale University
	3TC, Emtriva	Emory University
	Abacavir	University of Minnesota
	Fuzeon/T20	Duke University
Others	Prilosec	University of Alabama
	Remicade	New York University
	Epogen	Columbia University
	Xalatan	Columbia University
	Taxol	Florida State University
	Cisplatin	Michigan State University
	Alimta	Princeton University
	Vaccine for human papillomavirus	Georgetown University owns the intellectual property in the United States; University of Rochester for the European Union and Australia

Source: Amy Kapczynski, Samantha Chaifetz, Zachary Katz, and Yochai Benkler, "Addressing Global Health Inequities: An Open Licensing Approach for University Innovations," *Berkeley Technology Law Journal* 20 (2005), pp. 1031–1114.

this drug as widely as possible to impoverished populations (which would only occur if the costs were low, in turn implying low licensing revenues) on the other.

It should be emphasized, however, that some of the correctives have also come from within universities themselves, mainly because of activist students and faculty—a testimony to the strengths of U.S. universities. A student group, Universities Allied for Essential Medicines, has pressed universities that are major grant recipients from the federal government (the National Institutes of Health) to set low prices for developing countries when negotiating patent agreements. This, however, has not occurred at the time of writing. Universities fear that, in a competitive marketplace, companies will simply go to a competitor if they insist on any restrictive clauses.

In an effort to press universities to act on an issue uniquely within their power, in 2006 U.S. Senator Patrick Leahy introduced legislation (the Public Research in the Public Interest Act of 2006, S. 4040) requiring all federally funded research institutions to ensure that the drugs they develop are supplied to poor countries at the lowest possible cost. In introducing the legislation, Leahy argued:

> Universities are, before anything else, institutions dedicated to the creation and dissemination of knowledge in the public interest...leaders of universities have not yet been able to come together around a different approach. Regardless of how it is achieved, I believe that increasing the availability of the medical innovations that come from publicly funded research centers is a sound solution to a pressing global health concern.[29]

The bill, had it been passed, would have allowed generic manufacturers to supply drugs developed at federally funded institutions in eligible countries at affordable prices. Because these licensing terms would only affect the introduction of reduced-price drugs in poor countries, it did not threaten profits in wealthy nations.

Responding to these pressures, a group of leading U.S. research universities and members of the Association of American Medical Colleges released a set of guidelines for universities and nonprofit research institutes to consider when licensing internally developed technologies to private parties. The white paper, titled "In the Public Interest: Nine Points to Consider in Licensing University Technology," suggests a set of good practices.[30] Universities should strive to construct licensing arrangements in ways that ensure that poor populations have low- or no-cost access to adequate quantities of these medical innovations. These include provisions such as (1) facilitation of generic competition, (2) mandatory sublicensing clauses for developing countries, (3) specific access milestones, and (4) agreements that reduce royalty payments from the licensee to the university in exchange for fair pricing in poor countries on the part of the licensee.

In contrast to the very visible and profit-driven activities of technology transfer offices, the much less visible activities of librarians in major U.S. university libraries have been helping developing countries gain access to current scientific information. Examples include:

- OARE, Online Access to Research in the Environment, an international public–private consortium coordinated jointly by the United Nations Environment Programme, Yale University, and leading science and technology publishers;
- AGORA, Access to Global Online Research in Agriculture, led by the Food and Agriculture Organization and Cornell University. Its goal is to improve the quality of agricultural research, education, and training in low-income countries, and, in turn, improve food security. It enables developing countries to gain free or low-cost access to major scientific journals.[31]

EDUCATION

The increasing demand for higher education in developing countries is being met by U.S. universities in several ways. In decades past, U.S. universities attracted thousands of students from developing countries for graduate and postgraduate studies and research. This was a symbiotic relationship that fueled research in the United States relatively cheaply, while training tens of thousands of researchers from developing countries. It did contribute to a "brain drain" from developing countries, but at the same time added to the global stock of knowledge, and served developing countries to the extent that their nationals returned with augmented skills and human capital.

A growing phenomenon is the attempt by many U.S. universities to attract the children of elites of rich countries who can not only pay full tuition, but can provide future resources to the university, as well. What are the ethics of the world's richest universities raising money from elites of poor countries whose own higher education systems are weak and where the marginal impact of these resources might be much larger? In some cases, there are good reasons why this might serve the poor country better—for instance if the funds are for scholarships for students from that country or for research on problems specific to the country. However, when it is for another building or faculty chair, then it is hard not to conclude that the university's interests are trumping broader societal interests.

A very different approach is the attempt by many developing countries to attract U.S. universities to set up shop in their territories. Correspondingly, even U.S. public universities, whose primary mission is to educate in-state students, are trying to establish a global brand in an era of limited state financing. The government of Singapore has spent large resources to attract major universities as it seeks to transform itself into the primary educational hub in Asia. Many of the world's leading universities have either set up a physical campus in Singapore (including University of Chicago Graduate School of Business; Duke University; Digipen Institute of Technology; University of Nevada, Las Vegas; and New York University Tisch School of the Arts) or have joint collaborations/programs with local universities (local tie-ups). The latter includes Johns Hopkins, Georgia Institute of Technology, MIT, the Wharton School of the University of Pennsylvania, Stanford University, New York University School of Law, and Cornell University.

The Singaporean government has offered financial incentives to attract a number of foreign universities. For example, the government is paying Duke University $310 million over 7 years to establish a medical school in the country. Students will receive their degrees from the National University of Singapore, but Duke University will oversee the program and will receive a licensing fee for its curriculum. In many of these international partnerships, the government offers startup assistance but does not finance the costs of developing the curriculum.

Singapore has an effective government, but what about governments with much weaker capabilities? Most overseas campuses of U.S. universities offer only a narrow slice of American higher education, most often programs in business, science, engineering, and information technologies, for which there is money to be made on the U.S. brand name. Thus, although New York Institute of Technology may not be one of America's leading universities, it leads in overseas forays, with programs in Bahrain, Jordan, Abu Dhabi, Canada, Brazil, and China, "leveraging what we've got, which is the New York in our first name and the Technology in our last name," according to Edward Guiliano, the institute's president.[32]

The tension between the education mission of the university and the need to raise financial resources seems to be especially acute in the

forays of U.S. universities in the Gulf. Even prior to their recent efforts
in setting up overseas campuses, the countries of Qatar, the United
Arab Emirates, and Saudi Arabia funded U.S. universities to the tune of
nearly $300 million during the past decade.[33] In the past few years,
a host of U.S. universities have set up overseas outposts in the Gulf
(table 13.2).

Table 13.2 U.S. Universities with Branches in the Gulf

Location	University	Opened	Academic Program
Doha, Qatar	Carnegie Mellon University	2004	BS in computer science, information systems, and business
	Georgetown University	2005	BS in foreign service
	Texas A&M University	2003	BS and MS in engineering
	Virginia Commonwealth University	1998	BFA in communication, fashion design, and interior design
	Weill Cornell Medical College	2001	Medical program, leading to an MD
Abu Dhabi, UAE	Johns Hopkins University	2008	A graduate program in public health
	MIT	2009	Graduate science and technology programs at the Masdar Institute of Science and Technology
	New York University	2010	Full liberal arts curriculum, undergraduate and graduate
Dubai, UAE	Boston University	2008	Graduate dental training
	Harvard University	2004	Continuing medical-educational courses
	Michigan State University	2008	Full liberal arts curriculum
	Rochester Institute of Technology	2008	Graduate courses in finance, service management, and engineering; later, undergraduate program as well
Ras al Khaymah, UAE	George Mason University	2005	BS in biology, business administration, economics, and engineering
Sharjah, UAE	American University of Sharjah	1997	Undergraduate degree in liberal arts, engineering, architecture, and business

UAB, United Arab Emirates

Source: Zvika Krieger, "An Academic Building Boom Transforms the Persian Gulf: Western Universities Find Opportunities as 3 Arab Emirates Strive to Outdo One Another," *Chronicle of Higher Education* 54, p. A26.

Although improving the quality of higher education in that part of the world is the obvious goal of the Gulf states, it offers a lucrative business proposition for U.S. universities. The emirate of Qatar is "spending about $2 billion a year to bring U.S. universities."[34] The Qatar Foundation for Education, Science, and Community Development underwrote the operating expenses of Cornell's medical school for the first 10 years. The amount: $750 million.

Dubai has created a "Knowledge Village," a "Healthcare City," and an "Internet City" in the hopes of becoming the focal point of the knowledge economy in the Middle East.[35] In 2007, the Dubai International Academic City was launched as the first dedicated tertiary education cluster development in the world.[36] In 2004, Harvard Medical International, a nonprofit subsidiary of Harvard Medical School, announced that it would build a campus in Dubai, its first overseas bricks-and-mortar branch since the closure of its Shanghai campus in 1915. Dubai has raised $100 million to support this project, which Harvard Medical International estimates will eventually generate $4 million to $5 million in annual revenue. A $1.8 billion complex will contain private hospitals and clinics, pharmaceutical companies, and research centers, as well as residential villas, apartments, and five-star hotels. Boston University is opening a dental program in Healthcare City.

Abu Dhabi, which has deeper pockets than Dubai, has gone more upscale, paying a high-brand premium to top U.S. universities to set up shop, including New York University, Johns Hopkins, and MIT. When John Sexton, President of New York University, was first approached to open a branch campus in the United Arab Emirates, he asked for a $50 million gift. "It's like earnest money: if you're a $50 million donor, I'll take you seriously," Mr. Sexton said. "It's a way to test their bona fides." In the end, the money materialized from the government of Abu Dhabi.[37]

The most substantial commitment by U.S. universities is to the King Abdullah University of Science and Technology, a graduate-level research university with an endowment exceeding $10 billion (one of the largest endowments in the world and the largest on a per-student basis). Major U.S. research universities—the University of Texas at Austin, the University of California at Berkeley, and Stanford University—are each being paid $25 million or more for 5-year partnerships to jump-start this institution.[38] Although nominally it will be the first Saudi coeducational institution, the institution will not allow "any intermingling of the sexes within or outside the lecture halls, nor will it tolerate any classroom discussion of 'Western' subjects such as popular music, psychology, classical philosophy or—especially relevant to any research-led institution—evolutionary science."[39] And, as is the case with rest of Saudi Arabia, female academics cannot expect to drive a car or ride in a car driven by a man who is not a relation or spouse.

Should U.S. universities help build a campus where basic freedoms are curbed to an extent that would never be tolerated back at home?[40] The question is not an easy one, because a case could be made that the provision of better quality higher education itself can be a lever of change. Nonetheless, one has an uneasy feeling that the sheer size of the pecuniary payoffs are helping rationalize these arrangements.

SERVICE DELIVERY

In recent years, faculty members who work on health afflictions facing the world's poor have been arguing that universities should do more than merely researching the cause of their problems and researching solutions.[41] They argue that the typical outputs of a university in the health sphere—namely, the production of knowledge through research; its dissemination through teaching; and, through the teaching hospitals, the provision of services to local residents—will not permit the teaching hospitals in major universities to respond effectively to global diseases such as AIDS. Instead, this argument runs, universities need to leverage their greatest strengths in global health—the symbiosis between research and treatment—and to this end they need to create "effector arms," that provide an implementation mechanism to treat people. There is also the argument that translational or implementation research—a "science of global health delivery"—is also frontier research, and consequently well within the core functions of a research university.

U.S. universities have been receptive to these ideas, especially because of the massive increases in financing for global health. Consider PEPFAR (the President's Emergency Plan for AIDS Relief), a U.S. government initiative to combat the global HIV/AIDS pandemic. The plan was launched in 2003 with an original commitment of $15 billion across 5 years and a final funding level of $18.8 billion renewed. It was renewed in 2008 to provide $48 billion for an additional 5 years to tackle HIV/AIDS, tuberculosis, and malaria. Public–private partnerships were seen as a critical element to plan and implement the prevention, treatment, and care work aspects of PEPFAR. As a result, hundreds of organizations, including large international organizations, commercial firms, government departments, and universities partner PEPFAR in the 15 "focus countries." In 2007, 3 of the top 10 organizations receiving funds were universities: Columbia University ($111 million), University of Maryland ($80 million), and Harvard University ($70 million). In addition, in November 2007, Indiana University's School of Medicine was awarded $60 million over 5 years for its Academic Model for Prevention and Treatment of HIV/AIDS Program; the University of Washington and the University of California–San Francisco's joint International Training and Education Center on HIV received a $29.7 million grant in 2007 to support training of health care workers who provide HIV/AIDS clinical care. An affiliate of Johns Hopkins (Jhpiego) was awarded $20 million by USAID to improve HIV and AIDS treatment services in three South African provinces and received another $16.5 million 5-year grant in 2008 to improve access to counseling and testing services in Tanzania.[42]

However, these programs also provided for large indirect cost recovery to the universities, similar to that for research projects, even though the funds were meant to provide services to Africa's AIDS-ravaged populations. In 2004, the Harvard School of Public Health received a $107 million, 5-year grant to treat AIDS patients in Botswana, Nigeria, and Tanzania. Traditionally, such projects come under a university's sponsored projects administration, with rules that were originally designed for on-campus scientific research, not service delivery off-campus in the world's poorest countries. As a result, Harvard initially applied the same indirect cost recovery rate as it used for on-campus lab research (approximately $35.8 million). In effect, the university was using a grant to provide AIDS drugs to desperately poor people in Africa to spend on sundry campus expenses—be it library purchases or the maintenance of the university president's residence. Sustained pressure led Harvard to reduce its rates, but no standard policy exists on overhead costs for overseas service delivery projects. Universities have a justified need to recoup indirect costs, but to do it in such an aggressive manner has serious opportunity costs—and when done by the world's wealthiest universities, it is even less savory.

CONCLUSION

Many of the issues raised in this chapter arise from two key dilemmas. First, revenue generation for the support of unprofitable but socially valuable "public goods" is a never-ending challenge in the higher education industry. Even though the revenue and mission goods seldom conflict entirely, it is often the case that effective revenue-generating activities of universities contribute resources to support the collective-good mission, but also undermine the mission. As argued by Weisbrod, Ballou, and Asch, when a university sells scientific research to a specific firm, seeking to maximize its revenues through exclusive licensing rather than making the findings available freely to all, the conflict between a university's mission (creating and freely disseminating knowledge) and its revenue goals (restrictive sale and licensing of knowledge) is clear.[43] A corporation that would gain monopoly control over patent rights would be willing to pay more for the rights than would the total of a multiplicity of firms, all of which would gain rights to the new technology.

Second, higher education research capabilities are located in the North whereas many of the problems being researched are in resource-poor countries. When the locus of knowledge about a nation is located outside its borders, it exacerbates the already existing inequality between weak and strong countries. The incentives for development researchers in the United States are to give pride of place to *propositional* knowledge—the search for "universal" laws of development from the frontiers of academia—and using that to generate *prescriptive* knowledge.[44] Least developed country–based researchers are seldom, if ever, represented in the former. Does that matter? There are several good reasons why concerns on this score may not be warranted. First, typically there are participants from developing countries, even though their institutional base is in industrialized countries (primarily the United States). Second, the idea that one's analytical position is an isomorphic reflection of one's nationality or geographical base is rather specious. Third, one could argue that the problems facing poor countries are so difficult that they require the best talent to address them, and if that talent is based in North America, so be it. Fourth, the fears of lack of diversity are misplaced given the vigorous debates and differences that are integral to U.S. academic and intellectual cultures. And finally, the skewed participation may simply reflect the realities of the global production of knowledge in which least developed countries themselves have played a not insignificant role by running their own universities and knowledge production systems to the ground.

However, there are grounds for unease as well. Intellectual networks can be double-edged. Although they reduce selection costs and serve as reputational mechanisms, they can also be prone to a form of "crony intellectualism." There is an inherent tendency to inbreed, which has negative consequences for intellectual advancement. Researchers, like other societal groups, also have interests. Moreover, the very nature of academia means that academics (in the social sciences) are not accountable for the consequence, in the sense that their work responds to professional incentives, not to its development payoffs. These professional incentives place a large positive premium in academic papers on the novelty of ideas, methodological innovation, generalizability, and parsimonious explanations. Detailed country and sector knowledge, an acknowledgment that the ideas may be sensible but not especially novel, that uncertainty and complexity rather than parsimony—these are the ground realities of development, but have little place in top-tier academic journals. The professional payoffs of delivering a paper on Africa are substantially greater in Cambridge, Massachusetts, than in an African country. In turn, this means that the questions and methodologies will be geared to the priorities of the former, even though the latter has much more at stake. It also means that research priorities are more captive to the fads and fashions of academia, moving from one big idea to the next, rather than what might be most helpful to poor countries per se.

As a result, a half century into "development," a narrow set of institutions based in rich countries continues to dominate the discourse, reflecting (in part) their outstanding quality. Most poor countries still seem incapable of thinking for themselves on issues critical to their own welfare, without any agenda-setting power even on research related to their own welfare. This has several undesirable consequences. It skews the questions, methodologies, and other priorities of research. As a result, those directly affected by the policies of the institutions are underrepresented in setting the research and policy agenda. Furthermore, it narrows the diversity of views, which, given limited knowledge and the possibility of wrong advice, could amplify risk in the international system. The importance of diversity is particularly important in the context of an uncertain future.[45] Moreover, diversity may matter in and of itself on the grounds that there should be at least a minimum degree of participation by those likely to be affected by the consequences of the actions resulting from ideas emanating from these institutions. Diversity may also be important for its instrumentality; it diversifies risk, a not unimportant criterion, given limited knowledge and the consequences of misplaced advice.

Although there are no easy answers, three mechanisms could potentially address (albeit modestly) the complex issues raised by the role of U.S. universities and academics in developing countries. First, there should be greater transparency about any potential conflicts of interest that may bear on their advice. At the very least, those offering advice should provide greater information on their activities to allow the consumers of their advice to make more informed decisions. Second, in the case of acts of commission, the minimum that can be expected is that academic institutions whose talisman is transparency should undertake what even international organizations today practice: Set up independent and public investigations to ensure unbiased accountability.[46]

However, transparency and an independent and public investigative body to ensure unbiased accountability are unlikely to be effective unless there is prior agreement on what we can hold academics accountable for.[47] Indeed, the cloak of "notice and implicit consent" that accompanies transparency could simply sanitize problematic academic conduct and make matters worse for developing countries. If self-interest is a chronic condition of human behavior (including academics), then perhaps some fiduciary-like requirements on academics with respect to developing countries and other vulnerable groups they serve needs to be considered. These fiduciary responsibilities would entail being held accountable, not only for failure to disclose, but also for self-dealing (especially in the case of developing countries). Moreover, they would not only have to disclose potential conflicts of interest, but also actively avoid them and protect the interests of their clients.

A third mechanism would be to strengthen academia within developing countries, recognizing the reality that if the accountability of academics within a society is difficult, it is well nigh impossible across borders. Arguably, if universities in developing countries were strengthened, it would help developing countries to think for themselves—and take responsibility for the actions resulting from their ideas—rather than be the perennial objects of received wisdom.

Notes

I am grateful to Nancy Birdsall, Gobind Nankani, and Patricia Illingworth for their comments on an earlier draft; to Arjun Suri for his comments and help in health-related issues; and to Megan Crowley for research on some legal issues discussed in this chapter.

1. Statement of Theo A. Dillaha, Program Director, Sustainable Agriculture and Natural Resource Management (SANREM) Collaborative Research Support Program (CRSP) Office of International Research, Education, and Development, Virginia Polytechnic Institute and State University, Blacksburg, before the U.S. House of Representatives Committee on Agriculture Subcommittee on Specialty Crops, Rural Development and Foreign Agriculture. agriculture.house.gov/testimony/110/h80716/Dillaha.doc.

2. www.nasulgc.org/NetCommunity/Page.aspx?pid=776&srcid=288.

3. Burton A. Weisbrod, Jeffrey P. Ballou, and Evelyn Asch, *Mission and Money: Understanding the University* (New York: Cambridge University Press, 2008).

4. See Paul Drake, *The Money Doctor in the Andes—The Kemmerer Missions, 1923–1933* (Durham: Duke University Press, 1989).

5. On Chile, see Juan Gabriel Valdés, *Pinochet's Economists: The Chicago School of Economics in Chile* (Cambridge: Cambridge University Press, 1995). For an excellent account of the transformation of the Mexican economic technocracy from its nationalist left-leaning heyday in the 1960s to a bastion of neoliberals trained in elite U.S. universities such as the Massachusetts Institute of Technology, Harvard, Stanford, University of Chicago, and Yale, and their impact on Mexico see Sarah L. Babb, *Managing Mexico: Economists from Nationalism to Neoliberalism* (Princeton, N.J.: Princeton University Press, 2001). On the Berkeley Mafia, see Ford Foundation, *Celebrating Indonesia: Fifty Years with the Ford Foundation 1953–2003* (New York: Ford Foundation, 2003), web.archive.org/web/20070403150613/www.fordfound.org/elibrary/documents/5002/toc.cfm.

6. This account draws from a note by Edward Mason to Robert McNamara, World Bank Archives, 1972. At the time, Ed Mason was a distinguished faculty member in the economics department at Harvard.

7. *U.S. v. President and Fellows of Harvard College*, 323 F.Supp., 2d 151 (D. Mass., 2004).

8. In addition, Harvard's legal fees were estimated at between $10 million and $15 million. An employee who causes a loss to his employer to the tune of nearly $40 million would normally not be expected to enjoy the favors of his employer for long. But not in this case, perhaps because, as former Dean of Harvard College, Henry Lewis, put it: "An observer trying to make sense of the University's position on [faculty accused of misconduct] is driven to an unhappy conclusion. Most of all being a close personal friend of the president probably does one no harm." David McClintick, "How Harvard Lost Russia," *Institutional Investor* 40 (January 2006), www.iimagazine.com/article.aspx?articleID=1039086.

9. As Summers himself acknowledged when he testified under oath in the U.S. lawsuit in Cambridge in 2002: "The project was of enormous value.... Its cessation was damaging to Russian economic reform and to the U.S.–Russian relationship." McClintick, "How Harvard Lost."

10. Joann S. Lublin, "Travel Expenses Prompt Yale to Force Out Institute Chief," *Wall Street Journal* (January 10, 2005), p. B1.

11. www.yaledailynews.com/articles/view/12633.

12. At the beginning of the 1990s, 80 of the research staff at the World Bank had graduate degrees from U.S. and U.K. institutions (nearly two thirds from the United States). Although similar data from the IMF is unavailable, it is unlikely to be less. Since then, widening quality differences between U.S. and developing-country academic institutions are likely to have increased the skewness. Nicholas Stern, "The World Bank as Intellectual Actor," in Devesh Kapur, John Lewis, and Richard Webb, eds., *The World Bank: Its First Half Century* (Washington, D.C.: Brookings Institution, 1997), table 18–12–6.

13. In a recent analysis, Tetlock finds that "experts" who make predictions their business (and are paid for it) are scarcely better at it than anyone else, but are rarely held accountable. They rarely admit they were wrong, insisting that they were just off on timing, or blindsided by an improbable event, or almost right, or wrong for the right reasons. "In this age of academic hyperspecialization, there is no reason for supposing that contributors to top journals—distinguished political scientists, area study specialists, economists, and so on—are any better than journalists or attentive readers of the *New York Times* in 'reading' emerging situations." Indeed, "[e]xperts in demand were more overconfident than their colleagues who eked out existences far from the limelight." Philip Tetlock, *Expert Political Judgment: How Good Is It? How Can We Know?* (Princeton, N.J.: Princeton University Press, 2005), p. 233.

14. Devesh Kapur, "Academics Have More to Declare Than Their Genius," *Financial Times* (June 23, 2009), p. 11.

15. This is documented in the official history of the World Bank. See Devesh Kapur, John Lewis, and Richard Webb, eds., *The World Bank: Its First Half Century* (Washington, D.C.: Brookings Institution, 1997).

16. Debates about the roles and responsibilities of intellectuals are, of course, not new, ranging from those who espouse that intellectuals should be guided by a principle that, "My kingdom is not of this world" (Brenda) to those like Gellner, who believe that to "disregard consequences in the name of purity of principle can itself often be a kind of indulgence and evasion." Julian Benda, *The Treason of the Intellectual* (New York: The Norton Library, 1969), p. 43; Ernest Gellner, "La Trahison de la Trahison des Clercs," in Ian McLean, Alan Montefiore, and Peter Winch, eds., *The Political Responsibility of Intellectuals* (Cambridge: Cambridge University Press, 1990), pp. 17–28, 7. Nissan Oren, ed., *Intellectuals in Politics* (Jerusalem: The Magnes Press, The Hebrew University, 1984); Edward Said, *Representations of the Intellectual* (New York: Pantheon, 1994).

17. Harvard Business School case study, N9–109–032, November 6, 2008, by Professor Krishna Palepu and Research Associate Namrata Arora on the Emergency Management and Research Institute.

18. Rumi Dutta and Dev Chatterjee, *Economic Times*, "Palepu May Have to Quit DRL Board" (January 10, 2009), economictimes.indiatimes.com/Corporate_Announcement/Palepu_may_have_to_quit_DRL_board/articleshow/3958701.cms.

19. Walter W. Powell and Jason Owen-Smith, "Universities and the Market For Intellectual Property on the Life Sciences," *Journal of Policy Analysis and Management* 17 (1998), pp. 253–277.

20. Nannerl O. Keohane, "The Mission of the Research University," *Daedalus* 122 (Fall 1993), pp. 101, 122.

21. Shelia Slaughter and Larry L. Leslie, *Academic Capitalism: Politics, Policies and the Entrepreneurial University* (Baltimore, Md.: John Hopkins University Press, 1997).

22. Cited in Amy Kapczynski, Samantha Chaifetz, Zachary Katz, and Yochai Benkler, "Addressing Global Health Inequities: An Open Licensing Approach for University Innovations," *Berkeley Technology Law Journal* 20 (2005), pp. 1034–1114, 1055–1056.

23. National Institutes of Health, *Report of the National Institutes of Health (NIH) Working Group on Research Tools* (1998), www.nih.gov/news/researchtools.

24. Fifteen of the 21 drugs with the greatest therapeutic impact were derived from federally funded projects at academic centers, according to a 2000 senate report. www.essentialmedicine.org/cs/wp-content/uploads/2006/11/pipiabackgrounpaper.pdf.

25. Maura, Lerner, "AIDS Drug Puts 'U' in Debate over Access in Africa." *Star Tribune (Minneapolis)* (April 2, 2001), 1A.

26. Weisbrod, Ballou, and Asch, *Mission and Money*, p. 160.

27. Donald G. McNeil, Jr., "Yale Urged to Cut Drug Costs in Africa," *New York Times* (March 12, 2001), p. A3. In the article, Yale pharmacology professor William Prussoff, d4T's inventor, states, "I'd certainly join the students in that. I wish they would either supply the drug for free or allow India or Brazil to produce it cheaply for underdeveloped countries. But the problem is, the big drug houses are not altruistic organizations. Their only purpose is to make money."

28. World Health Organization, *Public Health, Innovation and Intellectual Property Rights: Report of the Commission on Intellectual Property Rights, Innovation and Public Health* (Geneva: World Health Organization, 2006), p. 74. Article 2.12.

29. Cited in www.essentialmedicine.org/cs/?page_id=14.

30. In addition to Stanford (which initiated and coordinated the effort), the paper was signed by the California Institute of Technology; Cornell University; Harvard University; MIT; the University of California system; the University of Illinois, Chicago, and University of Illinois, Urbana-Champaign; University of Washington; Wisconsin Alumni Research Foundation; Yale University; and the Association of American Medical Colleges news service. stanford.edu/news/2007/march7/gifs/whitepaper.pdf.

31. Another notable initiative in this direction is the *PLoS Neglected Tropical Diseases* journal, an open access journal published by the Public Library of Sciences and funded by the Gates Foundation to foster academic collaboration in addressing neglected disease research questions. www.plosntds.org/static/information.action.

32. Tamar Lewin, "U.S. Universities Rush to Set Up Outposts Abroad," *New York Times* (February 10, 2008), p. A1.

33. The data are from foreign gift disclosure requirements for American colleges and universities reported under Title 20, Section 1011f of the U.S. Code, "Disclosures of Foreign Gifts." The data can be found at www.nationalreview.com/kurtz/allforeigngiftsreport.html.

34. chronicle.com/weekly/v54/i29/29a02601.htm.

35. For many decades, Lebanon was the higher education hub of the Middle East, but it has steadily lost its advantage as a result of its political travails. Instead, Dubai is facing competition from nearby Qatar, which has launched a project to build an "education hub" in Doha, with programs from mainly U.S. universities, including Carnegie Mellon, Cornell University, Texas A&M, and Virginia Commonwealth universities. Katherine Zoepf, "International Business School to

Open Campus in Abu Dhabi," *Chronicle of Higher Education* (May 26, 2006), chronicle.com/article/International-Business-School/33147.

36. Eight million square feet will be used as an international higher education zone, 3 million square feet will be used for research and development centers, and another 3 million square feet will be allocated for sports facilities, student union buildings, and student and faculty housing.

37. www.nytimes.com/2008/02/10/education/10global.html?pagewanted=all.

38. Tamar Lewin, "U.S. Universities Join Saudis in Partnerships," *New York Times*, (March 6, 2008), www.nytimes.com/2008/03/06/education/06partner.html?_r=1.

39. David Cohen, "All the Perfumes of Arabia," *Guardian* (July 22, 2008), p. 4.

40. In some cases, such as the University of Connecticut, which suspended discussion over the construction of a campus in Dubai (paid for by the government of Dubai) because of concerns over human rights issues (specifically, the use of poorly paid migrant workers in construction projects for the program), universities have acted on principles. However, it is unclear whether this, rather than poor "market conditions" for attracting students, was the underlying cause.

41. This section draws on a paper by Luke Messac, "Cost Efficiency in University-Led Service Delivery in Poor Countries," Independent Study Paper for Professor Arachu Castro, Harvard University (January 5, 2007). Paul Farmer of the Harvard School of Public Health and founder of Partners in Health is a noted votary of this position.

42. www.avert.org/pepfar-partners.htm.

43. Weisbrod, Ballou, and Asch, *Mission and Money*.

44. The ideas in this paragraph and the next were initially developed in Devesh Kapur, "The Knowledge Bank," in Center for Global Development, *Rescuing the World Bank* (Washington, D.C.: Center for Global Development, 2006), pp. 159–170.

45. Andrew. Stirling, "On the Economics and Analysis of Diversity," SPRU Working Papers (Brighton: University of Sussex, 1998).

46. The creation of the independent inspection panels in the World Bank and IMF, and the Volcker commission in the case of the United Nations, are some examples.

47. This paragraph draws on comments by Patricia Illingworth on an earlier draft of this paper.

Index